THE HUMAN CHALLENGE
Seventh Edition

Mary Tucker
Ohio University

Anne McCarthy
University of Baltimore

Douglas A. Benton, Emeritus

Prentice Hall
Upper Saddle River, New Jersey

Library of Congress Cataloging-in Publication Data

Tucker, Mary L.
The human challenge: managing yourself and others in organizations / Mary L. Tucker, Anne M. McCarthy, Douglas A. Benton.
p. cm.
Rev. ed. of: Applied human relation / Douglas A. Benton. 6th ed. 1998.
Includes bibliographical references and index.
ISBN 0-13-085955-9 (alk. paper)
1. Organizational behavior. 2. Management. 3. Personnel management. I. McCarthy, Anne M. II. Benton, Douglas, 1937–. Applied human relations. III. Title.
HD58.7 .T83 2003
658.3—dc21 2002017081

Publisher: Steve Helba
Executive Editor: Elizabeth Sugg
Director of Production and Manufacturing: Bruce Johnson
Managing Editor: Mary Carnis
Manufacturing Buyer: Ilene Sanford
Production Liaison: Brian Hyland
Design Director: Cheryl Asherman
Senior Design Coordinator: Christopher Weigand
Cover Illustration: Tom White
Full Service Production/Formatting: BookMasters, Inc.
Editorial Assistant: Anita Rhodes
Printing and Binding: Courier Westford

Pearson Education LTD.
Pearson Education Australia PTY, Limited
Pearson Education Singapore, Pte. Ltd
Pearson Education North Asia Ltd
Pearson Education Canada, Ltd
Pearson Educación de Mexico, S.A. de C.V.
Pearson Education—Japan
Pearson Education Malaysia, Pte. Ltd
Pearson Education, Upper Saddle River, New Jersey

10 9 8 7 6 5 4 3 2 1
ISBN 0-13-085955-9

BRIEF CONTENTS

CONTENTS

PREFACE

The seventh edition of this book reflects changes in the theory and practice of human relations in organizations. The emphasis on *applied* human and organizational behavior continues. In addition, there is a concentration on student *skill development.*

As in previous editions, the book is designed to meet the needs of popular courses taught in junior colleges, four-year colleges, universities, adult education, and extension programs. The direct, straightforward language used attempts to emphasize the person in the organization rather than traditional theories of management philosophy. It is not a book on organizational theory, office management, or supervision. Instead, it is about the daily interaction between leaders/managers and other employees.

WHAT'S NEW

This seventh edition has been completely revised, and new topics have been added. The user-friendly, logical flow of the chapters remains the same. New material includes additions on emotional intelligence and workplace violence. Where appropriate, emotional intelligence is woven into other chapters as well. The discussions of leadership, workplace issues, and conflict management as well the technological and ethical implications of managing have been expanded. In many chapters, Internet action projects have been added.

The material focuses on the skills and thinking that lead to becoming an effective manager. Each chapter is introduced with "To Start You Thinking" questions and "Learning Goals." Most chapters contain experiential exercises, "Action Projects," and "Express Your Opinion" sections. Because the study of human relations involves self-discovery as well as interaction among people, the more participative the class can become, the more students learn from each other's experience. Within each chapter, marginal notes identify important information and are ideal for reviewing the chapter or finding necessary material.

Each chapter closes with summaries, case studies, and endnotes. The case studies are based on real-life experiences and can be used in or outside of class. Discussion and study questions—to keep you thinking—are included at the end of each chapter. A managerial skills assessment workbook, *The Prentice Hall Self-Assessment Library,* by Steve Robbins is available with this text as well as an instructor's manual and test bank with classroom-tested questions, learning aids, experiential exercises, and transparency masters.

In summary, the chapters contain:

1. "To start you thinking" questions
2. Learning goals
3. Key terms and concepts
4. Express your opinion and/or self-appraisal exercises
5. Marginal notes
6. Action projects
7. Summary
8. Case studies
9. Discussion and study questions—to keep you thinking
10. Endnotes

ACKNOWLEDGMENTS AND DEDICATION

Any book is the product of the efforts of many people. We are indebted to colleagues and students for their feedback and insights. Specifically, Jim McCambridge was instrumental in revising the chapters on leadership, conflict resolution, teamwork, and motivation. Gary Coombs provided insight and expertise in writing the chapter on creativity. David Kirch created a chapter on emotional intelligence. Chris Yost combined the two communication chapters from the sixth edition into one chapter and updated it for this edition. Ray Hogler lent his labor union expertise for the chapter on organized employee relations. Ray Bruce contributed to Chapter 3 on personal and organizational values. Mandi Tucker's formatting skills were priceless.

Editors and staff at Prentice Hall were a joy to work with. We are grateful to Elizabeth Sugg for her encouragement and to Anita Rhodes for keeping track of all the details.

This edition is dedicated to all our students and all those who have assisted and supported us throughout our careers. Without their encouragement, we would not have been able to accomplish our goals.

Mary Tucker, Anne McCarthy, and Doug Benton

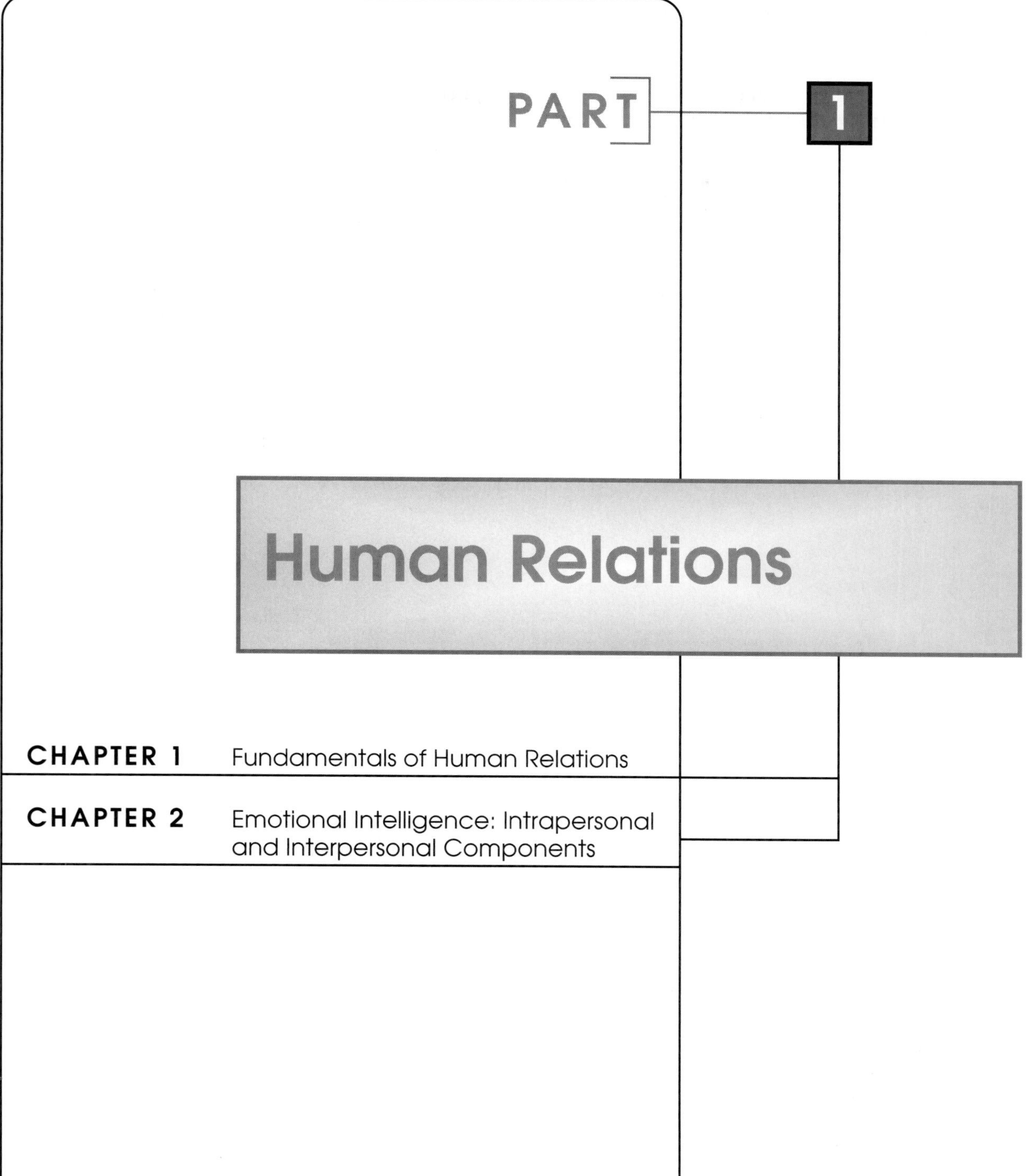

PART 1

Human Relations

CHAPTER 1

Fundamentals of Human Relations

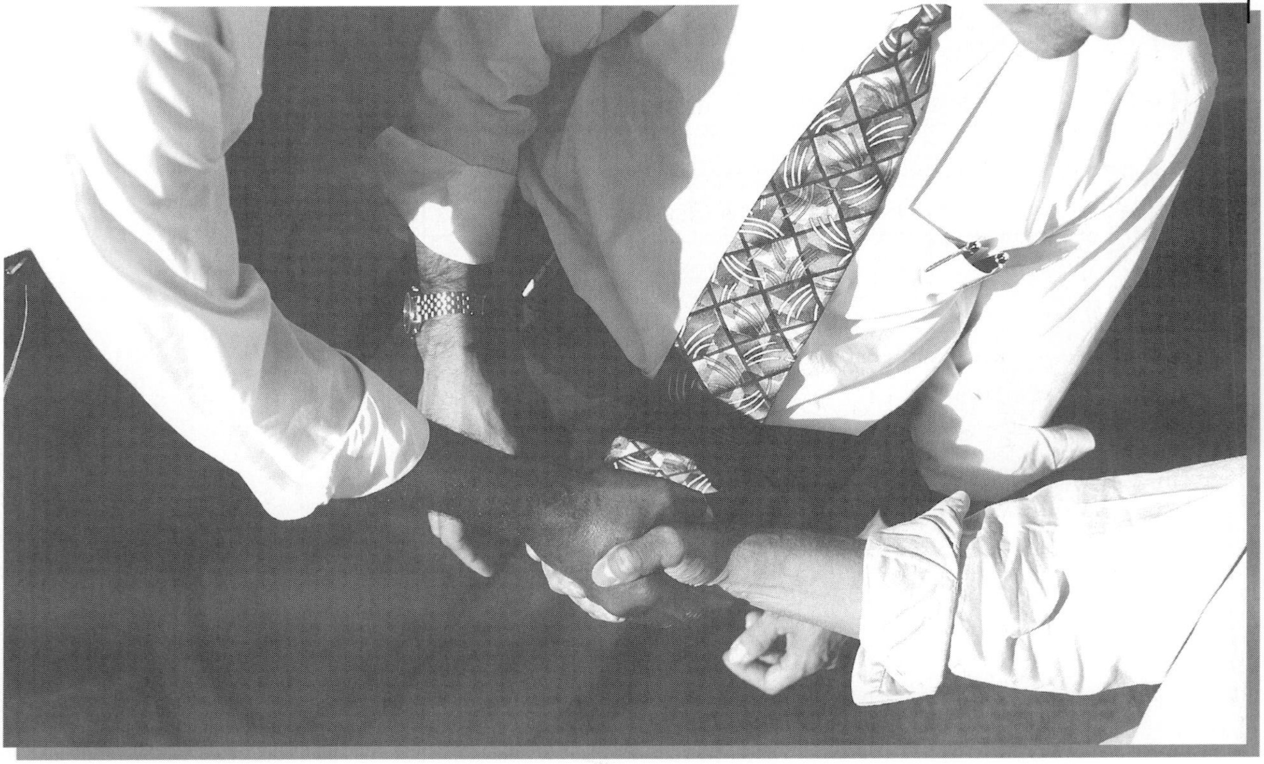

TO START YOU THINKING

At the beginning of each module, we provide a set of questions that is designed to stimulate your thinking. Some of the answers will be found in the readings; others will depend on your experience or personal opinion. Such open-ended questions are offered to generate discussion and an exchange of ideas.

- What is your definition of human relations?
- Why should we study human relations?
- Why would the study of human relations be more important to the supervisor than to the average worker?
- Is responsibility a two-way street between the employer and the employee?
- Are the skills required of managers changing?

LEARNING GOALS

After studying this chapter, you should be able to:

1. Dispel some myths about human relations.
2. Explain why there is a need for an interdisciplinary approach to human relations in business.
3. Define human relations as it is used in business and its importance to the individual.
4. Critically assess the concept of scientific management.
5. Explain recent developments in human relations, including quality management, employee empowerment, and organizational transformation.
6. Describe recurrent themes in human relations.
7. Describe the technical, human relations, and conceptual skills of management.
8. Distinguish among leadership, management, administration, and supervision.
9. Define and apply the following terms and concepts:

KEYWORDS

- **human relations**
- **organizational behavior**
- **management**
- **scientific management**
- **Hawthorne studies**
- **informal organization**
- **quality circles**
- **total quality management**
- **employee empowerment**
- **organizational transformation**
- **empathy**
- **individual differences**
- **whole person**

DEFINITION AND PURPOSE

Human relations is the study of interaction among people.

What is human relations? **Human relations**, in its most general sense, refers to all interactions that occur among people. The main focus of this book is human relations in organizations, also known as **organizational behavior**, which is the study of how people, groups, and organizations behave. Because organizations are made up of people, we focus on individual behavior and relationships between people.

COMMON GROUND

By the time most people reach adulthood, they have developed a system of interacting with others, socially and personally, that satisfies most of their needs. Frequently, however, people who feel confident and secure in their personal relationships lack confidence in their business relationships. Human relationships at work involve what is commonly referred to as management. **Management** can be defined as a group of people whose activities are to coordinate others in order to achieve specific objectives. Management depends on leadership and teamwork. To be productive and successful in our careers, it is in our best interests to learn as much as possible about human relations at work.

COMMON MISCONCEPTIONS

Human relations is not common sense.

Managers don't have to "manage" all the time.

Human relations is not just making people feel good at work. It is not manipulating others to get your way. Rather, it is being direct, honest, and positive in dealing with others. Unfortunately, human relations is not "common sense," because poor interpersonal relationships and communication are all too common.

Another understandable misconception is that managers should manage all the time. Managers should be leaders—setting good examples, being facilitators and standard setters, but not necessarily always bosses, order-givers, or directors.

NEED FOR HUMAN RELATIONS SKILLS

When people work together in groups to achieve a common goal, there is a strong possibility that the differences among their individual viewpoints will cause conflicts. Many people do not know how to resolve business conflicts in a constructive manner. The person who knows how to work harmoniously, even with those who hold different views or are motivated by different goals, will be successful in human relations in the world of work.

Daniel Goleman, cochair of the Organization for Research on Emotional Intelligence in Organizations, reports that the majority of those who fail in managerial positions do so because they lack intra- and interpersonal skills, even though they may be competent in technical matters.[1] The need to find new solutions to the day-to-day problems associated with modern job responsibilities has led to the development of human relations as a separate field of study in the business curriculum.

Human relations is a discipline within business.

A key to success in business is satisfying company objectives and personal goals.

From both the employer and employee point of view, good human relations are necessary if people are to achieve economic, social, and psychological satisfaction from the work they do. The study of human relations in business is the study of how people can work effectively to satisfy both (1) organizational goals and (2) personal goals.

ACTION PROJECT 1–1

DISTINGUISHING YOUR INDIVIDUAL GOALS FROM ORGANIZATIONAL GOALS

This exercise asks you to distinguish between individual and organizational goals. Check which of the following are personal goals and which are the organization's goals for using this course as the "organization."

Individual	Organizational	Element to Be Rated
____	____	Pass the course
____	____	Acquire a basic understanding of human relations concepts
____	____	Start class on time
____	____	Create classroom environment for learning
____	____	Build students' workplace skills
____	____	Learn from text readings, action projects, cases, and the instructor
____	____	Apply knowledge gained from readings and classroom activities
____	____	Provide an educational opportunity for community members
____	____	Learn to work with others in group settings
____	____	Learn expectations of group members
____	____	Teach human relations concepts

Compare your assessment with your classmates or as the instructor advises.

ORGANIZATION AND RATIONALE OF THIS BOOK

One of the tests of a good manager is the ability to meet organizational objectives and to fulfill employee needs at the same time. Another test is how well a manager balances efficiency (doing things right) and effectiveness (doing the right thing). These skills are a major emphasis of the book.

The book is arranged so that we take on the challenges of human relations first at the micro, or individual, level then at the macro, or group, level. We cannot communicate effectively with others until we know our own values and confront our own challenges of career development, motivation, and job performance. Therefore, unlike other books that take a piecemeal approach, we take a logical approach to applying human relations—knowing one's values, abilities, and goals, before trying to manage or lead others.

Short-term solutions do not solve long-term human relations problems.

Personal goals such as job satisfaction, recognition, and career advancement are influenced by many different kinds of social and psychological factors as well as by the organizational condition of the work environment. Short-term solutions, no matter how popular they may be, usually do not solve complex human relations problems. Such problems demand carefully thought-out measures that must be given enough time in actual practice to prove or disprove their worth.

We seek to understand how people manage or lead in the workplace in order to achieve (1) greater productivity at work and (2) greater human satisfaction within the organization (Figure 1–1). Patterns of behavior develop within groups of all kinds. For example, parents and children interact in a special kind of group called the family, while people at a football game are interacting in still another kind of human group. The focus of this book is on the patterns of human behavior at work within organizations.

FIGURE 1-1 *Human Relations Is a Study of How People Relate and Work Together to Achieve Satisfaction Within an Organization*

THE INTERDISCIPLINARY ASPECT OF HUMAN RELATIONS

Human relations is an interdisciplinary field because it includes the research of several social sciences. For example, psychologists have done extensive research on the relation of the individual to the work environment, including studies on job satisfaction, job placement, incentives, testing, and training.

Psychologists and sociologists have contributed to human relations.

Sociologists, anthropologists, and social psychologists have made major contributions to human relations with studies of group behavior and group dynamics. Their concepts of role behavior, status effects, and the influence of informal groupings have proved invaluable in understanding behavior in work environments.

Political science has contributed useful information about the relationships between organizational structure, power struggles, and the processes of leadership, management, administration, and supervision.

Following a brief history of the human relations movement, we will consider aspects of communication, motivation, leadership, and decision making, among others, keeping in mind that they are important not only in and of themselves, but also as elements of an integrated, interdisciplinary field of study.

A BRIEF HISTORY OF HUMAN RELATIONS

It is impossible to specify the exact date on which the human relations movement came into being, but it is fair to say that it was not until the second half of the nineteenth century that much attention was paid to workers' needs, nor was there much understanding of how those needs impacted productivity. Prior to that time, most employers viewed labor as a commodity that could be bought and sold like any other commodity. Long hours, low wages, and miserable working conditions were the commonplace realities of the average worker's life. Labor unions were still struggling for existence and had not yet won the right to represent the labor force.

SCIENTIFIC MANAGEMENT

At the beginning of the twentieth century, Frederick Taylor and his contemporaries introduced and developed the theory and practice of **scientific management**. This approach held that greater productivity could be achieved by breaking down work into isolated, specific, specialized tasks. This theory became popular at approximately the same time mass production became feasible, and it helped increase the efficiency of the assembly line.

Frederick Taylor developed the theory of scientific management.

Scientific management has often been described as a series of techniques for increasing production rates through the means of better cost accounting procedures, incentive payments, and time and motion studies. However, utilizing these techniques did not in itself constitute scientific management, because, as Taylor put it, the main objective of scientific management was "to remove the causes for antagonism between the boss and the men who were under him."[2]

Taylor and followers like Frank and Lillian Gilbreth, whose lives were depicted in the movie *Cheaper by the Dozen*, were criticized on the grounds that scientific management tended to exploit workers more than it benefited them. Critics said that scientific management paid no attention to the complex social networks created by workers within the work environment. These critics held that it was precisely those complex social networks that had the greatest influence on production rates.

THE DEVELOPMENT OF UNIONS

At the same time, in response to unsafe working conditions, low pay, and the use of child labor, unions were becoming an increasingly powerful force in industrial affairs. From 1897 to 1904, membership in trade unions grew from 400,000 to 2 million and kept on growing. By 1920 trade unions throughout the nation received a large measure of recognition from the owners and managers of businesses. Chapter 15, "Organized Employee Relations," explores the role of unions.

ELTON MAYO'S HAWTHORNE EXPERIMENT

Membership in unions increased at the start of the twentieth century.

In the mid-1920s, the focal point for the human relations approach in business was the famous **Hawthorne studies** conducted by Elton Mayo and his colleagues. Mayo's group began its work by studying the effects of illumination, ventilation, and fatigue on workers at Western Electric's Hawthorne plant.

Elton Mayo's famous Hawthorne experiment was the focus of human research.

In one study, two groups of employees working under similar conditions and doing similar types of work were selected; one was the experimental group, while the other was the control group. Output records were kept for each group. The intensity of the light under which one group worked was varied systematically, while the light was held constant for the second group. When the intensity of the light for the first group was increased, the unsurprising result was that the productivity of the group increased. Yet decreasing the intensity of the light also increased productivity. In fact, the productivity of the group continued to increase as the level of illumination was lowered and one of the highest levels of productivity was recorded during an extremely low level of illumination. Obviously other variables were contaminating the effects of the experiment.

After a few years of experimentation, researchers concluded that group morale and personal motivation factors were the most important in explaining increased productivity.[3] These studies started a revolution in how management treated workers and became the foundation for the human relations movement. Even though recent analysis of the Hawthorne data points out that the experimental group received higher pay, thus calling into question the original interpretation,[4] the Hawthorne experiments had a major impact on human relations and continue to do so by providing a foundation for the human relations movement.

THE INFORMAL ORGANIZATION

The Hawthorne studies also showed that the normal interactions of workers at work create a social network called the **informal organization**, which exerts tremendous influence over workers' behavior patterns and can offset the formal rules of the organization. For example, workers can informally agree to slow down their production pace despite organizational goals for production rates.

The informal group can have as much influence as the formal organization.

As a result of the Hawthorne studies, it was no longer possible for management to view workers as tools or as isolated units in the production process. They had to be seen as complex human beings whose normal interactions were bound to affect total production output, no matter how sophisticated the technological processes employed were. Mayo's findings developed the image of workers as whole persons, creatures of sentiment, whose basic human needs often resulted in complex outcomes, outcomes that cannot be predicted in a purely technological framework.

POST-HAWTHORNE DEVELOPMENTS

With the passage of the Wagner Act in 1935 and increasing militant unionism, business leaders turned again toward meeting workers' needs—particularly as those needs influenced total productivity. The industrial expansion during World War II and the prosperous postwar period stimulated and encouraged a deeper understanding of the relationship between productivity and employee satisfaction.

Countless studies on human relations were published by business theorists and social scientists. Three of the most important were Douglas McGregor's comparison of traditional management theory, Theory X, to his humanistic management approach, Theory Y; Abraham Maslow's studies on the hierarchy of human needs; and Frederick Herzberg's motivation/hygiene theory. All of these were milestones in human relations studies and still exert considerable influence, as discussed in later chapters.

THE INFLUENCE OF JAPAN AND OTHER COUNTRIES

By the beginning of 1980, management theories and human relations concepts from other countries began to influence American management practice. William Ouchi's Theory Z focuses on Japanese work philosophy, which includes a belief in lifetime employment, strong company loyalty, and group consensus. Japan's emphasis on loyalty, high productivity, group decision making, and efficient production were seen as underlying their industrial success. The Japanese philosophy of management is based on long-term planning, not short-term crisis management. The actual decision-making

Japanese management characteristics.

process in Japan is less efficient than that of the United States, but it produces a companywide consensus on the best course of action.

FURTHER HISTORICAL DEVELOPMENT IN HUMAN RELATIONS

The field of human relations is continuing to respond to changes in society and the workplace. Recent developments in human relations include quality management, employee empowerment, and organizational transformation.

QUALITY MANAGEMENT

Quality Circles. **Quality circles** (QCs) are voluntary groups of employees engaged in decision making at the lowest practical level of the organization. Quality circles have been in existence in the United States since the early 1970s and continue to be used under various names.

People want to be part of the solution. A good manager asks his or her staff "How can we do this better?" and "How can we achieve this goal?" Employees are being asked to help make decisions about their jobs through a process often called *industrial democracy,* which is also leading to basic changes in the worker-boss relationship. During the 1970s, several European countries adopted laws mandating worker participation plans that ranged from worker representatives on corporate boards to shop floor workers' councils to help make daily decisions.

Figure 1–2 is a poem from the autoworkers' underground and illustrates the approach of some businesses.

In the 1980s, the use of small problem-solving groups of workers at GM was typical of the revolutionary changes that took place between workers and managers across the nation. Ford, like GM, became fully committed to what Ford calls *employee involvement,* with worker-management committees jointly considering decisions at every level of the corporation from the highest executive suite to the shop floor.

Whether they are still called quality circles or some other name, QCs or other decision-making groups are used frequently in industry today. The input of many employees is invaluable in making more intelligent, rational decisions. Of course, these voluntary teams are not appropriate for all decision making. They ought to be used selectively for problems that can be solved within a relatively short time, and where they will give positive reinforcement to the group.

Total Quality Management. **Total quality management** is a comprehensive approach to quality that encourages everyone in the organization to provide customers with reliable products and services.

Figure 1–3 shows a comparison of organizations of the past and the future. Notice particularly the differences in the people and quality variables.

Oakley and Krug recommend that people be part of a TQM solution and that firms strive to accomplish the following:

- Constantly look for small successes you are achieving.
- Research extensively what you are doing to generate these successes.
- Continually reclarify the specific objectives.
- Clarify the benefits to all parties (customers, shareholders, team, each person) of achieving those objectives.
- Continually search for what you could do more of, do better, or do differently to move closer to the objectives.[5]

FIGURE 1–2 *THE IMMATURITY OF THE AMERICAN MANAGEMENT APPROACH*

Are these men and women
Workers of the world?
or is it an overgrown nursery
with children—goosing, slapping, boys
giggling, snotty girls?
What is it about that entrance way,
those gates to the plant? Is it the
guard, the showing of your badge—the smell?
is there some invisible eye
that pierces you through and
transforms your being? Some aura
or ether, that brain and spirit washes you
and commands, "For eight hours
you shall be different."
What is it that instantaneously makes
a child out of a man?
Moments before he was a father, a husband,
an owner of property,
a voter, a lover, an adult.
When he spoke at least some listened.
Salesmen courted his favor.
Insurance men appealed to his family responsibility
and by chance the church sought his help . . .
But that was before he shuffled past the guard,
climbed the step,
hung up his coat and
took his place along the line.

Source: Thomas J. Peters and Robert H. Waterman, Jr., *In Search of Excellence* (New York: Harper & Row, 1982), 235–236.

EMPLOYEE EMPOWERMENT

In recent years there have been many names for the concept of empowering employees: for example, "liberation management" from Tom Peters,[6] and "emancipation capitalism" from John Case.[7] **Employee empowerment** means to give power or authority to, enable, or enfranchise employees to do their jobs. If employees are to do their jobs effectively, they need tools and training to do those jobs.

FIGURE 1–3 *Organizations of the Past and Future*

OLD

- Hierarchical
- Centralized planning and decision making
- Separate data systems
- Internal focus
- Little interest in retooling workers
- People as variable cost
- Quality control through inspection

NEW

- Flatter and smaller
- Centralized planning process and decentralized decision making
- Making thinking strategic at all levels
- Integrated data systems
- Strong customer orientation
- Continuous retraining
- Built-in quality through process control

Source: David S. Bushnell and Michael B. Halus, "TQM in the Public Sector: Strategies for Quality Service," *National Productivity Review*, summer 1992, 368. Reprinted with permission from *National Productivity Review.* Copyright 1992 by Executive Enterprises, Inc., 22 West 21st Street, New York, NY 10010-6990. 212-645-7880. All rights reserved.

Employee empowerment increases power and effectiveness.

Tom Peters is noted for advocating employee empowerment. His guiding premises for empowerment are to "involve everyone in everything" and "use self-managing teams."[8] Peters goes so far as to say that "the power of the team is so great that it is often wise to violate apparent common sense and force a team structure on almost everything."[9]

Supporting and inhibiting prescriptions for empowerment are shown in Figure 1–4. Notice the admonitions regarding listening to and training people as well as simplifying structures.

ORGANIZATIONAL TRANSFORMATION

Empowerment requires organizational transformation. An **organizational transformation** is a way of thinking and acting—not so much techniques or gimmicks but a real commitment to change—and is required to create a new type of employee relationship. See Figure 1–5 for one view of the emancipation transformation necessary to create a company of empowered employees. This kind of commitment requires rethinking the use of people as factors of production to employees and managers who work together to achieve organizational goals.

FIGURE 1-4 *SUPPORTS AND INHIBITORS FOR EMPOWERING PEOPLE*

Five Supports (Add Them)

- Listen/celebrate/recognize
- Spend time lavishly on recruiting
- Train and retrain
- Provide incentive pay for everyone
- Provide an employment guarantee

Three Inhibitors (Take Them Away)

- Simplify/reduce structure
- Reconceive the middle manager's role
- Eliminate bureaucratic rules and humiliating conditions

Source: Adapted from Tom Peters, *Thriving on Chaos: Handbook for a Management Revolution* (New York: Alfred A. Knopf, 1988), 283.

FIGURE 1-5 *FOUR STEPS IN CREATING A COMPANY OF EMPOWERED EMPLOYEES*

1. First, people at all levels have to be able to make decisions, and the company must be structured to encourage it. This doesn't mean democracy, let alone anarchy; decisions obviously have to be coordinated, and some will require an okay from top management.
2. Second, people need the information necessary to make intelligent decisions. This is a truism, and any company that sets up quality teams with any other modification of the traditional systems makes sure its employees have some data to work with.
3. Third, employees need training. Few Americans outside of accounting classes are taught to understand the financial information that governs a business.
4. Fourth, people need a stake in the outcome of their decisions—and in the company itself. A stake cuts through cynicism ("Why should I work extra hours just so someone else can make more money?") and adds to the intrinsic satisfaction of helping to create a successful company.

Source: Adapted from Tom Peters, *Thriving on Chaos: Handbook for a Management Revolution* (New York: Alfred A. Knopf, 1988), 89–90.

RECURRENT THEMES IN HUMAN RELATIONS

There are several fundamental themes in human relations that help define and can help reduce human relations problems. Foremost among these are human dignity, empathy, individual differences and diversity, the whole person, communication, motivation, leadership, teamwork, and constant change.

HUMAN DIGNITY

The basic premise of all human relations is the dignity and worth of humans. People are not like other factors of production. All employees must balance individual concerns in their private lives with the demands of their jobs. Certainly there are times in the boss-subordinate relationship when both boss and subordinate must do very unpleasant jobs. For example, terminating a worthwhile employee because of economic conditions is difficult for a supervisor. It is best to remember that day-to-day work is most effectively accomplished by recognizing the inherent worth of the human beings upon whom we are dependent. Treating each other with human dignity is an important part of a successful workplace.

EMPATHY

To treat each other with dignity, empathy is required. **Empathy** is the ability to put yourself in someone else's place and to understand that person's point of view, needs, and reasons for his or her actions. Lack of empathy is a primary cause of conflict in organizations. Empathy is the chief quality that mediators of labor disputes must have, and successful salespersons are usually empathic to a very high degree. Empathy is an important element in leadership, and its absence can create barriers to communication.

The theme of empathy, in the form of understanding other people's needs and desires, is a unifying theme of this book. It is particularly important in interpersonal communication, conflict resolution, union relations, discrimination, and intercultural relations.

INDIVIDUAL DIFFERENCES AND DIVERSITY

The concept of **individual differences** indicates that people are not all the same. These differences have an important impact on organizations in the selection of applicants for employment and in their motivation in various jobs. Individual differences need to be considered in three contexts: (1) differences among individuals in terms of job potential (e.g., abilities to learn a job), (2) the effects of training on individuals, and (3) differences in job performance after training. All are the concern of managers who are responsible for the performance of their employees.

The concept of individual differences.

Each person is different, but similar in many ways, including the need for respect, recognition, socialization, and trust. It is individual differences that really make the management of human relationships a challenge. Some people have more need for recognition; others want more respect; still others want greater promotion opportunities.

The workforce is diverse.

The workforce is more ethnically, gender, and educationally diverse than ever before. The average age of the workforce is also increasing. These are dramatic shifts that have an impact on management and leadership styles. They point to the art as well as the science of managing human relationships.

THE WHOLE PERSON

If something at home is bothering an employee, it might be desirable from the organization's viewpoint to have him or her leave that concern at home, but it is often not possible to separate people from their problems that easily. We bring with us our personal and family problems and crises. The **whole person** refers to the interrelationships of the mind and the body and the total effect these interrelationships have on the individual.

In "More Than Just a Paycheck," Carol Clurman writes: "Essentially, employers are being forced to have a stake in the professional *and* personal well-being of their employees, realizing single parents and dual-income duos must be able to juggle things at home in order to hack it at work."[10]

COMMUNICATION

In modern organizations, all functions depend on communication. Communication is the way in which information and understanding are transmitted; it unifies group behavior and provides the basis for group cooperation. Without effective communication procedures, no business can survive, much less prosper. Managers who cannot communicate effectively with employees cannot motivate them or exercise leadership. If workers cannot communicate well with management, they cannot perform their jobs properly or receive adequate recognition for their work. If communication in an organization is not good, then there is no way in which the human relations in that organization can satisfy the people who work there.

Chapter 6 deals with communication principles and processes, and presents a number of principles and communication behavior patterns, the mastery of which will lead to more effective communication.

MOTIVATION

Although human relations is a vast and complicated subject composed of and influenced by many variables, it can be described simply as the total response of individuals to various motivating forces. In other words, people in organizations relate to each other in the ways that they do because they are driven by psychological, social, emotional, and economic forces that have the power to motivate them to behave in particular ways.

Performance is a function of motivation and ability. When someone's abilities and ambitions match the demands of a particular job, then motivation is likely to be high. If the demands of the job exceed a person's abilities or ambitions, the job will not be done well and personal frustration will result no matter how hard the individual tries. If the drives and abilities of the person far outdistance the job demands, he or she may experience boredom and the job may be done carelessly.

Chapter 7, "Motivation," introduces some of the approaches to motivation that have been influential in the human relations movement. As with communication, motivation is a pervasive theme in this book, most notably in the chapters on change, appraisals, and creativity.

LEADERSHIP

In a very real sense, the history of the human relations movement is the history of modern business leadership. A leader's fundamental responsibility in any kind of organization is to get work done through the combined cooperative efforts of others.

A leader must communicate with and motivate his or her subordinates in a just and satisfactory manner or the work will not get done. The human relations function is not, of course, the only responsibility a leader has. Leaders are also responsible for setting direction, dealing with external constituencies, and securing the financial and market success of the firm. Leaders must have good employee human relations to handle these other functions well. Chapter 11 is devoted to leadership.

There we discuss how leading and facilitating others' work are important parts of the leader's job.

TEAMWORK

If individuals and groups are to be effective, they must learn to work and communicate as a team. Teams have become an essential part of modern organizations. Employees often are members of multiple teams or groups. If managers are to work effectively with subordinates and associates, they must learn to work and be evaluated as a team. We discuss teamwork in Chapter 12.

CONSTANT CHANGE

A final major theme of human relations is constant change. Leadership, management, and organizational human relationships are always changing. No longer can organizations conduct business as usual. The manager's goal is to balance the organization's interests with its people's interests.[11] We will put these changes into perspective throughout the book.

Change is constantly accelerating.

The qualities of initiative, teamwork, and creativity, are part of the change process. These qualities are basic skills that all managers and other employees must have to be successful. We will look at the change process further in Chapter 16. Analysis, judgment, and problem solving, in an age of high technology, are necessary skills that will be explored in Chapter 5.

Additional emphasis is also being placed on cross-cultural management skills in a global environment for employee betterment. This will be explored in Chapter 13.

EXPRESS YOUR OPINION

Should all people:

1. Experience human dignity?
2. Experience empathy?
3. Recognize individual differences?
4. Be motivated, developed, and communicated with in different ways?
5. Exercise responsibility within the constraints of the whole person concept?
6. Be subjected to or capable of adapting to change?

WHAT IS REQUIRED TO GUIDE OUR ORGANIZATIONS?

Figure 1-6 shows a hierarchy of skills required to conduct operations within organizations. Notice that the top echelon must provide the greater part of organizational leadership, but there is also room for administrators and middle managers and supervisors to provide leadership. Similarly, supervisors are charged primarily with running day-to-day operations, but the top leaders must be willing to be "hands on" without micromanaging.

FIGURE 1-6 *Hierarchy of Skills Required to Guide Organizations*

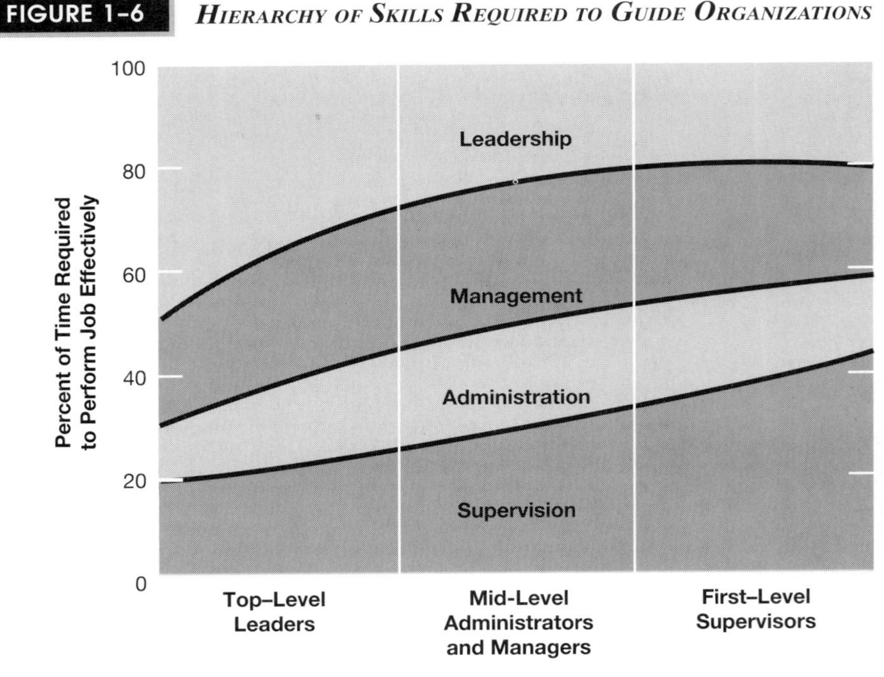

Increasingly, professional managers run our economy. How successful are they? What is really required of the people who run our organizations? Are they managers? leaders? administrators?

One view asserts that the best managers don't manage. The best managers lead, sponsor, and facilitate rather than order, direct, or tell others what to do. Good leaders and managers set good examples. Next, let us examine other management skills.

MANAGEMENT SKILLS

As we will discuss in Chapter 2, management has three broad aspects: technical, conceptual, and human relations. The technical aspect is the easiest to understand; most people obtain their jobs because of their ability to do certain tasks. However, the higher in management that a person goes, the more the ability to work with people and to handle abstract ideas becomes more important. At the upper levels, conceptual skills are more important—the ability to understand how parts of the organization fit together and how the organization interacts with its environment. The human relations aspect, or the ability to work well with people, is important at all levels, and thus is the focus of this book. This ability derives from a person's emotional intelligence, which is discussed in Chapter 2.

A supplementary view of the middle manager's role is presented in Figure 1–7 from an adaptation of an advertisement for Dun & Bradstreet Software.

Human relations skills are important at all levels.

Human relations skills are important now and will become even more so as technical and conceptual skills develop. Our major emphasis in this book, of course, is on the human relations skills that are needed for a successful career.

FIGURE 1-7 *"Is There a Middle Manager in the House?"*

If an accident happened and you YELLED,
"Is there a middle manager in the house?,"
would anyone come to the rescue?
What is a middle manager, anyway?
Valuable decision maker, or paper pusher?
How do you measure?
Sales per employee? Memo count?
Meetings per hour (MPH)?
And now that we're all trying to
re-invent the corporation,
what do we do with them?
Try asking *them* to re-invent their jobs.
From the ground up.
Maybe you can eliminate waste and inefficiency.
(Instead of people.)
Take advantage of the knowledge,
experience and ideas of your managers.
They'll probably surprise you.
(They can't wait to be asked.)

Source: Adapted from an advertisement by Dun & Bradstreet Software. Used with permission.

SELF-APPRAISAL

Of the basic themes mentioned in this chapter, which one do you feel most adept at performing?

1. Do you feel that you can communicate your ideas, feelings, and thoughts to others well?
2. Do you feel that you are best at giving pep talks and encouraging people to pursue their personal goals? Do you have a strong sense of direction and goal in life?
3. Perhaps responsibility and the desire for leadership are some of your strongest characteristics. Do you feel that you could, with a little time, lead a group of five students in a group discussion?
4. Finally, is the ability to empathize one of your assets? Do you feel that you really know how others feel and can place yourself in their shoes? Do people come to you for counsel and help on personal matters?

It is always exciting to see how you feel about the attitudes you expressed at the beginning of a course. At the end of the course look back and see if your feelings about certain ideas have changed. These questions will be hard to answer, but put the first ideas that come to mind down on paper. This exercise will hopefully have you thinking about these questions long after you have answered them.

1. Using a scale from 1 to 10 (1 = weakest, 10 = strongest), rate yourself in the following areas of human relations:
   a. Ability to communicate ______________________________
   b. Ability to motivate yourself and others ______________________________

(*continued*)

c. Ability to accept responsibility and lead others ______
d. Ability to empathize with others and understand their problems ______
e. Commitment to task ______
f. Commitment to people (boss, coworkers, customers, subordinates, etc.) ______

2. Which is more important, team spirit or individual achievement? Why?

______

3. Is today's fun more important than future accomplishments? Why?

______

4. What do you regard as your greatest personal achievement to date?

______

5. What do you regard as your greatest personal failure to date?

______

6. What two things would you most like to be said of you if you died today?

______ and ______

Compare your answers with classmates and friends to see how similar and different you are. While each individual is unique, we have overlapping and divergent values and goals, making the theory and practice of human relations both challenging and rewarding. Create an action plan for developing your weakest skills as you go through the course. By planning what you want from the class, you will maximize your learning.

SUMMARY

Human relations refers to the interactions that can occur among people, both organizational and personal. Organizational behavior is the study of how people, groups, and organizations behave. How you and others interact determines the quality of your work and personal lives.

Some common misconceptions about human relations are that it just makes people feel good at work, that it is common sense, and that managers manage all the time. There is a strong need to learn how people work together cooperatively—and sometimes in conflict—in organizations.

The approach that this book follows is a logical, applied approach to life and work. The study of human relations begins with you, the individual. Included in this is the study of emotional intelligence, values, self-esteem, time management, developing your career, and creative thinking. Our intention is to help you develop professionally. Then, we look at the knowledge and skills needed to interact effectively with others; communication, motivation, conflict management, leadership, and group behavior are explored. Finally, we look at contemporary issues in human relations, including diversity, workplace issues, labor relations, and managing change. That's the map for your trip through this book. Please enjoy the journey!

The history of human relations is approximately 100 years old. Frederick Taylor, the father of scientific management, and his followers were responsible for structuring management and allowing it to be studied as a science. Elton Mayo, one of the principals responsible for the Hawthorne experiment, learned that the social aspects of the job were as important, if not more so, than the technical aspects.

All the changes that have been taking place in management and employee human relations have been accelerated in recent years. Major contributing factors to this knowledge are quality management, people empowerment, and intercultural relations. Americans have learned much about management from the Japanese and others, and vice versa.

Fundamental concepts of human relations include the concepts of human dignity, empathy, individual differences, communication, motivation, leadership, and teamwork. How we relate to one another as human beings, how we put ourselves in others' places, and how we recognize individual needs make the management of human relations truly challenging.

People are hired primarily because of their technical skills. As a person is promoted to higher levels of management, the conceptual ability to handle abstract ideas becomes more important. Human relations skills are equally applicable to all levels of work and life.

There are major opportunities for leadership and management available today. We are more diverse as a culture and a workforce than ever before—a position that creates both opportunities and challenges. Managing in this dynamic environment will be fun. Enjoy it and your life!

CASE STUDY 1–1

JOE RILEY

Joe Riley is a charge nurse for the emergency room (ER) at Endo Valley Community Hospital. He is a technically competent nurse whose initial training as an emergency medical technician (EMT) took place during Desert Storm. After being discharged from the army, Joe completed his bachelor of science in nursing at a well-accredited university. He has expanded his proficiencies in nursing by taking advantage of continuing education in nursing offered through Endo Valley and local colleges and universities.

Joe is considered a good diagnostician by the people he works with and those he supervises. He is quick to spot life-threatening situations and to assist other members of the emergency room staff in alleviating physical pain and suffering of patients.

Joe's technical competence and expertise in providing nursing care is in sharp contrast to his people skills. He has managed to offend many patients, coworkers, doctors, and other members of the ER team. Some have complained to the hospital administration about his arrogance toward, impatience with, and rudeness to others—both patients and coworkers.

But the chief of ER medicine, Dr. Jake Banowetz, says that "there is no way we can terminate Joe. He has saved way too many lives by his quick actions to trade off some hurt, ruffled, or sensitive feelings." His subordinates resent Joe's "holier-than-thou" attitude; as a result, turnover is high among personnel in the ER. Turnover is sometimes higher in all emergency rooms because of the highly stressful environment, but much of the turnover here can be attributed to Joe's actions.

1. What is the problem? What "facts" do we need to know that we don't know? What courses of action are available to Joe and the administration/leadership of Endo Valley Community Hospital?
2. What do you recommend; that is, what would you do about Joe? Is this a problem with which you can identify in a different setting?
3. Can Joe and others like him learn people skills?
4. Is rudeness ever justified?

CASE STUDY 1-2

THE AEROBICS INSTRUCTOR

Jill Greenwood is the head aerobics instructor for the HealthCare Club. Jill and several other instructors conduct both high- and low-impact aerobics classes for men and women of different age groups. Jill recognizes that there are differences in the abilities of the various groups and even differences within the groups.

All the participants have a different reason for attending the aerobics classes; most want to attain and maintain a level of physical fitness, others enjoy the social atmosphere of the classes. Within any given class, some individuals desire autonomy—to be left alone to perform their exercises—while others want continual praise, recognition, and feedback, and still others want to increase their self-esteem.

Similarly, Jill finds that all the instructors are different in their abilities to communicate with, motivate, and lead their classes. Jill wants to know how to help her instructors better meet the needs of the participants. One of the instructors working with high-impact groups is Fred Billingsley. Fred likes to get the group "pumped up" and energized. He is a dynamic performer. The people in his class expect a tough workout, but they also expect a fun, entertaining time and they don't want to have to think. Fred attracts such a large following that it is difficult for him to pay attention to newcomers' and other individuals' aerobic needs.

Another instructor who desires recognition from her classes is Jan Grossman. Sometimes Jan has a great class, but other times it is a drag. Jan feeds off the mood of the class; if they are down, she is down. She takes her cues from the class instead of the other way around.

Jan is not as confident in her own aerobic and leadership skills as she would like to be. Jack Helmsley is very popular with students, but he is not keeping abreast of changes in the fitness industry. Some of his biomechanical moves are not as safe as they should be. HealthCare offers quarterly in-house training opportunities at no cost to all its aerobics instructors, but Jack very seldom takes advantage of the training.

1. What can Jill do to help her instructors better meet the needs of the participants?
2. Would you recommend training? If so, what specifically would you include in the training and how long would you recommend the training last? How would you structure any training?
3. Empathize with Jill—put yourself in her place—and try to communicate with Fred, Jan, and Jack in helping them perform their jobs better.

DISCUSSION AND STUDY QUESTIONS—TO KEEP YOU THINKING

1. What is your definition of human relations? Why would the study of human relations be more important to the supervisor than the average worker?
2. Can you name misconceptions about human relations that reading and studying this chapter may have helped clarify?
3. What are the various disciplines involved in human relations that require an interdisciplinary approach?
4. What is meant by the term scientific management?
5. What were major findings of the Hawthorne studies?
6. What are the newest developments in human relations?
7. What are recurrent themes in human relations?
8. What are the three basic skills required of all managers? Which set of skills is most important to the middle manager?
9. Distinguish among leadership, management, administration, and supervision.

NOTES

1. Daniel Goleman, "What Makes a Leader," *Harvard Business Review* (November–December 1998): 93–102.
2. Frederick Taylor, *Scientific Management* (New York: Harper, 1947), 128–129.
3. F. J. Roethlisberger, W. J. Dickson, and H. A. Wright, *Management and the Worker* (Cambridge, MA: Harvard University Press, 1939).
4. John G. Adair, "The Hawthrone Effect: A Reconsideration of the Methodological Artifact," *Journal of Applied Psychology* 69, no. 2 (1984): 334–345; and Gordon Diaper, "The Hawthorne Effect: A Fresh Examination," *Educational Studies* 15, no. 3 (1990): 1261–268.
5. Ed Oakley and Doug Krug, *Enlightened Leadership* (New York: Simon & Schuster, 1993), 116.
6. Tom Peters, *Liberation Management* (New York: Alfred A. Knopf, 1992).
7. John Case, "A Company of Businesspeople," *Inc.* (April 1993): 79–93.
8. Tom Peters, *Thriving on Chaos: Handbook for a Management Revolution* (New York: Alfred A. Knopf, 1988), 283.
9. Ibid., p. 302 (italics in original).
10. Carol Clurman, "More Than Just a Paycheck," *USA Weekend*, January 19–21, 1990, 4.
11. Denise Rousseau, "Corporate Culture Isn't Easy to Change," *The Wall Street Journal*, August 12, 1996, A1.

CHAPTER

2

Emotional Intelligence

Intrapersonal and Interpersonal Components

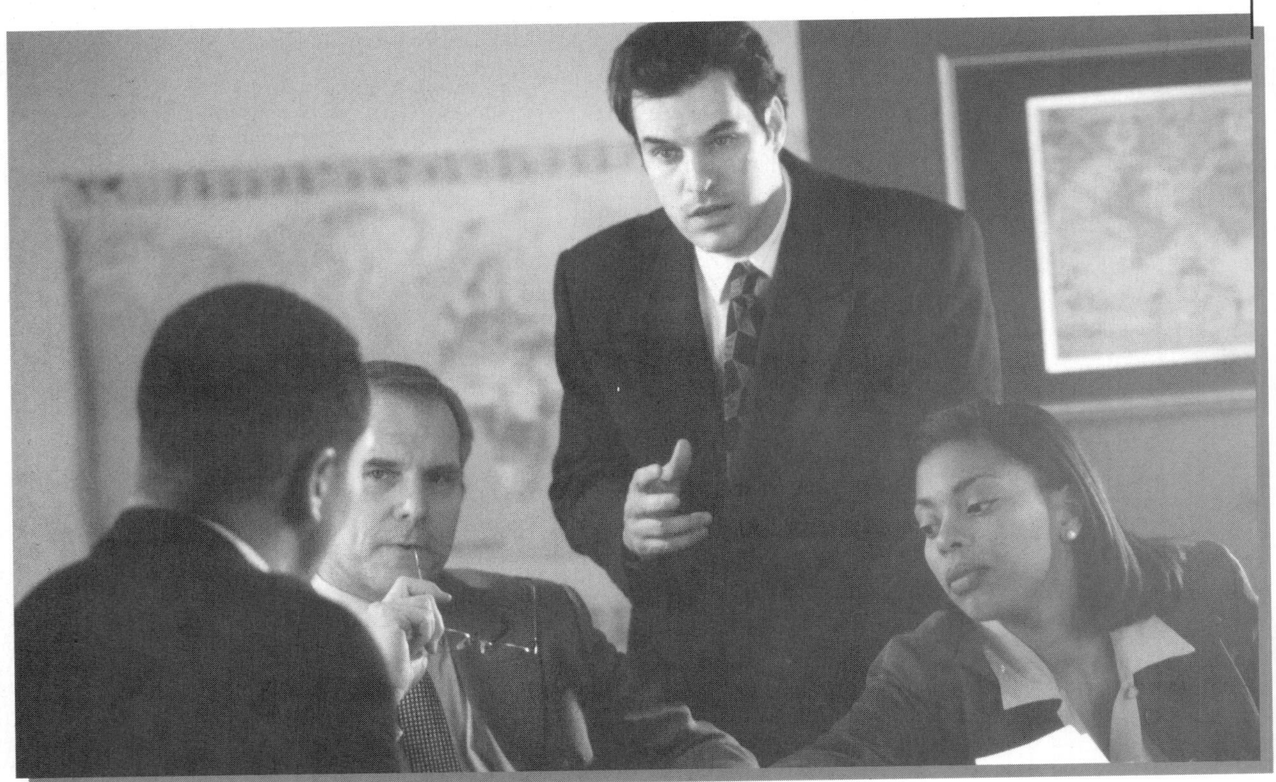

TO START YOU THINKING

Here are a few questions to think about before starting to read this chapter. In fact, these questions need to be answered before you can begin a meaningful career. Talk with classmates and others about your answers.

- Do you feel in control of your emotions?
- What is emotional intelligence?
- Is being emotional necessarily bad?
- How important is emotional intelligence in your personal life and career development?
- Do you know how to deal with people who are angry?
- Can you express how you are feeling without acting out how you are feeling?
- Is it possible to increase your emotional intelligence?
- How would managing emotions enhance today's workplace?

LEARNING GOALS

After studying this chapter, you should be able to:

1. Describe what role emotions play in human behavior.
2. Understand what emotional intelligence means.
3. Describe why emotional intelligence is important to human relations.
4. Distinguish between intrapersonal and interpersonal competencies.
5. Understand your emotional intelligence quotient.
6. Develop your own personal action plan for emotional intelligence development.
7. Define and apply the following terms and concepts (in order of first occurrence):

KEYWORDS

- **emotional intelligence**
- **intrapersonal competencies**
- **self-awareness**
- **managing emotions**
- **self-motivation**
- **interpersonal competencies**
- **relating well**
- **empathy**
- **emotional mentoring**
- **group intelligence**

WHAT IS MOST IMPORTANT?

If you could choose one area of study that would help you the most in your professional life, what would it be? Would accounting be the course of study to open the door of opportunity and success or would it be marketing? Could you sell your way to the top? Perhaps you would choose management so you could learn the latest theories and techniques to successfully lead your company into the future.

The answer is none of the above! The course of study that would help you climb the corporate ladder more than any other course is one not taught at most colleges. Research tells us that the majority of people's future success is not based on only their technical competence, though technical competence is important. Rather, career success is contingent upon a group of abilities known as emotional intelligence (EI). These are the abilities or competencies that allow people to create positive personal attributes and enhance their relationships with others.

EI enhances relationships with others.

This chapter addresses the emotional intelligence competencies that are necessary for success. To begin our study in this area, we will take a short trip into the distant past as we track the development of some pertinent parts of our brains, concentrating on the parts that affect our emotions. We will then look at the how and why of our reactions to certain situations. Next we will talk about how our actions are perceived by others and how we use emotional intelligence to become better skilled in our dealings with others. As you go through this chapter, keep in mind that these skills will help you in your professional career as well as with personal relationships.

WHAT ARE EMOTIONS?

We are all aware of times when we might have reacted to a friend or coworker in a way that, upon reflection, was completely inappropriate behavior. Maybe we reacted too angrily over something someone said or did. If it is any comfort, that same kind of reaction probably saved the life of our ancestors many times over. In fact, if our ancestors had not utilized that same type of emotional response, we probably would not be here today. We are all hardwired to react to certain stimuli before we even have a chance to think.[1]

Surviving in the primitive world was a matter of responding quickly to external threats. Over the centuries, human beings developed instincts, such as fight or flight, to deal with external threats. If they were being attacked by a large animal and stopped to think about whether or not they should run, by the time they reflected it probably would have been too late. Human beings are endowed with several highly specialized systems in their brain that exist simply to handle specific external problems. Our brain systems have the ability to cause our bodies to begin reacting before the thinking part of our brain, the cortex, even knows that anything is going on. It has been suggested that the truly important functions of our body, such as breathing, pumping blood, and reacting to danger, are too important to leave to the thinking part of our brain.[2]

SO HOW DO THESE "AUTOMATIC REACTION SYSTEMS" WORK?

Some emotional reactions are genetic.

Each emotion has evolved separately to handle specific situations. Some responses are innate: We are actually born afraid of certain things, such as loud noises. Other emotional reactions are learned. Thus, a newborn baby will be afraid of the loud bark of an angry dog, but will have to learn which spiders to fear. How do our automatic reaction systems work?

ACTION PROJECT 2-1

FOR DISCUSSION

Humans beings, because of their higher level of consciousness, have a whole set of fears that other animals do not have and that have an emotion-packed effect. These threats are created because of our ability to think. For example, people can be afraid of losing their jobs, losing money in the stock market, and losing a close friend. These are all fears that, as far as we know, other animals do not have. These fears differ across individuals. What are some of your fears? How do your fears affect how you interact with others?

Let's say you are taking a walk in the park. All of a sudden, out of the corner of your eye, you see movement in a bush. By the time you are cognitively aware that you have seen this movement, some parts of your brain are already reacting to the situation. First, all sensory input to your body through four of your five senses—hearing, seeing, feeling, and tasting are constantly being monitored by a group of nerve cells in the brain known as the thalamus (smell takes a different route).

The thalamus, working with the hypothalamus and the hippocampus, decides what information should be sent on to the cortex (the thinking part of the brain), what information should be acted upon immediately, and what information should be discarded. As the thalamus is receiving information, a small part of this information is also going to the amygdala. The amygdala is the alarm system of the body and houses all emotional memories. If the amygdala senses danger, based on previous experience or on genetically coded information that it has stored, it begins to flood the body with orders to produce hormones, instructions to specific muscles to commence certain actions, and so forth.

All of this activity is happening, indeed well into motion, before your thinking brain is even aware of what is going on! So you jump back, or focus on the danger, or begin whatever strategy is programmed genetically, or do what has been successful in the past in similar situations. How you handle these situations is an indication of your emotional intelligence; for example, if you are able to maintain your cool in a threatening situation, instead of displaying your anger, you are acting in an emotionally intelligent way. Because the amygdala only gets a part of the sensory flow, it must make judgments before it has all the facts. Many times people will react to situations totally inappropriately because their brains didn't have all the facts before they acted. Remember the last time your pet jumped up on your lap. If you didn't expect it, even though you could plainly see it was Rover or Fluffy, your body reacted as if it were a tiger coming after you.

If the amygdala assesses the threat to the human body as great, it can shut down communication to the thinking brain and take complete control of the response. You have probably had the experience of "seeing red" or being so angry that there was nothing you could do about it. Many times in those situations people will say, "I couldn't think straight." Probably a more accurate statement would be that "I could not think at all."

Indeed, we are born with certain genetic engineering that controls our actions in dangerous situations. We have little or no control over these reactions, at least during the first nanoseconds of experiencing them. People are also born with certain emotional tendencies; in areas such as bravery, temperament, and similar traits, the latest research shows that we inherit tendencies toward certain actions, but, we can choose to react differently. This ability to monitor and manage our temperament or emotions determines, in part, our emotional intelligence.

EMOTIONAL INTELLIGENCE

Emotional intelligence impacts our success in personal and career development.

So one of the major factors impacting our success in personal and career development is emotional intelligence. The study of **emotional intelligence** deals with how people handle their reactions to all the stimuli their brain is constantly receiving. In other words, how someone handles his or her emotions, as well as how he or she assists others in managing their emotions, plays an increasingly important role in how successful that person is in his or her personal life and career. Because emotional intelligence has emerged within the last decade as an indicator of career success, organizations such as Johnson & Johnson, AT&T, and American Express are training their leaders in the use of emotional intelligence skills.

You need strong technical skills to get a job.

Psychologists Jack Mayer and Peter Salovey theoretically established EI as a measurable intelligence similar to IQ (intelligence quotient). Daniel Goleman[3] popularized emotional intelligence in the business realm by describing its importance as an ingredient for successful business careers and as a crucial component for effective group performance. Goleman found that EI plays "an increasingly important role at the highest levels of the company, where differences in technical skills are of negligible importance. In other words, the higher the rank of the person considered to be a star performer, the more emotional intelligence capabilities show up as the reason for his or her effectiveness."[4] In comparing star performers in leadership positions with average performers, Goleman states that almost 90 percent of the difference in the profiles of the two groups was attributable to emotional intelligence factors rather than cognitive abilities.

What exactly would these differences involve? To answer this question, let's look at the skills required of managers to be successful.

MANAGEMENT SKILLS

Management has three broad aspects: technical, conceptual, and human relations. The technical aspect is of primary importance at lower levels in the organization. Most people obtain their jobs because of their ability to do certain tasks. Their first promotion may be based on how much they know about the department and the technical aspects related to their particular positions. A supervisor may deal with such technical contingencies as:

1. Variations in the product or raw material
2. Shortages of raw materials
3. Breakdowns of machines
4. Shortages and variations of tools and equipment
5. Shortages of space

The foundation of any career is, of course, technical expertise in a chosen field. While the majority of an employee's future success will not be correlated with the amount of his or her technical expertise, the employee must have a strong knowledge base in his or her chosen field in order to get the job and gain entrance to the game. However, as a person is promoted up the ranks, the technical aspects become less important, and the ability to handle abstract ideas and to work with people becomes more important. Figure 2–1 illustrates the varying mix of these three types of abilities.

At upper levels of the organization, conceptual skills become salient—the ability to understand how parts of the organization fit together and how the organization interacts with its environment. A company president spends time studying not only the firm's problems, but also new laws, community reaction, and, of course, the competition. Information about all these outside groups, as well as actions taking place inside the firm, are used by the president in deciding on the best direction for the company. Top management deals with more broadly conceptual problems, such as the following:

1. Strategic response to a new invention by a competitor
2. Community objections to a new plant
3. Failure to receive a large sales contract that was expected
4. An unexpected wildcat strike

Human relations skills are important at all levels.

The human relations aspect, or the ability to work well with people, is important at all levels; however, it becomes increasingly important as one moves up in the organizational hierarchy. Emotional intelligence forms the basis of a manager's human relations skills. We have stated that the majority of a person's career success will be based on EI or what some commonly refer to as "people skills," but this is the average over a total career. In the beginning, success is more dependent on technical ability. As managers move up the career ladder, effective managerial skills shift from the technical toward EI.

As you move up the career ladder the emphasis shifts to EI.

Think about some of the manager(s) you have now or you worked with in the past. Probably the more important or higher up the corporate ladder the manager was, the less he or she needed to handle the technical aspects of the job (Figure 2–2). At the top of the corporate ladder, most CEOs use little technical training in the performance of their job. In fact, some researchers believe that the only technical

FIGURE 2–1 *Three Skills Are Necessary in Management. Technical Skills Are More Important to the First-Line Supervisor. Conceptual Skills Are More Important to the Company President. Human Relations Skills Are Equally Important to All Levels*

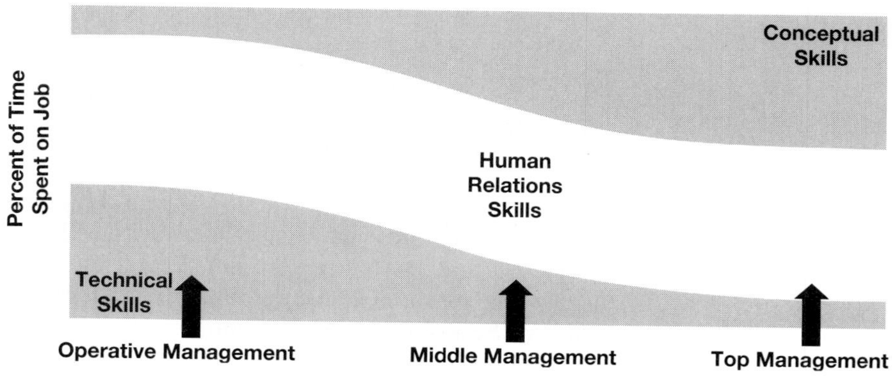

FIGURE 2-2 *Relationship of Your Technical Skills and Emotional Intelligence to Career Success*

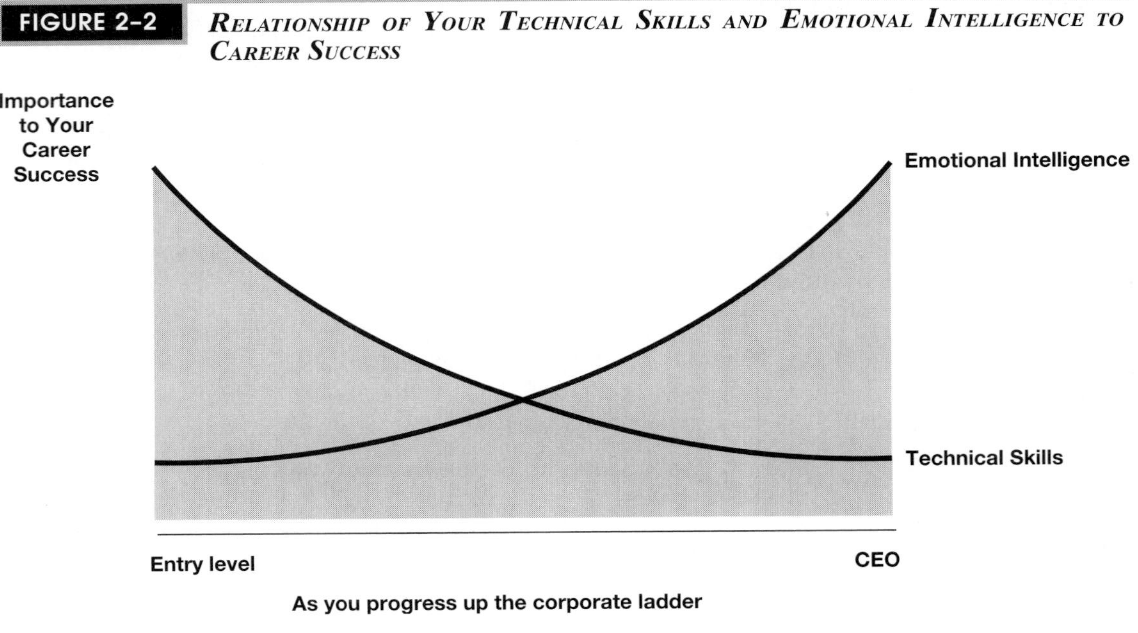

ability that is common among top CEOs is the ability to see the big picture and how the company and its products fit into that picture. All the rest of the pertinent abilities of these CEOs revolve around their ability to deal with people. Consider the number of companies that hire CEOs from outside the company and even outside the industry. For example, Lou Gerstner was a manager at American Express and then RJR Nabisco before taking the reigns at IBM. How much technical knowledge about computers did he bring to IBM?

Current changes in the work environment suggest that EI will be of increasing importance to workers at all levels in the new millennium. To deal with rapid technological and social change, individuals need the interpersonal competencies included in what we term emotional intelligence—the ability to recognize and respond to the emotions and feelings of others as well as the skill to help others manage their emotions.[5] In today's information technology-driven environment, teams, as opposed to individuals, are often the primary work unit. Research tells us that successful work groups have higher EI than unsuccessful ones.[6] We will take a closer look at teams and EI later in this chapter.

MEASURING YOUR EMOTIONAL INTELLIGENCE

The basic building block to enhanced EI is a high awareness of your emotions and how you handle those emotions. One way to estimate your current EI quotient is to complete a self-assessment. Action Project 2–2 provides alternative ways to learn more about your emotional intelligence quotient. This will assist you in fully understanding the remainder of this chapter.

Now you know how important EI skills are to your future, you have assessed your EI, and have an idea of your abilities in this area. For some of you, this has been a real eye-opening experience. There are two pieces of good news to consider. First, unlike a person's IQ, one's EI can be changed. People can learn strategies to help

ACTION PROJECT 2–2

ASSESSING YOUR EMOTIONAL INTELLIGENCE[7] (INDIVIDUAL EXERCISE) AND PLANNING FOR GROWTH

ASSESSING YOUR EMOTIONAL INTELLIGENCE

Entering the term *emotional intelligence* into a search engine will produce some Web site addresses for scoring your emotional intelligence. Here are some examples:

1. www.queendom.com/tests/iq/emotional_iq_r2_access.html

   This quiz has 70 items and will require about 35 minutes to complete. You will receive your score and some suggestions for improving your emotional intelligence competencies.

2. ei.haygroup.com/resources/default_ieitest.htm

   For a shorter version, try this 10-item quiz that quickly analyzes your emotional intelligence.

Hendrie Weisinger's book, *Emotional Intelligence at Work,*[7] has a section for assessing your emotional intelligence (pp. 214–215) and guidelines for developing a personal plan to increase your ability to intelligently handle your emotions (pp. 216–217). In addition, the book provides specific ways to develop these attributes that are clear and easy to follow.

PLANNING FOR GROWTH

1. Study your EI results.
2. Identify your strong EI skills and the EI skills you want to improve. You may also ask friends and coworkers to complete an EI assessment to see how they rate your EI. Often, seeing how others view our competencies compared to how we see ourselves reveals different strengths and weaknesses that assist us as we plan for professional growth. This will also help as you are analyzing your EI self-awareness. In fact, it is often the case that outside observers are far more accurate in judging a person's true emotional state than the individual being judged.[8]
3. List two strengths and two weaknesses that you identified.
4. Write out a plan for enhancing the two areas where you need the most improvement. Be very specific. For example, instead of saying, "I will not get angry with classmates," say, "When a classmate makes me mad, I will count to 10 before I respond."
5. Revisit the plan each Friday. Reflect on how you worked on your emotional intelligence competencies; congratulate yourself when you recognize improvements in how you handled your emotions and make any needed revision to the plan for the following week.

Following these steps will allow you to increase your emotional intelligence over time and assure you greater success in personal and workplace relationships.

them control their anger and make them a better team player. The second piece of good news is that an individual does not need to become an expert in all the EI skills to be successful. There is a critical mass of skills that, once mastered, will allow all of us to act and work effectively in most situations.

Your emotional intelligence can be increased.

It's uplifting to know that EI can be increased through committed effort. This can be achieved by utilizing the building-block approach to EI outlined by psychologists John Mayer and Peter Salovey when they developed the theory of EI in 1990. Each building block outlines abilities that increase EI. As you master each block, you incorporate and build onto the previous block(s). You can, in this way, increase your EI quotient through enhancing your ability to:

- Accurately perceive, appraise, and express emotion.
- Access or generate feelings on demand when they can facilitate understanding of yourself or another person.
- Understand emotions and the knowledge that derives from those emotions.
- Regulate emotions to promote emotional and intellectual growth.[9]

SO WHAT HAS ALL THIS GOT TO DO WITH ME?

Many of the things we do are in response to some emotion.

Many of our behaviors are in response to some emotion. Now we have an idea of why we do some of the dumb things we do. In order to work on those behaviors that might be holding us back in our human relations, we must first be aware of what they are. We now know the basics of the biology of our responses.

From the EI assessment you completed, you now have a picture of how you tend to react to certain situations. If you used Hendrie Weisinger's book you probably noticed, as you scored your EI assessment, that EI is divided into two components—the *intrapersonal* component and the *interpersonal* component.

INTRAPERSONAL AND INTERPERSONAL COMPETENCIES

INTRAPERSONAL COMPONENTS

Intrapersonal competencies, according to Weisinger, deal with increasing our EI within ourselves and are comprised of self-awareness, managing emotions, and self-motivation.

Self-Awareness. Developing high **self-awareness** involves the skill of monitoring oneself, observing oneself in action, and influencing one's actions so they work to one's benefit. How skilled are you at knowing what particular emotions are diving your actions right now? In order to begin any changes in your behavior, you must first know where you are. You have found an indication of your personal starting point through the EI assessment you completed and scored.

Not all emotions come from outside stimulus, or at least the connection between the emotion or feeling and the outside world is not that direct or obvious. You can be sitting in an armchair when all of a sudden you begin to worry about this or that. Sometimes you can trace why you began to worry about a certain thing, but at other times, worry and depression seem to come from out of the blue.

Try this exercise to increase your self-awareness. Take out a piece of paper, close your eyes, think hard, and then write down all of the emotional states you have experienced during the last 24 hours. If you are normal, and the last 24 hours have been normal, you have probably experienced a number of emotions. You have probably been happy, maybe a little sad, and perhaps a little angry.

If you were alone when you experienced these emotions, then you would not have shared them at the time with anyone else. If you were not alone, write down next to each of the emotions the name of the person who was with you when you were experiencing the emotion. If someone was with you whom you care about or who can affect your career or life, write down how that person reacted to your expression of your emotion. Was it positive or negative?

The first step in dealing with and possibly changing the management of your emotions is to be aware of what those emotions are at any time. You need to develop a system for constantly monitoring your emotional state. The real trick to monitoring your emotional state is the recognition of when it changes. We will talk about this more in the next section when we outline possible strategies for intercepting negative emotional surges and lessening or even nullifying their effect.

Managing Your Emotions. **Managing emotions**, rather than suppressing them, requires that a person understand those emotions and use that understanding to deal with situations productively. How good are you at managing what is going on as far as your emotions are concerned? Managing does not necessarily mean suppressing your emotions. The skills we are talking about here are more along the line of controlling how you express each emotion.

Most of the time we know when we are angry. Sometimes, however, we are slightly irritated, but do not think we are angry, yet others react to us as if we were. Sometimes we are so angry that others avoid us for a period of time. Anger that is inappropriately expressed is one of the more destructive emotions as far as relationships are concerned. What can you do when you feel angry? As we discussed earlier, our body is already reacting to protect itself; possibly it has already started to shut down your thinking brain—so you must act. You need to have a preplanned reaction to anger before you get angry. If you have such a plan of action, then you can begin reacting before or even during a thinking-brain shutdown and handle the situation more intelligently.

One strategy is to count to ten. Doing so gives the cortex (the thinking brain) time to engage. Hopefully, during this time, you will be able to analyze the real situation and think of a rational response. There are other strategies that focus on both getting your cortex engaged and on softening the feel of the anger. For example, you may think of a quiet place—somewhere you have actually been or a place you imagine in your mind. In this place you are so calm, so at peace that nothing bothers you; this place makes you feel so good that you could stay there forever. Pick a place and practice going there in your mind whenever you want. The first few times you let your mind take you there, do it when you are not angry. Then gradually work with this script when you feel angry.

AN INTERESTING POINT: EMOTIONS BUILD ON EACH OTHER

When you are angry about something and other things happen, no matter how insignificant, you will probably blow the situation out of proportion and act as if the second thing is much more of a problem than it really is. For example, on the way to work you got a traffic ticket; then you came into the office and found that someone took the last cup of coffee and failed to brew another pot.

Motivating Yourself. **Self-motivation** is recognizing and using available (internal and external) sources of motivation to enable you to effectively work through opportunity as well as adversity.

This is a very important part of EI. Motivation is an emotion that is partially the result of internal stimulus and partially the result of external stimulus. One of the most important emotions you can have is an overall positive attitude. If you are positively motivated to do something, you can engage all the energies of your body toward that goal, just as if you were being threatened. You also require motivation to go to your quiet place or to engage whatever strategy you have decided on to intercept harmful effects of emotions. The German philosopher G. W. F. Hegel said, "Nothing great in the world has ever been accomplished without passion."

INTERPERSONAL RELATIONS

Interpersonal competencies involve using EI in your relations with others.

Interpersonal competencies involve using EI in our relations with others and include relating well and emotional mentoring.

Relating Well. **Relating well** involves developing effective communication skills and engaging in effective communication practices to help with relationship building. People who relate well are able to monitor their emotions and, at the same time, recognize how their actions are affecting others. A crucial component of relating well with others is the ability to empathize with others. Empathy involves identifying the emotions of another person and being able to see the situation from that other person's perspective. Empathy does not mean agreeing with how the person feels, but involves acknowledging the person's feelings and trying to experience what he or she is feeling. Remember from Chapter 1 that lack of empathy is a primary cause of conflict in organizations. Here are some questions to ask yourself that will assist you in using empathy when dealing with others:

1. What is the general emotional state of this person?
2. How are my actions, communications, or reactions affecting this person's emotional state?
3. How can I change how I communicate and act to more precisely obtain the effect I want from this interaction?

Emotional Mentoring. **Emotional mentoring** is helping others to manage their own emotions, communicate effectively, solve problems, and ultimately perform to the best of their abilities. In addition, it encompasses basic business social skills—effective communication, appropriate manners, and interpersonal expertise. In combination, these competencies provide social polish.

As you can see, enhancing your intrapersonal and interpersonal competencies will increase your emotional intelligence. Strong emotional intelligence provides for increased success in your career and personal life. Just as EI is important to an individual's success, it plays a key role in the effectiveness of teams.

EMOTIONAL INTELLIGENCE AND TEAMS

Group intelligence is defined as "the functional intelligence of a group of people working as a unit."[10] Research conducted on group intelligence supports the idea that group members' interpersonal skills and compatibility are the key to effective group performance. Although it is important that at least one member of the team has a high IQ, EI skills—such as social skills, empathy, motivation, the ability to resolve differences, and effective communication—are better at predicting how well the team will do. This suggests that emotionally intelligent individuals, who work well with others and elevate the group's collective emotional intelligence, will be the most valued and sought-after employees.

Daniel Goleman, in his book *Working with Emotional Intelligence*, lists the following emotional competencies identified through research as the distinguishing attributes of star organizational teams:

- Empathy or interpersonal understanding
- Cooperation and a unified effort
- Open communication, setting explicit norms and expectations, and confronting under-performing members

- A drive to improve so that team members pay attention to performance feedback and seek improvement
- Self-awareness in the form of evaluating strengths and weaknesses as a team
- Initiative and taking a proactive stance toward solving problems
- Self-confidence as a team
- Flexibility in completing tasks
- Organizational awareness in terms of both assessing the needs of other key groups in the company and being resourceful in using what the organization has to offer
- Building bonds to other teams[11]

Utilizing these skills with technical competence will create team synergy. According to Stephen Covey, "when teams achieve synergy, gain momentum, and 'get on a roll,' they become virtually unstoppable."[12] Both talent and synergy are needed for developing unstoppable teams. Covey reminds us that:

> The value system in the United States is so focused on individualism and upon freedom of expression and freedom of action, without the corresponding sense of social responsibility, that it has created a culture of confrontation and adversarialism—the polar opposite of synergy and teamwork.[13]

This chapter has provided you with a glimpse of an extremely important topic. In fact, as we stated at the beginning of the chapter, it is probably the most important topic to you as far as your future success is concerned. This is especially true in today's fast-paced world, as Daniel Goleman reminds us in *Working with Emotional Intelligence*:

> The rules for work are changing. We're being judged by a new yardstick: not just how smart we are, or our expertise, but also how well we handle ourselves and each other.[14]

SUMMARY

This chapter addresses the competencies that are necessary for personal and career success. As human beings we are born with instinctual tendencies that impact, direct, and sometimes determine emotional responses, but we can change the way we react to certain emotions. Emotional intelligence encompasses how we handle our emotions as well as how we assist others in managing their emotions. EI plays an increasingly important role as one of the major factors impacting how successful we are in our personal lives and in our careers. EI can be increased through committed effort.

To increase EI, you need to accurately perceive, appraise, and express emotion; access or generate feelings on demand when they can facilitate understanding of yourself and another; understand emotions and the knowledge that derives from those emotions; and regulate emotions to promote emotional and intellectual growth.

Emotional intelligence is divided into intrapersonal and interpersonal components. Intrapersonal competencies deal with increasing your EI within yourself and consist of self-awareness, managing emotions, and self-motivation. Interpersonal competencies involve using your EI in your relations with others and include relating well and emotional mentoring.

Group intelligence refers to the functional intelligence of a group of people working as a unit. Research into group intelligence shows that a group members' interpersonal skills and compatibility is the key to effective group performance. While at least one member of the team needs to have a high IQ, EI skills, including social skills, empathy, motivation, the ability to resolve differences, and effective communication, are more important in determining how well the team will perform. This suggests that emotionally intelligent individuals, who work well with others and elevate the group's collective emotional intelligence, will be the most valued and sought-after employees.

CASE STUDY 2-1

THE FIRM

Paul has worked as a paraprofessional for the accounting firm of Max Wojcik and Associates since he graduated from high school in 1997. Although he does not hold a college degree, he has completed several training programs and incurred practical experience over the years. Amanda also works for the same firm. After graduating from high school in 1996, Amanda attended college by taking classes at night and on the weekends; she eventually (last June) earned a bachelor of business administration degree with a major in accounting. She has worked at the firm for five months.

Normally, Paul works with Gary, who is one of Amanda's peers. However, due to deadline pressures, Paul had been assigned to work for Amanda until Amanda's current auditing project is finished. The first task Amanda gave Paul was to enter some data into the computer. Problems began occurring almost immediately. Periodically, the computer program would have problems with the data. It just so happened that Paul was at the keyboard when the data was first rejected. From that moment, Amanda began blaming Paul for problems with this project. She even went so far as to complain to his supervisors that Paul was screwing up the engagement. Amanda periodically had to go to Paul's cubicle to confer on the project. Each time that she went over, she made cutting remarks to Paul, blaming him for the problems.

Paul takes great pride in his work and was offended that a person, especially a new person, would criticize the quality of his work. The two had a major "blow up" when something in the final presentation to the client had to be changed. Although it was no one's fault, Amanda blamed Paul. Paul exploded, yelling at Amanda about the way he was being treated. Feeling the pressure of the deadline that stood despite the technical difficulties, Amanda's nerves were also stretched thin. She, too, began yelling and throwing things in Paul's cubicle. The situation ended when the firm's manager took both employees into the president's office to "talk it out."

1. Discuss the cause for the tension in this office situation. Who is at fault and why?
2. A higher emotional intelligence rating in what areas would have benefited Amanda in this situation?
3. How would you suggest that Amanda plan for further professional development? What are some specific things that she might focus on?

CASE STUDY 2-2

THE BANK

Mandi, a recent business graduate, began working as a manager trainee at Uptown Bank, which employs about 45 employees. Her first month went wonderfully as she began to learn the ropes by rotating through the different departments of the bank. She gained hands-on experience working as a teller and assisting in the accounts division. She also shadowed trainers in new accounts and the loan department. Mandi is an easy-going person, who gets along well with her co-workers. Her trainers had many positive things to say about her work. Overall, Mandi greatly enjoyed her first month at the bank.

After training, Mandi was placed with a supervisor. Upon meeting Mandi for the first time, her supervisor, Theodore, chastised Mandi for the suit she was wearing. Theodore didn't like the short length of Mandi's suit skirt, and told Mandi that she was stupid to buy a skirt that fell above the knee, and even more stupid to wear short skirts to work. At first Mandi thought that the older man was joking, however, a glance at Theodore's serious expression told her otherwise. Her feelings hurt, Mandi could only mumble, "Oh, I'm sorry" before she hurried out of her supervisor's critical eye and retreated to her own desk.

Since that initial first slam, Mandi's relationship with Theodore has increasingly worsened because Theodore's temper flares often and he shouts at Mandi daily. Mandi feels that Theodore overlooks all of her good work, and seeks her out only to reprimand and belittle her. As a result, Mandi constantly avoids her supervisor, even attempting to hide from Theodore whenever possible. Because Mandi continuously avoids him, Theodore believes that Mandi is a slacker. He thinks that Mandi hides to avoid being assigned tasks. Furthermore, since Mandi constantly avoids him, Theodore cannot explain new tasks to her, or critique the work that she does.

Theodore has come to expect a lower level of performance from Mandi, and continuously views Mandi's work in a negative light. The situation in the office is in a downward spiral. Someone must take action to correct the situation.

1. Before the situation can be corrected, who do you think is responsible? Why?

2. When Mandi avoids Theodore, why is Theodore unable to understand Mandi's true reason for this avoidance? How should this problem be solved?

3. How could this situation have been handled with more emotional intelligence? What specific steps could Mandi and Theodore take to become more emotionally intelligent?

DISCUSSION AND STUDY QUESTIONS—TO KEEP YOU THINKING

1. How important is emotional intelligence to your career and personal relationships? Explain.

2. Describe the difference between intrapersonal and interpersonal competencies.

3. What does the term emotional intelligence mean to you?

4. Describe your emotional intelligence profile. Where are your strengths? Which area(s) of EI do you believe you should work to improve? What is your plan for improvement?

NOTES

1. Nigel Nicholson, "How Hardwired is Human Behavior?" *Harvard Business Review* (July–August 1998): 135–170.

2. Daniel Goleman, *Emotional Intelligence* (New York: Bantam, 1995).

3. Ibid.; Daniel Goleman, *Working with Emotional Intelligence* (New York: Bantam, 1998).

4. Daniel Goleman, "What Makes a Leader?" *Harvard Business Review* 77 (1998): 93–102.

5. D. C. Schmidt, "Organizational Change and the Role of Emotional Intelligence" (paper presented at the Academy of Management meeting, Boston, MA, 1997).

6. W. Williams and R. Sternberg, " Group Intelligence: Why Some Groups Are Better Than Others," *Intelligence* 12 no. 4 (1988): 351–377.

7. Hendrie Weisinger, *Emotional Intelligence at Work* (San Francisco: Jossey-Bass Inc., 1998), 214–217.

8. Joseph LeDoux, *The Emotional Brain* (New York: Simon & Schuster, 1996), 65.

9. Ibid., xvii–xviii.

10. W. Williams and R. Sternberg, "Group Intelligence: Why Some Groups Are Better Than Others." *Intelligence* 12 no. 4 (1988): 351–377.

11. Daniel Goleman, *Emotional Intelligence* (New York: Bantam, 1995), 219–220.

12. Steven R. Covey, "Unstoppable Teams," *Executive Excellence* 13 no. 7 (1996): 7.

13. Steven R. Covey, "Unstoppable Teams," *Executive Excellence* 13 no. 7 (1996): 8.

14. Daniel Goleman, *Working with Emotional Intelligence.* (New York: Bantam, 1998), 3.

PART 2

Developing Professionally

CHAPTER

3

Personal and Organizational Values

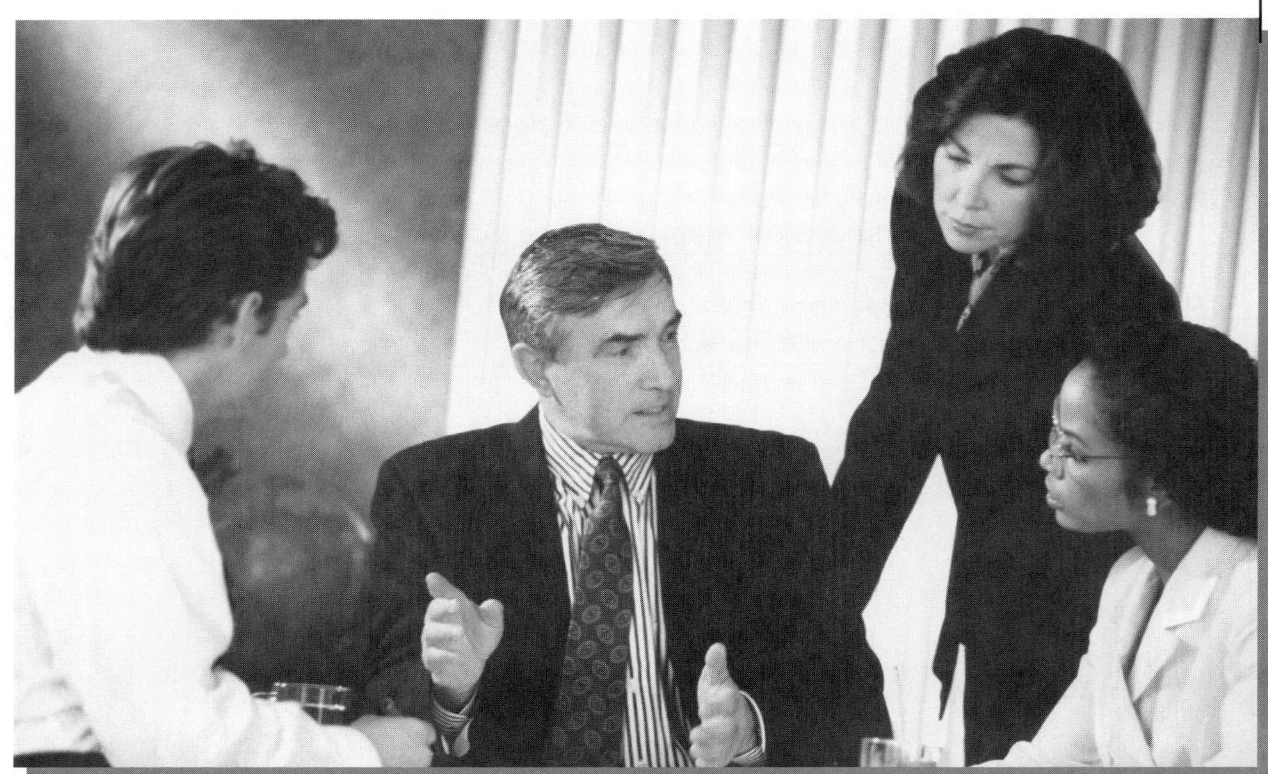

TO START YOU THINKING

Before you read this chapter, take time to ask and begin to answer the following questions:

- What are values?
- Are there differences between organizational and personal values?
- Is there some overlap in organizational and personal values?
- What are your most important values with respect to how you treat others? Where did they come from—parents, grandparents, teachers, peers, others?
- Do more mature individuals have more mature values?
- Are our values as a society changing?
- What importance do we put on ethics, honesty, loyalty, trust, and commitment, among other values?
- What importance do we put on courtesy, compassion, dependability, and perseverance, among other personal values?
- What importance do we put on equity and fairness, entrepreneurship, teamwork, and leadership, among other organizational values?
- Which of these values are most important in how other people treat you?

LEARNING GOALS

After studying this chapter, you should be able to:

1. Define values generally and specifically for yourself.
2. Discuss organizational or corporate values that work in concert with personal values.
3. Discuss unique personal values that hold the key to most people's success.
4. Discuss the organizational values that are common to most organizations' success.
5. Examine personal and corporate values and their impact on the organization of work.
6. Define and apply the following terms and concepts (in order of first occurrence):

KEYWORDS

- **values**
- **personal values**
- **organizational values**
- **business ethics**
- **honesty/integrity**
- **loyalty**
- **commitment**
- **stewardship**
- **attitudes**
- **courtesy**
- **compassion**
- **perseverance**
- **equity**
- **entrepreneurship**
- **intrapreneur**
- **teamwork**
- **visionary leadership**

DEFINITIONS AND PURPOSES

Human relationships are based on our personal and organizational values.

In this chapter, we study the personal and organizational values that are the basis of all human relations. We are in a position to interact effectively with other human beings—human relations—only when we know what we stand for and what the underlying principles of behavior are. In short, we can experience meaningful human relations only when we know the underlying values.

Values are those standards or qualities within a society that are regarded as guiding principles for behavior and action. **Personal values** are values held by individuals that guide their activities, including work. **Organizational values** are a composite of these personal values and more. There is a synergistic effect to organizational values; that is, the sum of all the parts is greater than the individual values. The values considered in this chapter include:

- business ethics
- commitment
- honesty/integrity
- loyalty
- mutual trust/ mutual respect
- courtesy
- work/leisure attitudes
- visionary leadership
- action orientation

We will start with some values that are both personal and corporate.

COMBINED PERSONAL AND ORGANIZATIONAL VALUES

Some values are critical to organizational success.

Some values are so critical to the successful performance of an organization that they pervade both personal and organizational life. Examples are mutual trust and respect, honesty/integrity, and loyalty.

BUSINESS AND WORK ETHICS

The most basic values governing personal and organizational lives are ethics. **Business ethics** can be defined as taking into consideration the effects of one's decisions on all of the stakeholders of the organization—employees, customers, owners, vendors, and competitors. Failure to consider these diverse stakeholders can result in negative outcomes for individuals and organizations. Many say that adopting the golden rule makes decision making and action in the ethical areas easier: "Do unto others as you would have them do unto you."

Organizational ethics emulate the leader's ethics.

Organizational ethics often mirror the ethics of the leader. Some research has shown that just because an organization has a code of ethics does not make it more ethical. To the contrary, there is some evidence that having a code causes employees to rely more on it than their own innate senses of right and wrong.[1]

Professor Mark Pastin writes that, "the ethics of a person or firm is simply *the most fundamental ground rules by which the person or firm acts.* Understanding these ground rules is the key to understanding how organizations function and to changing the way they function."[2]

A useful approach for making ethical decisions is to ask and answer the following 12 questions developed by Laura Nash:

1. Have you defined the problem accurately?
2. How would you define the problem if you stood on the other side of the fence?
3. How did this situation occur in the first place?

4. To whom and what do you give your loyalties as a person and as a member of the organization?
5. What is your intention in making this decision?
6. How does this intention compare with the likely results?
7. Whom could your decision or action injure?
8. Can you engage the affected parties in a discussion of the problem before you make your decision?
9. Are you confident that your position will be as valid over a long period of time as it seems now?
10. Could you disclose, without qualms, your decision or action to your boss, your CEO, the board of directors, your family, or society as a whole?
11. What is the symbolic potential of your action if understood? If misunderstood?
12. Under what conditions would you allow exceptions to your stand?[3]

Some of the best business ethics advice available comes from Kenneth Blanchard and Norman Vincent Peale's *The Power of Ethical Management.* They suggest three "ethics check" questions:

1. ***Is it legal?*** Will I be violating either civil law or company policy?
2. ***Is it balanced?*** Is it fair to all concerned in the short term as well as the long term? Does it promote win–win relationships?
3. ***How will it make me feel about myself?*** Will it make me proud? Would I feel good if my decision was published in the newspaper? Would I feel good if my family knew about it?[4]

Blanchard and Peale also remind us that the most difficult part of being ethical is doing what is right, not deciding what is right. Of course, it is easy to say we would do one thing or decide to do something in an abstract situation, but it is quite another to act in an ethical manner. Figure 3–1 reviews five principles of ethical power for individuals.[5]

FIGURE 3–1 *FIVE PRINCIPLES OF ETHICAL POWER FOR INDIVIDUALS*

1. *Purpose.* I see myself as being an ethically sound person. I let my conscience be my guide. No matter what happens, I am always able to face the mirror, look myself straight in the eye, and feel good about myself.
2. *Pride.* I do feel good about myself. I don't need the acceptance of other people to feel important. A balanced self-esteem keeps my ego and my desire to be accepted from influencing my decisions.
3. *Patience.* I believe that things will eventually work out well. I don't need everything to happen right now.
4. *Persistence.* I stick to my purpose, especially when it seems inconvenient to do so! My behavior is consistent with my intentions. As Winston Churchill said, "Never, never, never give up!"
5. *Perspective.* I take time to enter each day quietly in a mood of reflection. This helps me to get myself focused and allows me to listen to my inner self and to see things more clearly.

HONESTY/INTEGRITY

Honesty is being truthful, trustworthy, and sincere; it is refraining from lying, cheating, or stealing. Fundamental principles such as "honesty is the best policy," "giving a fair day's work for a fair day's pay," and the importance of truth are worthwhile values that strengthen our organizations. Even when the truth hurts, it is best in the long run to be open and honest with others in our human relationships. Failure to do so simply allows us to dig ourselves deeper into a hole—whether on an employment or a personal level.

In his book, *Honesty in the Workplace*, Kevin Murphy explores the psychology surrounding workplace honesty. He says:

> If you are concerned about ethics, dishonesty and crime in the workplace, the best thing you can do is promote programs, ideas and a workplace environment that encourage a healthy commitment to the organization. . . . People who identify with the organization are less likely to steal from it or to engage in behavior that harms it.[6]

Related to honesty is **integrity**. Arthur C. Nielsen, Jr., CEO of the Nielsen marketing research and ratings company, relates that integrity is the willingness to take charge, be decisive, and suffer the consequences of defeat—that is, be able to accept the blame when things go wrong. He suggests that integrity is a sense of responsibility that extends to personal principles and to others—"to customers, to employers, to fellow workers. This kind of integrity means more than adherence to some vague code of business ethics. It means always doing what is right, as simple and as terribly difficult as that sometimes may be."[7]

> Integrity is not a conditional word. It doesn't blow in the wind or change with the weather. It is your inner image of yourself, and if you look in there and see a man who won't cheat, then you know he never will.
>
> *Source:* John D. MacDonald, *The Turquoise Lament.*

Honesty and integrity in making business decisions have significant long-term effects. Lack of honesty and integrity eventually drive away customers and suppliers and demoralize employees.

LOYALTY

Employee **loyalty** comes from managers being aware of employee needs, having the foresight to appreciate and involve employees, rewarding employees, and being responsive to their needs. Treating employees with respect creates loyalty and a healthy work environment. Like the other values and principles discussed here, loyalty is fundamental to long-term success in an employer-employee relationship.

William Werther writes:

> Employee loyalty can do wonders for a company if it's channeled in the right direction. Yet, not only do executives perceive employee loyalty in their organizations as low, but they are not quite sure how to raise it. . . . For loyalty at work to flow freely, however, it must begin somewhere. That place is senior management, whose mem-

> bers realize that the loyalty they earn for the organization reflects the loyalty the organization gives to its member.[8]

Employee loyalty is a two-way street, a reciprocal relationship. Many would argue that management loses considerable credibility and productivity with its employees if they have a cavalier, take-the-employees-for-granted attitude.

MUTUAL TRUST AND RESPECT

Like honesty and loyalty, mutual trust and mutual respect are the cornerstones of healthy relationships. Without trust and respect, the relationship is destined to fail—in spirit if not in time.

Leaders must earn employee trust. A leader without trust will have no followers. That does not mean that we must always agree with the leader; it means that we must always know where that leader stands. Trust is the conviction that leaders mean what they say—whether in national politics, business, or other types of organizations.

"As soon as you trust yourself, you will know how to live." Goethe

Trust and respect must be earned and developed over time. They cannot be mandated. Both personal and organizational trust are based on predictability, dependability, and faith as well as open communication. Open communication may create stress in organizations, but, as we shall see, stress is not necessarily bad.

COMMITMENT AND RENEWAL

Commitment, like trust and loyalty, is a two-way street.

Commitment is an attachment to an organization that allows people to willingly do things on their own. Managers need to get others to make a commitment to people, goals, values, and systems. People need commitment for themselves and their organizations. A commitment to improved quality and doing things right the first time has become the keystone of renewed productivity and profitability in many organizations.

Honoring a commitment to one's job, word, and others, including employees, employers, and customers, is a fundamental value. Organizational commitment results from management's ability to turn grand causes into small actions so that everyone can contribute to the mission. The renewal factor is the opportunity that transforms threat into issue, issue into cause, cause into quest. The result: enthusiasm is generated. Everyone is pulling for the same purpose regardless of how small the task may seem.[9]

The complacent manager merely presides. Robert Waterman emphasizes that what is needed instead is renewal of commitment to the organization. These renewal factors apply to people as well as organizations. In summary, Waterman argues that people should be prepared for diverse opportunities through (1) both internal and external information; (2) seeking stability in our relationships in the form of teamwork and trust, adaptability, and flexibility; and (3) decisive and visible commitment to achieve goals.[10]

QUALITY, SERVICE, AND STEWARDSHIP

> Look at a well-run company and you will see the needs of its stockholders, its employees, and the community at large being served simultaneously.
>
> Arnold Hiatt, Former CEO, Stride Rite Corporation

Hewlett-Packard is notable for its commitment to people and values such as quality. For retail and other types of business firms, honesty and other values mean good business. Customers demand quality and service in an increasingly competitive environment. Clearly, providing quality products and services is not just a matter of being nice to customers and employees. In fact, it means showing and acting on real, substantial concern for employees and providing real, substantive service to customers. Peter Drucker notes:

> Everybody in retailing talks of "service" as the key to success, if not to survival. So do the new retailers. But they mean something different. For traditional merchants, service means salespeople who personally take care of an individual customer. But the new retailers employ very few salespeople. Service to them means that customers do not need a salesperson, do not have to spend time trying to find one, do not have to ask, do not have to wait. It means that the customers know where goods are the moment they enter the store, in what colors and sizes, and at what price. It means providing information.[11]

Service is the reason for any organization.

When an organization gives value in the form of high-quality products and services, it can expect to survive in the long run. Current research has established a positive relationship between organizational citizenship and a company's financial performance.[12]

Professor Leonard Berry offers "Seven Rules of Service" regarding quality. He says quality service is:

1. Defined by the customer
2. A journey, a full-court press, all the time; continuously changing needs and expectations
3. Everyone's job
4. Inseparable from leadership and communication; leaders coach, praise, and model service; face-to-face communication; communicate to inspire, not to command; communicate by deeds, not words
5. Inseparable from integrity
6. A design issue
7. Keeping the service promise: "Not promising more than you can reliably deliver."[13]

Another positive view of service is offered by Peter Block in his book *Stewardship: Choosing Service Over Self-Interest.* Block says that organizations practicing stewardship offer equity, partnership, and choice at all levels for their employees. **Stewardship** is the willingness to be accountable for the well-being of the larger organization by operating in service, rather than in control, of those around us. Managers who act as stewards choose service over self-interest and hold themselves accountable to all over whom they exercise power.[14]

OTHER COMMON VALUES

Competitiveness. There is a competitive intensity in business. Foreign competition, new technology, deregulation, and other variables such as market maturity have caused firms to go out of business or lose ground because of their reliance on doing things the way they have always been done. There is a need to identify a competitive advantage and to determine how that advantage can be achieved and sustained.

Patience. Patience is a unique value for both individuals and organizations. Not many entities possess this valuable attribute, but it can be the difference between success and failure in business or personal relationships. Patience is the ability to accept delay graciously.

In a world filled with reasons to react, a quiet, understanding response may be the one example that brings peace and serenity to those around you—including employees and customers. Of course, there is a limit to what any organization can or should do to show its patience, but this quality may be the one that sets it apart from the competition.

Confidence. Confidence is a two-pronged value—self-confidence and confidence in others—that needs cultivation from both an individual and organizational perspective. Individuals need self-confidence before they can build confidence in and with others; organizations, too, need the self-confidence to handle appointed tasks.

Confidence is based on applying skills.

Students who are about to graduate and enter the world of full-time work need self-confidence that they can do a job—not unrealistic expectations, but a spirit of "can do" based on the application of their learned skills. To succeed at building confidence, they need to develop skills and a strong belief in their capabilities. The key to achieving a goal is confidence in the ability to control one's life or perceived self-effectiveness.

Diversity and Fun. Two last contemporary values are diversity and fun. Although seemingly unrelated, they have more in common than initially meets the eye. In deciding to act on certain matters like personnel staffing, we worry about things like sameness, personality, and a personal (although probably biased) assessment of "can he or she do the job?" The latter is, of course, very important, but there are better ways to assess it than by subjectively stating a feeling that a person can or cannot do the job.

Stereotyping and discriminating against certain segments of our society cause us considerable loss of talent. Whether the stereotypes are based on gender, ethnic origin, religious preferences, or any number of other classifications, they have a negative effect on the talent pool as well as the morale of the existing workforce. As human beings, we like to be appreciated. Further, we perform at a higher level when we enjoy doing the task at hand. Combining the impact of accepting others and celebrating our mutual strengths with the fun of doing what we enjoy while someone else can do work they enjoy provides everyone with a more productive work environment.

"Loosen up."

When a woman does a construction job better than the men applying for the job, then let her do it—do it well—and have fun doing it. Don't get trapped by the stereotypes that suggest a group can or cannot do certain things. Celebrate diversity and enjoy the uniqueness of individual differences. In fact, we complement one another rather well, and that makes for more effective teamwork and total organizational effectiveness.

PERSONAL VALUES

As noted earlier, organizational values are, in large part, a composite of individual, personal values. How we conduct our personal work activities and lives in general determines the total ethics of organizations.

An NBC-*Wall Street Journal* poll of Americans shows that the vast majority—75 percent—believe that traditional values have grown weaker. They define traditional values as honesty, integrity, respect, trustworthiness, loyalty, commitment, self-discipline, caring, among others. On discussing the poll, one writer concludes, "Everything in life that works really boils down to good people doing their best to do what's right. That was true yesterday. It's true today. And it'll be true tomorrow, when the debate about 'traditional values' will still be going on."[15]

ATTITUDE AND HUMOR

A fundamental concept and value of human relationships is attitude. In fact, it is often the impact of decisions and choices made as the result of attitudes that really count. A person's approach to customers and other employees is a critical part of the job.

Assume positive attitudes.

Attitudes are predispositions, mental states, emotions, or moods. Contrary to popular opinion, they are not easily measured nor is it appropriate to measure performance based solely on attitude. Above all, it is important to maintain positive attitudes about ourselves, our work associates, even our bosses. If there are great differences between managers' expectations and employee performance, then other arrangements—training, job changes, and so on—can be made. As inept as we may think some of our work associates or bosses are, it is best to assume that they are doing the best they can at their jobs and that we should do the same.

Elwood Chapman notes that positive attitudes are appreciated and that the most popular and productive people in any work environment are usually those with the best attitudes. Their positive attitudes cause the following results:

- Inject humor into what otherwise would be just work. Everyone misses these individuals when they are on vacation.
- Add to the team spirit by bonding everyone together in a more positive and productive mood.
- Make it easier for coworkers to maintain their upbeat attitudes. This, in turn, helps coworkers maintain productivity and enhance their own careers.[16]

The wrong attitude may become a turnoff for others and spell defeat for ourselves if not held in check. If people spend most of their time griping about their jobs or whining about other organizational issues, opportunities for networking and possible change or advancement may be foregone. There is nothing wrong with the person who takes time off from work to enjoy family, hobbies, and relaxation activities. In fact, the converse is probably true—there is something wrong with the workaholic who feels guilty about being away from work. We enjoy our leisure activities—and should—but we should also enjoy our work activities.

Attitudes are important.

A positive mental outlook that puts emphasis on drive and determination to see dreams come true are part of positive attitudes. But the attitudes of individuals toward their jobs and total organizations are what make a difference in building an enjoyable workplace. Figure 3–2 shows the ABCs of a positive attitude.

Humor is related to attitude. In *Hope for the Troubled Heart*, Dr. Billy Graham observed that a keen sense of humor helps us to

- Overlook the unbecoming
- Understand the unconventional
- Tolerate the unpleasant
- Overcome the unexpected, and
- Outlast the unbearable[17]

COURTESY/ENTHUSIASM

Closely related to attitudes and mutual respect is the handling of the public—especially customers and coworkers—with courtesy. **Courtesy** goes beyond politeness or kindness. It means being civil to other people—customers, coworkers, subordinates, even the boss!

Courtesy can spell the difference between profit and loss.

Courtesy is so important to the successful conduct of business that it can spell the difference between profit and loss, between survival and extinction of an organization. It is important in acquiring new customers and employees, as well as in keeping old customers and employees. Research indicates that almost 75 percent of banking customers cite teller courtesy as a prime consideration in choosing a financial institution.[18]

Other research suggests that, as the population increases, we will become less courteous to each other.[19] Overcrowding, changes in social status, and the ascendancy of special interest groups all contribute to an increasing need for a renewed commitment to courtesy.

How managers treat employees is also important. Most people respond more positively to polite, considerate instructions than to orders. An ordinary conversation

FIGURE 3-2 ***A Positive Attitude Is as Simple as ABC***

Avoid negative sources—people, places, things, and habits.
Believe in yourself.
Consider things from every angle.
Don't give up, and don't give in.
Enjoy life today; yesterday is gone, and tomorrow may never come.
Family and friends are hidden treasures. Seek them and enjoy their riches.
Give more than you planned to give.
Hang on to your dreams.
Ignore those who try to discourage you.
Just do it!
Keep on trying. No matter how hard it seems now, it will get easier.
Love yourself first and most.
Make it happen.
Never lie, cheat, or steal. Always strike a fair deal.
Open your eyes, and see things as they really are.
Practice makes perfect.
Quitters never win, and winners never quit.
Read, study, and learn about everything important in your life.
Stop procrastinating.
Take control of your own destiny.
Understand yourself in order to better understand others.
Visualize it.
Want it more than anything.
"Xccelerate" your efforts.
You are unique of all God's creations. Nothing can replace you.
Zero in on your target, and go for it!

—Wanda Carter
St. Augustine, Florida

Source: "A Positive Attitude Is as Simple as ABC," *The Coloradoan* (Ft. Collins), March 28, 1992, B5. Reprinted with permission.

between boss and subordinate does not have to be rude or punctuated with barbs from the boss. Related to this type of interaction is the amount of enthusiasm managers exhibit and, in turn, can generate in others.

Be "fired up" with enthusiasm, or you may be fired with enthusiasm.

Finding ways to generate and maintain enthusiasm for people, product, and the organizational mission is very important to successful leaders. Means of increasing enthusiasm include training and development, and healthy competition among internal groups—not a negative type of competition but an approach that says "We want to do better than we have done before." In essence, then, the competition is with self.

SHORT COURSE IN HUMAN RELATIONS

- Five most important words: You Did a Good Job.
- Four most important words: What Is Your Opinion?
- Three most important words: If You Please.
- Two most important words: Thank You.
- One most important word: We.
- Least important word: I.

According to Ralph Waldo Emerson in his essay "Circles,"

> Enthusiasm is one of the most powerful engines of success. When you do a thing, do it with your might. Put your whole soul into it. Stamp it with your own personality. Be active, be energetic, be enthusiastic and faithful, and you will accomplish your object. Nothing great was ever achieved without enthusiasm.

COMPASSION/CARING

Compassion and a caring attitude are closely related to empathy. **Compassion** is a feeling for and understanding of another person's difficult situation. Tied to it is a desire to help the person alleviate personal discomfort. However, it is important to remember that it is impossible for a person to always understand others' perspectives; even in similar circumstances, individual perceptions, feelings, and resulting behaviors will be different.

As managers, family members, and human beings, we should try to put ourselves in others' footsteps. How does this person feel? How would he or she react if experiencing something like a job dispute or layoff? Our organizations and the people in them will judge us by how we treat people. Treating people without regard for their feelings, or in other cavalier ways, extracts significant costs in morale and job performance.

DEPENDABILITY/RELIABILITY

Dependability and reliability are basic values. "Be on time," "be predictable" (in a positive sense!), and "do a good job" are truly fundamental values that provide the contrast between effective and productive organizations and those ineffective, less productive entities. Motivated, positive people who can be depended on to turn out reliable products and services make the difference in those organizations.

Be dependable, reliable, and persevering.

Like so many other values discussed in this chapter, dependability and reliability are two-way streets in which both managers and subordinates are expected to be dependable and reliable—in short, "to be there."

PERSEVERANCE/DILIGENCE

Closely related to dependability and reliability is perseverance or diligence. Suzanne Chazin has called **perseverance** the ultimate key to success, noting that it can matter more than talent, brains, or luck. She says it is a simple trait that anyone can master and suggests, "successful people understand that no one makes it to the top in a single bound. What truly sets them apart is their willingness to keep putting one step in front of the other—no matter how rough the terrain."[20]

According to Tom Peters, employees can succeed in business by really trying harder than others. What separates winners from losers:

- *Attention to details:* superb execution will win the day.
- *Culture counts:* spirit, energy, and professionalism are important.
- *Keep meticulous books:* not necessarily complex but accurate and timely. Present a crystal clear picture of how the business is working.
- *Perseverance itself:* learn from early mistakes. Peters says that Sam Walton (Wal-Mart) and Anita Roddick (The Body Shop) "learned from their early pratfalls, made adjustment after adjustment, and eventually came up with a winning formula."[21]

Another frequently heard term for perseverance or diligence is "stick-to-itiveness," a fundamental distinction that makes a difference in successful individuals and organizations.

ACTION PROJECT 3–1

INDIVIDUAL GOALS AND VALUES (INDIVIDUAL EXERCISE)

The following survey is designed to start you thinking about certain goals and values—now and in the future. Like most of the exercises in this book, there are no right or wrong answers. The demographic information (age, gender, and major) is for classification and tabulation purposes only.

Age: ____ Male or Female: ____ Major: ____

On Questions 1 through 6, you are asked to rank goals in order of preference (eca = extracurricular activities, 1 = most prefer, 6 = least prefer). On Questions 7 through 9, check the appropriate answer.

1. As a college student, rank your present "living" goals:
   ____money ____where to live ____career ____family ____friends ____eca
2. In 5 years, how will your goal preferences rank?
   ____money ____where to live ____career ____family ____friends ____eca
3. In 10 years, how will your goal preferences rank?
   ____money ____where to live ____career ____family ____friends ____eca
4. In 20 years, how will your goal preferences rank?
   ____money ____where to live ____career ____family ____friends ____eca
5. In 40 years, how will your goal preferences rank?
   ____money ____where to live ____career ____family ____friends ____eca
6. Rank these compensation benefits in order of preference if all offered are of equal value:
   ____cost-of-living increase
   ____opportunity to buy stock at reduced rate every year
   ____medical and life insurance
   ____paid 15-week leave of absence every 5 years

Do Not Rank the Following. Check the appropriate answer.

7. How often do you change career goals? (If more than 5 years leave blank.)
   ____every term ____every year ____every 2 years ____every 5 years
8. For your career goals, do you feel
   ____overeducated ____educated enough ____undereducated
9. Have your parents influenced your chosen career goals?
   ____yes ____no ____partial input

ORGANIZATIONAL VALUES

EQUITY

Three types of equity: internal, external, and individual.

Equity manifests itself in internal, external, or individual consistency within an organization.

These equity principles are fundamental to effective compensation and other human resource management practices. One type of equity is *internal equity,* how fairly each job is paid within an organization. A second type is *external equity,* how pay for a job compares to pay for jobs in other, perhaps competing, organizations. Finally, there is *individual equity* or performance pay, based on how well individuals perform in their jobs.

Emphasis on short-term equity based on performance is increasing. Of course, long-term equity is important too, so that job incumbents perceive fairness in pay and other employee treatment. However, two researchers find that

> perceived fairness no longer means job security, steady cradle-to-grave growth, and ever-increasing benefits. Rather, employees should expect appropriate rewards based in large part on their performance during the past year, as well as the company's performance. . . . Flexibility is changing from a longer-term, financially-based curve to a shorter-term, performance-based series of sharp turns [adjustments].[22]

RISK TAKING/ENTREPRENEURSHIP/INTRAPRENEURS

Entrepreneurship adds value.

A necessary value in today's ever-changing business world is risk taking. Traditionally, we think of entrepreneurs as risk takers. **Entrepreneurship** is the creation of wealth by adding value, usually through the creation of a new business enterprise. Usually, the entrepreneur benefits directly from his or her efforts. **Intrapreneurs**

HOW TO BE A GREAT BOSS

Regardless of whether it is long-term or short-term equity, the concept of equity has always been important to American workers. Its importance appears to be increasing. Fairness, openness, and honesty are consistently mentioned as qualities that employees most appreciate in a boss. Experts say that bosses can learn to be great by doing the following:

- Be a good and willing communicator.
- Specify job performance expectations.
- Make contact daily with as many team members as possible.
- Loosen the reins.
- Have a sense of humor and admit mistakes.
- Provide direction and strive to be consistent.
- Look for ways to improve and to learn from others.

In the future, bosses will succeed when they promote teamwork and value a diverse workplace.

Source: Roberta Maynard, "How to Be a Great Boss," *Nation's Business* (December 1991): 44–45.

are individuals within existing organizations who create wealth for that organization by using existing resources and capacities in new ways. Sometimes intrapreneurs benefit directly from their efforts through stock options or bonuses; sometimes their experience is leveraged into new positions of responsibility or other opportunities.

The challenge for organizations is to balance risks. Of course, there are risks in taking an action—risks that we will be wrong, too soon with a decision, and so on. There is also a risk that we will lose market or a key person because of inaction, or because of drawn-out negotiations or unnecessary detail. By the time someone finds something acceptable after many revisions, the opportunity may be lost.

The effective leader knows that there is risk inherent in making decisions. It is important to risk failure rather than to live in mediocrity. Vic Sussman writes that failure is not to be feared. He offers several specific suggestions:

1. Stop using the "F" [failure] word.
2. Don't take it [failure] personally.
3. Be prepared [insulate yourself by mapping a catastrophe plan].
4. Learn to fail intelligently.
5. Never say die.[23]

Allow entrepreneurs and intrapreneurs to work and grow in an organization by loosening the restrictions so common to bureaucratic organizations. Allow employees to make some mistakes within predefined constraints.

TEAMWORK/COOPERATION/COLLEGIALITY

Teamwork is working together to identify and solve group-related work problems. Teamwork has become a fashionable buzzword in recent years and for good reason. Americans have always cherished their independence and individuality—sometimes at the expense of cooperation and teamwork. Figure 3–3 shows a valuable team builder's checklist that emphasizes the roles of all members but especially the leader's roles.

A spirit of cooperation and collegiality pervade effective organizations. By definition, an organization means teamwork toward common goals and objectives. Teamwork is essential in athletic teams, businesses, and musical groups, as well as in civil, religious, and other kinds of organizations.

However, teamwork can be carried too far, lessening the degree of individual motivation. There should always be opportunities for individual growth as well as team development. Not everything has to be or should be done as a team. There needs to be a balance between teamwork and individual effort.

A final lesson for universal teamwork is provided by Marian Edelman:

> *Remember and help America remember that the fellowship of human beings is more important than the fellowship of race and class and gender in a democratic society.* Be decent and fair and insist that others be so in your presence. Don't tell, laugh at, or in any way acquiesce to racial, ethnic, religious, or gender jokes or to any practices intended to demean rather than enhance another human being. Walk away from them. Stare them down. Make them unacceptable in your homes, religious congregations, and clubs. Through daily moral consciousness counter the proliferating voices of racial and ethnic and religious division that are gaining respectability over the land, including on college campuses. Let's face up to rather than ignore our growing racial problems, which are America's historical and future Achilles' heel.[24]

FIGURE 3–3 *TEAM BUILDER'S CHECKLIST*

1. Does each team member, including myself, have a crystal clear understanding of the agreed goals of the team?____
2. Is every team member, including myself, sufficiently committed to the team goals to devote the necessary effort to achieve them?____
3. Does every team member, including myself, clearly understand his or her assigned role on the team and the importance of that role to team success?____
4. Is every team member, including myself, committed to fulfilling his or her assigned role to the best of his or her ability?____
5. Does every team member, including myself, clearly understand the plan for reaching team goals and, especially, does every team member understand precisely the part of the planned activity he or she is responsible for?____
6. Does every team member, including myself, understand and accept the performance standards for individual activity and the total team activity necessary for the team to achieve its goals?____
7. Am I providing frequent, timely, and useful feedback on each team member's performance, and to the team as a whole on team performances?____
8. Am I providing the coaching and facilitating necessary to help each team member and the group as a whole reach the required performance standards?____
9. Am I providing the initiative, the enthusiasm, the sense of purpose, and an example of the appropriate behavior and attitudes that team members expect of their leader?____
10. Am I creating and maintaining a supportive group climate, and am I constructively controlling the group process?____

VISIONARY LEADERSHIP

An old adage says "Where there is no vision, the people perish." John Gardner, former secretary of Health, Education, and Welfare, states:

> Leaders have a significant role in creating the state of mind that is the society. They can serve as symbols of the moral unity of the society. They can express the values that hold the society together. Most important, they can conceive and articulate goals that lift people out of their petty preoccupations, carry them above the conflicts that tear a society apart, and unite them in the pursuit of objectives worthy of their best efforts.[25]

Tom Peters, Nancy Austin, and many others point out the importance of having **visionary leadership** if we are to succeed. Organizations and individuals both need to know what their objectives and goals are. People need time to reflect and plan. Organizations like Disney, General Electric, McDonald's, and Wal-Mart are where they are today because their founders and successive leaders had entrepreneurial spirit and vision, and demonstrated the leadership necessary to be successful.

HUMAN RELATIONS CHALLENGES

Human relations problems have many different causes. Five of the most common are:

Your talents

1. Every person brings a unique set of talents, ambitions, and work experience to a job. These personal attitudes change over time, often as a result of the degree of success or failure the person experiences in the work world. Matching so many unique sets of personal qualities to a standardized technology can create problems.

Organization needs

2. The organizational aspects of a company, such as its size, geographic location, economic health, and degree of automation, define the scope of work and the activity in each work division. Frequent arbitrary structural definitions often cause difficulties in human relations.

Technological growth

3. Innovations in technology and production methods generally require the restructuring of job roles and responsibilities. Radical changes in basic organizational structure can cause severe strains between workers and management, thus creating intense problems in human relations.

Need for responsibility

4. Promotions of individuals to positions of greater responsibility and authority generally create a need for changed behavior patterns between the new supervisors and their former peers, which, in turn, can create human relations problems.

Inexperienced workers

5. Inexperienced or young workers may not be able to perform their roles or tasks in work groups in a competent manner. The time they require to adjust can create problems with production schedules and lead to human relations problems between these workers and their coworkers or supervisors.

SUMMARY

People are most effective in their interactions with other human beings when they know the underlying values of their own and others' behavior. Values are those standards or qualities that are regarded as guiding principles for behavior and action. There are at least three sets of values: personal, organizational, and those that combine personal and organizational values.

Specific combinations of personal and organizational values include business ethics, honesty, loyalty, mutual trust, commitment to organizational and personal quality, and service. Some of the values basic to successful personal relationships are positive attitudes, courtesy, compassion, dependability, and perseverance.

Organizational values worthy of our attention include equity, risk taking, teamwork, and visionary leadership. These values and their implementation are fundamental to the continued transformation of organizations.

Finally, we are challenged by human relations problems that have many different causes. Among the most common causes are individual talents, organizational needs, technological change, the need to accept responsibility, and the need to train inexperienced workers in human as well as technological skills.

SELF-APPRAISAL

Since human relations problems have many different causes and perspectives, it might be interesting to identify your thoughts about the five causes just listed. Then, it might be interesting to share them with members of your class. Listing your immediate thoughts may help you clarify your own values as well as determine your place in the working world.

1. Every person brings a unique set of talents, ambitions, and experience to a job. What three outstanding things do you feel that you can bring to a job?
   a. ______________________________
   b. ______________________________
   c. ______________________________
2. With regard to the organizational aspects of a company,
   a. In what size company would you like to work?
      (1) 10–50 employees, (2) 50–150 employees, (3) over 150 employees
   b. Where would you like your company located?
      (1) locally, (2) within 100 miles of home, (3) anywhere in the United States, (4) outside the United States
3. Do you enjoy changes at work?
   a. Look forward to change
   b. Occasionally enjoy changes
   c. Seldom like to see change
   d. Change makes it difficult to get the work done
4. Promotions mean greater responsibility and authority. In my next job I would like to see a promotion
   a. in three months.
   b. in six months.
   c. in one year.
   d. when I deserve it.
5. One way to handle untrained and inexperienced workers is to
   a. have training classes frequently for new employees.
   b. hire only experienced employees.
   c. have a trainee work with you to learn the trade.

Your ideas may change in a few months or remain the same. In any case, if you compare your answers with others and share your thoughts about your answers, you may clarify some of your attitudes about work and discover some of your career expectations.

CASE STUDY 3–1

THE ETHICAL NURSE

Violet "Vi" Curtis is a registered nurse who graduated from Uptown University some years ago with a baccalaureate degree in nursing and completed a master's degree in clinical family nursing. Since receiving her master's degree, Vi has been employed as a nurse practitioner by the Metropolitan City Health Department, working with a number of individuals and families needing the services of a nurse practitioner.

Vi is a competent and professional nurse. She provides her patients with first-class nursing care and advice. The challenges of working within a big-city bureaucracy are becoming more strenuous for Vi. Limited municipal budgets are declining and paperwork for each case is increasing. In fact, Vi has decided to leave the city health department and begin her own business as a nurse practitioner.

Starting one's own business involves many functions—financing, marketing, and accounting as well as producing the product or services. Vi is not concerned about her ability to provide quality care as a nurse practitioner. She also has other well-qualified individuals interested and willing to work for her if her business grows.

One of Vi's major concerns is that she does not have a marketing plan. She does not have a client base outside of the city health department. She knows that many of her current clients would become future, private clients, but she is not sure how to go about attracting them. She has the mailing list for the city health department's clients available to her on computer and wonders if it would be ethical to mail announcements and other promotional literature to them.

1. Can you help Vi resolve her ethical dilemma?
2. Should she use the city health department's list?
3. Can you identify some factors that would start her toward developing a plan?
4. How can you reconcile Vi's entrepreneurial and ethical dilemma?

DISCUSSION AND STUDY QUESTIONS—TO KEEP YOU THINKING

1. What are your most important guiding values?
2. What are the differences and similarities between personal and organizational values?
3. What are important "ethics check" questions? What are important principles of ethical power for individuals and organizations?
4. How do honesty, loyalty, and mutual trust impact business and employee relationships?
5. How do attitudes and other personal values impact business and employee relationships?
6. What are important organizational values?
7. What are major human relations challenges or problems?

NOTES

1. Henry W. Tulloch and W. Scott Bauman, *The Management of Business Conduct* (Charlottesville, VA: Center for Applied Ethics, University of Virginia, 1981), 9.
2. Mark Pastin, *The Hard Problems of Management: Gaining the Ethics Edge* (San Francisco: Jossey-Bass, 1986), xii (italics in original).
3. Laura L. Nash, "Ethics Without the Sermon," *Harvard Business Review* (November–December 1981): 79–90.
4. Kenneth Blanchard and Norman Vincent Peale, *The Power of Ethical Management* (New York: Fawcett Crest, 1988), 20.
5. Ibid., 79.
6. Kevin Murphy, quoted in Carol Borchert, "Book Addresses Honesty in the Workplace," *Comment* (November 12, 1992): p. 4.
7. "Nielsen Shares Secrets of Success," *Beta Gamma Sigma* [professional business] *Newsletter* (summer 1988): 2.
8. William B. Werther, Jr., "Loyalty at Work," *Harvard Business Review* (March–April 1988): 28, 35.
9. Robert Waterman, "How the Best Get Better," *Business Week* (September 14, 1987): 99.
10. Ibid.

11. Peter F. Drucker, "The Retail Revolution," *The Wall Street Journal*, July 15, 1993, A14.
12. S. Waddock and S. Graves, "The Corporate Social Performance-Financial Performance Link," *Strategic Management Journal* 18 (1997): 303–319.
13. Based on research and private communication from Dr. Leonard Berry, chair and professor of marketing, Texas A & M University.
14. Peter Block, *Stewardship: Choosing Service Over Self-Interest* (San Francisco: Berrett-Koehler Publishers, 1996).
15. Judith Clabes, "Be a Good Person, and Values Follow," *Rocky Mountain News*, June 25, 1993, 38C.
16. Elwood N. Chapman, *Your Attitude Is Showing*, 7th ed. (New York: Macmillan, 1993), 4.
17. Billy Graham, *Hope for the Troubled Heart* (New York: Walker & Company, 1992).
18. Barry Leeds, " 'Mystery Shopping' Offers Clues to Quality Service," *Bank Marketing* (November 1992): 24–26.
19. John D. Long, "Common Courtesy: Less Common?" *Business Horizons* (January–February 1990): 133–143.
20. Suzanne Chazin, "The Ultimate Key to Success," *Reader's Digest* (April 1992): 21, 26.
21. Tom Peters, "How to Succeed in Small Business by Really Trying Harder Than Others," *Rocky Mountain News*, November 17, 1992, 95.
22. Mircea Manicatide and Virginia Pennell, "Key Developments in Compensation Management," *HR Focus* (October 1992): 3–4.
23. Vic Sussman, "Don't Fear Failure," *Reader's Digest* (June 1990): 116–118.
24. Marian Wright Edelman, *The Measure of Our Success: A Letter to My Children and Yours* (Boston: Beacon Press, 1992), 54.
25. John W. Gardner, "The Antileadership Vaccine," *Annual Report of the Carnegie Corporation* (New York: Carnegie Corporation, 1965), 12.

CHAPTER

4

Managing Yourself

Stress, Time, and Career Management

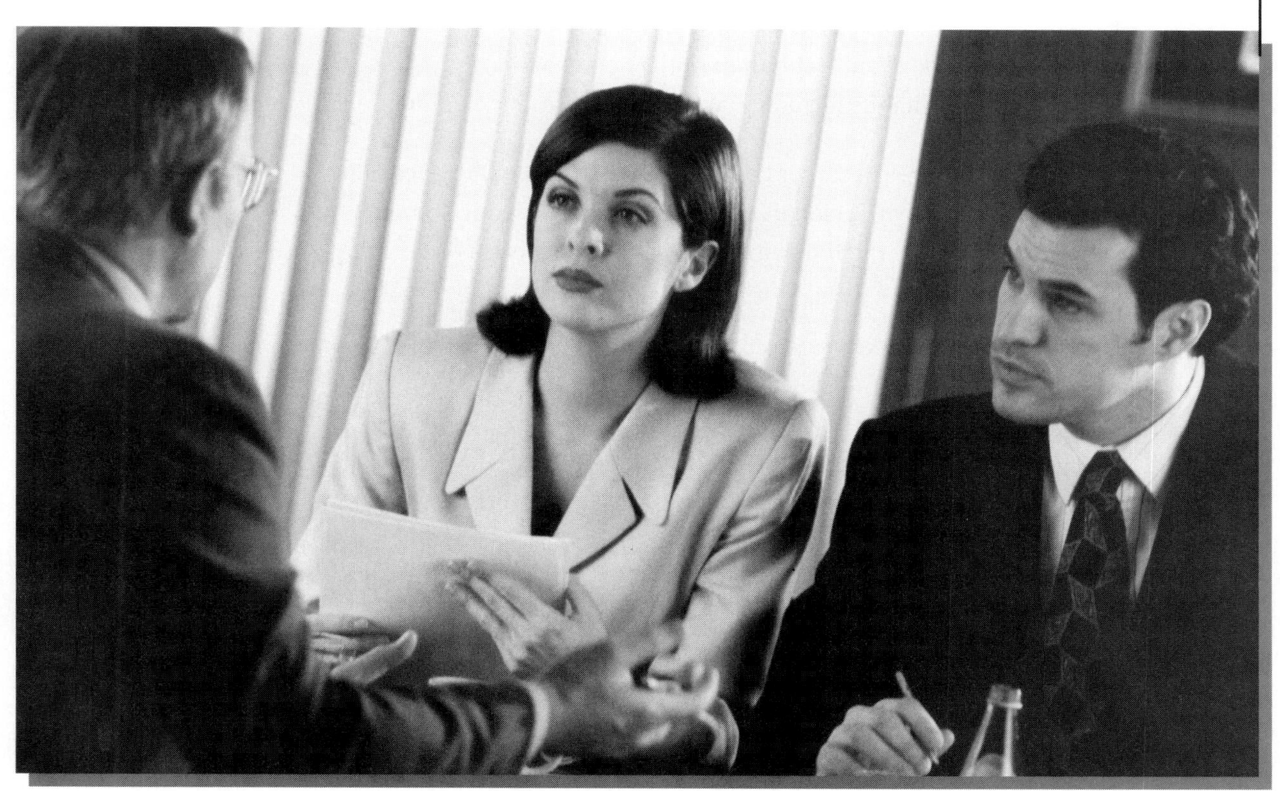

TO START YOU THINKING

Here are a few questions to think about before starting to read this chapter. In fact, these questions need to be answered before you can begin a meaningful career. Talk with classmates and others about your answers.

- Is stress good or bad? What types of stress are good? What types are bad?
- What roles do stress and time play in my personal development?
- How can I better manage my time? Am I in control of my time?
- Whose responsibility is career development?
- When should I start thinking about my career development?
- What do I want to be doing five years from now? Ten? Twenty?
- How many times do I anticipate changing jobs before then?
- How do I measure success?

LEARNING GOALS

After studying this chapter, you should be able to:

1. Distinguish between stress and tension, and between distress and eustress.
2. Describe the differences between Type A, H, and B behaviors.
3. List at least four ways to manage stress.
4. Set time priorities consistent with goals.
5. Use various tools and techniques of time control.
6. Improve work habits including reading, paperwork, telephone, e-mail, and other workplace activities.
7. Discuss the stages in career development and career advancement.
8. Develop your own personal action plans for career development.
9. Define and apply the following terms and concepts (in order of first occurrence):

KEYWORDS

- **work**
- **stress**
- **eustress**
- **distress**
- **Type A behavior**
- **Type H behavior**
- **Type B behavior**
- **workaholic**
- **anger**
- **career development**
- **career paths**
- **resume**
- **flextime**
- **job sharing**
- **telecommuting**

PLANS FOR MANAGING YOUR PERSONAL DEVELOPMENT

Introducing the concepts of career and other types of personal development early in this book helps to put the rest of the book in perspective. How we meet individual, group, and organizational challenges and adapt to change and different cultures can be personally rewarding.

Work—sustained physical or mental effort to achieve an objective or result[1]—is as natural as other life activities. People thrive on things they do well, and work can be one of those things. To make work and life truly rewarding, it is necessary to have personal development and career plans. Putting stress to work for you by managing your time avoids burnout and enhances personal success. Having a goal and a charted, but flexible, course of action enables planning for all the other human relations opportunities that arise in life.

STRESS

Among the factors impacting our personal development is stress. Not all stress is bad. Positive stress and tension, in large part, create and play major roles in personal development. Stress and tension also help us learn how to cope with multiple demands and develop our personal skills. However, unmanaged stress can lead to emotional, cognitive, and physical consequences. The American Psychological Association reports that

- Forty-three percent of all adults suffer adverse health effects from stress.
- Seventy-five to ninety percent of all physician office visits are for stress-related ailments and complaints.
- Stress is linked to the six leading causes of death—heart disease, cancer, lung ailments, accidents, cirrhosis of the liver, and suicide.
- The Occupational Safety and Health Administration declared stress a hazard of the workplace.[2]

Stress refers to pressure, strain, or force on a system. Human stress includes physical and psychological stress. Too much of either can lead to fatigue or damage of the affected system. According to Hans Selye, an expert on stress, there are two types of stress. **Eustress** is the positive type that has its foundations in meeting the challenges of a task or job. This type of stress manifests itself in achievement and accomplishment. The effects of eustress are beneficial in that they help us to overcome obstacles.

Distress is negative in that it allows us to be overpowered. Anger, loss of control, and feelings of inadequacy and insecurity are all manifestations of distress. We teeter on the edge of collapse when we experience these phenomena. If not alleviated, serious physical and psychological health problems can result.

Stress and tension are natural. These feelings help us to do our best work because they start our adrenaline flowing. We cannot hope to—nor would we want to—eliminate all the excitement and accompanying stress from our jobs. However, too much stress and tension on or off the job can have a negative effect. In most cases the person, not the job, creates the tension. Many causes of stress originate off the job and serve to disrupt job performance.

Most stress is created by the person, not the job.

Negative stress results in lower and poorer production, difficult relationships with other workers, inadequate attention and concentration, memory lapses, tardiness, and absenteeism. About 80 percent of the emotional problems of employees are caused by distress. Effective supervisors must be prepared to help with these problems.

A promotion frequently creates added stress that can ruin a person's work and spill over into his or her home life. Some people welcome and thrive on heavy stress and pressure at work. Some employees recognize when they have had enough and refuse an advancement, which often confounds people in management. Most people want the promotion, but do not want the added headaches, stresses, and responsibilities that accompany it.

ACTION PROJECT 4–1

STRESS-PRONE PERSONALITY QUIZ (INDIVIDUAL EXERCISE)

Rate yourself using the following scale on how you typically react in each of the situations given:

4 = very often; 3 = frequently; 2 = sometimes; 1 = very seldom

1. I try to do as much as possible in the least amount of time. ______
2. I become impatient with delays or interruptions. ______
3. I have to win at games to enjoy myself. ______
4. I find myself speeding up the car to get through amber lights. ______
5. I hesitate to ask for or indicate I need help with a problem. ______
6. I seek the respect and admiration of others. ______
7. I am critical of the way others do their work. ______
8. I have the habit of looking at my watch or clock often. ______
9. I strive to better my position and achievements. ______
10. I spread myself "too thin" in terms of time. ______
11. I have the habit of doing more than one thing at a time. ______
12. I get angry or irritable. ______
13. I have little time for hobbies or time by myself. ______
14. I have a tendency to talk quickly or hasten conversations. ______
15. I consider myself hard-driving. ______
16. My friends and relatives consider me to be hard-driving. ______
17. I have a tendency to get involved in multiple projects. ______
18. I have a lot of deadlines in my work. ______
19. I feel guilty when I relax and do nothing during leisure time. ______
20. I take on too many responsibilities. ______

Now, add your ratings. Use the following guidelines to determine your susceptibility to stress:

20–30	Nonproductive
30–50	Good balance
50–60	Too tense
60+	Good candidate for heart disease, especially if hostile

TYPES A, H, AND B BEHAVIOR

Type A is impatient and goal oriented.

Type A people are highly competitive, feel time pressures, and may have several projects going at the same time. The Type A person is likely to set personal deadlines or quotas for work and home at least once a week. The Type A person frequently brings work home. Such people are highly achievement oriented and push themselves to near capacity. Hard-driving Type A students earn more academic honors than do their peers.

Some Type A personalities risk more health problems than other Type A's. Research shows that it is not being a hard worker that puts a person at high risk of having a heart attack. It is being a hostile, hard worker. Redford Williams, M.D., director of the Behavioral Medicine Research Center at Duke University, observes that the most dangerous Type A characteristic is hostility. Anger, cynicism, and aggression are strong expressions of hostility. **Type H**, is a subset of Type A behavior. The "H" refers to hostility, and some Type A people show a lot of hostility. Recent studies show that hostility is the trait most closely associated with heart disease. Dr. Williams told an American Heart Association forum that, of all the aspects originally associated with the Type A personality, only those traits related to hostility contribute to coronary disease.[3]

Type H stands for hostility.

While Type A workers are often called workaholics, fast paced, competitive, and impatient, these traits do not contribute to disease. However, Type H workers who are hostile and display anger, cynicism, and aggression are risking health problems.

Type B people put their time in at work and seldom bring work home. They are more inclined to have interests in sports or leisure activities. Time is not a master, and proving their worth to themselves or to others is not a strong requirement of their personalities. They can be as intelligent as Type A's, but they do not work hard to prove it. Type B personalities are less likely to demand strong control of their lives and environments. The heartbeat is much quicker to slow down after mental stress in the Type B person than in the hostile Type H.

SELF-APPRAISAL

ARE YOU A TYPE H? MEASURE YOUR HOSTILITY

1. Do you think you have to yell at subordinates so they do not mess up? ____________
2. Do you assume cashiers will shortchange you if they can? ____________
3. If your child spills milk, do you immediately yell? ____________
4. After an irritating encounter, do you feel shaky or breathless? ____________
5. Do you feel your anger is justified? Do you feel an urge to punish people? ____________
6. Do you get angry every time you stand in line? Get behind the wheel? ____________

"Yes" answers show you are Type H, but check here to see how far it has progressed. (A "Yes" to Question 1 shows the lowest level of hostility; a "Yes" to Question 6 shows the highest level of hostility.):

- A "Yes" to Questions 1 or 2 indicates cynical mistrust—that you expect the worst from people and take it personally.
- A "Yes" to Question 3 shows that you are expressing anger—whether your responses are automatic or slightly disguised.
- A "Yes" to Question 4 shows that your body is experiencing the effects of hostility.
- A "Yes" to Question 5 indicates reactions that are aggressively hostile.
- A "Yes" to Question 6 means that hostility has become a habit.[4]

WORKAHOLICS: FORTUNE'S FAVORITE CHILDREN

Workaholics exhibit many type A traits. A **workaholic** is a person who takes great satisfaction in work but may carry that commitment to an extreme preoccupation. Workaholics put in long hours, often neglecting their families. Workaholics enjoy their work; it is not a sacrifice or an imposition. What sets them apart is their attitude toward work, not the number of hours they work. Work is the dominant role in life, and spouses and family seem to suffer; inactivity is intolerable and having free time means boredom. Even vacations are hard to take.

Workaholic behavior in all probability is permanent and can only be modified. Hans Selye, an expert in the field, has said that a racehorse cannot become a snail; the best it can become is a slow trotter. Being a workaholic is usually part of the person's makeup and is difficult to change—the trait is even noticeable in childhood.

Yet as Winston Churchill stated, "Those whose work and pleasures are one are fortune's favorite children." At times, workaholic tendencies can become a problem for individuals and organizations. Figure 4–1 lists some of its symptoms and gives tips on coping with workaholism.

FIGURE 4–1 *How to Detect and Treat Workaholism*

SYMPTOMS

- Rigid, inflexible, narrow, and over-focused thinking.
- Need to be in control and often engage in ritualistic behavior.
- Unable to delegate work; overly concerned about details.
- Can't say no; poor at setting priorities.
- Intolerant, impatient, and demanding of others; poor personal relationships.
- Not team players; uncooperative.
- Can't handle criticism; need constant approval.
- Can't rest or relax; constant feelings of inadequacy, guilt, and loneliness.

TIPS

- Focus on results, not hours at the workplace; manage by objective.
- Restructure jobs that carry too much responsibility.
- Find a steady pace at work; create challenges that don't involve crises.
- Don't deliberate over minor decisions; use time wisely.
- Learn to delegate tasks and do so without interfering.
- Schedule time away from the office or workplace.
- Develop friends and relationships outside of work.
- Determine what you are avoiding by overworking.
- Do not take work home and avoid thinking about work at home.

Source: John Butterfield, "Unbad Stress for '94," *USA Weekend*, December 31, 1993–January 2, 1994, 18.

HOW TO SURVIVE STRESS

Stress is more than a matter of emotional problems and personality; it is a problem that affects the corporate balance sheet. Manifestations of stress such as ulcers, stroke, heart attack, alcoholism, drug dependency, and social breakdowns can also lead to low productivity, absenteeism, hospitalization, and premature death.

Several corporate programs are designed to take stress out of the job, or at least to minimize distress and reduce costs. Many companies, like Texas Instruments and John Hancock Mutual Life Insurance, provide training sessions on relaxation and coping skills. Similarly, gyms and wellness centers are becoming integral components of many organizations. PepsiCo provides worker incentives that include rebates on fees for programs for losing weight and keeping it off. Adolph Coors Company holds stress classes, including one on the stress of child rearing.

A person undergoing stress feels "keyed up." Stress is usually accompanied by feelings of agitation. The problem is that when such agitation occurs, thoughts and actions become more primitive. As people become more and more agitated, their thoughts become more simplistic; they notice less in the environment, revert to older habits, and ignore all complicated responses.

MAKE STRESS WORK FOR YOU

Don't fight tension.

Do not fight tension—use it. Built-up tensions can cause grave consequences, and telling ourselves not to be tense rarely works. We cannot always remove the source of our tensions. However, when you are tense, you are temporarily more energetic, alert, and aggressive. Begin a job you have been putting off for a long time or one that seems to be a tremendous task. You will enjoy the feeling of accomplishment that such drive can give; your tension will ease and perhaps even disappear.

Tackle one thing at a time.

Tackle one thing at a time. Anxiety gives us a restless dissatisfaction with ourselves when we attempt to do too many things at once. For example, you find that you are not as successful at work as you would like so you decide to go to night school to work on your degree. You barely get started and you are asked to join a civic club that would provide some good contacts. You wish you had more money to buy better clothes, and you think of moonlighting to buy a new wardrobe. If you suffer persistent anxiety by starting things, dropping them, and becoming hopelessly distracted, then tackle one thing at a time. Stick with it until you have done all you can do about it.

Laugh at yourself.

Finally, laugh at yourself on occasion. The way to tell whether you are leaning too heavily toward role playing or pretense is to ask yourself, "When was the last time I had a good laugh at my own expense?" In fact, the following three rules for stress management offer humorous but helpful, tongue-in-cheek advice:

1. If you can't flee, flow.
2. Don't sweat the small stuff.
3. It's all small stuff!

Situations are not inherently stressful.

We have to get away from the assumption that a situation is inherently stressful or not stressful. We are the ones who assign those labels and we can also remove them. It is not the stress itself that is painful and disabling but the impression that it will never end. It is this erroneous projection of a feeling, rather than the pain itself, that reduces people's ability to cope.

People like to control their own fate.

People like to see themselves as able to control their own fate. A primary contributor to stress is the feeling of losing control. The painfulness of the subsequent stress may not result from the actual fact of losing control but from the individual's unwillingness to admit that he or she is capable of losing control.

If people can accept both their strengths and their weaknesses, they can control stress. If individuals regard themselves as capable of controlling events, even while recognizing that there are occasions when they cannot, they will be in a much better position to manage stress. If they are unable to adapt, a physical or mental breakdown may result.

CONTROLLING ANGER

Anger is an emotional feeling of distress. The physical manifestation of anger is hostility. Anger may be a manifestation of stress, but it is not a productive result. All jobs have or perhaps should have an element of at least positive stress, yet anger and hostility can have fatal consequences.

Psychologists advise that controlling your emotions is an important skill. Anger signals that something is wrong. For example, it can be a sign of faulty communica-

SURVIVING STRESS

Here is a seven-step survival plan. Remember to PLEASE yourself to a "T."

P **Plan.** Disorganization can breed stress. Having too many projects going on simultaneously often leads to confusion and forgetfulness when uncompleted projects are hanging over your head. When possible, take on projects one at a time and work on them until completed.

L **Learn to tolerate.** Many of us set unreasonable goals, and because we can never be perfect, we often have a sense of failure no matter how well we perform. Set reasonable goals for yourself.

E **Enjoy life.** You need to escape occasionally from the pressures of life and have fun. Find activities that are absorbing and enjoyable no matter what your level of ability or skill.

A **Assert positive attitudes.** Learn to praise the things you like in others. Focus on the good qualities that those around you possess.

S **Set tolerance limits.** Intolerance of others leads to frustration and anger. An attempt to really understand the way other people feel can make you more accepting.

E **Exercise.** Check with your doctor before beginning any exercise program. Then, select an exercise program you will enjoy. You will more likely stay with a program you chose, especially if you pick one that you really enjoy rather than one that is drudgery.

T **Talk out tensions.** Find a friend, a member of the clergy, a counselor, or a psychologist with whom you can be open. Expressing your bottled-up tension to a sympathetic ear can be incredibly helpful in relieving that tension. Even if no solutions are reached, you may feel better about addressing your problems after releasing these tensions.

tion. Psychologists Jeanne Plas and Kathleen Hoover-Dempsey urge everyone to plan in advance how to react to negative feedback.

> Learning to understand your emotions and coping with them when problems arise can make a tremendous difference in how you are perceived by others. Whenever anger flares at work, remember that good communication often makes hostility disappear. So even if a conversation is interrupted, make sure you get back to it. When you can effectively replace anger with good communication, you've learned one of the hardest but most important lessons of building effective interoffice relationships.[5]

Some companies, in an effort to manage anger, are implementing strict rules that prohibit angry behavior.[6] However, psychologist Jerry Deffenbacher says that it is unrealistic to expect to eliminate anger:

> The goal of intervention should be on *anger management,* not anger elimination. It is idealistic to believe that anger will or can ever be eliminated. Frustration, pain, injustice, and disagreement will continue. People become ill, jobs are lost, relationships end, others are inconsiderate and obnoxious. Even when anger regarding these events is well managed, a residue of mild anger (e.g., frustration, disappointment, annoyance, irritation) remains, and difficult choices remain to be made and implemented.[7]

Becoming aware of when we are becoming angry and using that knowledge to circumvent rash outbursts is key to managing anger and increases emotional intelligence.

AVOIDING BURNOUT

A recognized syndrome related to stress is job burnout, which follows a period of stress. Individuals in the counseling occupations such as lawyers, nurses, teachers, and mental health professionals are especially prone to burnout. Recognizing the symptoms, phases, and methods of overcoming burnout will help reduce its impact.

Symptoms of Burnout (Beyond Stress)

1. Chronic fatigue and low energy.
2. Irritability and negative attitude.
3. Idealistic, inflexible, and indecisive viewpoints.

Four Phases of Burnout

1. Emotional exhaustion.
2. Cynicism and defensiveness.
3. Isolation, tendency to eat alone and act antisocial.
4. Defeatism, feeling of having been unsuccessful with all job effort having been fruitless.

How to Overcome Burnout

1. List priorities. Schedule yourself to do less.
2. Set goals that are achievable.
3. Compartmentalize by focusing on one job at a time.
4. Make changes in your job routine. Schedule fun times.
5. Listen to your body. Your listless feeling may indicate you need more exercise, a better diet, or more sleep.
6. Develop a detached concern. Be concerned with your clients, but do not make them your problems. Build support groups by having contacts with people outside of work.

TIME MANAGEMENT

Another potentially positive and negative stressor is time. Time can be a positive stressor if we manage it rather than letting it manage us. If we become constantly rushed for time, always taking our work home with us and working all of the time, then time becomes a negative stressor.

How we manage our time is also a major determinant of our personal development. All of us have the same amount of time in any given day. What we do with that time can determine our priorities, our future opportunities, our career options, and can help determine how successful we are.

WE ALL HAVE THE SAME AMOUNT OF TIME

Keep a "to do" list.

It makes good business sense to keep a calendar of appointments and a "to do" list. There will be a big payoff for a small amount of time spent in planning for the upcoming day. In addition to this planning time, we all need some quiet time during the day to get organized, to set priorities, and to think.

Some people's internal clocks and habits allow them to do their planning and organizing early in the morning; others prefer late evening. Regardless, we all have the same amount of time each day and planning that time can help us maximize its use.

If you have difficulty keeping track of time, it might be helpful to keep a detailed sample log of your time for a week or two. To see how you are doing, record your time in 10-, 15-, or 30-minute intervals; at the end of the week categorize and tabulate how you spent your time (see Figure 4–2).

SET PRIORITIES ON YOUR TIME

The key to time management is setting priorities.[8] Most time management authorities recommend keeping a prioritized "to do" list. Tasks to be accomplished on a given day are listed with a space for assigning a priority code. One way to order daily tasks is by using the ABC priority system. "A" is for activities with the highest priority, "B" for medium priority, and "C" for low priority. After this "first cut" at prioritizing the list, the A's can be prioritized as A_1, A_2, A_3, and so on. Likewise for the B's and C's. Work on the A's first or at least during your peak hours of performance. Alan Lakein explains:

> Some people do as many items as possible on their lists. They get a very high percentage of tasks done, but their effectiveness is low because the tasks they've done are mostly of C-priority. Others like to start at the top of the list and go right down it, again with little regard to what's important. The best way is to take your list and label each item according to ABC priority, delegate as much as you can, and then polish off the list accordingly.[9]

Figure 4–3 shows a prioritized daily "to do" list. Using a prioritized list allows us to spend 80 percent of our time on the most important items rather than the all-too-common practice of spending 80 percent of our time on routine activities.

THE TECHNOLOGY PARADOX

Technology can be a tremendous time saver. A quick telephone call can answer questions that must be determined before you can proceed on an A-priority project. Similarly, e-mail and the Internet assist in gathering information with greater efficiency than ever before. Yet, phone calls, e-mails, and the Internet can contribute to wasting time by taking you away from "A" activities. Successful businesspeople allow certain hours of the day for phone calls, e-mails, and Internet activities. This allows more time to focus on "A" tasks and gives you control of your own time.

FIGURE 4-2 ***Log for Intermittent Time Analysis***

Day of the Week__________________ Date __________________

Time:	Activity:	Interruptions:
pre-6:00 A.M.		
6:00 A.M.		
6:15		
6:30		
6:45		
7:00		
7:15		
7:30		
7:45		
8:00		
8:15		
8:30		
8:45		
9:00		
9:15		
9:30		
9:45		
10:00		
10:15		
10:30		
10:45		
11:00		
11:15		
11:30		
11:45		
Noon		
12:15 P.M.		
12:30		
12:45		
1:00		
1:15		
1:30		
1:45		

(continued)

FIGURE 4–2 *(CONTINUED)*

2:00
2:15
2:30
2:45

3:00
3:15
3:30
3:45

4:00
4:15
4:30
4:45

5:00
5:15
5:30
5:45

6:00
6:15
6:30
6:45

7:00
7:15
7:30
7:45

8:00
8:15
8:30
8:45

9:00
9:15
9:30
9:45

10:00
Post-10:00 P.M.

FIGURE 4–3 *Abbreviated Example of Daily "To Do" List*

C_2	____	Call Morgan about Reardon project
B_1	____	Complete paper on Tech Transfer for next month
A_1	____	Finish report due next Friday
A_2	____	Work on proposal for SBA
C_3	____	Arrange itinerary for next month's trip—Call travel agent
B_2	____	Plan local travel and appointments for next week
A_4	____	Letter to Bill Jones (fire problem)
A_3	____	Refine goals with boss (make appointment)
B_4	____	Call Johnsen about maintenance service
B_5	____	Call City of Greeley engineer about new process they want
C_1	____	Revise filing system
B_3	____	Recreation time—call M.R.

MANAGE YOUR OWN TIME

It is essential to make time for yourself. Be in control of your own schedule so that you can work on A-priority projects. Organize your schedule and workplace so that you are most productive. Table 4–1 presents 10 summary tips for effective time management.

Iacocca's time planning.

It is also necessary to set long-term priorities on an annual basis. Planning time for major projects and also for major relaxation is equally important. Lee Iacocca, in his autobiography, tells about the importance of planning and time.

> The ability to concentrate and to use your time well is everything if you want to succeed in business—or almost anywhere else, for that matter. Ever since college I've always worked hard during the week while trying to keep my weekends free for family and recreation . . . Every Sunday night I get the adrenalin going again by making an outline of what I want to accomplish during the upcoming week . . .

TABLE 4–1

Ten Tips for Effective Time Management

1. Keep an intermittent time log for a week or two to see how you spend your time.
2. Plan daily, intermediate, and long-term goals.
3. Keep "to do" lists.
4. Prioritize activities.
5. Schedule your time realistically.
6. Improve your communication skills, including meeting management.
7. Make big projects manageable.
8. Balance your personal and professional life.
9. Organize your physical space.
10. Control interruptions and be willing to say "no."

> I'm constantly amazed by the number of people who can't seem to control their own schedules. Over the years, I've had many executives come to me and say with pride: "Boy, last year I worked so hard that I didn't take any vacation." . . . I always feel like responding: "You dummy. You mean to tell me that you can take responsibility for an $80 million project and you can't plan two weeks out of the year to go off with your family and have some fun?"[10]

Increasingly, most managers want their subordinates to take vacations to avoid burnout. Of course, the vacation has to be planned so that it is not a bad time for the business.

YOUR DESK AND WORKPLACE

A survey of 100 executives by Accountemps, a temporary employment service, found that "people with neat desks stand a much better chance of promotion than coworkers with messy desks."[11] But there were perceived differences between top executives and middle managers. Desks used by middle managers were much more likely to be cluttered than those of the top executives, according to the survey.

A clean desk, however, does not guarantee job success—just as a messy desk would not be the only factor considered in a promotion or demotion. It is a point that many managers have a strong opinion about, and may consider with other factors in advancement or firings. What you want to achieve is a workspace that is organized so that you have no more than 10 items on your desk at a time and you are able to find what you need without lost time.[12]

MEETINGS—TIME WASTERS OR COMMUNICATION TOOLS?

WHERE TO MEET?

Tradition suggests that subordinates go to the boss's office—out of deference to status and to save the boss time in getting to the meeting. Techniques such as Management by Walking Around (MBWA), practiced at Hewlett-Packard and other companies, have changed that.

Management by Walking Around (MBWA).

There is some benefit to be gained by going to the other person's office. You usually remain in control of your time by being able to exit more freely than if someone is in your workplace. Even if someone is in your office or workplace, you can still control the meeting and her or his departure by your summary of the meeting and movement away from or out of your workplace.

FORMAL MEETINGS

Use an agenda.

For successful formal meetings, solicit agenda items from participants, distribute the agenda in advance, and announce the beginning and ending meeting times. Having meetings just because they are routinely scheduled at that time is a time waster if there are no agenda items to be discussed.

Meetings are information dissemination and participation tools.

Meetings provide an opportunity for significant participation. Strive to obtain balanced participation by controlling the long-winded participants and drawing out the silent ones.

Unless you know what your time is worth and how to evaluate the time cost of what you do, it is almost impossible to make a correct decision or to evaluate prop-

ACTION PROJECT 4-2

TYPICAL TIME WASTERS (INDIVIDUAL EXERCISE)

This exercise is designed to give you insight into some typical time wasters that may currently be part of your lifestyle. Please complete the form by rating yourself using the following scale:

4 = very often; 3 = frequently; 2 = sometimes; 1 = very seldom

1. Indecision regarding what to do next ____________
2. Daydreaming ____________
3. Drawn-out conversations ____________
4. Lack of concentration ____________
5. Procrastination ____________
6. Unclear priorities ____________
7. Unnecessary socializing ____________
8. Prolonged phone calls ____________
9. Excessive TV watching ____________
10. Little self-direction ____________
11. Inability to say "no" ____________
12. Too many commitments ____________
13. Stressed out/too anxious ____________
14. Partying ____________
15. Inability to find anything ____________
16. Not using time between classes (and all other short periods) ____________
17. Shuffling papers ____________
18. Staring at the books ____________
19. Oversleeping ____________
20. Trouble getting organized ____________

Now, add your ratings. Use the following guidelines to determine your time efficiency:

20–30	Relatively time efficient
30–50	Good balance
50–60	You waste a lot of time
60+	Good candidate for a time management course

erly what action to take in a given situation. Too many people spend $50 worth of time on a $1 job. Table 4–2 illustrates what your time is worth by the hour, based on 244 eight-hour working days per year (a 5-day week less vacation and holidays).

The chart shows the broad average of the entire day based on annual income. You should also decide what your priority of time is for each activity in which you are engaged. Some things you do are more important, and more profitable, than others.

SEVERAL RULES FOR EFFECTIVE MEETINGS AND THEIR LEADERSHIP

Preparation for Meeting

- Limit the number of participants to those persons who are needed to reach a decision on the topic confronting the group.
- Schedule the meeting properly: (1) allocate time according to the relative importance of each topic, and (2) schedule meetings before natural quitting times, such as lunch.
- Determine the specific purpose of the meeting in your own mind.
- Develop and distribute the agenda in advance.

Leading the Meeting

- Start the meeting on time. Do not wait for latecomers.
- Start with the most important item on the agenda. Then stick to the agenda; permit only emergency interruptions.
- Be sensitive to hidden agendas and the social-emotional needs of members.
- Summarize group progress and restate conclusions to ensure agreement.
- Make specific assignments for the next meeting.
- End the meeting on time to allow participants to plan their own time effectively.

Follow-Up Meeting

- Distribute the minutes or a summary of the proceedings. It is especially important to communicate group decisions to the group members.

TABLE 4–2

What Is Your Time Worth?

IF YOUR ANNUAL EARNINGS ARE	EVERY HOUR IS WORTH
$10,000	$ 5.12
12,000	6.15
15,000	7.68
18,000	9.22
20,000	10.25
25,000	12.81
30,000	15.37
35,000	17.93
40,000	20.49
50,000	25.61
60,000	30.74
75,000	38.42
100,000	51.23

CAREER DEVELOPMENT

INDIVIDUAL RESPONSIBILITY

Each individual has the primary responsibility for his or her career development. **Career development** includes all of the activities necessary to become aware of and acquire the knowledge, skills, and competence to perform different jobs. Career development, like time management, is a personal, goal-oriented activity. No one can set your goals or plan your career for you.

Career development starts with self-awareness.

No matter how sophisticated an organization's training program or job rotation system might be, you must take the initiative in planning your career. Career development starts with self-awareness, knowing where you are and where you want to be in 5, 10, or 20 years. Any gaps between your present situation and your future goals provide the basis for career planning.

Individuals must be willing to take short-term trade-offs for long-term gains. Some positions may be lateral transfers in today's increasingly flat organizations. An individual must also be prepared to leave an organization and perhaps a geographic region. The most important aspect of career development is to keep one's options open.

There are several stages in a person's career and life development. Become aware of career opportunities by talking with job counselors and researching literature, such as the *Occupational Outlook Handbook* published by the U.S. Department of Labor and found online at stats.bls.gov/oco. Lists of the best companies to work for are available in current periodicals, such as *Fortune*, *Fast Company*, and *BusinessWeek*.

ORGANIZATIONAL RESPONSIBILITY

Organizations can help you in various stages of your career development process. Many organizations are involved in some type of career development activity, ranging from one-on-one counseling to announcing available training and development seminars. To capitalize on an employer's help, you need to recognize the stages in career development, which are as follows:

1. Job search
2. Settling down and settling in
3. Changing with the organization
4. Mid-career changes and personal crises (burnout, lack of job challenge, plateauing, etc.)
5. Changing jobs within and outside of the organization
6. Preparing for retirement; identifying and grooming potential successors
7. Continuing to work, but at a reduced rate, in retirement

Career development is a part of an organization's human resources planning.

An organization's career development program will be more meaningful if it is a formalized process included in the organization's human resources planning. That means that your manager as well as a centralized database should have knowledge of your skills, training, and career aspirations and that these data are used in making personnel decisions. It pays to take the initiative in discussing these items with your manager and, if appropriate, personnel and career counselors in your organization.

Whether or not an organization incorporates career planning into its human resources development process may be a determinant in where you decide to work. Some organizations have taken on part of the responsibility for helping employees grow and prepare for lateral, upward, and sometimes retrenchment moves. Career planning programs also include demand analysis, career pathing, and career advancement.

DEMAND

Demand for certain occupations is cyclical.

Many careers are cyclical. Engineers, lawyers, and medical doctors are classic examples of fluctuating but fairly constant high-demand careers. Demands for nurses and teachers have fluctuated in recent years, partly because of increased technology and population. As health care services rely on more sophisticated technology, there is less demand for nurses who do not have technical skills and more demand for clinical nursing specialists and other technologists.

The demand for secondary school teachers, once considered a glutted market, is variable. Some school districts now have to recruit teachers the way businesses recruit managers. Others may be cutting back or experiencing hiring freezes or even layoffs because of cost-cutting measures.

Businesses, too, have their opportunity areas. Demand for sales and marketing jobs and for computer specialists continues to grow. The outlook for first-level and middle managers may continue to be less than optimal because of the "lean-and-mean" downsizing or "rightsizing" approaches to management that evolved in the 1990s. Still, there will always be a shortage of really good managers—in other words, there is always room for a truly outstanding leader/manager. The primary factor in individual career advancement is the quality of current job performance.

There is always room for a truly outstanding person in any occupation.

CAREER PATHING

Career planning involves making detailed plans relating to career goals. Included in these plans will be career options and potential career paths. **Career paths** are alternative progressions planned by both the individual and the organization through jobs in an organization. Figure 4–4 shows an example of possible career paths in a savings and loan or bank branch office. Titles may vary and there may be additional steps, such as assistant cashier or administrative assistant. The point is to indicate alternative paths to promotion within an organization.

Career paths point out necessary skills, knowledge, abilities, and training.

Once the career paths are known, it is necessary to determine what skills, knowledge, and abilities a person needs to progress.

CAREER ADVANCEMENT

Certain steps should be followed to ensure success in pursuing a career. Learning how to learn, learning your current job well, and identifying and understanding potential future jobs are important first steps in the pursuit of a career.

How well you do your current job—including being a student—is the best, but not the only, indicator of promotability and success in another job. Additional assessment techniques are needed to predict success. However, poor performance in your current job is a very good predictor of nonpromotability or failure in another job. One of the truest pieces of advice on career development is to produce in your current job in order to get ahead.

In addition to doing your current job well, it is necessary that it be well documented for performance appraisal and promotion purposes. Build your own database or record of your achievements even if management does not require it.

In a sense, you are being encouraged to keep a brag sheet, but it is really a working document for a **resume**—a summary of your accomplishments and goals. Keep your resume up to date at all times, even if you think you do not have a lot of accomplishments. You can include part-time and summer jobs, and extracurricular activities and interests, like specific sports. You never know when job or other

FIGURE 4–4 *Potential Career Paths in a Financial Institution Branch Office*

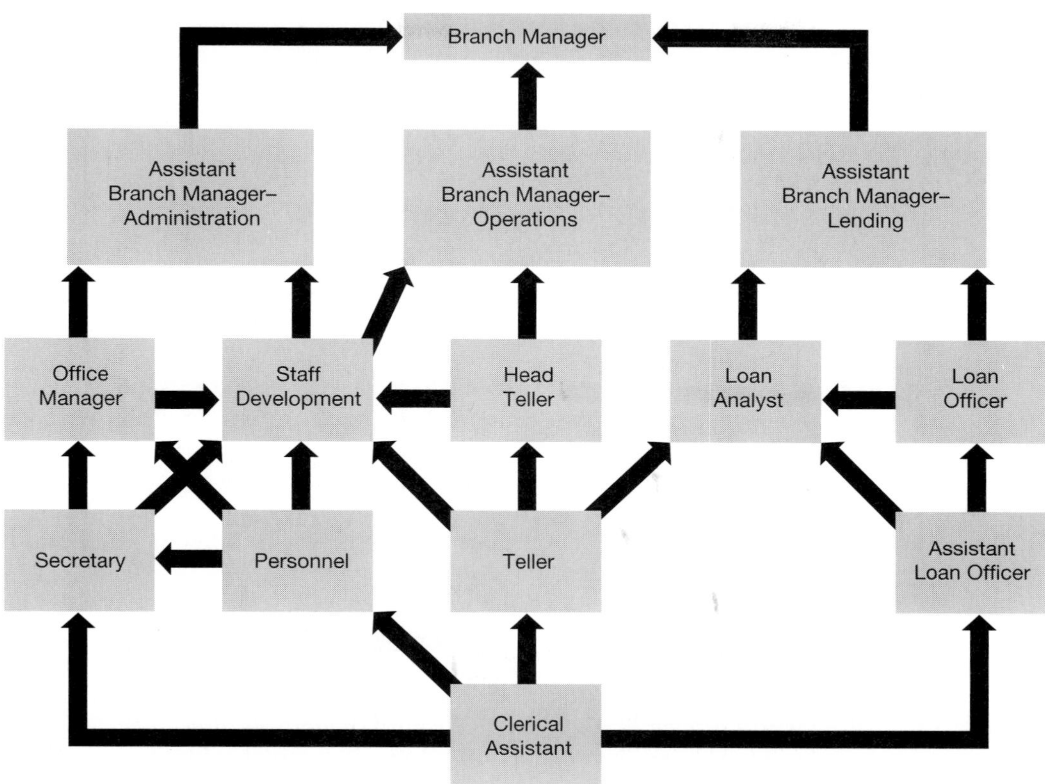

STEPS IN CAREER ADVANCEMENT

1. Learn how to learn.
2. Learn your job.
3. Perform your job well.
4. Know your potential next jobs.
5. Try to understand your next job.
6. Find a mentor and develop a network.
7. Build a performance database.
8. Make clear career choices.

social interest opportunities will present themselves to you, and you want to be prepared.

Have a career plan. The plan may change, but if you do not have a goal or a career plan, then anything will do, won't it? Seek the help of mentors and develop networks. A mentor is an advocate for you who takes you under his or her wing to advise, encourage, and facilitate contacts for you. Networking is the construction and nurturing of personal contacts for business and social use, both in and outside of an organization.

Finally, make clear career choices. Ask others in a job about the demands, expectations, and frustrations of the job before taking it. Jobs change, but it is important for the job applicant to learn as much as possible before making a career commitment.

ALTERNATIVE SCHEDULE CHOICES

There are many alternatives to the traditional 9-to-5 workday.

As we moved into the Information Age, advances in technology and the aging of the workforce have contributed to alternative work schedules. Several alternatives exist for accomplishing alternative schedule choices:

1. *Alternative career paths.* Individuals work part-time for a salary and may receive longevity credit for part-time work, but they lower their odds of becoming partners or other senior-level managers.
2. *Extended leave.* Employees can take leave with benefits and the guarantee of a comparable job on return.
3. *Flexible scheduling.* Employees create customized schedules and work at home, allowing a phase-in period after taking a leave.
4. *Flextime.* Employees shift the standard workday forward or back as long as they work a common core of hours. **Flextime** allows employees to set their own work schedules within defined limits. Flexible time is most frequently used in service and retail industries to accommodate peak hours, but it can be adapted to manufacturing operations. Hewlett-Packard, Federal Express, and Merck are just a few of the types of manufacturing and service companies that have used flextime successfully.
5. *Job sharing.* **Job sharing** occurs when two or more employees share a title, workload, salary, benefits, and vacation. Job sharing allows individuals who might have time constraints, because of other work, home, or school responsibilities, to be productive for their organizations by dividing a job usually held by one individual into jobs held by two or more employees.

   Job sharing involves additional coordination and management of variable work schedules, but one of the major advantages is that it allows for employee cross-training and sets the stage for skill-based pay systems. Although many managers remain highly resistant to job sharing, research of 131 firms shows that job sharing increases employee motivation, loyalty, and commitment.[13]
6. *Telecommuting.* Employees are allowed to limit the time they spend in the office by using personal computers, fax machines, and e-mail at home. **Telecommuting** has already allowed organizations to improve their productivity by allowing employees to work when and where they are at their peak or prime times of performance. Telecommuting eliminates commuting time as well, decreasing one negative impact on our environment.

   > Telecommuting is the springboard for a reengineering of how work is done. The more than 6 million employees who telecommute do so during work hours and are in fairly regular contact with the office. There are already signs that in the future the telecommuting concept will evolve into the idea that work can and will be done anytime and anyplace.[14]

Another consideration in career advancement is created by opportunities for dual-career couples and geographic transfer. A career opportunity may arise for one individual that is problematic for that person's spouse, who cannot secure meaningful employment at the new location or who hesitates to leave an established, successful job. As a result, there is a rise in commuter marriages.

Franklin Becker at Cornell University says that the key to the office of the future is diversity. "Diversity is going to take on many different forms, including age, ethnicity, gender, and work style. The key shift will be to support the varied ways in which people actually work, emphasizing performance" instead of focusing on just being visibly present at the office all day.[15]

Flextime, job sharing, telecommuting, and other alternative choices continue to become increasingly popular. Because home computers can now be part of networks through modems and fax machines, it is much easier to modify schedules and, in fact, to be even more productive than at the office.

ACTION PROJECT 4-3

CAREER DEVELOPMENT (GROUP EXERCISE)

The following exercise requires that you choose/recommend your replacement. You are the manager of a men's wear department at a major department store. You have just been promoted and will be moving to another store. You have two full-time and three part-time employees from whom you must choose a replacement for your position. The job requires 40 hours per week, and the starting pay is $32,000 yearly. You are looking for someone who is reliable and industrious.

These are the five candidates:

Frank—Full-time employee, 32 years old, family man with two children; been with the store for 2 years; great public relations, no management skills, makes mistakes due to sloppiness.

Charmaine—Full-time employee, 17 years old, high school drop-out; been with store for 6 months; quick learner, makes few mistakes, does not plan on attending college.

Greg—Part-time employee, 21 years old; been with the store for 3 years; most knowledgeable in business aspects, excellent with customers, will be leaving in 2 years due to college graduation.

Lisa—Part-time employee, 58 years old; been with the store 15 years, working 12 hours a week; most familiar with store routine, makes few mistakes, good public relations, health is failing—misses work about 3 days per month due to illness.

Susan—Part-time employee, 25 years old, pregnant; college graduate with degree in marketing; been with store for 2 years; best overall worker but prefers part-time hours.

First, rank your preferences for the person to get the job (1= first preference). Then, compare your rankings with others in your group.

Your Individual Ranking		Group Ranking	Analysis/Reasons
_____	Charmaine	_____	_____
_____	Frank	_____	_____
_____	Greg	_____	_____
_____	Lisa	_____	_____
_____	Susan	_____	_____

SUCCESS

Being ready to act is the key to capitalizing on opportunities—and opportunities along with hard work are the keys to success. Success is not just a destination—it is a journey.

The concepts of success and failure as fundamental motivating forces are constantly being redefined. More and more, people are realizing that success can be measured by personal standards as well as by public ones. Some people march to different drummers. Success can be defined in terms of one's attitudes or material wealth. Is material wealth an adequate dimension by itself? Does it depend on how and why you acquire wealth?

Success depends on your goals.

Success is goal oriented. If you set demanding but attainable goals and achieve them, then you are successful. If you perform well in your job, as well as in other relationships within your family and other social institutions, you are successful.

SUCCESS IS RESPECT

Success is attitudinal.

Success is not a popularity contest.

A more universal meaning of success relates to the attitudes of others. Respect from others is a more recognized dimension of success than any other. People need to be accepted by others. A person is successful who has gained the respect of intelligent men and women. Respect does not necessarily imply admiration or popularity. Respect means that a person is recognized and given consideration. The person does not have to be loved, or even liked, to be successful. Individuals should have respect from some, preferably a majority, of their coworkers, customers, and others with whom they interact.

MATURITY

Success includes being magnanimous.

A mature attitude is another sign of success. Magnanimity, or the ability to rise above petty matters, is in itself a sign of maturity and success. The art of being successful includes being concerned with the important rather than the petty. Positive attitudes have a profound effect on success.

Negative attitudes and preoccupation with what is wrong with oneself, others, the organization, or society can drain energies away from the important matters and from ultimate success. We may spend our time tilting at windmills in a quixotic manner while success is getting away—or we win the battle and lose the war.

Whether applied to international relations, national politics, or interoffice squabbles, magnanimity is a means of translating hostility into harmony and success. There are times when it is better to turn the other cheek. Obviously there is also a limit beyond which we cannot go in both international and interpersonal relations.

Certainly, there are circumstances that call for a person to take a firm stand on major issues, but as in time management, it is important to make sure the issues are really important before we spend the majority of our time and emotional energies defending them. From a likability viewpoint, magnanimity does much to facilitate human relationships.

YOU DO NOT HAVE TO BE PERFECT TO BE SUCCESSFUL

Success does not necessarily imply perfection. Effective workers aim for success—not perfection—because the pressure and discouragement that perfectionists feel leads to decreases in productivity and creativity. Success, then, is a matter of feeling that we are doing our very best and having our boss, coworkers, customers, and others respect, acknowledge, and accept our efforts.

SELF-APPRAISAL

PERFECTION VERSUS SATISFACTION

If you are a compulsive perfectionist, you may find it hard to believe that you can enjoy life to the maximum or find true happiness without aiming for perfection. You can put this notion to the test. On a piece of paper, list a wide range of activities such as mowing the lawn, preparing a meal, or writing a report for work. Record the actual satisfaction you get from each activity by scoring it from 0 to 100 percent. Now estimate how perfectly you do each activity, again using a scale of 0 to 100. I call this an "antiperfectionism sheet." It will help you break the illusory connection between perfection and satisfaction.

Here is how it works: A physician I know was convinced he had to be perfect at all times. No matter how much he accomplished he would always raise his standards slightly higher and then he would feel miserable. I persuaded him to do some research on his moods and accomplishments, using the antiperfectionism sheet. One weekend a pipe broke at his home and flooded the kitchen. It took a long time, but he did manage to stop the leak. Because he was such a novice at plumbing, had taken a long time, and required considerable guidance from a neighbor, he recorded his expertise as only 20 percent. On the other hand, he estimated his level of satisfaction with the job as 99 percent. By contrast, he received low degrees of satisfaction from some activities on which he did an outstanding job.

This experience with the antiperfectionism sheet persuaded him that he did not have to be perfect at something to enjoy it. Furthermore, striving for perfection and performing exceptionally did not guarantee happiness; rather, it tended to be associated with less satisfaction. He concluded he could either give up his compulsive drive for perfection and settle for joyous living and high productivity, or cling to his compulsions and settle for emotional anguish and modest productivity. Which would you choose? Put yourself to the test.

Source: Excerpts abridged from David D. Burns, M.D., *Feeling Good* William Morrow & Company, 1980, 303–304, as it appeared in "Aim for Success, Not Perfection," *Reader's Digest*. By permission of William Morrow & Company.

President Theodore Roosevelt summarized the maturity, magnanimity, and orientation necessary to be successful in one's personal and career development:

> It is not the critic who counts, nor the man who points out how the strong man stumbles or where the doer of deeds could have done them better. The credit belongs to the man who is actually in the arena, whose face is marred by dust and sweat and blood. And who strives valiantly. Who errs and comes short again and again. Who knows the great enthusiasms, the great devotions and spends himself in a worthy cause. Who at the best knows in the end the triumph of high achievement and who at the worst, if he fails, at least fails while daring greatly. So that his place will never be with those cold and timid souls who knew neither victory nor defeat.

Finally, a quote from former secretary of Health, Education, and Welfare, John W. Gardner, is appropriate to close this chapter.

> The things you learn in maturity aren't simple things such as acquiring information and skills. You learn not to engage in self-destructive behavior. You learn not to burn up energy in anxiety. You discover how to manage your tensions. You learn that self-pity and resentment are among the most toxic of drugs. You find that the world loves talent but pays off on character. You come to understand that most people are neither for you nor against you; they are thinking about themselves. You learn that no matter how hard you try to please, some people in this world are not going to love you—a lesson that is at first troubling and then really quite relaxing.[16]

SUMMARY

We need eustress—or positive stress—to help us to develop personally and professionally. However, distress, or negative stress, can be dysfunctional. Stress is natural, but can be our worst enemy when it leads to emotional and physical ills. People with Type A personalities are compulsive, hardworking achievers and are more likely to experience physical ailments, especially if their Type A behavior is associated with hostility, or Type H behavior.

Negative stress, or even too much positive stress, can lead to burnout. People who are fatigued and irritable express negative attitudes and make mistakes. Feelings of burnout can be overcome in part by managing time.

Time management is largely a matter of scheduling activities and setting priorities. When we are in control of our own time, we manage our schedule and make time for ourselves. Telephones and meetings can be either time savers or time wasters depending on how we manage them and get them to work for us.

Both stress and time factors contribute to career development and success. Our job environment and lifestyle create an ambiance that allows us to be successful. By not letting the petty things bother us, we give ourselves more time to concentrate on our important goals. Success should not be confused with perfection.

Focus on one job at a time and schedule fun times; this helps to overcome the failure syndrome. Build support groups by having contacts with people outside of work. Finally, develop a somewhat detached concern for problems at work; this helps and can spell success in life as well as work. Recognize that personal and career development is primarily an individual responsibility. Organizations can help guide current and prospective employees through careers by providing realistic job previews and assessments of individuals' skills and abilities. There may even be times when it is advantageous for employees to move on to other opportunities.

Ultimately, success depends in large measure on how well we (1) cope with stress and tension; (2) manage our time, meetings, and other human interactions; and (3) plan and otherwise manage our personal careers.

CASE STUDY 4-1

I DO NOT HAVE ENOUGH TIME

Joan Flickinger is a branch manager for Home National Bank in the growing suburban community of Sylvan Dale. Ten years ago, she started at another suburban branch as teller and was gradually promoted to assistant manager. When the Sylvan Dale office opened, she was promoted to branch manager.

Joan sat in her office at 6:15 P.M. wondering why she had not accomplished more that day. She had arrived just after 8 A.M. as usual. Her day had been filled by appointments with subordinates and customers, and was fairly typical, she thought, insofar as day-to-day operations were concerned.

She was frustrated because she had not spent any time on the report that the main office expected from her next week on expansion plans for her branch. She knew that she would have to take that work home with her again tonight. It was difficult to work on it in addition to spending time with her family—her husband and two teenage daughters. Joan had never really had any training in staff development positions and found it difficult to write such reports.

Joan's administrative assistant, Sue Tate, schedules appointments for her. The last meeting for the day was scheduled for 4:30 P.M., right after the office closed, with Sue. Sue wanted to talk about a raise because of increased responsibilities in answering the phone, scheduling appointments, working for other branch officers, and typing correspondence and reports for the main office. Sue's request for a raise caught Joan by surprise, and the meeting was a little tense at times. It lasted over an hour and a half. No resolution was achieved.

1. What is Joan's problem?

2. Could career development and a career path help alleviate some of Joan's problem?

3. What should Joan do about her problem?

DISCUSSION AND STUDY QUESTIONS—TO KEEP YOU THINKING

1. Why did we introduce, study, and discuss personal development—coping with stress, time management, and career progression—now? Why not at the end of the book, or at the end of the academic term?

2. What are the differences between eustress and distress?

3. Why are workaholics "Fortune's favorite children"?

4. Can or should anger be eliminated?

5. What is meant by the technology paradox?

6. Are meetings time wasters or communication tools?

7. Who has the responsibility for career development?

8. What are career paths? How can they help you?

9. What are examples of alternative schedule choices?

10. What is success?

NOTES

1. *Webster's Ninth New Collegiate Dictionary* (Springfield, MA: Merriam-Webster Inc. 1984): 1359.
2. American Psychological Association, "Psychology at Work: How Does Stress Affect Us?" helping.apa.org/ (accessed January 2000).
3. David Levine, "The Secrets of People Who Never Get Sick," *Good Housekeeping* (December 1995): 70–73.
4. "Are You a Type H?" *USA Weekend*, July 7–9, 1989, 8.
5. Jeanne M. Plas and Kathleen V. Hoover-Dempsey, "Keeping Anger in Check," *National Business Employment Weekly* (spring 1989): 18, 20.
6. Mark P. Couch, "Fight Fire with Fire to Squelch Anger in Workplace," *Fort Collins Coloradoan*, October 9, 1995, C1.
7. Jerry L. Deffenbacher, "Anger Reduction," in *Anger, Hostility, and the Heart*, ed. A. Siegman and T. Smith, (Hillsdale, NJ: Lawrence Erlbaum, 1994), 267.
8. Lesley Alderman, "You Can Achieve More in a Lot Less Time by Following Five Key Steps," *Money* (October 1995): 37–38.
9. Alan Lakein, *How to Get Control of Your Time and Your Life* (New York: Signet, 1973), 28.

10. Lee Iacocca with William Novak, *Iacocca: An Autobiography* (New York: Bantam, 1984), 20.
11. "Clean Desk for Success," *USA Today*, June 28, 1985, 1.
12. Hal Lancaster, "Managing Your Career: Is Your Messy Desk a Sign You're Busy or Just Disorganized?" *The Wall Street Journal*, January 30, 1996, B1.
13. Malia Boyd, "Job Sharers Are More Motivated," *Incentive* (February 1995): 13.
14. Julie Cohen Mason, "Workplace 2000: The Death of 9 to 5?" *Management Review* (January 1993): 15.
15. Ibid., 16.
16. John W. Gardner, Commencement address at Stanford University, Palo Alto, California, June 16, 1991.

CHAPTER

5

Creativity, Innovation, and Entrepreneurial Thinking

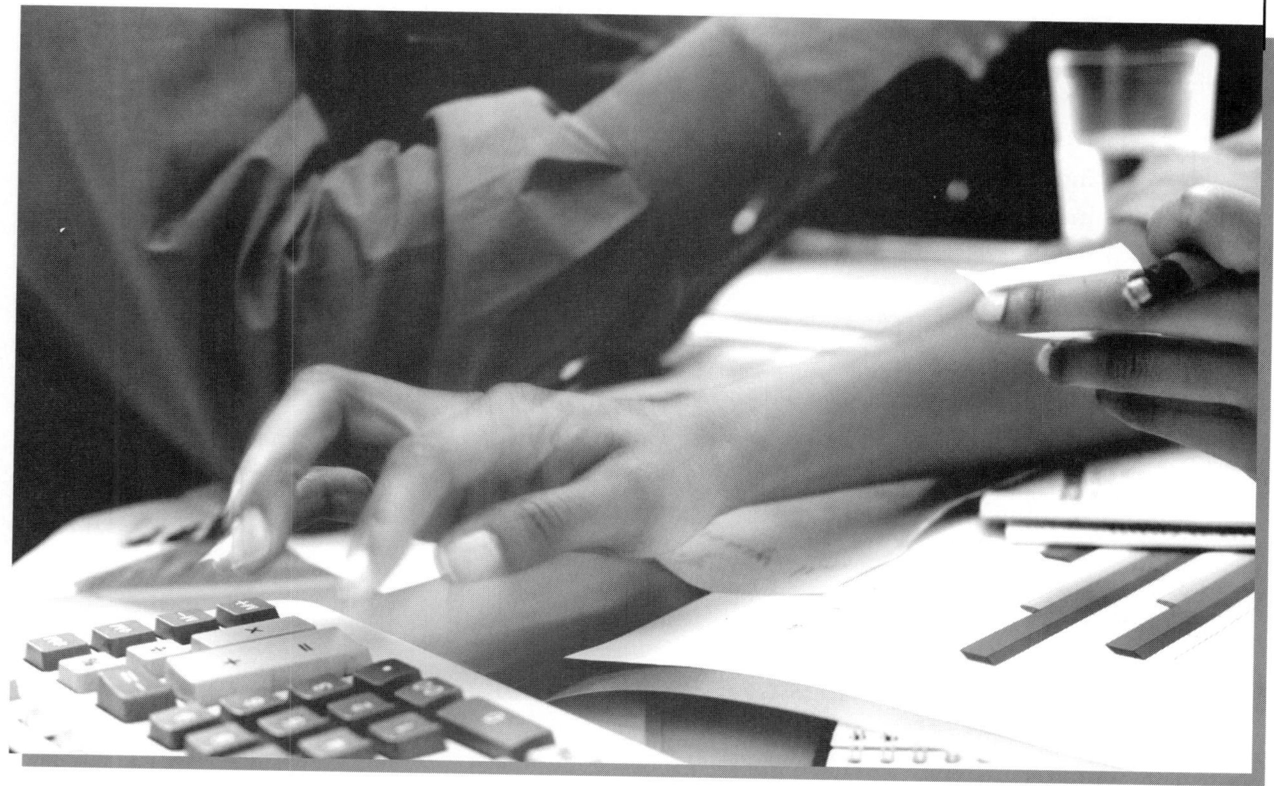

TO START YOU THINKING

Consider the following questions before you read the chapter.

- Are only artists creative?
- Is creativity something you are born with or a skill you can develop?
- Is it possible to become more creative?
- Why is innovation critical to doing business in the twenty-first century?
- What makes a person an entrepreneur?
- What impact does management have on creativity and innovation?
- How can organizations support creativity and innovation?
- What techniques can you use to improve individual and group creativity?

LEARNING GOALS

After studying this chapter, you should be able to:

1. Describe the relationships among creativity, innovation, and entrepreneurship.
2. Identify instances of innovation in organizations.
3. Explain the role of management in supporting creativity and innovation in organizations.
4. Describe and apply various techniques for enhancing individual and group creativity.
5. Be able to define the following (in order of first occurrence):

KEYWORDS

- **creativity**
- **innovation**
- **product/service innovation**
- **process innovation**
- **marketing innovation**
- **managerial innovation**
- **learning innovation**
- **divergent thinking**
- **convergent thinking**
- **flexibility of thinking**
- **fluency of thinking**
- **multifunctional teams**
- **groupthink**
- **brainstorming**
- **nominal group technique**
- **devil's advocate**
- **entrepreneur**
- **intrapreneurship**

WHAT DEFINES CREATIVITY AND INNOVATION?

The definition of creativity has been the subject of debate for a long time among theorists, artists, and philosophers. We all have our own unique and intuitive understanding of what we mean by creativity. Some describe it as a trait or internal predisposition that people have toward certain behaviors. Others see it as an unconscious process resulting in sudden illumination. Still others think it is an associative process through which new associations are made among disparate ideas; and yet others believe it to be a linear set of steps in problem solving.[1] For our purposes, we will distill that debate down to a relatively simple definition. **Creativity** is the process of generating something new.

Creativity is the process of generating something new.

As simple as that definition is, it bears some explanation. First, creativity is a *process.* It consists of a series of actions or changes, using resources at our disposal, directed toward a goal. The goal that spurs the creative process may be expressive, artistic, practical, or playful; it may be lasting or transient; it may spring from necessity or whimsy. The resources we use may include materials, the inputs of others, our life experiences, and our intellect and skill. Second, it is a *generative* act, meaning that something is produced as a result of the creative process. The product may be as tangible as an invention, a work of art, or a piece of writing. It may be as intangible as an idea, a theory, or a vision. Finally, creativity results in something new or novel. This element of the definition reminds us that creativity is about producing something original, something that did not exist before.

Creativity results in something new.

In the business context, we require additional criteria when defining creativity. Those additional elements are *utility* and *value.* In business, we want creativity to result in something useful and valuable. These become overriding goals in the creative process for an established or entrepreneurial organization. This leads us to the definition of innovation. **Innovation** is the process of generating a new idea, finding the value in that idea, and capturing that value. It begins with an act of creativity—the generation of the new idea—but innovation goes beyond the creative act and focuses on finding and exploiting the utility and value of the creation, whether it is a new product, a new service, or a new way of doing things. Innovation can also be a way to capture the value in another person's creative idea, not just one's own idea.

Innovation is the process of generating a new idea, finding the value in that idea, and capturing that value.

Organizations of the twenty-first century will rise and fall based on the ability to innovate. James Higgins identifies 10 forces in the twenty-first century business environment that will drive the necessity of innovation.[2]

Organizations of the twenty-first century will rise and fall based on the ability to innovate.

1. Accelerating rates of change: As we enter a new century, it is clear that change is occurring faster and with greater impact.
2. Increasing levels of competition: Organizations face more competition, both domestic and international, from established players and entrepreneurial start-ups.
3. Globalization of business competition: Competitors may come from anywhere in the world.
4. Rapid technological change: The pace of change in the technologies that most organizations have come to depend upon leads to rapid obsolescence.
5. A more diverse workforce: The workforce that organizations are drawing from is increasingly heterogeneous along various demographic characteristics.
6. Resource shortages: Different industries will face decreased availability of critical material, human, and/or capital resources.
7. Transition from an industrial to a knowledge-based society: Information has become an increasingly critical resource in organizations, and knowledge will be fundamental to survival.

8. Unstable market and economic conditions: The increasingly global nature of the business environment has led to the potential for greater volatility, as capital and other resources move more freely around the world.
9. Increasing demands of constituents: Organizations are discovering that various stakeholder groups are becoming more vocal in their demands and more willing to push for their needs to be met.
10. Increasing complexity of the environment: Managers are faced with more problems and more variables that they must consider in doing their jobs effectively.

What Higgins's list makes abundantly clear is that organizations in this century must find new, useful, and valuable ways to do business—to innovate. In order to survive and thrive, companies must:

- come up with new products and services to meet the changing demands of existing customers and to enter new markets (**product/service innovation**),
- find new ways to produce products and deliver services that reduce costs, use fewer resources, reduce production time, and increase flexibility (**process innovation**),
- create new ways to present their product or service to a wider array of customers (**marketing innovation**), and
- find innovative ways to organize and manage their human resources (**managerial innovation**).

Learning innovation improves the ability to gather, process, and retain information and knowledge.

A category that does not appear on Higgins's list, but which will be increasingly important in our contemporary environment, is that organizations must improve the ability to gather, process, and retain information and knowledge. This might be termed **learning innovation**.

Higgins also defines innovation as "*the* core competence because it makes competitive advantage by any other strategy possible."[3] Creating new products and product enhancements provides differentiation. Process innovation can lead to lower costs and improved customer satisfaction. Tom Peters places innovation as the top priority in liberating an entire organization.[4]

LEFT-BRAIN, RIGHT-BRAIN, OR WHOLE-BRAIN THINKING?

Creativity has often been discussed as a function of the right side of the brain. Our brains are structured so that the left and right hemispheres are specialized with respect to the ways that each processes information. In most people, the left side contains the segments of the brain that are involved in speech and analytical thinking, and it controls the right hand. The right side has the segments that handle spatial perception, idea synthesis, and our sense of aesthetics, and controls the left hand.

The two sides are connected by the corpus callosum, which regulates exchanges between the left and right hemispheres. Only a few people, often victims of accidents that sever the corpus callosum, operate purely in left- or right-brain mode.

So while this split-brain approach is of passing interest as a way of understanding processes occurring at a physiological level, the more important reality is that we operate holistically using both sides of the brain, particularly when we are creative and innovative. James Adams identifies our tendency to label people based on the left-right brain model as a cultural barrier to creativity because it creates an inaccurate stereotype of innovators as nonanalytic or illogical thinkers.[5]

Divergent thinking expands alternatives.

Convergent thinking narrows alternatives.

Alternatively, creativity can be characterized as a sequence of divergent and convergent thinking events. **Divergent thinking** involves expanding the alternatives under consideration while **convergent thinking** is a narrowing down of alternatives. We are thinking divergently when we scan the environment for new information, when we generate alternative ideas, and when we attempt to consider the implications of our creative work. We are thinking convergently when we discard some information as irrelevant, when we eliminate some alternatives from consideration, and when we prioritize and make choices. Creativity and innovation in business require both sets of activities. One model proposes that there are seven "universal" stages to creative problem solving.[6] These stages are commitment to complete the task, research and analysis, defining the issue(s) and primary cause(s), idea generation, selection, implementation, and evaluation.

First, we commit ourselves to trying to solve a problem or find an opportunity. We also commit to investing the necessary time and resources to complete the task. Then we must seek out information to expand our understanding of the world around us. We seek opportunities, look for new markets, and identify unmet needs. This is divergent activity. Then we evaluate those opportunities to determine which are most likely to have value and eliminate some alternatives that offer too few rewards, present too great a risk, or exceed our capabilities. This is a convergent act, narrowing the set of ideas under consideration.

We again act divergently by generating alternative approaches to capitalize on the reduced set of opportunities. Then we must again converge by selecting the alternative we will actually pursue. In the last two stages we implement the alternative we have selected, opening up the opportunity and evaluating the results, then converging to a conclusion. This alternating sequence of divergence and convergence continues, utilizing both sides of our brains—the creative and the analytical—in a coordinated process.

ARE THERE CHARACTERISTICS OF CREATIVE INDIVIDUALS?

Many researchers have tried to develop a profile of the creative individual. E. P. Torrance, one of the most prolific creativity researchers, suggests that courage, independence of thought and judgment, honesty, perseverance, curiosity, tolerance for moderate risk, and, most importantly, a love for what you are doing are the keys to being creative.[7] To this list, others would add a tolerance for ambiguity, a willingness to overcome obstacles, an ability to make associations among diverse concepts, and a drive for recognition.

Creative people challenge assumptions.

What does seem clear is that creative people are unwilling to simply accept things as they are. They are not only willing, but also driven, to challenge the assumptions that others take for granted, to question the limitations that others perceive, and to seek new ways to accomplish their goals. Koberg and Bagnall refer to three basic strengths needed for creativity: awareness (curiosity and appreciation of life), passion (love of the quest and determination to interact with the world), and self-control (taking charge of one's behaviors).[8]

One characteristic that is often associated with creativity is intelligence, but the research record does not bear this out, at least not with traditional, logical/rational definitions of intelligence. The work of Howard Gardner on multiple intelligences contends that we have limited our definition of intelligence to a narrow reliance on logical and analytical skills—the convergent approach—instead of recognizing and appreciating the many varieties of intelligence that are manifested in ourselves and others.[9] His work may offer opportunities to reexplore the connection between creativity and other definitions of intelligence, including spatial ability.

HOW DO YOU TAP YOUR CREATIVE POTENTIAL?

Being creative improves with practice.

Being creative, like anything else, improves with practice. Unfortunately, we are not challenged to think creatively as often as we are forced to think analytically. Our educational process from grade school through college emphasizes logic and analysis (the left-brain stereotype) through courses in mathematics and science (even literature courses focus on the analysis of written works), with creativity often relegated to marginal status in elective courses like creative writing, music, and art.

Business courses fail to teach creativity; instead, they emphasize quantitative analysis of industry trends, marketing research, financial data, and accounting information over managerial intuition, entrepreneurship, and new product development. Organizations often carry on this pattern by focusing solely on short-term results, following formalized procedures, and "if it ain't broke, don't fix it" thinking.

Additionally, we encounter many barriers to our creativity. Adams classifies these barriers, or blocks, into several categories: perceptual, emotional, cultural, environmental, intellectual, and expressive.[10] First, perceptual blocks prevent us from accurately perceiving the situation or the necessary information. One form of perceptual block is the stereotype that constrains our thinking to oversimplified, and often inaccurate, generalizations. Others include the inability to distinguish the problem from the surrounding chaos or to effectively select relevant information from the overload of data available.

Another set of blocks is emotional, the most damaging of which is fear: fear of failure, of embarrassment, of trusting others, of taking risks, and of dealing with ambiguity. Also within this set is the inability to allow time for ideas to incubate and to refrain from judging ideas too early in the process.

The third set of blocks is cultural and environmental. Among the cultural barriers are taboos, traditions, reliance on rational thinking approaches, and, at the same time, the devaluing of fantasy, playfulness, intuition, and humor. The environmental barriers include distractions, lack of trust among coworkers, lack of support for implementation of ideas, and autocratic bosses. Finally, Adams examines the intellectual and expressive blocks that inhibit our creativity. These reflect limitations in our strategies, tools, and information for attacking problems or generating alternatives and for capturing and communicating our ideas effectively.

For an individual interested in revitalizing his or her creativity, these barriers must be overcome. There are many resources available in trade publications and the popular press to help you do so. Authors like James Adams, Edward DeBono, Roger Van Oech, and James Higgins offer techniques identifying our self-limitations on creativity, ways to loosen up our thinking patterns and to practice more creative approaches to problem solving. Try a few of the better-known creative problem-solving activities that follow.

The Nine Dots exercise points out one of the typical barriers to creativity that James Adams refers to as perceptual blocks. We often impose limitations on our thinking and problem solving that are not really there. Many people, when challenged with the Nine Dots, mentally draw a boundary line at the edge of the square defined by the dots themselves. Once they place themselves in this "box," the exercise becomes insolvable. Only those who are able to "think outside the box" are able to make the creative leap to solve the puzzle. The Japanese saying is "don't think like a frog in a well." Thinking outside

ACTION PROJECT 5–1

CREATIVE PROBLEM SOLVING (INDIVIDUAL EXERCISE)

THE NINE DOTS EXERCISE

Draw four straight lines, without lifting your pencil from the paper, that cross through all nine dots.

• • •

• • •

• • •

USES FOR A BRICK EXERCISE

List as many uses as you can think of for a common brick.

the box has entered the managerial lexicon as a mantra and a description of any ideas that go beyond the generally perceived, and usually false, limitations.

The Uses for a Brick exercise asks you to freely list alternative uses for a common item. This type of exercise may reveal your flexibility and fluency of thinking. **Flexibility of thinking** is reflected in the total number of unique solutions you generate and indicates an ability to produce many alternatives. These alternatives may be variations on the same theme, for example holding things, such as using the brick as a doorstop, to block a car's tire on a hill, to hold open a window, and as a paperweight. When you produce many such variations, you are being flexible.

Flexibility of thinking indicates an ability to produce many alternatives.

Fluency of thinking refers to how many unrelated ideas you generate and reflects an ability to move among diverse alternatives rather than simply producing variations on one or a few dominant themes. Thus, those who suggest using the brick for a doorstop, a water conservation device in a toilet tank, an abrasive, and a weight for exercising, are demonstrating fluency by considering multiple attributes of the brick in generating alternative uses.

Fluency of thinking reflects an ability to move among diverse alternatives.

How do you improve your skills? There are many techniques suggested for freeing your creative potential. Several of these are discussed below.

Ask lots of questions.

One skill that can be developed is that of asking questions. To start, one might want to use a checklist of questions to be answered about problems to be solved, solutions developed, or new ideas generated.[11] These lists can guide you in your thinking and help you develop the habit of questioning assumptions, evaluating goals, and considering extensions to the ideas you generate. James Adams, in his book, *The Care and Feeding of Ideas*, provides a list of questions suggested by Alex Osborne that provides a great way to loosen up one's thinking.[12] Notice how each set of questions pushes you to move beyond your current idea to consider alternatives that you might not otherwise have thought about. Once you have used the list a few times, you will probably discover additional questions that apply to the types of situations with which you deal most frequently. After you have used a checklist enough times, you may no longer need to refer to it as it will become second nature to you.

OSBORNE'S LIST

Put to other uses? New ways to use as is? Other uses if modified?
Adapt? What else is like this? What other idea does this suggest? Does past offer a parallel? What could I copy? Whom could I emulate?

Modify? New twist? Change meaning, color, motion, sound, odor, form, shape? Other changes?
Magnify? What to add? More time? Greater frequency? Stronger? Higher? Longer? Thicker? Extra value? Plus ingredient? Duplicate? Multiply? Exaggerate?
Minify? What to subtract? Smaller? Condensed? Miniature? Lower? Shorter? Lighter? Omit? Streamline? Split up? Understate?
Substitute? Who else instead? What else instead? Other ingredient? Other material? Other process? Other power? Other place? Other approach? Other voice tone?
Rearrange? Interchange components? Other pattern? Other layout? Other sequence? Transpose cause and effect? Change pace? Change schedule?
Reverse? Transpose positive and negative? How about opposites? Turn it backward? Turn it upside down? Reverse roles? Change shoes? Turn tables? Turn other cheek?
Combine? How about a blend, an alloy, an assortment, an ensemble? Combine units? Combine purposes? Combine appeals? Combine ideas?

Another technique suggested by Adams and others is to list as many attributes of the situation or solution as possible and then generate multiple alternatives for each one. By considering random combinations of attributes and alternatives, one may come up with a new idea or trigger a new way of thinking about the problem.

Beyond attempts by individuals to expand their creative potential, we also need to be concerned with environmental and cultural barriers. That means that we need to consider the organizational context and how it may impact on creativity and innovation of employees.

WHAT CAN ORGANIZATIONS DO?

Before examining what organizations can do to encourage creativity in their employees, let us look at what they often do to discourage it. If we were to create a list of barriers to creativity in a typical organization it would probably include many of the following.

1. Punishment of failure
2. "If it ain't broke, don't fix it" thinking
3. Not-invented-here syndrome
4. Avoidance of risk and ambiguity
5. Fear of change
6. Pressures for conformity
7. Failure to act on suggestions
8. Overcontrol of information
9. Isolation of employees
10. "It's been tried before and didn't work"

Each of these can be logically supported as an organizational value and argued for by traditional managers as necessary to the efficient running of a business. Organizations that follow these approaches may linger on for years if they are in a stable or stagnant industry, but they are unlikely to grow and thrive, particularly in the dynamic markets that hold the most opportunities.

By contrast, organizations that wish to encourage creativity among their employees need to take different approaches. First and foremost, management needs to make creativity and innovation organizational values. One company that has long been considered as an icon of creativity and innovation is 3M (Minnesota Mining and Manufacturing, Inc.). Dr. William E. Coyne, the senior vice president for research and development, has indicated that innovation is not only 3M's goal, it is its strategy, and is reinforced in many ways.[13]

At 3M, failure is an expected outcome and is valued as an opportunity to learn rather than as something to be avoided and punished. Technical employees are encouraged to spend 15 percent of their time working on projects of their own choice in pursuit of breakthrough ideas upon which the company can capitalize. Managers are given a great deal of autonomy in deciding how to accomplish organizational goals. Divisions act as strategic units focused on specific customer groups. Despite this autonomy, the divisions have access to the resources of 3M as a whole. Reward systems reinforce innovation as an organizational value at individual and team levels, and across both technical and nontechnical areas. Formal and informal structures are in place to encourage cross-pollination of ideas and information among technical people.

What lessons can we learn from 3M's example? First, innovation must be an element of the organization's strategy and integrated into everything the organization does. While 3M has made innovation an encompassing focus of its strategy, other organizations may choose to apply it on a more limited basis, but nonetheless it should be explicitly included in their strategic planning.

Second, 3M, like other innovative organizations, embraces innovation as part of its organizational culture and has developed organizational value systems that support employee creativity. Two of the most important of these values are risk taking and "failing forward."[14] Being creative and breaking away from the way things are entails risk. An organization can create a culture that tolerates risk by taking risks itself, by encouraging risk takers who fail to try again, and by ensuring that the organization is viewed as a safe environment in which to take risks. That is not to say that employees should be encouraged to engage in behaviors that place themselves, their coworkers, or the organization in danger.

"Failing forward" is taking risks to advance the organization's goals.

"Failing forward" refers to taking risks that are calculated to advance the organization's goals. The risks should be known or anticipated and accompanied by contingency plans that are in place in case of failure. Innovative organizations learn from failures and extract value from each experience, so that the next risk-taking attempt occurs with greater knowledge than the last. Peters refers to this as supporting fast failures (and learning from them).[15] This may require a postmortem examination of failed projects to determine the reason they failed and what could have been done better. The focus during these examinations should be on what can be learned from the failure, not who is to blame for it. Equally important, organizations must celebrate and reward successful risk taking.

Third, 3M has created structures that support and reinforce its focus on innovation. Linking mechanisms, reward systems, and job characteristics remove barriers to creativity and innovation. Opportunities are provided for cross-fertilization of ideas across units and areas of expertise. Innovators are frequently given the lead role in implementing their ideas, sometimes even to the point of creating new business units.

John Kao, professor at the Harvard Business School, recommends multiple ways for organizations to improve creativity, including:[16]

1. Create an open, decentralized structure
2. Encourage experimental attitudes
3. Circulate success stories
4. Emphasize the role of the champion
5. Stress effective communication at all levels

6. Provide the freedom to fail
7. Make resources available for new initiatives
8. Minimize administrative interference
9. Provide financial and nonfinancial rewards for success
10. Loosen deadlines

WHERE CAN ORGANIZATIONS GO FOR HELP?

Sometimes even an innovative organization finds itself at a loss for new ideas or stuck in a rut. When this happens, there are consulting firms that specialize in assisting organizations with creativity development. One of the best known is Eureka Ranch, the training facility of Richard Saunders International, Inc. This organization, located outside of Cincinnati, Ohio, is the brainchild of Doug Hall and provides intense training in creativity and innovation to a diverse clientele including Compaq, Kellogg, and even the Walt Disney Company. The training is both fun and challenging and draws on the company's extensive database of information about successful and unsuccessful innovations. Clients are led through a fast-paced series of exercises designed to loosen up their thinking, shake up their preconceptions, and set them off to generate literally thousands of possible product or service ideas.[17]

GROUP-LEVEL CREATIVITY

With the increasing reliance on teams in contemporary organizations, we should take some time to examine how creativity can be encouraged in that setting. First, what characteristics are likely to allow a group to be creative or innovative?

Diversity brings multiple perspectives to the act of innovation.

Heterogeneity seems to be a key element. A team that is more diverse along a variety of parameters—age, experience, ethnicity, discipline—is able to bring multiple viewpoints and perspectives to the process of innovation. The more varied and complex the situation under consideration, the more internal diversity is needed to adequately address it. This is referred to as the concept of "requisite variety."[18] **Multifunctional teams** bring together representatives from different functional areas in the organization and represent a broader array of knowledge, skills, and abilities, as well as differing perspectives. This is highly advantageous in ensuring both flexibility and fluency at the group level.

Diverse groups are more likely to engage in a contest of ideas that leads to the generation of more numerous and more varied alternatives for consideration. This "creative abrasion" may come at the cost of higher levels of conflict within the team.[19] Organizations and individuals often fear conflict, yet a reasonable level of well-managed conflict is necessary for vigor and energy in innovation. Innovation in high-performing organizations is associated with substantive, but not personal, conflict within teams.[20,21]

One danger associated with homogeneous groups or other highly cohesive groups is the concept of groupthink. **Groupthink** occurs when the members of the group are more committed to maintaining good relationships within the team and avoiding conflict than to generating better ideas and challenging the ideas presented by teammates. Teams that experience groupthink often prematurely close the generation of alternatives and converge on a solution without first being diligent in the divergence stage. A number of techniques have been suggested to help groups remain focused on idea generation at the early stage of the creative or innovative process.

Among the techniques most commonly associated with group creativity is **brainstorming**. While often viewed as a free-for-all sharing of ideas, brainstorming should follow some specific rules if it is to be effective. First, all participants must be encouraged to contribute ideas to the effort. A silent participant is withholding the diversity that he or she brings to the group. The goal is often to generate the longest list of possibilities. Second, participants must refrain from evaluating or judging the ideas being generated. No idea is too strange or too impractical at this first divergent stage. Evaluations and judgments belong in the convergent stage that will follow when the list is winnowed to identify those ideas worthy of pursuit. Third, participants should be encouraged to build on, extend, or otherwise piggyback on the ideas of others. One person's idea may trigger additional ideas in others in the group.

While commonly used, and sometimes misused, brainstorming is not the only approach available. In the **nominal group technique**, individuals first work in isolation to generate ideas. These ideas are then shared in a round-robin fashion until all of the ideas previously generated and any new ideas inspired by others are listed. The advantage is that this approach eases the way for more reticent participants to share their ideas rather than finding themselves overwhelmed in the more freewheeling brainstorming session. A variation on this approach uses a computer-based decision-support system to allow virtual groups to share ideas, sometimes anonymously. The possibility of anonymity can often free up an individual to share ideas that might otherwise be self-censored out of fear of embarrassment or because the idea goes against the prevailing opinions of the group. This approach can also head off the tendency of groups to quickly fall in line with the ideas of members with higher levels of power or authority.

Another approach is to assign one or more members of a group to act as a **devil's advocate**. This term derives from the process of selecting saints within the Catholic Church. One priest is assigned the task of challenging the credentials of the candidate for sanctification. Similarly, a team member can have the job of challenging the ideas put forth within the team by questioning the underlying assumptions, pursuing the implications, and inquiring about the practicality of the alternatives under consideration.

The individual must be skillful at keeping the focus on content and not on people, as well as on the idea rather than the person who generated it. By the same token, the group must recognize that the individual is performing an important role as devil's advocate in the group and should not be punished for her or his comments.

ENTREPRENEURS AND ENTREPRENEURIAL THINKING

Entrepreneurs are individuals who start their own businesses rather than pursuing careers within existing organizations.

There is a special class of businesses that are worth discussion. These are the new ventures that seem to spring up overnight and capture the imagination of investors and the media alike. New ventures or start-ups are usually the handiwork of a special type of individual, the entrepreneur. **Entrepreneurs** are individuals who start their own businesses rather than pursuing careers within existing organizations. These individuals have a dream and are willing to put in hard work, long hours, and sleepless nights to see that dream become a reality. They are also willing to risk financial hardships and even failure in pursuit of their dreams.

HOW DOES CREATIVITY AND INNOVATION CONNECT WITH ENTREPRENEURSHIP?

An entrepreneur creates a new organization. At an even more basic level, no one can start a new business without an idea. While many new businesses may be repetitions of existing businesses, the ones that make the big splash are those that reflect a creative and innovative idea. Entrepreneurs see an unmet need and develop a way to meet that need in a unique and novel way. He or she must then find a way to convert that need-fulfilling idea into a viable business concept.

Here is the most fundamental demonstration of both creativity and innovation, for the entrepreneur must take the creative new idea and convert it, through innovation, into an actual business that creates value and generates the profits needed to sustain the business. Not all of these new ventures are ideas of earthshaking proportions. Many reflect the recognition of a small opportunity that larger companies either do not recognize or do not consider worth the effort to pursue.

Unlike their creative counterparts in existing organizations who have access to the resources of the organization, entrepreneurs must gather all of the resources necessary to launch and sustain the new venture. The specific resources that are needed will vary with the type of business the individual hopes to build, but one common element is money. It is the rare (and fortunate) entrepreneur who has all of the financial resources he or she needs to start the business. Most often, entrepreneurs demonstrate additional creativity by finding the money they need to start their business.

WHAT MAKES A GOOD ENTREPRENEUR?

Many researchers have tried to identify the characteristics that make someone successful as an entrepreneur and there is agreement on some aspects. First and foremost, they must be *risk takers.*

Entrepreneurs are risk takers.

New businesses face many obstacles, and the chances of failure are often high. To move forward despite these risks indicates a high level of self-confidence in their abilities to overcome the odds through their persistence, hard work, and drive. Entrepreneurs must be able to *tolerate ambiguity* because they face situations that have high levels of uncertainty. Research indicates that they have a high *internal locus of control.* This reflects the belief that they control their own destiny rather than being at the mercy of external forces. They also have a high *need for achievement;* they are motivated to take on challenging goals for the sense of accomplishment that comes with successfully completing the project.

Entrepreneurs tolerate ambiguity.

Entrepreneurs have a high need for achievement.

Notice the similarities between the characteristics of entrepreneurs and those of innovative organizations, particularly with respect to intelligent risk taking and tolerance for ambiguity. Innovative organizations have learned well from the success of entrepreneurs and have attempted to emulate their best practices. The term **intrapreneurship** was coined to describe the practices of an established organization that encourages employees to behave like those starting up their own businesses.

In this chapter we studied creativity and innovation as central forces needed for organizations to be successful in the twenty-first century. Author Gordon MacKenzie, in his book *Orbiting the Giant Hairball*, provides some sage advice to assist in developing our creativity and innovativeness:

> If we do not let go, we make prisoners of ourselves. To be fully free to create, we must first find the courage and willingness to let go:
>
> Let go of the strategies that have worked for us in the past . . .
> Let go of our biases, the foundation of our illusions . . .
> Let go of our grievances, the root source of our victimhood . . .
> Let go of our so-often-denied fear of being found unlovable.
>
> You will find it is not a one-shot deal, this letting go. You must do it again and again and again. It's kind of like breathing. You can't breathe just once. Try it: Breathe just once. You'll pass out.

SELF-APPRAISAL

SQUARES IN A BOX

- How many squares are in the box?
- Now, count again.
- Only sixteen?
- Take away your preconception of how many squares there are.
- Now, how many do you find?

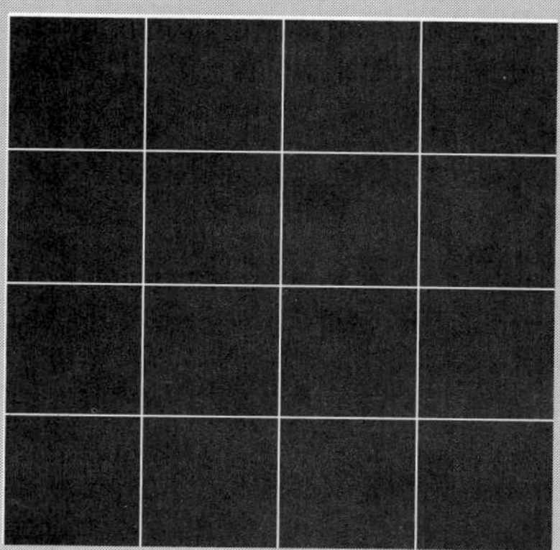

If you stop letting go, your creative spirit will pass out.

Now when I say let go, I do not mean reject. Because when you let go of something, it will still be there for you when you need it. But because you have stopped clinging, you will have freed yourself up to tap into other possibilities—possibilities that can help you deal with this world of accelerating change.[22]

FIGURE 5–1 ***Creativity Exercise. Can You Draw a Circle with a Dot in the Center without Lifting Your Pencil?***

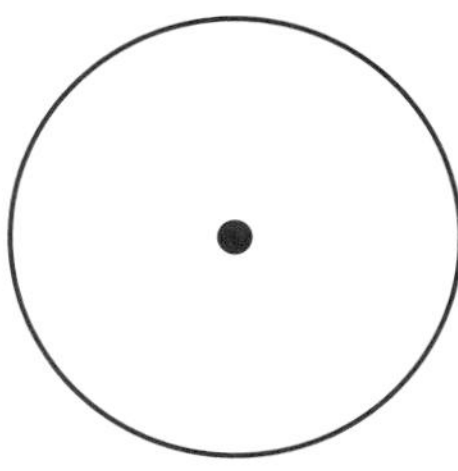

FIGURE 5-2 *Solution to Creativity Exercise in Figure 5-1*

Step 1

a. Fold corner of paper over.
b. Start dot at corner, making sure that part of dot is on both sides of paper.
c. Without lifting pencil, draw radius on back of paper to circumference of circle.
d. Start circle.

Step 2

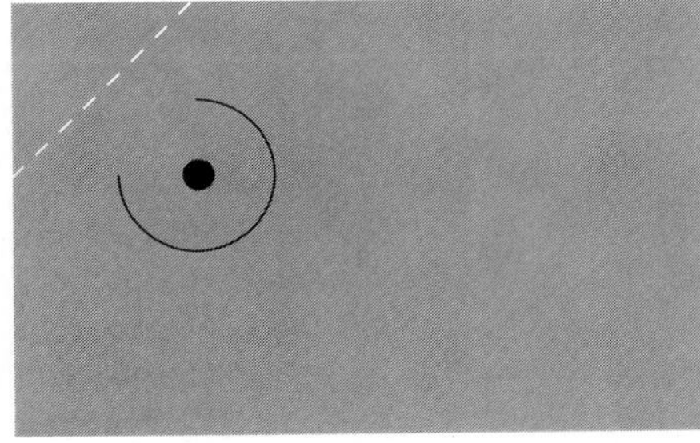

e. Unfold.

Step 3

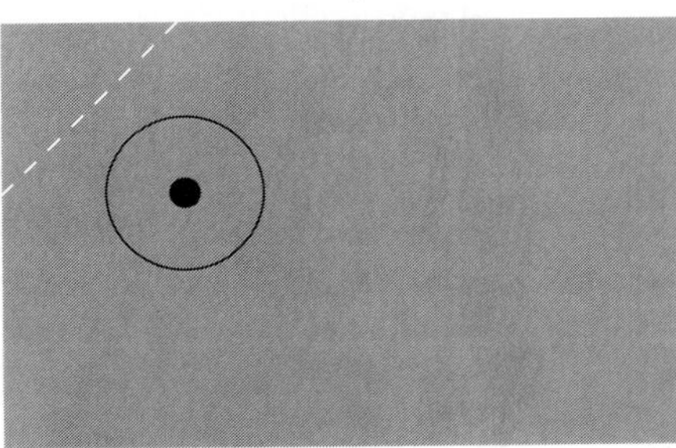

f. Complete circle.

SUMMARY

Creativity is the process of generating something new. Creativity is a process because it consists of a series of actions or changes, using resources at our disposal, directed toward a goal. It is a generative act because something is produced as a result of the creative process. Creativity results in something new; it is about producing something original, something that did not exist before.

Innovation is the process of generating a new idea, finding the value in that idea, and capturing that value. Organizations of the twenty-first century will rise and fall based on their ability to innovate.

Creativity has often been discussed as a function of the right side of the brain; the reality is that we operate holistically using both sides of the brain, particularly when we are creative and innovative.

Many researchers have tried to develop a profile of the creative individual. E. P. Torrance, one of the most prolific creativity researchers, suggests that courage, independence of thought and judgment, honesty, perseverance, curiosity, tolerance for moderate risk, and, most importantly, a love for what one is doing are the keys to being creative. Others would add to this list a tolerance for ambiguity, a willingness to overcome obstacles, the ability to make associations among diverse concepts, and a drive for recognition. Being creative, like anything else, improves with practice.

Because of the increasing reliance on teams in contemporary organizations, it is important to examine how creativity can be encouraged in that setting. Heterogeneity seems to be a key element of a creative team because it is more diverse along a variety of parameters, such as age, experience, ethnicity, discipline, and is able to bring multiple viewpoints and perspectives to the act of innovation. Multifunctional teams bring representation from different functional areas in the organization and represent a broader array of knowledge, skills, and abilities, as well as differing perspectives. This is highly advantageous in ensuring both flexibility and fluency at the group level.

Entrepreneurs are individuals who start their own businesses rather than pursue careers within existing organizations. Thus, an entrepreneur creates a new organization. Characteristics of entrepreneurs include the ability to take risks, a tolerance for ambiguity, and the need for achievement. Intrapreneurship describes the practices of organizations designed to encourage employees to behave like those starting up their own businesses.

Finally, being creative and innovative will help you succeed in this world of accelerating change.

CASE STUDY 5-1

YOU MAKE THE DECISION: SHOULD THIS BUSINESS EXPAND?

Joe Sanchez and his partner, Wiley Othero, own a copy and print shop that caters to customers in a regional shopping center. They employ two part-time workers in addition to themselves. Additionally, Joe's girlfriend handles the front desk and office bookkeeping. Joe wants to expand the business to draw more customers—students, faculty, and staff—from a local college.

1. Should they expand or not?
2. What are important factors to consider in making this decision? (Hints: Remember that decision making is a process that includes identifying what you don't know as well as what you know.)
3. Brainstorm to identify alternatives.
4. What are the pros and cons of each alternative?

DISCUSSION AND STUDY QUESTIONS—TO KEEP YOU THINKING

1. Distinguish between creativity and innovation.
2. What are the 10 forces in the twenty-first century business environment that will make innovation necessary?
3. What is meant by the term "learning innovation"?
4. Discuss creativity in relation to left-brain/right-brain or whole-brain thinking.
5. Explain the alternative way that creativity can be characterized as a sequence of divergent and convergent thinking.
6. Can creative ability be increased? What are the characteristics of a creative individual?
7. What are some personal barriers to creativity? What are some organizational barriers to creativity?
8. Compare flexibility of thinking with fluency of thinking.

9. What are the characteristics that are likely to allow a group to be creative or innovative?

10. How does creativity and innovation connect with entrepreneurship?

11. What makes a good entrepreneur?

NOTES

1. Robert T. Brown, "Creativity: What Are We to Measure?" in *Handbook of Creativity*, ed. J. A. Glover, R. R. Ronning, and C. R. Reynolds (New York: Plenum Press, 1989).
2. James M. Higgins, *Innovate or Evaporate* (Winter Park, FL: New Management Publishing Co., Inc., 1995).
3. James M. Higgins, "Achieving *the* Core Competence—It's as Easy as 1, 2, 3, . . . , 47, 48, 49," *Business Horizons* (March–April 1996): 27–32.
4. Tom Peters, *The Tom Peters Business School in a Box* (New York: Alfred A. Knopf, Inc., 1995).
5. James Adams, *Conceptual Blockbusting: A Guide to Better Ideas* (Reading, MA: Perseus Books, 1986).
6. Don Koberg and Jim Bagnall, *The Universal Traveler: A Soft-Systems Guide to Creativity, Problem-Solving, and the Process of Reaching Goals* (Los Altos, CA: Crisp Publications, 1991).
7. E. Paul Torrance, "The Nature of Creativity as Manifest in Its Testing," in *The Nature of Creativity: Contemporary Psychological Perspectives*, ed. R. J. Sternberg (Cambridge: Cambridge University Press, 1988).
8. Don Koberg and Jim Bagnall, *The Universal Traveler: A Soft-Systems Guide to Creativity, Problem-Solving, and the Process of Reaching Goals* (Los Altos, CA: Crisp Publications, 1991).
9. Howard Gardner, *Frames of Mind* (New York: Basic Books, 1983).
10. James Adams, *The Care and Feeding of Ideas: A Guide to Encouraging Creativity* (Reading, MA: Addison-Wesley Publishing Company, Inc., 1986).
11. Ibid.
12. Ibid, 108–109.
13. Rosabeth Moss Kanter, John Kao, and Fred Wiersema, *Innovation* (New York: HarperCollins Publishers, Inc., 1997).
14. Dorothy A. Leonard, and Walter C. Swap, *When Sparks Fly: Igniting Creativity in Groups* (Boston, MA: Harvard University Press, 1999).
15. Tom Peters, *The Tom Peters Business School in a Box* New York: Alfred A. Knopf, Inc., 1995).
16. John Kao, *Managing Creativity* (Upper Saddle River, NJ: Prentice Hall, 1991).
17. Todd Datz, "Romper Ranch," *CIO Enterprise* (May 15, 1999) www.cio.com/archive/enterprise/051599_doug.html.
18. Gareth Morgan, *Images of Organization* (Thousand Oaks, CA: Sage Publications, 1997).
19. Jerry Hirshberg, *The Creative Priority: Driving Innovative Business in the Real World* (New York: Harper Business, 1998).
20. Kathleen M. Eisenhardt, Jean L. Kahwajy, and L. J. Bourgeois III, "Conflict and Strategic Choice: How Top Management Teams Disagree," *California Management Review* (winter 1997): 42–62.
21. Kathleen M. Eisenhardt, Jean L. Kaywajy, and L. J. Bourgeois III, "How Management Teams Can Have a Good Fight," *Harvard Business Review* (July–August 1997): 77–85.
22. Gordon MacKenzie, *Orbiting the Giant Hairball: A Corporate Fool's Guide to Surviving with Grace* (New York: Viking Penguin, 1998), 216.

PART 3

Interacting Effectively with Others

CHAPTER 6

Communicating in the Workplace

TO START YOU THINKING

As you read this chapter, think about these questions. The answers to some of these questions can be found in your reading; others can only be answered based on your own experiences.

- What are barriers to effective communication?
- How does formal communication differ from informal communication?
- How can you use the "positive sandwich" technique?
- Is it easier for you to speak or to listen?
- Do you work just as hard when listening to a speech as you do when preparing a speech?
- Does your body language contradict your verbal messages? Which is more honest? Why?

LEARNING GOALS

After studying this chapter, you should be able to:

1. Restate in your own words the idea that meanings are in the person, not in the message.
2. Describe the communication process and discuss barriers to effective communication.
3. Describe the importance of the following elements in the communication process.
    - Attitudes
    - Emotions
    - Roles
    - Nonverbal behavior
    - Feedback
    - Perception
4. Describe why listening is an active, not a passive, activity. List six general guidelines for more effective listening.
5. Define and give examples of the four basic levels of communication.
    - Conventional
    - Exploratory
    - Participative
    - Intimate
6. Describe how proxemics affects our actions.
7. Describe the kind of information that vertical communication usually conveys, both upward and downward. Describe the basic elements involved in improving upward and downward communication.
8. Understand the Pygmalion (self-fulfilling prophecy) effect.
9. Explain the importance of good horizontal communication in coordinating group effort and how it can be improved.
10. Describe the role that ethics plays in the organizational communication process.

11. Explain how technology impacts how we communicate.
12. Define and apply the following terms and concepts (in order of first occurrence):

KEYWORDS

- **communication**
- **perception**
- **feedback**
- **distortion**
- **stereotyping**
- **filtering**
- **semantics**
- **organizational communication**
- **informal communication**
- **formal communication**
- **horizontal communication**
- **vertical communication**
- **self-fulfilling prophecy**
- **positive sandwich technique**
- **self-disclosure**
- **listening**
- **body language**
- **kinesics**
- **neurolinguistic programming (NLP)**
- **proxemics**

THE MEANING OF COMMUNICATION

Communication of all types is so common but so complex that it continues to justify study. Communication is the process of transferring information and understanding from one or more persons to one or more persons. In the simplest form of communication, one person transfers information to another. In more complex kinds of communication, members of a group transfer information to other members of a group. Comprehension is the only test of a message's success as communication. If the message is understood, communication has succeeded. If not, communication has failed.

This chapter addresses both the more formal types of communication found in organizational settings as well as the not-so-simple interpersonal communication. In today's work organizations, communication is the foundation on which all other functions rest. Communication transfers information and enhances understanding among individuals and groups; it also unifies group behavior. Unified behavior provides the basis for continuous group cooperation.

Interpersonal communication processes include the sending and receiving functions as well as the concepts of listening and understanding. We spend more than 70 to 80 percent of our work lives receiving messages, but we are usually not trained to be listeners. We will explore several fundamental principles that will help us become better communicators, and especially better listeners. Finally, the chapter presents a discussion on nonverbal communication, communication style, ethics in communication, and how technology is impacting the way we communicate.

MEANINGS ARE WITHIN US

How many times have you asked, "What do you mean by that?" When confronted with this situation, most communicators choose to use different words in order to get their meanings across. Although the original meaning has not changed, the words

The meaning of words exists within ourselves.

have. Hence, meaning exists within ourselves, not in the words we use to express that meaning. The meaning of a message is also called its *semantic content.*

Meaning is what the speaker intends to be understood. With the exception of mathematical, computer, and scientific communication, meaning is somewhat subjective. *Objective meaning* is found in mathematics and science because in those "language systems," one term is only allowed one meaning. There is no ambiguity. "Plus" does not mean "minus," nor can it imply "equal to." The rules of mathematical language leave no room for disagreement. On the other hand, and outside of the mathematical realm, words can mean different things to different people and can also have a slightly different meaning to the same person in a different set of circumstances.

Subjective meaning has multiple meanings.

A word's *subjective meaning* is the personal significance of that word to an individual. For some people, rap music means stimulating, exciting rhythms. To others it is a noisy assault on human ears. Words sometimes have different emotional and intellectual meanings for each of us. Even ordinary terms can have a variety of meanings attached to them because the meaning attached to any object or experience is experienced personally.

Semantic meaning can vary.

The more the speaker's messages relate to and overlap with the listener's mental and emotional experiences, the more effective communication will be. Because people can assign different meanings to words, good communication demands a high tolerance for ambiguity. This is especially true for more abstract terms. Consider the various meanings that different people have for abstract terms such as "justice," "freedom," and "faith."

Because words can have ambiguous meanings, to fully understand another's meaning, we must pay as much attention to the person speaking as to the words spoken. Voice tones, facial expressions, and body language communicate meaning as much as words do. Effective communicators are person oriented and word oriented.

PERCEPTION

Although perception is an individual view of facts and emotions, our world and our organizations are more complex than one person's view. **Perceptions** are the way in which we interpret circumstances—either in an accurate or in a distorted manner. The things we notice, or our perceptions of both verbal and nonverbal cues, lead us to meaning.

Our value systems have a profound effect on what we see or hear. We are also influenced by our needs for economic, social, and psychological fulfillment: recognition, love, and self-worth, among others. In other words, we frequently see and hear what our backgrounds lead us to perceive.

THE COMMUNICATION PROCESS

Communication is largely a matter of style. Psychologist Robert Hecht says,

> Paying attention to communication styles when you do business can help you avoid people problems. As the old song title explains, "It Ain't What You Do, It's the Way That You Do It." Becoming a student of communication styles can help you be more persuasive, working with other people's natures rather than against them . . .
>
> Each of us, it seems, has a preferred way of approaching people, tasks, and time. Yet, adapting occasionally to another's communication style can yield impressive results.[1]

Hecht recognizes four basic communicator styles and advocates using different styles to meet the needs of the intended receiver.

- A **forecaster** is interested in ideas; is imaginative, visionary, and innovative.
- An **associator** is interested in personal relationships; is agreeable, adaptable, and perceptive.
- A **systematizer** is impressed by details, plans, and order; seems rational, steady, and methodical.
- An **energizer** is results-now oriented; is spirited, dynamic, decisive, and impatient.[2]

To speak coherently, we must select 10 percent of the words and thoughts in our minds and, at the same time, discard or "put on hold" the remaining 90 percent. This is an amazingly complex process. When we listen, we can hear and comprehend at least double the number of words that we can speak. Therefore, it would seem that listening to and understanding a message would be easier than speaking it, because listening requires less mental activity than does speaking. However, in our culture, verbal messages are frequently received inaccurately, understood poorly, and garbled in retelling. If you have played the "Pass It Along" whisper game, you know how garbled the message may become.

The keys to effective verbal communication are speaking clearly, listening actively, and providing ample feedback. Having ideas and not knowing how to express them is the same as not having them at all. Now let's look at how the communication model works.

COMMUNICATION MODEL

One way to find out what takes place during any communication is to construct a model of the process. A model is a visual representation that names, describes, and classifies the separate parts of the process. It also shows how the separate parts connect, interact, and influence one another.

Figure 6–1 is a model of human communication. The clarity of the transmission is shown as a function of the speaker's attitudes, emotions, relationship with the listener, and nonverbal behavior. Similarly, the clarity or the reception is shown as a

FIGURE 6–1 *Complex Communication*

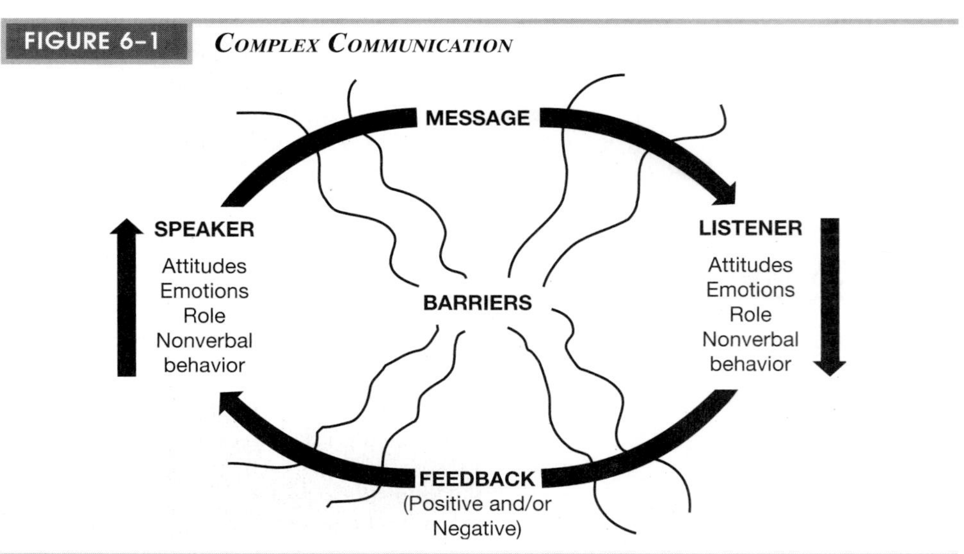

function of the listener's attitudes, emotions, role relationships with the speaker, and nonverbal behavior. **Feedback** is the process of reacting to a person's messages, either verbally or nonverbally. The listener is shown as responding to the message by either positive or negative feedback or by a combination of both.

Figure 6–2 is the famous drawing of the woman. Look carefully. What do you see first—a fashionably dressed young woman or a much older woman with a scarf over her head? Actually, both figures are present. The younger woman is looking away from you, to your left at an angle. The older woman is also looking to your left but toward you at an angle. Do you see both? Which woman you see first or whether you can see both is a matter of perception—your view of facts, age, and physical characteristics.

BARRIERS TO COMMUNICATION

Many barriers block communication. These include distortion, language/semantics, defensiveness, noise, and mistrust, among other emotional responses. Let us now examine these barriers.

DISTORTION

There are many distractions to the communication process. Environmental considerations, other demands on our time, and thought processes are just a few of the things that can distract and, consequently, distort the communication process. **Distortion** includes any distractions. For example, one experiment shows that at any given time in a college classroom, only 20 percent of the students are paying attention to the lecture. No wonder we fail to hear, let alone understand, what is being said.

FIGURE 6–2 *What Do You See—a Young Woman, an Old Woman, or Both?*

Figure 6–3 shows an area of distortion common in most communication. The area or arc of distortion is a function of what the sender intends to communicate, and what both the sender and receiver actually do communicate. There may always be some distortion, but effort should be made to maximize clarity and to avoid deceitful practices that increase misunderstandings.

Stereotyping is an unfortunate type of distortion. Our preconceived notions or ideas about people, situations, or cultures get in the way of the truth. Remember the saying, "Don't confuse me with the facts, my mind is made up!" We hear and perceive what we want to hear.

Filtering is another example of distortion where the receiver hears only what she or he wants to hear. The receiver acknowledges only certain information and may use that information to make the message clearer.

EXPRESS YOUR OPINION

Should Illegal Aliens Be Allowed to Stay?

Here is a topic that might develop some strong contrasting feelings between people. Pair off with another student and take opposite views on the topic. Argue for 5 minutes for your special viewpoint; then repeat the view of the sender. See if you develop a new appreciation or understanding for the other person's point of view.

Thousands, perhaps even millions, of illegal aliens are in the United States, and many are working in our industries. They are depriving our citizens of potential employment; they are not paying taxes, yet they are receiving welfare.

Many businesses argue that they must compete in the open marketplace. If they can pay illegal aliens less than the prevailing wage rate, they can in turn sell a product cheaper to the public. By such a method, the public benefits. It is certainly cheaper than sending our raw goods or parts to a foreign country to be processed or assembled and then bringing them back to the United States to sell.

Are you for or against illegal aliens remaining in the United States?

FIGURE 6–3 *AREA OF COMMUNICATION DISTORTION*

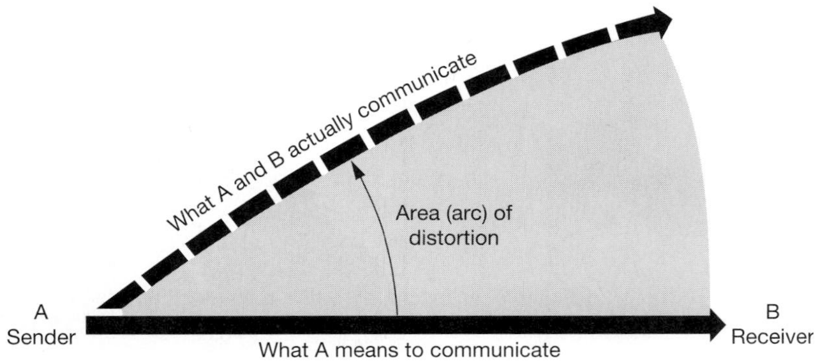

LANGUAGE/SEMANTICS

There are honest differences in language among cultures and even within families. **Semantics** refers to the meanings given to individual words. Each of us may give different meanings to the same word. We may even give different meanings to the same word under different circumstances. The word "love," for example, has many different meanings.

DEFENSIVENESS

Good communication depends on the organizational and communication climate or culture. If there is open communication, we can expect an entirely different climate than if all transactions are conducted with suspicion or wariness on the part of both sender and receiver. Supportive and defensive characteristics are contrasted in Figure 6–4.

The defensive climate can be distinguished from a supportive climate where there is more mutuality of objectives, openness, and understanding. In a supportive climate:

1. People seem interested; they listen.
2. People do not seem hurried; they imply by body movements that they want to hear what an individual has to say.
3. People who are receivers invite the sender to proceed by asking questions that are directly tied to the sender's preceding statements.
4. People who are receivers do not judge or criticize what is being said for the sake of criticism, but request clarification and allow time to correct misunderstandings.

FIGURE 6–4 *A Contrast of Communication Climates*

DEFENSIVE CLIMATE		SUPPORTIVE CLIMATE
Evaluation	Communication that appears to judge the other person—increases defensiveness.	Description
Control	Communication that is used to control the receiver—evokes resistance.	Problem orientation
Strategy	Perception of the sender engaging in a strategy involving ambiguous motivations—causes receivers to become defensive.	Spontaneity
Neutrality	Perception that neutrality in communication indicates a lack of concern for the receivers' welfare—causes receivers to become defensive.	Empathy
Superiority	Communication that indicates superiority in power, wealth, or in other ways arouses defensiveness	Equality (as human beings)
Certainty	Dogmatic speakers who seem to know the answers, and require no data—tend to put others on guard.	Provisionalism (willing to listen)

Source: Adapted from Jack R. Gibb, "Defensive Communication," *Journal of Communication* (September 1961): 141–148.

NOISE

The sender must often compete with a number of other stimuli in getting the message through to the receiver; that is, there is physical noise or other externally generated sensations in the system or process. "Noise is . . . an irritant that can prevent employees from working efficiently, and which can prevent managers from being able to collect their thoughts."[3] Physical noise is one of the many sources of confusion and, therefore, can become a barrier to effective communication. So-called background noise may include loud or even soft music or noise in an office and may be distracting.

Human-generated noise, like a nearby loud conversation, can be as distracting as loud machinery because of the irregular peaks and valleys of decibels. Some organizations have attempted to cope with noise by restricting phone calls during certain hours of the day or by providing "think tanks" where employees can go to work in a stress-free environment. Employees can also reduce noise by coming early to the office, staying late, or using earplugs or earphones to mask sporadic noise.

MISTRUST

A distinct mistrust between the sender and receiver of a message can become a barrier to effective communication. In the workplace, such a condition can be very negative and telling in explaining poor performance and productivity. According to a survey by pollster Louis Harris, an organizational climate with restructuring, mergers, and acquisitions may contribute to the workers' mistrust of management. The survey revealed that top executives do not always show a thorough understanding of their employees.[4]

There is a direct link between employee communication and the trust relationship between management and employees. Understanding the goals of the organization and the results of their work gives meaning to employee efforts. Valorie McClelland finds that five factors are essential in building communication trust: openness, feedback, congruity, autonomy, and shared values. Mistrust can arise from mixed signals sent by management. Managers need to consider the consistency of their communication to their audiences. Finally, to achieve better communication and less mistrust, managers must consider emerging issues and plan together to make decisions consistent with long-term goals.[5]

We have just discussed the communication process, detailing ways to break down the barriers of effective communication. Now, let's look at those aspects of communication most prevalent in the organizational context.

COMMUNICATING IN ORGANIZATIONS

Organizational communication is any communication that takes place within a total organization—usually formal and written messages, as opposed to informal, interpersonal communication. Many of the human relations problems that we encounter today have their origin in organizational communication or miscommunication.

Good communication unifies group behavior.

In today's work organizations, communication is the foundation on which all other functions rest. Communication serves not only to transfer information and to help understanding among individuals and groups, but it also unifies group behavior. Unified behavior provides the basis for continuous group cooperation.

COMMUNICATION CHANNELS

Communication channels are the paths along which messages travel from one person to another, from one group to another, or both. All organizations use both formal and informal channels of communication. Informal channels are bound by convention, custom, and culture, not a formal chart on the wall; formal channels are the communication chains and networks that determine the direction and flow of official messages to all the different members and divisions of an organization.

INFORMAL COMMUNICATION CHANNELS

Although not bound by an organizational chart, informal communication is bound by convention, custom, and culture. **Informal communication** grows out of the social interactions among people who work together. Most theorists believe that informal relationships cannot be charted because they change so rapidly and are so complex. One of the major functions that informal channels serve is to provide communication routes for members of small groups. Every successful business has at least one healthy, if invisible, communication channel through which the messages of the informal organization are communicated. One major source of employees' information about their companies is the grapevine.

THE GRAPEVINE

The grapevine is the unofficial news carrier.

The grapevine is the informal channel of communication between people. It is fast and selective in disseminating limited information. The term is believed to have come into use during the Civil War when the first telegraph lines, used to carry military intelligence, were strung from tree to tree in the pattern of a grapevine. Often messages were garbled or interfered with, and all rumors or unofficial messages came to be known as carried "by the grapevine."

In a complex organization, depending on its size, there can be dozens or hundreds of grapevines. These channels carry information that is not, or cannot be, transmitted by formal means. Information of this sort includes "I would not ask for that raise today, if I were you. The boss is in a foul mood, and you better wait for a better time."

You cannot eliminate the grapevine.

It is impossible to predict the direction, speed, accuracy, or final content of a message carried by the grapevine. Messages may be abbreviated, magnified, restructured, elaborated, or generally twisted out of shape. Sometimes official messages must be issued to counteract the inaccuracies of the grapevine. At other times, the grapevine can spread information very quickly and accurately.

Even though the grapevine's reliability can never be determined with complete certainty, it does serve some useful functions.

The grapevine develops relationships.

1. It satisfies a need that employees have to enjoy friendly relations with their fellow employees.
2. It helps workers make sense out of their work environment, especially in interpreting unclear orders from supervisors.
3. It acts as a safety valve. When people are confused and unclear about what is going to happen to them, they use the grapevine to relieve their anxieties.

The grapevine also relieves anxieties.

Research indicates that the grapevine has a role to play in socializing employees to a company, initiating behavioral change, and providing information. To increase the accuracy of grapevine messages, regular management contact should provide honest, reliable information.[6]

FORMAL COMMUNICATION

Formal communication is a part of all organizations.

Formal communication includes structured, stable methods of communicating between people and their superiors, subordinates, or peers. Customs are followed with regard to authority, rank, and type of work. Official communication usually must travel between and within separate divisions along structural paths.

HORIZONTAL COMMUNICATION

Horizontal communication involves the flow of messages across functional areas at any particular level of the organization. When members at the same level in the hierarchy of authority communicate with one another (i.e., one worker to another worker or one manager to another manager) horizontal communication takes place.

Horizontal communication increases flexibility within the organizational structure, facilitates problem solving, and enhances information sharing across work groups. The problems associated with horizontal communication seldom stem from a lack of messages among individuals or groups, but rather from the large number and various types of messages that are sent and received. Work is often duplicated or delayed unnecessarily because information needed in one department is available only in another, and sometimes no one in the department needing the information knows that it exists.

VERTICAL COMMUNICATION

It is easier to communicate downward than upward.

Vertical communication flows in two directions, up and down. Although downward and upward communication travels along the same paths, the content, nature, and challenges of the two vary considerably. Official top-to-bottom communication channels flow down with great force and reach a great many people, but official bottom-to-top channels flow up with difficulty and reach relatively few people.

DOWNWARD COMMUNICATION

To increase the effectiveness of their firms, many executives have decided to shift decision making related to everyday operations to middle-level employees, who are closer to operations and customers.

Downward communication is the fastest form of communication.

Downward communication is the fastest form in the vertical chain of communication, is accepted more at face value, and is reacted to more vigorously.

Managers only think they know the problems of their employees.

In order for downward communiqués to be effective, managers must fully understand the problems of their employees. Yet, often, employees tend to think that their superiors do not understand their problems.

To combat this dilemma, some of the more successful companies hold regularly scheduled departmental meetings between managers and employees each Monday morning where everyone is required to participate. Many banks, savings and loan associations, and retail stores do this during the 15-minute period just prior to the morning opening. There is an increasing use of short meetings that include warm-up exercises and singing of company songs—spin-offs of Japanese management ideas. Shared meaning, and hence communication, are enhanced in these settings.

WRITTEN VERSUS ORAL DOWNWARD COMMUNICATION

Written communication traveling along downward channels ranges from handwritten messages pinned to bulletin boards to typed interoffice memos, printed job descriptions, circulars, handbooks, job manuals, and electronic mail. Research suggests that those who rely principally on memos, letters, and manuals for communicating messages downward not only fall short of achieving understanding, credibility, and acceptance, but actually contribute to new problems of misunderstandings, disbelief, and rejection.

On the other hand, sharing information in a brief meeting can serve at least two purposes: (1) less paperwork and (2) better interpersonal communication, relationships, and overall understanding. Yet some employees are informed best in writing, some orally, and some both ways. Sensitive topics are best handled orally rather than in writing. For example, firing an employee or arbitrating conflicts among workers are issues best handled in person.

When emotions are high, communicate in person.

Use oral messages for quick decisions.

Many companies have begun to change their basic views about internal communication systems. One corporation banished its "Never say it—write it!" slogan, and replaced it with "Talk it over—jot it down."

SELF-FULFILLING PROPHECY

A **self-fulfilling prophecy** occurs when what you expect of others determines the reactions of others. If you expect low achievement, people will produce little. If treated as inferior, lazy, materialistic, or irresponsible, people become so. In contrast, if treated as responsible, independent, intelligent, motivated, and creative, people tend to become so. The term *Pygmalion management* describes this concept. Pygmalion was a mythological character who created a statue of the perfect woman; Aphrodite brought the statue to life. A Pygmalion in modern terms is a person who re-creates another person, making him or her into something different from what he or she was. In organizations, management can also create effective workers by treating employees as worthy of respect. Management can expect elegant performance from an employee when the training is good and, most important, when the expectations and responsibilities are high and clearly understood.

EXPRESS YOUR OPINION

Do you believe that there is some truth to the self-fulfilling prophecy concept or the Pygmalion theory? Do you believe that your parents or teachers may have influenced you either in a positive or negative way? Can you name people who have influenced you in your accomplishments or career direction? It is usually easier to see how others have influenced us, but harder to see how we have influenced others. Whom do you feel you have influenced through the self-fulfilling prophecy? Have you expressed such feelings subtly to a coworker or to those at home?

Do you suppose that such an attitude or belief in the Pygmalion theory might be an excuse for not being successful? "I am not successful because my father did not expect much out of me!" Can we overcome such a negative influence?

HOW TO HANDLE NEGATIVE NEWS

In addition to relaying positive, informative, and instructional messages, managers frequently must transmit negative messages, such as denying salary raises, job promotions, or transfers. While positive and informative messages are more directly conveyed, the positive sandwich approach may work most effectively in bad news situations.

Use the positive sandwich technique to handle negative news.

Basically, the **positive sandwich technique** provides bad news between slices of good feelings and can be used in handling negative news. Start with a good slice of bread spread generously with good news and information that is true and supportive. Then express the bad news quickly and simply as a thin slice of ham, and follow with another piece of bread bearing supportive reasons and assurances.

Whether the message is written or oral, you must prevent the disappointing news from turning your subordinate against you. The opening remarks or sentences should strengthen whatever good feeling exists. Certainly, by asserting the bad news right at the beginning, you would be giving too much emphasis to it and jeopardizing existing goodwill. Equally vital to bad news situations is the last third of the positive sandwich—a positive ending that can tip the scales toward retaining the employee's goodwill.

There is another viewpoint on delivering bad news. Give the bad news directly, and then positively reinforce the recipient of the bad news. Advocates of this approach say the positive sandwich technique is phony and only delays the inevitable. What do you think?

UPWARD COMMUNICATION

Upward communication occurs when someone in a lower position in the company communicates information, ideas, suggestions, opinions, or grievances to someone in a higher organizational position. Examples include a receptionist putting an idea in the company suggestion box or a supervisor reporting a breakdown in the machinery to the plant manager.

The first step toward building a successful upward communication program is to gain the endorsement of top management. Next, an anonymous communication audit of all employees will provide insight into how employees understand the goals of the business and how employees feel about their jobs and the communication climate. Including open-ended questions in the audit survey provides a better opportunity for employees to express their true concerns.

The best "open door" is when the supervisor walks around and talks to workers.

Mechanisms available for encouraging upward communication include (1) employee-management meetings, (2) speak-out sessions, (3) quality circles, (4) employee ombudsmen positions, (5) newsletters, and (6) the open-door policy. Employees consider access to upper management, involvement in making decisions, information about the business, feedback to suggestions, and a climate of trust to be effective methods of communication.[7]

For upward communication to be effective, managerial staffs and their subordinate employees must work together in a spirit of trust and goodwill. Suppose that a company maintains a conspicuously placed suggestion box that gets a great deal of use but the employees never receive managerial feedback on any of their suggestions. In this case, the employees may take a cynical view of management's sincerity.

On the other hand, when workers know that their messages are treated with respect and attention, the company benefits in at least four important ways. The acronym OPEN (offers ideas, prevents problems, encourages acceptance, notably increases participation) captures the reasons why upward communication is of value. Being open creates good upward communication:

O **Offers ideas.** Employees often have valuable ideas and suggestions about improving product quality and production rates.

P **Prevents problems.** When messages travel upward easily, managers can stay informed about potentially troublesome situations.

E **Encourages acceptance.** Effective upward communication reveals to management the degree of acceptance and credibility that company policies have among employees and customers.

N **Notably increases participation.** Open upward communication stimulates employees to participate more when they have some say in planning or evaluating policies.

SMALL-GROUP COMMUNICATION

Groups satisfy needs.

Most people spend a great deal of time communicating in small groups—families, classes, work teams, quality circles, athletic teams, committees, and so on. The groups that most influence people's behavior become their reference groups: the people with whom values, attitudes, and beliefs are shared. Groups also provide people with opportunities to satisfy their needs for recognition and achievement. They satisfy other wishes too, such as those for dominance and autonomy.

A person with high credibility has great influence.

Small-group interaction is dynamic and involves a lot of feedback. The social relations within a small group influence the kind of communication that takes place, and, in turn, the nature of the communication will influence social relations. For example, a person who has high credibility will have much more influence than will someone of high status but low credibility.

In business organizations especially, the power relations within a group determine, to a large extent, the kind of communication that exists. When power is concentrated in a few high-status people, lower-status group members may feel that their needs are not being met, and communication will be less than effective. Communication is also affected within a group by the degree of cooperation and competition among the group members.

FEEDBACK

It is said that the three principles of real estate are location, location, location! Likewise, the three principles of communication are feedback, feedback, feedback! Our communication is only as good as the message that gets through; hence, the sender needs feedback. In any organization, when employees know when they are doing a task well, they continue that behavior; likewise, when a task is not done well, employees need to know in order to change the behavior.

Feedback connects, influences, and interacts with all other parts of the communication process. Originally, the term *feedback* was used by engineers to refer to the transfer of electrical energy from the output to the input of the same electrical circuit. In computer technology, feedback is used to describe a computer's coded responses or answers to messages. These responses are usually very simple. In this manner, the computer tells the source of the message whether the message has been received accurately. In similar fashion, people tell one another whether their messages are being received correctly.

Feedback is verbal and visual.

In face-to-face communication, both the listener and the speaker continuously give feedback to each other nonverbally and verbally. Nonverbal feedback includes nodding agreement or disagreement, frowning or smiling, engaging in or avoiding eye contact, or yawning. Verbal feedback is contained in the listener's questions and responses in relation to what is being discussed.

Those responses perceived as rewarding (smiling or nodding) are called *positive feedback.* Those perceived as punishing (frowns or yawns) are called *negative feedback.* Feedback enables us to recognize misunderstandings while the miscommunication is occurring so that the messages can be modified and redefined.

Feedback in its broadest usage includes all the verbal and nonverbal responses to a message that are perceived by the sender of that message. Constructive and responsible feedback meets the following criteria:

1. Specific, not general
2. Focused on behavior, not the person
3. Considerate of the needs of the receiver
4. Focused on something the receiver can act on
5. Solicited, not imposed
6. Shared information, not advice
7. Well-timed and not overloading
8. Concerned with "what" and "how," not "why"
9. Checked for accuracy

SILENCE

Have you ever let silence speak for you? Silence is one type of feedback. Some experts feel that it is never good to rush in and break the silence in a small conversation. The more secure the person, the less fearful he or she is of silence. Here are some reasons for believing that "silence is golden."

Silent power is used frequently by interviewers and others to force a person to speak. Another example is the *silence of uncertainty;* if a person has a thoughtful look of concentration, it may be risky to break their concentration if you are trying to convince that person or communicate a specific message. The more important the subject, the greater the patience required. *Silent accord,* accompanied by a smile or a nod, is a good way in which to respect another's choice of communication. A studied frown, pursed lips, or a shake of the head often accompanies *silent disapproval.* Do not rush to speak—wait for the person to verbalize his or her feelings. Then you can direct your comments to the misgivings rather than to a mere guess.

LEVELS OF VERBAL COMMUNICATION

There are four levels of verbal communication (see Figure 6–5). We communicate with strangers and casual acquaintances on the *conventional* level: attempting to be polite, to get acquainted, to fill silences, to seek or convey incidental information, or relieve tensions. Remarks such as "Hi, there!" "Do you have the time?" and "Good

ACTION PROJECT 6–1

ONE-WAY AND TWO-WAY COMMUNICATION (GROUP EXERCISE)

Have you ever wondered how well you are understood? Can you really tell others exactly what you are thinking? Here is your opportunity to prove to yourself how well you can tell others what is on your mind. To set the stage for the exercise, consider this story:

> This is the case of a night supervisor in a machine shop who did not know how to do a job on a lathe because there was no blueprint available. The day supervisor was angry at being telephoned at home, but described the blueprint over the phone. Because the supervisor was angry, the night foreman hesitated to ask any questions. The result of the telephone conversation was seen the next day in $1,000 worth of ruined parts.

PART 1: NO FEEDBACK

Your instructor will ask the class to pair off and move your chairs so that you are sitting back-to-back. One partner will be able to see the chalkboard and the other will not. The partner who can see the chalkboard will describe the configuration that is drawn there. The other partner will draw what she or he hears described on a piece of paper. It is important that the student who is drawing asks no questions and gives no verbal feedback.

The person giving the instructions will be the day supervisor. The other individual will be the night supervisor and will need a full blank sheet of paper and pen ready to draw the sketch.

PART 2: CHECK RESULTS

After everyone has finished the drawing, all the night supervisors may turn around and compare their sketches with the configuration drawn on the chalkboard.

PART 3: FEEDBACK

This time the students will reverse roles. The person who first drew the sketch now describes the second configuration to the other partner. This time, both individuals may ask questions. Repeating questions and repeating answers sometimes helps both to understand exactly what is meant.

PART 4: CHECK RESULTS

Again, after everyone has finished the drawing, all of the night supervisors can check their work. There should be real improvement.

FIGURE 6–5 *Levels of Communication in Building a Relationship*

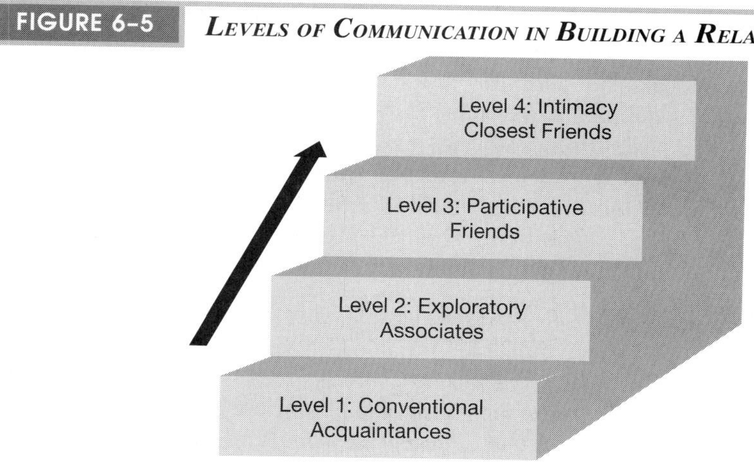

morning" may open the door to further communication, but are minimal attempts at communicating.

On the second or *exploratory* level, communication is fact and problem oriented. Here, too, conversation is usually impersonal. At times our relationships with our coworkers, neighbors, and business contacts are developed on this level and remain there for many years. Your relationship is friendly but not open to much self-disclosure. The topics of conversation are almost always related to business, not to personal matters. Classroom lectures are usually conducted on the exploratory level. Often, in personal transactions, a relationship must be established on this level before the participants can move on to the third level.

The third level is *participative.* Here people talk about themselves and engage in self-disclosure. They express their own feelings, describe their own experiences, and discuss their own ideas. While these are personal subjects, they are expressed in fairly safe ways: "I feel happiest with people my own age" or "I would say that I am more conservative now than I was 5 years ago." The fourth level, *intimacy,* we reserve for a select few. Here again people reveal themselves, but now they share more of themselves with one another in ways that involve risk: "I get the feeling that you do not really care about me" or "I want you to know I have been on drugs." Intimate relationships are characterized by communication of this kind, which evolves from deeply felt mutual understanding.

SPEAKING

Speaking is a form of communication that should be confirmed in writing if it is lengthy, complex, or technical. Studies have shown that college freshmen, immediately following a 10-minute lecture, retain only 50 percent of it and forget half of that material within 48 hours.

Matters important to a subordinate are particularly susceptible to misinterpretation and should be confirmed in writing. The most common example is the spoken promise of a raise or promotion, which is often misinterpreted after a lapse of time. About 30 percent of a message is lost or distorted after having passed through the first two recipients. When communication is urgent, the message should be given directly to the person affected.

VOICE TONE

"There are no dull subjects . . . only dull ways of talking."[8] The basic point and purpose of communication must be clear. In addition, our intent and enthusiasm for the subject matter must also be clear.

Often our tone of voice will indicate our emotional state. Voice tones can transmit as much or more emotional information as words. Loudly pitched voices can communicate anger no matter how emotionally neutral the dictionary meanings of the words being shouted. Also, anger can be conveyed through very intense whispering. The same emotion can be expressed by different tones of voice, and people differ in their reactions to these tones.

EMOTIONS

Perhaps the most important emotional factor in good communication is desire. When the desire to understand is strong, understanding usually results. However, one of the largest drawbacks to effective communication is that, as human beings, we do not

Emotions can make it hard to listen accurately.

separate ourselves from our emotions. In fact, we identify with them. We become our emotions. We say, "I am angry" or "I am happy." The intensity of our feelings colors everything we think and talk about. When we talk about a problem, we cannot help seeing it in terms of our own past experience and of how we feel at that very moment. Naturally, this can make it more difficult to see the other person's point of view, especially if he or she is also in the throes of some strong emotion.

SELF-DISCLOSURE

When people communicate with each other, especially face-to-face, their physical and emotional states of being are exposed to some degree. **Self-disclosure** is the act of opening up your self—your weaknesses as well as your strengths—to others. This exposure is sometimes disturbing because our culture places a high value on self-concealment. In a competitive society, concealment is frequently more useful than self-exposure or self-revelation. Yet if we were to reveal more of ourselves, we would understand each other better.

When people wish to reveal themselves to each other, they talk about personal matters such as loves, hates, beliefs, fears, worries, and perceptions about work, about themselves, and about each other. Of course, the atmosphere for self-disclosure must be one of mutual acceptance and goodwill. If not, mutual self-defense systems will automatically switch our psychic early-warning systems to "red alert," thereby raising defensive barriers and short-circuiting communication.

LISTENING

Listening is an active, not passive, activity.[9] Listening can be described as a combination of (1) *hearing*—the physical reception of sound; (2) *understanding*—the interpretation and comprehension of the message; (3) *remembering*—the ability to retain what has been heard; and (4) *acting*—responding by either action or inaction. It is not enough to hear. It is necessary to understand, remember, and act.

Henry Thoreau once wrote, "It takes two to speak the truth—one to speak and another to hear." Sometimes people think they are communicating when all they are really doing is talking a lot and taking very little time to get the feedback on what they have said. This has been called the echo-chamber approach to communication. Feedback is important, but there is much more to listening than just feedback.

The "echo chamber" is not worthwhile feedback.

Bad listening can result in people being injured or killed. The sinking of the *Titanic*; the attack on Pearl Harbor; the Waco, Texas, incident; and some disasters such as the one in Bhopal, India, are classic examples of breakdowns in communication and judgment. Messages were sent but the listening process broke down.

One of the reasons that we are not more careful when we listen is because we do not view communication from different listening perspectives. Bennett and Wood say that there are three perspectives or listening styles: results, process, and reasons. Results-style listeners want to hear only the bottom line. Process-style listeners want to be led into a subject with some background on how it all came about. Reasons-style listeners must be convinced that whatever is being proposed is reasonable, logical, and correct for the situation.[10]

How many times have you had a conversation with someone and not heard a word that was said? Listening is a form of paying attention, which is an active process involving much more than hearing and seeing. When we pay attention to each other, we are focusing our awareness on what is being said and are excluding other external and internal stimuli. This is not always easy because our senses are constantly scanning the environment for incoming stimuli, much like switched-on radar screens, and our minds are often preoccupied with our own thoughts.

Good listening is paying attention.

Under normal circumstances, people listen with only about 25 percent efficiency.[11] Good management requires good listening. People who force themselves to talk less begin to lose the desire to talk too much and, in turn, begin to enjoy listening. The ability to listen well is not an inherent trait; it is a learned behavior and a skill that must be developed.[12] As you advance in a business career, effective listening skills become increasingly critical.

Preoccupation.

Most of us can speak about 140 words per minute, but we can comprehend at a much faster rate. This permits us to take mental excursions as we listen. Later we return, hoping not to have missed anything important.

Prejudgment.

Opinions and prejudices can also cause poor listening. The style of the speaker's clothes, facial expression, posture, accent, color of skin, mannerisms, or age can cause a listener to tune out. Trying to put aside preconceived ideas or prejudgments allows us to open our minds to worthwhile listening.

One sales manager studied the percentage of the sales interaction done by the salesperson and the percentage done by prospective customer. He found that there was usually an inverse correlation between the amount of talking by his salesperson and the amount of the resulting order. In addition, the high-percentage talkers tended to be the newer people in the field, whereas the low-percentage talkers were the more experienced and successful ones.

There are no specific rules to follow for effective listening because what might work well for one person might not work for another. There are, however, some general guidelines that will help you to construct your own rules for more successful listening:

1. **Listen without evaluating.** A good listener is not judgmental and does not guess what the speaker is saying.
2. **Do not anticipate.** Sometimes we think we know what people are going to say before they say it and we say it for them. Often we are wrong. Try not to anticipate the next statement; stay in the present and listen.
3. **Note taking.** Note taking is important given that we forget one-third to one-half of what we hear within 8 hours. However, if too much time is spent on note taking, real listening can suffer.
4. **Listen for themes and facts.** Listen for the major themes as well as for important facts.
5. **Do not fake attention.** Really paying attention actually takes less energy than faking does. Acting is hard work.
6. **Review.** Periodically review the portion of the talk given so far. Plan to tell the contents to someone within 8 hours.

NONVERBAL COMMUNICATION

Nonverbal communication plays an important role in transmitting and decoding messages. Nonverbal cues include body language or kinesics, posture, eye contact, space or proxemics, and touching.

BODY LANGUAGE

Body language can convey the opposite of our words.

Body language, or in more scientific terms, **kinesics**, is any nonflexive or reflexive movement of the body. Body language can often communicate one's thoughts or feelings more honestly than verbal communication.

Studies show that at least 70 percent of what is really being communicated between individuals is done nonverbally.[13] This type of communication involves various dimensions: body posture, eye contact, gestures, distance, and proximity, among others.

Our eyes, hands, and bodies send and receive communication signals constantly. Over 30 head and facial movements that communicate specific messages have been isolated. Nearly all people tend to imitate the sitting and standing postures of someone they admire. They may cross their arms and legs and orient their bodies in specific withdrawal postures to shut out those who are perceived as threatening, and most people, regardless of sex or age, will touch each other when they are moved by strong emotions.

Avoid rigid interpretations of body language.

Here is a tip: Consider deliberately mirroring movements to enhance rapport when you feel it would be useful. Avoid rigid interpretations of nonverbal clues. Rarely make an interpretation based on a single cue or read too much into body language. Maybe some people just fold their arms a lot!

Observation and intuition are part of NLP.

Body language has now become part of the study of communication. People have distinctive ways of expressing themselves. Observation and intuition along with verbal and nonverbal language create the basis of neurolinguistic programming. **Neurolinguistic programming (NLP)** is a model for understanding human behavior and a set of communication and learning techniques based on the belief that people have preferred modes of acquiring and processing information.[14]

NLP indicates that people have a preferred way of learning and communicating. It is a communication technique that is easily learned. *Neuro* refers to the human nervous system and the way it receives and uses communication. *Linguistic* refers to the manner of communication including the words, tone, inflection, and timing. The *programming* aspect refers to the mechanisms for achieving consistency of responses given the message and manner of communication. It is becoming increasingly important in understanding the total message of communication.

POSTURE

A person's posture is a good clue as to how that individual feels about him- or herself. Stooping indicates that the person feels burdened, whereas a rigid walk or stance may indicate emotional stress.

Body language even speaks to muggers. Two researchers secretly videotaped people walking in Manhattan's garment district on 3 working days between 10 A.M. and noon.[15] Each pedestrian was taped for 6 to 8 seconds. The researchers assembled 60 taped segments of an equal number of men and women of varying ages. Then 12 prisoners who had been convicted of assaults on persons were asked how muggable the videotaped people were. More than half the convicts rated the same 20 people as either easy or very easy victims. Movements that characterized easy victims included their strides, which were either very long or very short, and their postures, which were awkward. Overall, the people rated most muggable walked as if they were in conflict with themselves.

EYE CONTACT

Everyone knows that a few seconds of eye contact can transmit meanings that might require hundreds of spoken words. Such idioms as "to make eyes at," "to keep an eye on," or "if looks could kill" reflect the importance of eye contact in many kinds of communication. Someone who sits at a crowded lunch counter looking straight ahead and an airplane passenger who sits with tightly closed eyes are both communicating that they do not wish to speak or to be spoken to. Their message is usually interpreted correctly without any need for words.

SPACE OR PROXEMICS

Proxemics is the physical distance that people put between themselves and others. There are two types of space as a form of communication: social and public. In the social type, for example, the distance in a normal business transaction would be 4 to 7 feet. This distance is used for casual social gatherings, but it can be used as a tool by a salesperson as well. As the salesperson steps closer to the customer, he or she invades that person's inner circle, making the customer feel uncomfortable. The salesperson pressures the customer psychologically into a sale. The social space of 7 to 12 feet is used for more formal business relations. It is the distance between the big boss and you—a way of showing the boss's authority. Public space of 12 to 25 feet, as in a teaching situation, allows many to focus their attention on more than one person.

You will discover that the closer an individual chooses to sit or stand to another, the more comfortable that person feels about the relationship. In business, the more confident a person is, the closer he or she will decide, even subconsciously, to sit to a partner or associate. Notice that two coworkers usually sit closer to each other than an employee and the boss.

TOUCHING

When we allow ourselves to touch and be touched, we become more open and vulnerable to one another. This openness, in turn, creates a greater sense of receptivity and, consequently, a greater willingness to listen attentively and try to understand the other person's point of view.

There is an interesting relation between the words touch and tact. The word *tact* is the root of the Latin word for touch. There is a psychological relationship between the two terms, for we say of a tactless person that he or she has a "heavy touch." We do not trust tactless people because they are likely to wound or betray us. We do trust those we allow to touch us and those we feel are safe to touch. Trust, or the lack of it, often determines the kind of feedback that is generated during a conversation.

We trust those we allow to touch us.

COMMUNICATION STYLE

The most common definition of communicator style involves "the way one verbally and nonverbally interacts to signal how literal meaning should be taken, interpreted, filtered, or understood."[16] This process of filtering and communicating is vital to the effective operation of an organization. Norton's Communicator Style Measure, a self-report instrument, assesses communication style. Norton's instrument involves nine sub-constructs described below in terms of communication behavior:

1. Dominant—takes charge of social interactions.
2. Dramatic—manipulates and exaggerates stories, voice, and other factors to highlight content.

3. Contentious—is argumentative.
4. Animated—provides frequent and sustained eye contact, uses numerous facial expressions, and frequently gestures.
5. Impression leaving—centers on being remembered, based on projected stimuli.
6. Relaxed—is relaxed, not tense, or anxious.
7. Attentive—makes sure that the receiver knows she or he has an attentive audience.
8. Open—conversational, affable, unreserved, and extroverted.
9. Friendly—ranges from being unhostile to intimate.

The Communicator Style Measure is but one measure that helps us to understand our communication type. Complete the following activity to more fully discover your communication skills.

ACTION PROJECT 6-2

HOW DO I COMMUNICATE? (INDIVIDUAL-DYAD EXERCISE)

Complete the following exercise by rating each question on a scale of 1 to 5 (where 5 = strongly agree/very high). When you are through, ask a friend, classmate, or other associate to rate you using the same scale. Then, compare your responses. Too much disparity suggests room for improvement.

	Strongly Disagree	Disagree	Neutral	Agree	Strongly Agree
1. I think before talking.	1	2	3	4	5
2. I think before writing.	1	2	3	4	5
3. I listen to others without distraction.	1	2	3	4	5
4. I listen to others without interrupting.	1	2	3	4	5
5. I encourage feedback from others by soliciting questions and by other verbal means.	1	2	3	4	5
6. I encourage feedback from others by my body language.	1	2	3	4	5
7. I am careful in selecting understandable words and phrases.	1	2	3	4	5
8. I am brief and to the point in communication.	1	2	3	4	5
9. I encourage free exchange of ideas by withholding judgment about others' ideas.	1	2	3	4	5
10. I listen even if I do not like the person who is talking or otherwise communicating.	1	2	3	4	5
11. I encourage others to communicate by my facial expressions and body language.	1	2	3	4	5
12. I restate what I understand others to have said and/or ask questions to clarify positions.	1	2	3	4	5

ETHICS/VALUES CONSIDERATIONS

Given the changes that are occurring within the formal organization, a new emphasis is placed on the values under which the organization functions. Trends in organizations include less hierarchy, integrated structures, teams and teamwork, empowered employees, and labor-management partnerships.[17] A myriad of new ethical considerations abound in the workplace and communication plays its inherent role in the process. Much of the controversy found within the workplace centers around ethics and the ways in which employees express their views. Issues such as insider trading, employment interviewing, racial or sex discrimination, gender equality, and cross-cultural communication are commonly found in organizational life. One place to look for guidance is the legal system, which has worked to assist organizations to work within ethical boundaries.

Ethics is inextricably tied to communication. Each rhetorical act of persuading is deeply rooted in an individual's ethical perspective. An effective communicator shows courage to deal with ethical issues related to sensitive or unpleasant topics. The familiar directive "with power comes responsibility" should be applied in each communication encounter. Because effective communication is such a powerful tool, communicators must accept responsibility for embracing both their personal values as well as the standards of their company. To assure ethical communicative acts, consider the following questions:

- Are negative messages expressed in a manner that protects the recipient's self-worth and sustains the relationship?
- Are messages expressed in a clear and understandable manner?
- Is the conveyed message truthful, honest, and fair?

Managers and employees should consider whether sensitive material is appropriate for written modes of communication; for example, legal matters that must be kept confidential or employee misconduct issues. Although written documentation is required for most important events within the workplace, care and caution should be used before putting some kinds of information into internal documents to be read by large numbers of people.

TECHNOLOGICAL IMPLICATIONS

Rapid changes in the economic, social, and technological climates contribute to changes in the nature of work in this country. With the advent of cellular phones, laptop computers, pagers, fax machines, electronic mail, and voice mail, American workers are finding it quite easy to stay attached to the workplace, even while on vacation. One study of U.S. workers in higher household income brackets shows that American workers tend to work while on vacation. More than 50 percent carry cellular phones and nearly one-third check their voice mail.[18] While technology facilitates the communication process among workers within the organization, face-to-face communication has seemingly decreased. Do you think this is a positive trend?

SUMMARY

Communication is the process by which information and understanding are transferred from one person to another. Effective communication enables people to exercise control over their environment. It is an essential tool for the establishment and maintenance of good social and working relationships. If the messages being communicated are not understood, then communication is poor or nonexistent. Effective communication is a dynamic process that involves constant change and interaction among many verbal and nonverbal elements.

The meaning of a message is sometimes subjective. A word's meaning is the significance that word has for both speaker and listener, and that significance can vary from person to person. Good communication requires paying as much attention to the person speaking as to the verbal message itself, because words can have ambiguous meanings. Barriers to effective communication include distortion, language/semantics, defensiveness, noise, mistrust, and other emotional responses. Failure to listen is another major barrier.

Two kinds of communication channels serve to accomplish effective communication: formal and informal. Formal channels are the official paths by which official messages travel. They are called the vertical and horizontal channels because they relate to and grow out of the vertical and horizontal relationships pictured on an organization's structural chart. Informal channels stem from the social relationships between individuals who work together and serve to transmit unofficial messages.

Although the downward and upward channels both move vertically, the nature, content, and volume of messages going up and down are completely different. The downward channel is dominated by orders from above dealing with policies and procedures. Vast amounts of printed matter are generated in the top-down channel in the form of memos and reports.

Horizontal channels exist for members of the same organizational rank to communicate with one another. Horizontal communication can be observed on a formal organization chart, but it also exhibits a number of characteristics associated with informal modes of communication. It has been demonstrated that open horizontal communication is essential for the success of any complex organization, from the managerial level to the assembly line.

Effective listening depends on paying attention and focusing. It requires understanding, remembering, and acting, as well as hearing. Although there are no specific rules that everyone must follow to become a good listener, there are some general guidelines for developing good listening habits.

The communication process can be described in terms of a model in which attitudes, emotions, roles, nonverbal behaviors, perceptions, and feedback are interacting constantly. There are four levels of communication that depend on the degree of intimacy existing between speaker and listener: conventional, exploratory, participative, and intimate.

Body language, or kinesics, is used to interpret a person's attitudes by observing his or her body movement. Nonverbal cues are usually more honest than are verbal cues. Remember to avoid rigid interpretations of nonverbal clues, particularly those based on a single clue. Proxemics is the study of the distance people put between themselves and others. The closer they are to each other, the more comfortable they are in their relationship.

A new emphasis on values and technology must be considered in regard to communication in today's organizations. Ethical issues, such as gender equality, insider trading, and cross-cultural communication, must be addressed in today's organizations. The rapid development of new technology allows us to communicate with those at work even when we are away.

CASE STUDY 6-1

BODY LANGUAGE SPEAKS LOUDLY IN THE ESCROW OFFICE

An escrow department of a large national bank recently hired a new employee. Mona Chatman is 25 years old and single. Prior to being hired as an escrow officer, she worked as a teller and later as a secretary of an escrow office in another firm. Before leaving her former location, Mona was given some training in escrow procedures. Mona is an attractive woman, and this is highlighted by her stylish, yet conservative, method of dress.

Although Mona has had previous on-the-job training in escrow, she has not yet reached complete proficiency. In some areas she is still in need of further training and advice. The person closest to Mona, both in physical distance and job responsibilities, is John Baxter—the only other escrow officer. When Mona was hired, the department supervisor informed her that John would be the person to go to for help and advice, primarily because both Mona and John would be working on the same tract of homes for some time.

Being a rather shy person, Mona has not made a habit of asking John for his help. She has tended to keep to herself for the most part, and John has not gone out of his way to help break the ice between them. Mona does not really know if John is capable of giving her any worthy advice, let alone taking the time to help her. Judging from appearances, she feels that John is a pretty sloppy individual both in appearance (John's clothes look almost as if he has slept in them) and in his work. He seems to have trouble handling his own duties. It looks as if he is always a week behind in his work, and his desk is constantly a mess.

In spite of his overly casual appearance and method of handling work, John is competent and qualified in the escrow business. When Mona began working in the department a few weeks back, John had planned on giving her any assistance she would need in handling her new position. However, John soon began to feel that Mona really did not want his help. Even though Mona seems shy, John believes that she is more stuck up and cold than anything else. John has admitted to a close friend in the bank that he is somewhat jealous of Mona's promotions all the way from teller to escrow officer by the age of 25. He also finds it irritating that Mona manages to type so quickly and has her desk clean at the end of each day. It is also John's opinion that Mona looks down on his appearance. As a family man, he cannot afford the quality of clothes that Mona, as a single woman, wears each day. As far as John is concerned at the present time, if Mona wishes any help from him, she will have to come and ask for it.

As the supervisor of the escrow department, you have become aware of the problem existing between Mona and John. They should be working together and yet they are not.

1. Given the information supplied, what would you identify as the main problem?
2. What steps would you take to improve the situation?
3. From the description of Mona, what other assumptions might you make about her personality? Could these assumptions lead to faulty generalizations?
4. From the description of John, what other assumptions might you make about his personality? Could these assumptions lead to faulty generalizations?
5. How can you, as supervisor, help both Mona and John overcome their misconceptions of each other?

DISCUSSION AND STUDY QUESTIONS—TO KEEP YOU THINKING

1. Explain what is meant by the phrase "meanings are within us."
2. How does perception affect communication?
3. What are the major barriers to effective communication?
4. How does formal communication differ from informal communication?
5. How do the processes and effects of downward communication and upward communication differ?
6. How are vertical messages likely to be different depending on whether they move up or down?
7. Describe what is meant by the echo-chamber effect in listening.
8. What is the Pygmalion (self-fulfilling prophecy) effect and how does it impact management?
9. What does small-group communication accomplish besides the obvious transmitting and receiving of information?
10. What are some ways you can assure that communication is ethical?
11. How is technology impacting communication?

NOTES

1. Robert M. Hecht, "Key Words: Use the Right 'Communication Style,'" *Success* (December 1989): 14.
2. Ibid.
3. J. H. Foegen, "Quiet, Please!" *SAM Advanced Management Journal* (winter 1987): 17.
4. Louis Harris cited in Stanley J. Modic, "Whatever It Is, It's Not Working," *Industry Week* (July 17, 1989): 27.
5. Valorie McClelland, "Employees We Trust," *Personnel Administrator* (September 1988): 137–139.
6. David Cathmoir Nicoll, "Acknowledge and Use Your Grapevine," *Management Decision* (1994): 25–30.
7. Valorie A. McClelland, "Upward Communication: Is Anyone Listening?" *Personnel Journal* (June 1988): 124–131.
8. Ralph Proodian, "There Are No Dull Subjects," *The Wall Street Journal*, January 4, 1985, 18.
9. Margaret Brody, "Listen Up! Do You Really Hear What People Are Saying?" *The American Salesman* (June 1994): 14–15.
10. Ruth T. Bennett and Rosemary V. Wood, "Effective Communication via Listening Styles," *Business* (April–June 1989): 45–48.
11. Glenn Pearce, "Doing Something About Your Listening Skills," *Supervisory Management* (March 1989): 29–34.
12. Jo Procter, "You Haven't Heard a Word I Said: Getting Managers to Listen," *IEEE Transactions on Professional Communication* (March 1994): 18–20.
13. C. Barnum and N. Wolniansky, "Taking Cues from Body Language," *Management Review* (June 1989): 59–60.
14. Barbara Dastoor, "Speaking Their Language," *Training and Development* (June 1993): 17–20.
15. Betty Grayson and Morris Stein, "Body Language That Speaks to Muggers," *Psychology Today* (August 1980): 20.
16. R. W. Norton. "Foundation of a Communicator Style Construct," *Human Communication Research* 4, (Winter 1978) 99–111.
17. Ellen F. Harshman and Carl L. Harshman. "Communicating with Employees: Building on an Ethical Foundation," *Journal of Business Ethics* (March 1999): 3–19.
18. Andersen Consulting, "Andersen Consulting Survey Finds That 83% of American Workers Stayed Connected to Their Offices While on Summer Vacation." businesswire.com/webbox/bw.090100/202452001.htm (accessed January 2001).

CHAPTER 7

Motivation

TO START YOU THINKING

Here are some questions that may stimulate your thinking. The answers to some will be found in the readings; other answers will come from your experiences and personal opinions.

- What motivates you?
- Why do people work when they don't need the money?
- What makes some people work harder than others?
- Does everyone have the same needs? Are needs hierarchical?
- Are people motivated internally or externally?
- How can routine jobs be redesigned to be more productive and satisfying?
- Do managers motivate subordinates by listening to them?

LEARNING GOALS

After studying this chapter, you should be able to:

1. Describe what motivation means.
2. Explain how the individual's need to be motivated may differ from the company's and supervisor's need to motivate.
3. Describe the schools of psychology and how they relate to motivation.
4. Discuss the various behavior defense mechanisms we exhibit when we cannot achieve our goals easily.
5. Describe the five elements of Maslow's hierarchy of needs. Contrast them with Herzberg's two-factor theory.
6. Contrast intrinsic and extrinsic motivators and list several of each type.
7. Compare the expectancy, equity, and needs approaches to motivation.
8. Describe the nature of incentives and their relationship to motivation.
9. Summarize some of the important methods of job enrichment.
10. Describe the job characteristics model of work motivation.
11. Describe barriers to achievement and how to overcome them.
12. Define and apply the following terms and concepts (in order of first occurrence):

KEYWORDS

- **performance**
- **motivation**
- **goal congruency**
- **behavior modification**
- **reinforcement**
- **belonging needs**
- **self-actualization**
- **need prepotency**
- **hygiene factors**
- **expectancy theory**
- **equity theory**
- **ERG approach**
- **incentive**
- **intrinsic motivators/rewards**

- **defense mechanisms**
- **job design**
- **job enlargement**
- **job enrichment**
- **job rotation**
- **job sharing**
- **core job dimensions**

This chapter is devoted to human motivation processes and accompanying strategies for improving them.

WHAT IS MOTIVATION?

Motivation results from the existence of a person's needs and the fulfillment of those needs. Too often, we think that we motivate another person, but as we shall see, it is not something that we do to or for another person; it is not a set of needs externally imposed on another person. In its simplest sense, motivation is a process that enables internal need fulfillment.

In business, motivation is used to describe the drive that impels an individual to work. A truly motivated person is one who wants to work. Employers want to know what motivates employees so they can encourage employees to work more productively. The motivation to work is integral to successful organizations and to employee job satisfaction. Ultimately, employers are concerned with performance. **Performance** may defined as a function of individual ability (A), opportunity (O) to perform (e.g., sufficient resources to get the job done, including appropriate training), and motivation (M). If any one of these components is lacking, an organization's performance will be diminished. Our focus in this chapter in on the "M" in the aforementioned equation—motivation.

MOTIVATION AND BEHAVIOR

Motivation is an internal need satisfied by external expression.

The term **motivation,** originally derived from the Latin word meaning "to move," refers to those components and processes that are associated with the manner in which human behavior is activated. The three essential components of motivated behavior include the direction, intensity, and persistence of effort toward attaining a goal.[1]

Direction refers to the behaviors an individual chooses to perform when confronted with a number of possible alternatives. In organizations, the objective is to maximize the likelihood that the behavioral alternative(s) chosen by an individual will be consistent with the overall objectives of the organization, and more specifically, with the individual's tasks in the work unit. Such behaviors are termed *functional.* Workers may also be motivated to perform in ways that hinder an organization's ability to achieve its goals. Such behaviors are termed *dysfunctional.*

Direction provides focus; it defines the purpose or result that the behavior is attempting to achieve. *Intensity,* or level of effort, refers to the strength of the motivated behavior in the pursuit of the particular objective. *Persistence* refers to how long an individual will devote effort to a chosen alternative.[2]

Concept of individual differences revisited.

People are motivated to perform similar actions by very different internal drives. Recall that individual differences are emotional, physical, and social qualities unique to each individual human being. The concept of individual differences is illustrated by the fact that two employees may work hard for a raise, but for different reasons. To one, the raise is important because it will provide more money for retirement; to the other, the raise is important because it provides money for instant consumption.

In addition, similar internal motivations can have different results. Two employees who feel a strong need for job security may handle their needs in very different ways. One might decide to work hard, but never to "rock the boat" for fear of being fired. The other might choose to be innovative, even at the risk of being controversial, as a way of becoming indispensable.

MOTIVATION AND ORGANIZATIONS

Studies of motivation try to discover the incentives that will cause workers to work more productively. Managers try to increase the motivation of workers by creating incentive systems, but they cannot motivate the workers—only the workers themselves can do that.

An important task of management is to achieve **goal congruency,** maximizing the overlap between organizational objectives and individuals' goals. Managers can do this by helping employees achieve personal goals like salary maximization, autonomy, and empowerment, while at the same time accomplishing organizational objectives (see Figure 7-1).

Harvard professor and management theorist Chris Argyris examined the proposition that individual growth needs and organizational objectives are often in conflict. He found that as people mature, they grow more independent and want to make more decisions for themselves. They seek to take on more responsibility and become more competent. He also found that some organizations exert pressures that directly oppose these patterns. For example, in the interest of efficiency, some organizations require employees to submit to rigid forms of authority, demand few skills of them, and make as many decisions as possible for them.

Argyris believes that the "incongruence between the individual and the organization can provide the basis for a continued challenge that, as it is fulfilled, will tend to help people to enhance their own growth and to develop organizations that will tend to be viable and effective."[3]

FIGURE 7-1 *Goal Congruency. The Objective Is to Make the Shaded Area as Congruent as Possible.*

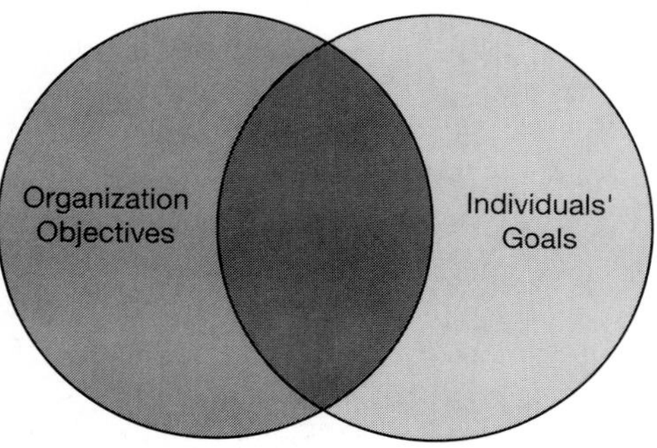

In its simplest form, motivation can be understood as a three-step process: (1) an internal need exists, (2) a behavioral action or direction is taken to satisfy that need, and (3) the need is satisfied. Note that the need is internally, not externally, generated and creates tension in the person. Need may be physiological, economic, social, psychological, or emotional. For example, you may have a desire for food that can be satisfied by various actions: grabbing a snack or waiting several hours for a more substantial meal. Alternatively, you may wish to become the top salesperson in your company and set about engaging in behaviors leading to that objective.

Efforts to understand these complex processes have stimulated considerable research. In the next section we will begin to explore how various schools of psychology have attempted to explain motivation.

PSYCHOLOGY AND ITS IMPACT ON MOTIVATION

Three schools of psychology discuss human motivation: the psychoanalytic, behaviorist, and human relations schools of behavior. Each represents a different way of perceiving motivation and how to motivate others.

PSYCHOANALYTIC SCHOOL

Iceberg theory.

Sigmund Freud, the founder of the psychoanalytic process, stressed the complexity of human motivation and pointed out that the outward manifestation of an individual's psyche is like the tip of a submerged iceberg (see Figure 7-2). The submerged portion of the iceberg represents the unconscious needs and motivations of the individual. To Freud, motivated behavior was a result of what resided below the surface and was not something of which the individual was consciously aware. Freud believed that the interpersonal and social environments influenced the outcome of the individual's efforts, but the real motivation for those efforts was typically not available to the conscious mind.

FIGURE 7-2 *Iceberg Theory: A Large Portion of Our Personality Is Hidden from Our Conscious Perception.*

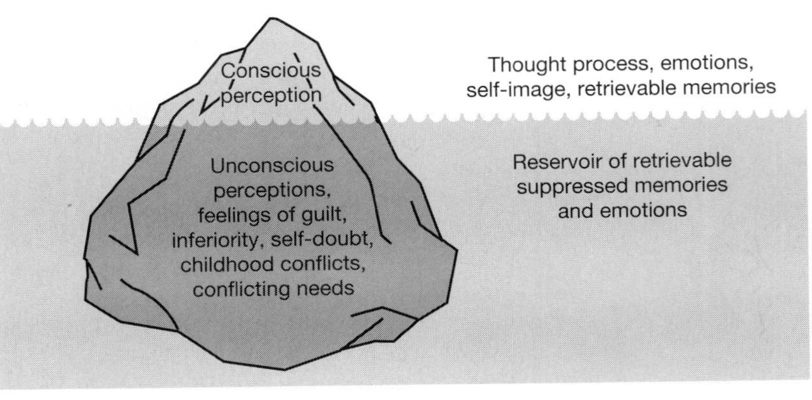

BEHAVIORIST SCHOOL

Behavior modification.

More than fifty years ago, psychologist B. F. Skinner developed a theory of motivation known as behavior modification. **Behavior modification** is the process of influencing behavior by rewarding the individual for proper responses and not rewarding improper responses. A basic tenet of behavior modification is the *law of effect,* which states that positively reinforced behavior tends to be repeated while behavior that is not reinforced tends not to be repeated.

Principle of reinforcement.

Anything that causes a certain behavior to be repeated or inhibited is known as **reinforcement.** Skinner found that, for effective reinforcement, a carefully planned schedule must be followed. The most effective rewards are those that immediately follow the desired behavior.

Positive reinforcement is the administration of a pleasant or rewarding outcome following a behavior, while *negative reinforcement* is the removal of a negative consequence when a worker performs a desired behavior. When managers use positive reinforcements, workers learn the connection between behaviors the organization wants them to perform and the positive consequences they want to obtain. Conversely, when managers use negative reinforcement, workers learn the connection between desired behaviors and a consequence they wish to avoid. A positive reinforcement, such as praise, is generally more effective than negative reinforcement.

Extinction is the withdrawal of a positive reward. Behaviors that do not receive positive rewards will tend to disappear. When a manager cannot wait for extinction to remove the undesirable behavior, he may choose to use punishment. *Punishment* is the administration of a negative consequence when undesired behavior occurs.[4] Behavior modification has some intriguing possibilities for motivation. One of the best-documented examples of the potential of behavior modification in industry is at the Emery Air Freight Company. The supervisors at the company were trained to praise work done correctly by the employees, such as keeping records of all their activities, improving delivery times, or responding quickly to telephone requests. The program saved over $2 million in 4 years.

HUMAN RELATIONS SCHOOL

Classical organizational theory says that employees are lazy, work only for money, and need to be supervised closely if they are to produce up to standard.

The human relations school, on the other hand, believes in looking to people rather than to the organization for resolving interpersonal problems or opportunities. There is a heavy emphasis on the study of informal groups, group decision making, employee satisfaction, and leadership styles. People have many different feelings and collectively develop a group personality that should be managed differently from that of other groups. Primary examples of the human relations approach are Maslow's hierarchy of needs and Herzberg's motivator/hygiene theory. Both of these approaches to understanding motivation and job satisfaction are discussed on the following pages.

MASLOW'S BASIC NEEDS

Abraham Maslow conjectured that basic needs are the same for all human beings.[5] He found that, although different cultures satisfy these needs in different ways, the needs themselves are the same. What are the basic needs that motivate people to act in the ways they do? Figure 7-3 illustrates Maslow's hierarchy.

FIGURE 7-3 ***Maslow's Hierarchy of Needs.***

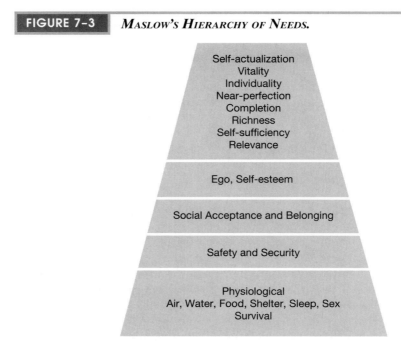

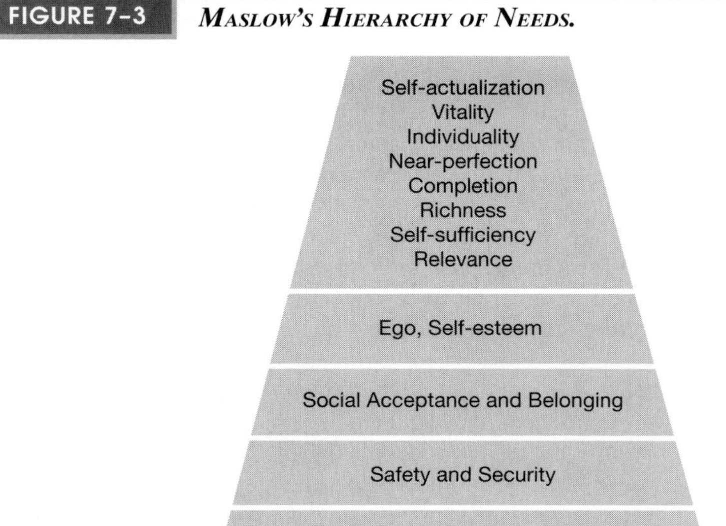

PHYSIOLOGICAL NEEDS

Maslow believed that not much can motivate a person who has not reasonably satisfied his or her basic physiological needs; when a person is starving, the only need that is important is food.

Maslow's five basic needs start with the physiological needs.

Physiological needs include such basics as food, water, sleep, air, satisfactory temperature, and protection from the elements by clothing and shelter. For most people, the physical needs are indirectly satisfied with the money earned from the work they do.

SAFETY OR SECURITY NEEDS

People also want to feel safe from harm. For most adults, safety needs are expressed by the desire to be stable and secure. To prefer the familiar to the unfamiliar or unknown reflects the basic need for safety.

Your chosen career may reflect your need for security.

For example, the type of career we choose may reflect our need for security. Secure careers are often found in teaching, accounting, or civil service. You may prefer to work for a larger, stable company whose future is predictable. Alternatively, you may prefer to work for a high-tech start-up firm that lacks the track record of stability and performance offered by a more established firm, but perhaps holds the promise of a more exciting and rewarding employment opportunity. Your choice depends, to some extent, on your unique level of security needs at the particular time in your career.

SOCIAL OR BELONGING NEEDS

Once people have satisfied their physiological and safety needs, they seek to satisfy their needs for acceptance, affection, and the feeling of belonging. It is important to remember that a person needs to give as well as receive affection. Supervisors can see the strength of the social need by observing conversations during coffee breaks or groups leaving work together.

People need a sense of belonging.

Social needs may more aptly be called **belonging needs.** One way for managers to build team spirit is by addressing social or belonging needs. People have the desire to be successful as a group or team as well as individually.

ESTEEM NEEDS

Status symbols satisfy self-esteem needs.

Maslow classifies the need for esteem into two categories: (1) the desire for a sense of internal worth and (2) the desire for prestige or reputation that can only be conferred by other people. People who value themselves have highly developed feelings of confidence, worth, strength, capability, and adequacy. Lack of self-esteem produces feelings of inferiority, inadequacy, weakness, and helplessness. These feelings of self-dislike can lead to discouragement and a sense of failure.

In today's organizations, esteem needs may be met in a variety of ways: for example, stock options, flextime, travel, opportunities to participate in special project assignments, and office perks.

Belonging needs can be in conflict with esteem needs.

Sometimes our needs are in conflict. The need to be an accepted member of a group may conflict with the need to be a leader. A good worker who is selected as a supervisor may become an ambivalent leader because the need to be an accepted member of the group proves stronger than the ego drive to be a supervisor.

SELF-ACTUALIZATION NEEDS

The realization of one's fullest potential is called **self-actualization.** The need for self-actualization is demonstrated by doing a job well merely for the sake of doing it well and by striving toward more creative endeavors of all kinds. Maslow classifies the needs concerned with physiology, safety, belonging, and esteem as *deficiency* needs—without their satisfaction, people lack the necessary components for developing healthy personalities. Conversely, self-actualization is a *growth* need.

THE HIERARCHY OF NEEDS

Maslow explains the five categories of needs in terms of a hierarchy and believes that needs at a lower level in the hierarchy must be relatively satisfied before needs at the next level can become motivating (e.g., the concept of **need prepotency**). Although this description of a hierarchy of needs is convenient, it is slightly misleading. One need does not require full satisfaction before the next need on the hierarchical ladder makes itself felt.

People are constantly driven by internal forces—they are increasingly motivated toward new goals. One of the chief reasons that the positive feelings accompanying the achievement of a goal are short-lived is that another goal, based on the same or a different need, soon takes its place. When a need is satisfied, it no longer motivates. The ever-changing nature of needs plays an important role in the theory and practice of incentive systems and job development programs. The truly motivated person will look for opportunities to satisfy his or her desires, as demonstrated in "To the Kid on the End of the Bench" (Figure 7-4).[6]

FIGURE 7-4 ***To Be Motivated to Long-Term Goals Means Determination, Sacrifice, and Strong Desire.***

TO THE KID ON THE END OF THE BENCH

Champions once sat where you're sitting, kid.

The Football Hall of Fame (and every other Hall of Fame) is filled with names of people who sat, week after week, without getting a spot of mud on their well-laundered uniforms.

Generals, senators, surgeons, prize-winning novelists, professors, business executives started on the end of a bench, too.

Don't sit and study your shoe tops. Keep your eye on the game. Watch for defensive lapses.

Look for offensive opportunities.

If you don't think you're in a great spot, wait until you see how many would like to take it away from you at next spring practice.

What you do from the bench this season could put you on the field next season, as a player, or back in the grandstand as a spectator.

Source: Compliments of United Technologies, Box 360, Hartford, CT 06141.

EXPRESS YOUR OPINION

You have now read about Maslow's hierarchy of needs. Assume that most of your physiological needs are satisfied and focus on your other needs. Sometimes the self-esteem need seems to prevail, like when you need considerable recognition as an individual. At other times there may be a strong need for social acceptance to overcome loneliness in your daily life. Which need seems to be the strongest and most desirable one to satisfy in the next few months? Can you say why? What one accomplishment could satisfy it most?

What do you think is the strongest need of your closest friend? Is it the same as yours? What is the strongest need of your parents? Do you think that people may go through life cycles that, at different stages, reflect the importance of different needs?

HERZBERG'S MOTIVATOR/HYGIENE APPROACH

Another approach to motivation and job satisfaction resulting from needs is provided by Frederick Herzberg. Herzberg classified needs into two categories: motivators and hygiene factors.

SATISFIERS AND DISSATISFIERS

Herzberg found that the factors that make a job satisfying are different than the factors that make it dissatisfying. He termed the factors that make jobs satisfying, **motivators**. Those factors that make jobs dissatisfying are termed **hygiene factors.** For example, Herzberg found that offering workers more money could lead to less dis-

SELF-APPRAISAL

CAN YOU RECOGNIZE THE NEED?

Each of the following work situations stresses the denial of one of four basic needs: (1) security, (2) social, (3) self-esteem, and (4) self-actualization. After each situation write the number of the need being denied. Refer to the text if necessary. (Answers are given at the end of the chapter.)

1. A rumor of imminent layoffs is being circulated in the company, and the employees are upset. _____
2. A new employee felt left out when she was not asked to join her fellow workers for coffee. _______
3. A machine operator developed a way to cut production time. His supervisor adopted the plan for operators on similar machines without giving him credit. The man was resentful. _______________
4. A man who had worked hard on behalf of the union wished to be elected shop steward. At the last election he was not nominated and felt let down by his friends. _______________
5. A worker received $15 extra in his weekly paycheck. He felt ashamed that he did not report the mistake. _______________
6. A group of employees liked to go for coffee together. The boss divided them into two groups and made them go at different times. The employees were unhappy about the ruling. _______________
7. An employee who felt he could not work smoothly with others wanted to take a human relations course. The course required him to leave work 15 minutes early once a week, and he offered to make up the loss by coming in 15 minutes early on those days. The supervisor denied his request, thereby causing the employee a setback in his planning. _______________
8. A store manager set a goal of a 15 percent sales increase in the next 6 months. She failed to attain her goal, but she did increase sales by 5 percent. She was keenly disappointed. _______________
9. A salesman is worried because he has experienced a substantial drop in sales for no apparent reason. _______________
10. A manager resented having to cancel, at the last minute, elaborate plans for a camping trip with his family. _______________

satisfaction, but not to true job satisfaction. Employees who hold jobs they consider intrinsically rewarding are satisfied with their jobs; with less rewarding work, they become less satisfied. Offering them more money does not replace the satisfaction gained from doing fulfilling work.

Workers are often in a neutral position—neither satisfied nor dissatisfied, but simply doing their jobs. Certain negative job factors (hygiene factors) decrease job satisfaction. Alleviating these hygiene factors brings employees back to a neutral position. Other positive factors (motivators) can create employee satisfaction on the job. Without them, employees become neutral, but not dissatisfied.

MAINTAINING MOTIVATION

Herzberg believes certain factors are used to keep a person from being dissatisfied (Table 7-1), much in the same way that food keeps us from being hungry. Just as eating breakfast in the morning does not keep us from being hungry in the afternoon, factors that keep employees from being dissatisfied can be short-lived. For example, a salary raise makes us happy, but not forever. Six months or a year later, we may feel that we are deserving of a raise again. Employees report that receiving more money in routine amounts, such as the annual raise, is largely taken for granted, anticipated

TABLE 7-1

Hygiene Factors and Growth Needs

HYGIENE MAINTENANCE FACTORS	MOTIVATORS AND GROWTH NEEDS
Salary, status, and security	Growth and advancement to higher level tasks
Company policies and administration	Achievement
Supervision	Recognition for achievement
Work environment and interpersonal relations	Interest in the task
	Responsibility for enlarged task

Source: Frederick Herzberg et al., *The Motivation to Work* (New York: John Wiley, 1959), p. 81.

before it arrives, and viewed as a justly deserved reward for past services, not as a stimulus to a new effort. In Herzberg's terminology, money and fringe benefits are known as *negative motivators.* Their absence from a job will unquestionably make people dissatisfied, but their presence doesn't necessarily make employees happier or more productive.

Satisfying a hygiene factor keeps us from being unhappy.

Hygiene factors are conditions conducive to maintaining mental and physical health. Satisfying hygiene factors only keep us from being unhappy; once satisfied, they cease to motivate individuals.

Satisfying a hygiene factor does not make us happy or productive.

Another way of viewing Herzberg's approach is that once certain hygiene factors are present, they are adequate and keep a person from being dissatisfied. Such factors can include company policies, supervision, interpersonal relationships, status, money, and security. However, the factors that strongly motivate people to do more on the job are real opportunities for professional growth, responsibility, the work itself, recognition, and achievement.

Dissatisfiers relate more to hygiene factors.

When employees are asked what is dissatisfying about their jobs, they usually complain about things that are not associated with the actual work itself, but rather with the work environment. These complaints include matters such as supervision, relations with others, physical conditions, organizational policies, administrative practices, pay, fringe benefits, status, and job security. Such complaints suggest that the context in which the work is done "is unfair or disorganized and as such represents . . . an unhealthy psychological work environment."[7]

Satisfiers relate more to the job itself.

When employees are asked what satisfies them about their work, they tend to describe aspects of the job itself. Employees are satisfied when the work they do is interesting, when they achieve job goals and receive recognition for their achievements, and when they are given increased responsibility. Factors that lead to job satisfaction are related to the need for self-actualization.

In summary, Herzberg believes that both *hygiene* and *motivator* needs must be satisfied. Employees with exciting jobs will usually be willing to tolerate unpleasant circumstances, such as low pay or an unfriendly supervisor. However, the fewer the possibilities for growth and personal fulfillment on a job, the greater the number of hygiene factors that must be offered in compensation.

OTHER APPROACHES TO MOTIVATION

Additional theories on motivation include the expectancy approach, equity approach, and ERG approach.

ACTION PROJECT 7–1

SELF-MOTIVATION COMES WHEN YOU HAVE GOALS (INDIVIDUAL EXERCISE)

Answer the following questions as they pertain to you. You should not be asked to turn in your answers or to react to these questions in class, unless you wish to verbalize your feelings. The idea for this exercise is to see if you can focus on your needs and goals at this point in your life.

1. What is your most important physiological need at this time?

___

2. What is your most important security need at this time? Is it being basically satisfied? If it is not currently being satisfied, identify some steps can you take in order to fulfill that need.

___

3. What is your most important social need at this time? Is it being basically satisfied? If it is not currently being satisfied, identify some steps can you take in order to fulfill that need.

___

4. What is your most important self-esteem need at this time? Is it being satisfied? If it is not currently being satisfied, identify some steps can you take in order to fulfill that need.

___

5. What one goal would you like to accomplish in 3 months?

___

6. What one goal would you like to accomplish in 3 years?

___

7. What would you like to accomplish in business in the next 3 years?

___

Every month for the next 6 months, review your list and see how you are doing. Are your goals realistic? Are you working to make your dreams come true? You may find that as your life circumstances change, you will need to modify or change your goals.

EXPECTANCY THEORY

How we expect to do influences how we do.

Expectancy theory relates to the strength of an individual's belief that a particular course of action will result in a given outcome (reward). That belief is a function of the expectation itself (*expectancy*), the method for making it happen (*instrumentality*), and the degree of attractiveness of a behavioral goal (*valence*) that the individual places on the outcome (reward). The formula for the relationship is shown in Figure 7-5.

A good example of the expectancy approach is the grade that you expect to earn in a class. That expected grade influences how hard you work and the value you place on the outcome. In this example, the grade is the expectancy. The instrumentality is how hard you work to achieve that grade, and the valence is how much you want a particular grade. The reward is the grade itself. Expectancy theory suggests that managers link the expectations employees have about their work to what the employees want from their work in terms of rewards. In addition, employees must believe that the work performed, when done so at an appropriate level, will result in receiving the rewards or outcomes they feel are important. When that is accomplished successfully, both work performance and work satisfaction will increase.[8]

FIGURE 7-5 *FORMULA FOR EXPECTANCY APPROACH.*

Motivation	=	(or is a function of) Expectancy × Instrumentality × Valence
where		
Expectancy	=	the person's belief that effort will result in performance
Instrumentality	=	the person's belief that performance will be rewarded
Valence	=	the perceived strength or value of receiving the rewards

EQUITY THEORY

Equity theory says that motivation is based on perceived fairness. Its central tenet is that employees strive to maintain balance between their own inputs and their rewards in comparison to other employees.

Equity is in the eye of the beholder.

Our perception of fairness is based on how we see others rewarded for more, the same, or less effort. Individuals want their efforts to be judged fairly. According to equity theory, people make judgments about whether they are being treated fairly and take action based upon those perceptions. If individuals perceive inequity, they can reduce that inequity by changing how hard they work or by seeking a change in rewards.

Employees compare their input/output ratio with others' input/output ratios. Figure 7-6 shows the relationship and consequences of imbalances in the input/out-

FIGURE 7-6 *EQUITY APPROACH RATIOS AND CONSEQUENCES.*

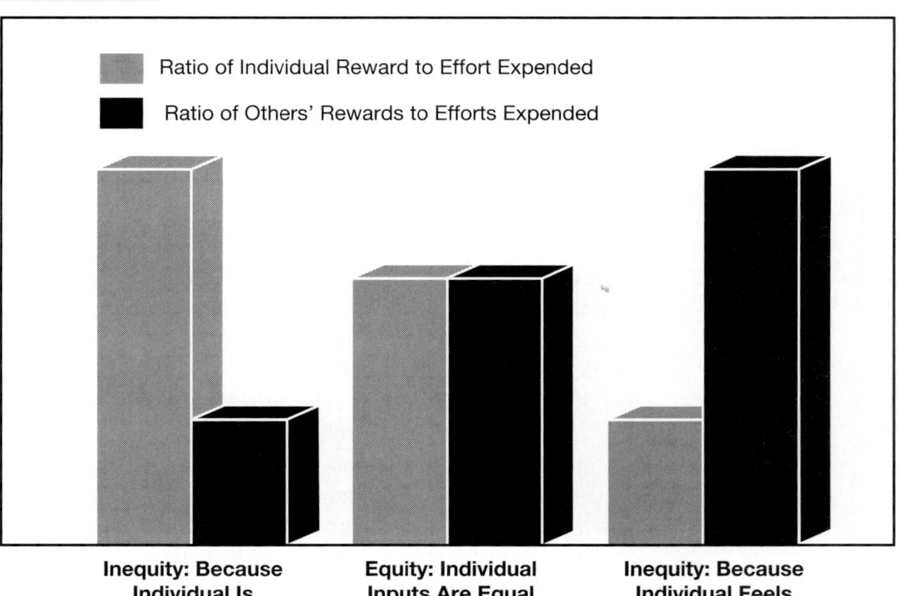

put ratios. Rewards can be monetary or nonmonetary, such as recognition, praise, advancement opportunities, or special privileges.

If individuals feel inequity because others are receiving more than they are for similar work, they may not work as hard (e.g., reduce their inputs into the equity ratio). If individuals perceive inequity because they are being overrewarded (getting more money than they deserve relative to their colleagues) they may feel guilty, leading them to work harder or perhaps change their associations in the workplace.[9] In today's more enlightened workplace, with individuals knowing more than ever before about how the organization is performing, managers have a responsibility to ensure that individuals are treated fairly. In instances where that is not occurring, having mechanisms in place for concerns to be expressed is essential.

ERG APPROACH

Another modern model is the **ERG approach,** based on the work of Clayton Alderfer.[10] Like other needs-based models, Alderfer's model looks at three sets of needs: (1) existence (subsistence) needs, (2) relatedness (social) needs, and (3) growth needs. ERG recognizes that although there is no one best way to motivate all employees, there are some broad guidelines to follow and a recognizable hierarchy that makes motivation problems easier to resolve. Effective managers strive to know employees and tailor motivation techniques to meet their needs.

The ERG approach follows a stair-step structure similar to Maslow's hierarchy of needs, except that while Maslow argued for need prepotency, Alderfer believed that multiple needs could be addressed at the same time. The existence (E) needs include material and physical needs, and must be relatively satisfied; if frustrated, the E needs will be more important. The relatedness (R) needs are the next step up in the hierarchy and involve relationships with other people; if they are not relatively satisfied, both the R and E needs are important. Growth (G) needs include creative efforts and are the pinnacle of needs; if they are not relatively satisfied, they will be greatly desired. Thus, real motivation is based on growth, not existence or even relatedness.[11] ERG theory has a stronger base of empirical support than does Maslow's theory and is somewhat more advanced in terms of its view of the complex process of need-based motivation.[12]

OTHER MOTIVATIONAL PROCESSES

Considerable research has been done on other specific needs that affect motivation, including achievement, affiliation, and power. The achievement approach holds that a person's performance is a function of the strength of that individual's need for achievement. The affiliation approach measures the need to be with other people in meaningful relationships including business. The power approach measures the need for control and influence over others.

Another type of motivation is *tensional* or *deficiency motivation.* In essence, Freud's approach is a tensional or "a-deficiency-must-exist-before-you-can-have-a-motivating-situation" approach. *Hedonistic motivation* is another type. The hedonists believe that an individual will try to attain or maintain a pleasant state, and strive to change or leave an unpleasant state: If it feels good, do it; if it hurts, don't do it.

Versions of the *management-by-objectives/results* method (MBO) are widely practiced in industry today. In MBO the supervisor and the employee together develop realistic goals for the employee to accomplish by some future date, usually 6 months to a year; emphasis is then placed on results. The employee's next review focuses on how well he or she has met the mutually agreed-upon goals. Current performance management initiatives in many companies use an MBO-like approach to link corporate objectives with individual performance goals, and tie employee and work unit compensation plans to those agreed-upon performance levels.

INCENTIVES

THE NATURE OF INCENTIVES

What is an incentive? An **incentive** is anything other than the job itself that motivates employees to perform. Incentive systems assume people must be persuaded, rewarded, pushed, punished, or otherwise externally encouraged to take action.

Some past incentives have become today's rights.

Most managers believe rewards are incentives to work harder to achieve organizational goals. However, many of these incentive schemes have become a source of frustration because they have not increased output consistently. One reason for this disappointing state of affairs can be explained by Maslow's principle: A need that is satisfied ceases to motivate. Employees adjust rapidly to changing conditions, particularly when they are for the better.

Thus, management needs to continually identify new incentives that will be perceived as motivating by employees. As Douglas McGregor, a college president and management theorist who was introduced in Chapter 1, said:

> . . . the carrot and stick theory does not work at all once man has reached an adequate subsistence level and is motivated primarily by higher needs. Management cannot provide a man with self-respect, or with the respect of his fellows, or with the satisfaction of needs for self-fulfillment. It can create conditions such that he is encouraged and enabled to seek such satisfaction for himself, or it can thwart him by failing to create those conditions.[13]

To create these conditions the manager must know a great deal about human nature.

INTRINSIC AND EXTRINSIC MOTIVATORS

Intrinsic motivators/rewards take place on the job and help us to enjoy working. Intrinsic rewards are the internal satisfactions that a person receives as a result of doing well a particular task in an organization. *Extrinsic motivators/rewards* are those job outcomes, typically administered by another person (e.g., a pay bonus from a supervisor or kudos from a coworker), which are given as a result of doing well on a particular job-related task.

During the past 40 years, employee benefits (extrinsic rewards) have become an important aspect of the overall employee compensation package. They are no longer "fringes." In some organizations, they amount to 50 percent of payroll. For example, companies provide paid vacations and sick leave, medical and dental plans, child care, flexible work schedules, and free legal aid. All of these benefits were established to encourage employees to show more loyalty and to (hopefully) increase employee motivation.

Extrinsic motivators may undermine intrinsic motivators.

Interestingly, recent research suggests there is a danger that extrinsic rewards may undermine intrinsic motivation—that a person's intrinsic interest in an activity may be undermined by inducing him or her to engage in it only as a means to some extrinsic goal. The joy of performing a task for itself may disappear when it is done simply for the reward offered by the supervisor. Today's increasing use of pay for performance (incentive) plans may, in fact, be counter-productive to having employees focus on the organization's longer-term vision.[14]

Intrinsic motivators benefit employees on the job. Logically, people work harder when they are provided with comforts and when work is enjoyable. In one University of Michigan survey, 1,533 workers were asked to rate the importance of various aspects of work, and intrinsic motivators led the list. Of the five top-ranked features, only the fifth had to do with tangible economic benefits:

1. Interesting work
2. Enough help and equipment to get the job done
3. Sufficient information to get the job done
4. Enough authority to do the job
5. Good pay

EXPRESS YOUR OPINION

Up to this point in your career, you may have held many or only a few jobs, but within a short time you were able to state that you enjoyed the job or were looking eagerly for another. Concentrate on one company and list the major extrinsic motivators. Then list the job's intrinsic motivators.

Now ask yourself, if you enjoyed the job, was it because of the extrinsic or the intrinsic motivators? If you disliked the job, was it because of the extrinsic or the intrinsic motivators?

By your own experience and the experiences that might be shared by others in the class, which seems to be the most important? Which motivators do companies tend to advertise and spend most of their time developing? Why?

BARRIERS TO ACHIEVEMENT

From the organization's perspective, motivated behavior should result in performance related to the achievement of both individual and organizational goals. Not infrequently, the work environment is encumbered by situations and circumstances that can lead to diminished motivation and lowered productivity. Figure 7-7 highlights several barriers that can deter us from reaching our goals.

DEFENSE MECHANISMS

Barriers cause frustrations that persist and become stronger. Some external barriers encountered by employees are discriminatory practices, hostile supervisors, monotonous jobs, and economic insecurity. Some internal barriers that frustrate employees are lack of clear goals or purpose, poor work habits, or a poor aptitude for a particular job.

The existence of these barriers can lead to defense mechanisms in the individual. A **defense mechanism** is a response that an individual will engage in to cope with his or her frustration.

COMMON DEFENSE MECHANISMS

Aggression.

Aggression or *hostility* may be either verbal or physical, and expressed as attacks against the people perceived to be the cause of frustration. *Displaced aggression* can

ACTION PROJECT 7–2

Suppose you were to die tomorrow! How would you like people to remember you? What words would you like to be said about your personality during your eulogy? What kind of accomplishments would you like listed?

Now make out your own epitaph. List your name, date of birth, and date of death—tomorrow. Then list your accomplishments.

Finally, below the epitaph, list the accomplishments you wished you had done. Perhaps these are the goals and tasks you would like to accomplish in the future!

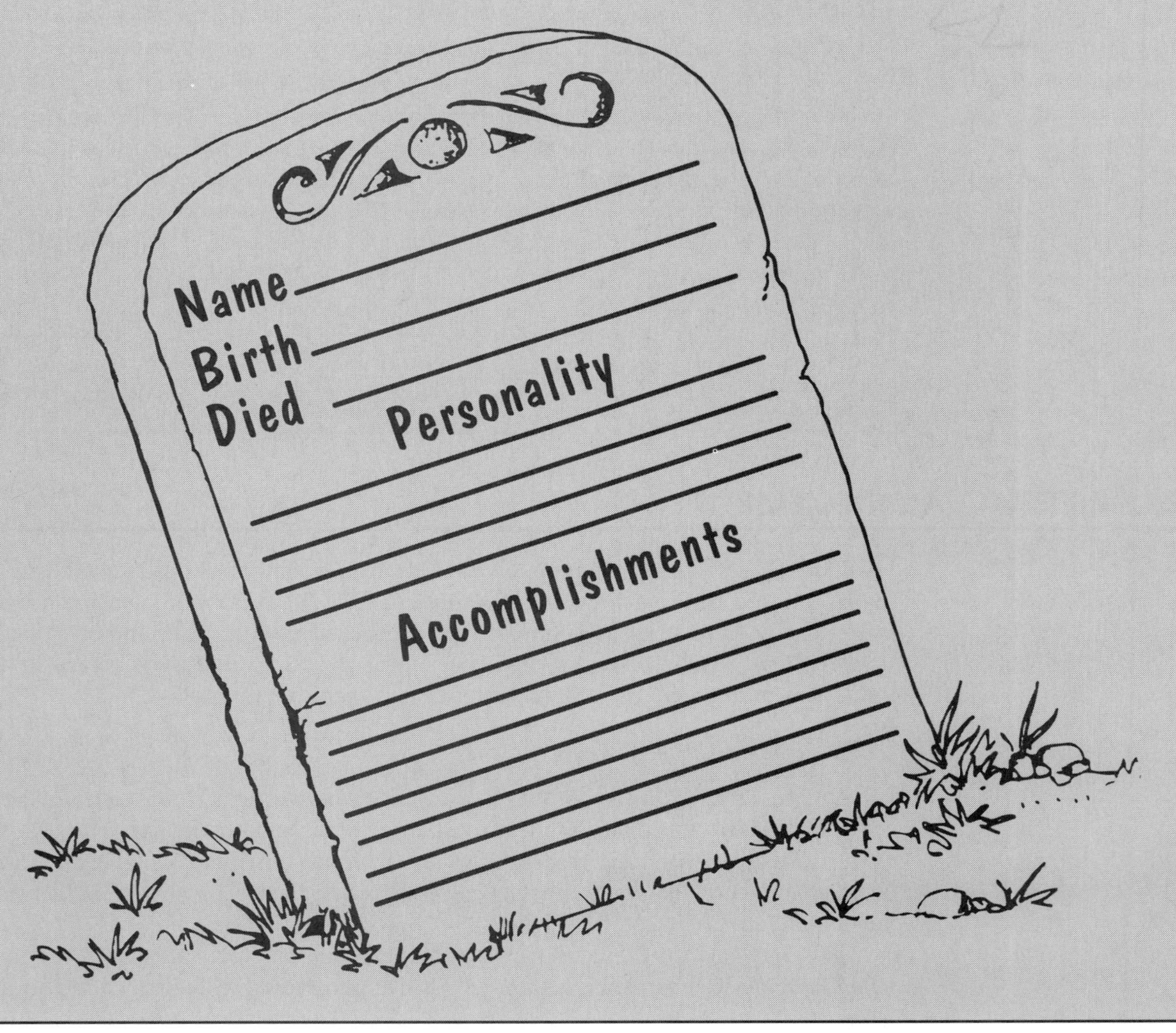

FIGURE 7-7 ***Barriers to Motivation.***

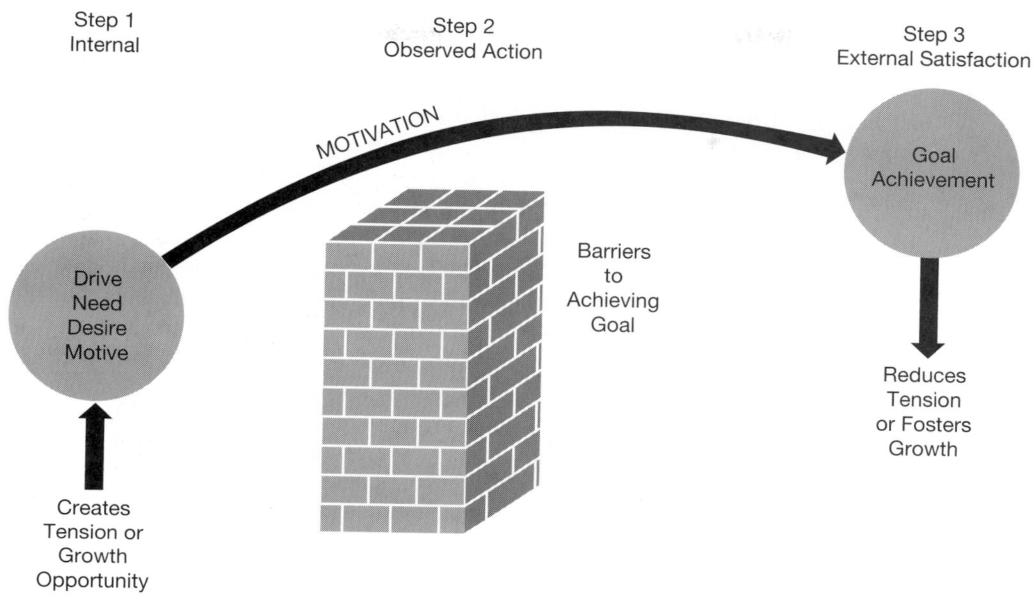

be seen in a supervisor who feels that he or she is not able to communicate with a superior and, in turn, verbally abuses his or her subordinates.

Individuals who can tolerate a high degree of abuse or aggression by others are said to have a high degree of tolerance to frustration. People with an "inner calm" are able to handle their own frustrations as well as those of others more easily.

Regression.

Regression is defined as reverting to an earlier form of behavior to find satisfaction. It can be seen best through childish actions such as temper tantrums or pouting. We can even see this in the case of a newly appointed supervisor who starts doing segments of the old job he or she enjoyed because he or she cannot master the duties of the new position.

Fixation.

Fixation behavior is the persistence of doing the same thing over and over again in the same way. Have you ever encountered an ATM machine that eventually confiscated your credit card because you repeatedly tried to enter the same series of numbers over and over? Such behavior can continue even when several demonstrations show that it won't work. This type of stubbornness can also be seen in a salesperson who has been taught to use several sales techniques, but slips back into an old, worn-out technique that has become ineffective.

Resignation.

Resignation is displayed when someone gives up all sense of emotional or personal involvement. By failing to achieve some goal, a person may lose any positive concern about his or her job and adopt an apathetic attitude toward the situation.

Withdrawal.

Such feelings can lead to *withdrawal,* in which the frustrated individual simply removes himself or herself from the situation in question—either physically or psychologically. A person who is not able to cope with a business adversary may avoid situations that would put him in contact with that individual. A person who is the target of jibes and jokes may become a loner by adopting withdrawal behavior.

Repression.

Repressive behavior is exhibited by the person who blocks out from their conscious mind those cognitive associations that are disturbing. It is an unrealistic form of behavior because it implies that the problem will simply go away if one doesn't think about it.

Compensation, rationalization, projection.

Other common reactions are *compensation, rationalization,* and *projection.* The office clerk who is frustrated with his limited education may try to compensate by using multisyllabic words and complicated language to impress others. The manager who is frustrated with having little or no authority may attempt to impress others by his or her bossiness, which is really a form of compensation. An employee may rationalize when he has been passed over several times for a promotion by saying, "It would hardly have been worth the small difference in pay; I can find other good ways to spend my time." Projection is the act of subscribing to someone else's attitudes or thoughts and can take the form of blaming others for your own thoughts, feelings, and behaviors. Some employees continually blame others because they sincerely believe they are not at fault for their own actions.

Defense mechanisms are common in all of us and are often unconscious. Unless used to an extreme degree, defensive behavior is considered quite normal; perhaps not acceptable at all times, but certainly normal.

JOB DESIGN

The world is filled with boring jobs. While managers rely on incentives to encourage workers to perform their jobs well, they can also have significant influence on the design of even the dullest jobs. Ideally, jobs should be structured to expand employee capabilities. Many workers are motivated when managers allow them to assume increased responsibility and participate in a productive way in making decisions about their jobs and their work environment. (see Figure 7-8).

FIGURE 7-8 ***Workers Can Be Motivated Most Effectively When Managers Allow Them to Assume Responsibility and to Participate in a Productive Way in Making Decisions.***

Source: Michael Mayman/Photo Researchers.

Job design includes all the variables that increase the quality and quantity of worker performance. It is a conscious effort to organize tasks, duties, and responsibilities into a work unit.

Jim Tunney, motivational speaker and former NFL referee, said: "Most of the time people go through life doing the things they do because they're supposed to do them. They've been conditioned."[15] A manager's challenge is to get people to motivate themselves by helping them realize their own strengths and weaknesses, by helping them achieve self-confidence and a belief in themselves and their capabilities. Although the following approaches are not equally effective, each provides a solid foundation for understanding how jobs can be designed to be challenging.

JOB ENLARGEMENT

Job enlargement is a job design strategy in which employees are given multiple tasks to accomplish instead of a single task. The idea of job enlargement is to introduce more task variety into the workplace to minimize employee boredom with the job.

Typically, enlarged jobs are more interesting and call on different employee skills. The intent is that workers will be motivated to work harder and be more satisfied with their work. For example, a customer service representative (CSR) may be given multiple products on which to respond to customer inquiries, rather than only one product.

JOB ENRICHMENT

Try to create a job where the person is self-motivated.

Job enrichment changes jobs to include larger areas of responsibility. Jobs are restructured so they will become intrinsically more interesting. The worker is motivated because the job is more challenging and meaningful. For instance, the same customer service representative referred to in the previous paragraph would have an enriched job if he/she was also asked to monitor the length of time calls were waiting in the queue to be answered and decide when to notify the supervisor that additional help was needed.

Greater challenge or responsibility motivates.

Job enrichment implies that employees should be given as much responsibility as possible. Employees should be encouraged to be accountable for their work with little supervision. Job enrichment includes the idea of "closure." Employees have an understanding of the organization of which they are a part; they are no longer just cogs in a wheel, but instead participate in and contribute to the entire work process. To provide for closure, tasks that belong together logically are grouped into one job—steps that one employee can carry through from beginning to end.

Thus, job enrichment means:

1. Less direct control of the employee
2. Increased employee accountability
3. Assignment of complete tasks
4. Greater freedom on the job
5. Better skill utilization

A former bank clerk remembers her job well. Even a machine would have grown bored with it. "As part of our bank's effort to convert all records to an online system, my job was to pull pertinent loan documents from loan files, scan them, and then rebuild the original paper files for subsequent review (audit). There were thousands of those files! After 2 months of this I was so bored I would have quit within another month." After 18 more months, she was still at the bank, but instead of performing a single boring task in the scanning room, she had assumed responsibility for all phases of branch technical operations. Her job had expanded significantly to include activities well beyond the original tasks. "Being able to be involved in more things than just the scanning project is so much more interesting. It changes all the time and really enables me to feel as if I am accomplishing something meaningful for the bank."

JOB ROTATION AND JOB SHARING

Change of tasks relieves monotony.

In **job rotation,** workers learn to do all the different activities necessary in one operation or unit of work. Teams that are used to working together adapt well to the rotation method. Using job enlargement, monotony may be relieved by rotating similarly meaningless tasks, but this does not help to make the job more significant. However, it is also possible to arrange for job enrichment, where both routine and complex tasks are passed around and new skills must be applied to each job in the operation.

As noted in the earlier discussion relating to job stress (Chapter 4), **job sharing** allows individuals who have time constraints, because of other work, home, or school responsibilities, to be productive for their organizations by dividing a job usually held by one individual into jobs held by two or more employees. The ultimate purpose of job design efforts is to improve performance and quality of work life.

DELEGATION

Delegation of authority is a motivator.

Another way to satisfy the needs for achievement, recognition, and responsibility is to give employees a task and the authority to carry it out. Authority is one of the most important positive motivators delegated to employees by supervisors. With authority, employees are more willing to take on new challenges. Not all supervisors are eager to delegate authority or responsibility to subordinates, despite today's emphasis on employee empowerment. To them, delegation is seen as an abdication of their responsibility as a supervisor.

Delegation of authority—used by transformational leaders—is examined along with leadership in Chapter 11. Managers should look for new ways in which to expand, rather than limit, subordinates' scope of activities. One company that does try new methods is 3M. 3M allows its scientists to pursue their own creative ideas. They are expected to come up with new products as part of their ongoing responsibilities, rather than being directed to do so by management.

FLEXIBILITY GIVES SELF-DIRECTION

Firms such as General Foods and Motorola banished time clocks years ago. Other companies have staggered the working hours to best fit employee needs. One company has five shifts starting every 15 minutes. The morning shifts start at 8:00, 8:15, 8:30, 8:45, and 9:00 A.M. The evening shifts end at 4:00, 4:15, 4:30, 4:45, and 5:00 P.M. Each shift puts in 8 hours, but employees can pick their time schedule, provided they are around for "core time," from 10:00 A.M. to 3:00 P.M., and that they put in a 40-hour week. Supervisors must trust their workers to maintain or increase productivity under decreased supervision.[16]

Flextime helps employees decide for themselves.

LET WORKERS SEE THE END PRODUCT OF THEIR EFFORTS

In today's technology-dominated society, employees have an opportunity to see much more clearly how their specific task(s) fit into the entire process of producing their company's products or services. Historically, it was more common for employees to work on parts for pieces of equipment that they would never see. In those cases, employees commonly had no idea of the type of equipment that would hold their handiwork. Such a limiting view of the product led to a more complacent, bored attitude on the job.

Some manufacturing firms sent employees from their supply plants to assembly plants to see where their parts fit into the finished product. Other firms put the assembly-line workers on inspection jobs for 1-week stints. Said one welder, "I now see metal damage, missing welds, and framing fits that I never would have noticed before." The employee who sees more of the company as a whole can identify with it in more positive terms. There is a greater chance of loyalty and motivation under these conditions.

SUPERVISORS WHO LISTEN

Listening to employees motivates more than talking to them.

Studies indicate that employees with supervisors who listen have higher morale than those without such supervisors.

As one manager said, "I don't understand why the employees don't perform better." In reply, another manager commented: "Perhaps they don't want to be treated better, but want to be better utilized, and the only way we can find out how to make things better is to listen to them."

As the work environment has changed, so have many of the factors that are seen to serve as motivators of today's technical professionals. Rosenbaum identified several motivational components sought by today's technical professionals in their jobs. These elements are:

Autonomy: a high level of independence in controlling work pace, working conditions, and work content.
Challenge: jobs that demand the highest skill level and considerable effort.
Accomplishment: Because the greatest challenge is found in the jobs demanding high skill levels and considerable effort, when those jobs are completed, these individuals want to experience the intrinsic satisfaction of having achieved what for many may have appeared nearly impossible.
Collegial support: to work with people who have the same high levels of skills and high expectations about the nature of their work. Working in an environment where those shared values define the culture is seen as highly motivating to these individuals.
Recognition: acknowledgement from their peers about the significance of their achievements when a difficult job is accomplished.

When these elements are present in a work environment, technical professionals will be more likely to experience increased job satisfaction.[17]

JOB CHARACTERISTICS MODEL

The job enrichment and job enlargement research completed in the 1960s and 1970s led to subsequent efforts to identify the aspects of jobs that were the primary contributors to intrinsic motivation. Richard Hackman and Greg Oldham developed a model, known as the Job Characteristics Model of work motivation and effectiveness (JCM), which was intended to identify the job characteristics that contribute to intrinsically motivating work. These scientists reasoned that when workers are intrinsically motivated by their jobs, good performance on the job will make the workers more likely to perform at a high level, feel good about their performance, and, therefore, be more likely to continue to perform at that high level. This principle of self-reinforcement is one of the reasons that the JCM is one of the most popular approaches to job design today.

Through their job analysis efforts, Hackman and Oldham identified five core dimensions present in jobs. They determined that managers can increase internal work motivation (intrinsic motivation) and quality work performance of employees when a particular job scores high on all five dimensions. Also, as illustrated in Figure 7-9, workers are more satisfied with their jobs, rarely absent from work, and more loyal to their company when these five core job characteristics are implemented. The good feelings that result from good performance help motivate workers to continue to perform at a high level, thereby enabling good performance to become self-reinforcing. Hackman and Oldham define five core tasks and two interpersonal dimensions.

Job characteristics model.

Core Task Dimensions. The following are key influences on employee motivation:

- **Skill variety.** The degree to which the job requires a variety of operations, and the degree to which employees must use a variety of procedures in their work.
- **Task identity.** The extent to which employees can identify and complete an entire piece of work.
- **Task significance.** The extent to which the job has a strong impact on others and their work.
- **Autonomy.** The extent to which employees have a say in scheduling and controlling decisions affecting their work.
- **Feedback.** The degree to which employees receive information regarding level and quality of performance.

Hackman and Oldham propose that the five **core job dimensions** contribute to three critical psychological states that help determine how employees react to the design of their jobs. The first psychological state, *experienced meaningfulness* of the work, is a result of employee perceptions about the extent to which their jobs are high in the

FIGURE 7-9 *THE JOB CHARACTERISTICS MODEL.*

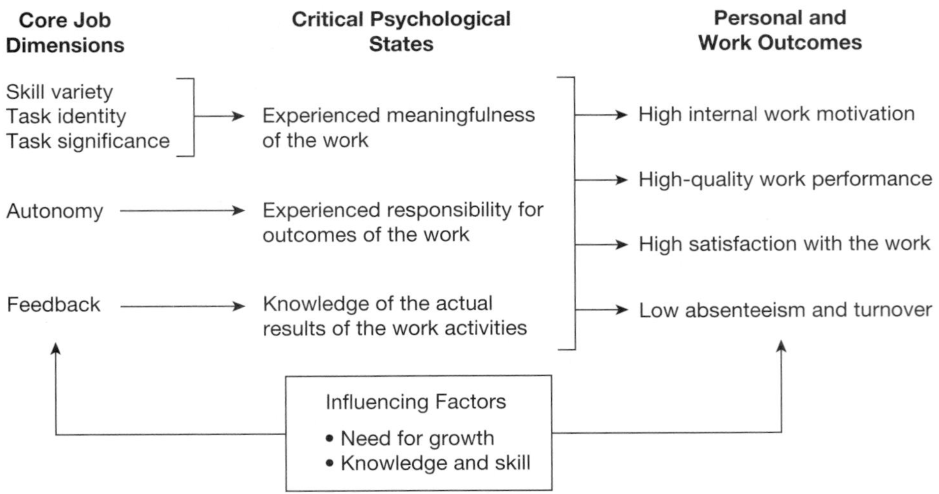

Source: Adapted from J.R. Hackman and Greg Oldham, *Work Redesign* (Reading, MA.: Addison-Wesley, 1980), 77–80.

core dimensions of skill variety, task identity, and task significance. The second psychological state is *experienced responsibility* for work outcomes. This state stems from the core dimension of autonomy. *Knowledge of results,* the degree to which employees know how well they perform their jobs on a continuous basis, is the third psychological state and stems from the extent and nature of the feedback that each employee receives.

The authors propose that these critical psychological states determine four key outcomes for employees and the organization: high intrinsic motivation, high job performance, high job satisfaction, and low absenteeism and turnover. When a job is high on all five core dimensions, workers experience the three psychological states and are intrinsically motivated. In such circumstances, workers enjoy performing a job for its own sake. Good performance becomes self-reinforcing and leads workers to feel positive about and satisfied with their jobs because the opportunity for personal growth and development is increased. Finally, increased job satisfaction leads to increased employee commitment to the job and the organization, thereby reducing turnover and absenteeism.[18]

SUMMARY

Motivation is concerned with the components of behavior and the processes that are associated with how human behavior is activated. The three essential components of motivated behavior include the direction, intensity, and persistence of effort toward attaining a goal.

Each of us has reasons for acting in the ways that we do. While some generalizations can safely be made about the nature of motivation, it is inadvisable to judge the reasons for motivation on observed behavior alone.

At least three schools of psychology deal with motivation. The psychoanalytic perspective argues that because much of a person's motivational thrust is hidden in the unconscious realm of the psyche, the actual reasons for a person's behavior can be very difficult to discover. B. F. Skinner believed that people could be motivated to act through behavior modification, which involves the rewarding of desired behavior and the ignoring of undesirable behavior. Any attention to a behavior, either positive or negative, will impact the likelihood that the behavior will or will not be repeated. The third school of thought, developed by Abraham Maslow and Frederick Herzberg, widened the scope of motivational theory with observations on the hierarchy of needs and motivator/hygiene theory, respectively. Several contemporary motivation concepts include the expectancy, equity, and ERG theories.

Incentives are punishments and rewards, extrinsic to the job itself, which are used to try to motivate people to work better or harder.

Some motivating factors are intrinsic to the job, while others are considered extrinsic. While both work, research tends to support the conclusion that intrinsically satisfying jobs lead to greater job satisfaction, less turnover, and lower absenteeism.

Job enlargement increases workers' duties at the same level, without giving workers higher levels of responsibility. Job enrichment, on the other hand, adds new dimensions to jobs. Employees become responsible for entire operations, including many levels of tasks and skills. Job rotation is the concept of trading jobs, which often relieves monotony and can increase responsibility. Through job enlargement programs, assembly lines have been disbanded and teams formed that build entire assemblies together. *Job enrichment* and *job development* are terms now used to indicate vertical job-loading methods.

The job characteristics model outlines five core job dimensions—skill variety, task identity, task significance, autonomy, and feedback—that link to individuals experiencing three psychological states. Those states help workers determine how they will react to their jobs, which, in turn, lead to the following four worker outcomes: high intrinsic motivation, high-quality work performance, high satisfaction with work, and low absenteeism and turnover.

CASE STUDY 7-1

HOW DO YOU MOTIVATE MOTEL MAIDS?

Western Motels is part of a franchise operation with 12 locations in the San Diego area. For the last several years, employee turnover, especially among the lower paid workers, has been a major problem. The turnover rate for maids alone reached the level of three employees per month per motel, representing a staggering 45 percent on an annual basis.

The maid is probably the most important representative of the motel, even though the maid is seldom seen by the guests. It is the way in which the job duties are performed that determines whether a guest will return to the motel for a second stay. Repeat customers make a motel's reputation—especially through word-of-mouth recommendations, the best and the least expensive kind of advertising.

Not only are these motels faced with the expense of hiring, processing, and bonding employees, but low morale has produced a low-grade, careless approach to the job. In several instances, a complete refund of room charges has been necessary. In addition, maids have often quit without notice, and the cost to train a new employee has increased.

The maids for Western Motels were being paid the top wages for similar employment, even though those wages were still in the bottom quarter of wages in the area. The working conditions seemed good. The maids were allowed one meal per shift at the motel's coffee shops and to use the pool facilities during their off-hours at four of the locations.

The managers tried to interview the workers who had left their employ, but they could get no useful information from them. They spoke in generalities, such as "I'm just tired of working here." Finally, the operators approached the franchise's main office in Phoenix, and a general meeting of the concerned managers was called. You were chosen as the franchise representative to the conference.

The meeting was held over a 2-day period at one of the San Diego locations. Only 7 of the 12 motels sent representatives. One manager claimed that the whole thing was "just a waste of time and money." After lunch on the first day, your group sat down to discuss the situation.

It was the general consensus of the group that efforts should be made to try to increase the commitment of the maids to their jobs and to the company. Personal commitment to and pride in their jobs seemed to be the ingredients most lacking, but how could these feelings be created for the motel maids?

1. Put yourself in the role of the motel maid. What physical changes could be made to enhance the job?
2. Personal identity and pride in the job should be given top priority in redesigning the position. Can changes be made in uniform, job functions, reporting times, personal recognition, or off-duty privileges to enhance the employee's personal identity?
3. What psychological factors can be developed to help the maid's personal image?
4. What intrinsic motivators can help the situation?

DISCUSSION AND STUDY QUESTIONS—TO KEEP YOU THINKING

1. What are various schools of psychological thought related to motivation that are discussed in the chapter?
2. Is all motivation based on internal motivation?
3. Describe barriers to achievement and how to overcome them.
4. Compare Maslow's need classification with Herzberg's motivator/hygiene approach; compare with Alderfer's ERG approach.
5. What is meant by the term need prepotency?
6. Compare the expectancy and equity approaches to motivation.
7. Explain the differences between intrinsic and extrinsic motivators.
8. What are the differences between job enrichment and job enlargement?
9. Describe the job characteristics model of work motivation.

ANSWERS TO SELF-APPRAISAL: CAN YOU RECOGNIZE THE NEED?

1. (1)	2. (2)	3. (3)	4. (3)	5. (3)
6. (2)	7. (4)	8. (4)	9. (1)	10. (3)

NOTES

1. Richard M. Steers, Lyman W. Porter, and Gregory A. Bigley, *Motivation and Leadership at Work,* 6th ed. (New York: McGraw-Hill Companies, Inc., 1996), 8.
2. R. Kanfer, "Motivation Theory and Industrial and Organizational Psychology" in M. D. Dunnette and L. M. Houghs, eds., *Handbook of Industrial and Organizational Psychology,* Vol. 1, ed. M. D. Dunnette and L. M. Houghs (Palo Alto, CA: Consulting Psychologists Press, 1990), 75–170.
3. Chris Argyris, *Integrating the Individual and the Organization* (New York: John Wiley, 1964), 7.
4. Jennifer M. George and Gareth R. Jones. *Organizational Behavior,* 2nd ed. (Reading, MA: Addison-Wesley, 1999), 150–158.
5. A. H. Maslow, *Motivation and Personality* (New York: Harper & Row, 1954).
6. J. P. Campbell and R. D. Pritchard, "Motivation Theory in Industrial and Organizational Psychology," in *Handbook of Industrial and Organizational Psychology,* Vol. 1, ed. M. D. Dunnette (Chicago, IL: Rand-McNally, 1976), 66–130.
7. Frederick Herzberg, Bernard Mausner, and Barbara Bloch Snyderman, *The Motivation to Work* (New York: John Wiley, 1959), 113.
8. Victor H. Vroom, *Work and Motivation* (New York: John Wiley & Sons, 1964).
9. J. Stacey Adams, "Toward an Understanding of Inequity," *Journal of Abnormal and Social Psychology,* 67 (1963): 422–436.
10. Clayton Alderfer, *Existence, Relatedness, and Growth* (New York: The Free Press, 1972).
11. Pat Buhler, "Motivation: What Is Behind the Motivation of Employees?" *Supervision* (June 1988): 18–20.
12. C. Pinder, *Work Motivation* (Glennview, IL: Scott-Foresman, 1984).
13. Douglas McGregor, *The Human Side of Enterprise* (New York: McGraw-Hill, 1960), 121–122.
14. Richard M. Steers, Lyman W. Porter, and Gregory A. Bigley, *Motivation and Leadership at Work,* 6th ed. (New York: McGraw-Hill, 1996), 496–498.
15. Jim Tunney, "Motivating People," *USA Today,* June 7, 1985, 13A.
16. David Hull, "No More 9 to 5?" *Computer Decisions* (June 1982): 160–178.
17. B. L. Rosenbaum, "Leading Today's Technical Professionals," *Training and Development* (October 1991): 55–66.
18. Richard Hackman and Greg R. Oldham, *Work Redesign* (Reading, MA: Addison-Wesley, 1980), 77–80.

CHAPTER

8

Orientation, Training, and Development

TO START YOU THINKING

Take a look at these questions and check your reactions to them.

- How important is an orientation program when you begin a new job?
- What specific factors would you want covered in an orientation?
- Are you aware of how much a company's orientation can affect job attitudes?
- What is the difference between job training and general education?
- What are the differences between training and development?
- Do you know what sensitivity and assertiveness development cover?
- What are two experiential training methods and what do they cover?

LEARNING GOALS

After studying this chapter, you should be able to:

1. Relate the need for employee orientation on a new job.
2. Distinguish between training and development.
3. Discuss training from the point of view of needs assessment, goals, methods, and follow-up.
4. Describe the experiential method used in training and development. Discuss how the following methods simulate business situations.
    - In-basket method
    - Case method
    - Management games
    - Role playing
5. Distinguish between aggressiveness and assertiveness.
6. Define and apply the following terms and concepts (in order of first occurrence):

KEYWORDS

- **orientation**
- **policy orientation (induction)**
- **procedural orientation (process orientation)**
- **training**
- **development**
- **learning**
- **on-the-job training (OJT)**
- **programmed instruction (PI)**
- **computer-assisted instruction (CAI)**
- **experiential methods**
- **simulation**
- **in-basket training**
- **case method**
- **management games**
- **role playing**
- **sensitivity development**
- **assertiveness development**

INTRODUCTION

This chapter discusses the functions that can make a leader's job easier and more effective: orientation, training, and development. Ultimately, the leader has responsibility for all these functions, but leaders can enhance their effectiveness by empowering others through employee orientation, preparedness (training), and development. All managers play an important role in recruitment and hiring, but their role in training and developing employees once they are hired is frequently underestimated.

ORIENTATION

When a new employee accepts a job, he or she has some perceptions about the company. The job interview provides a glimpse of the company's environment. However, the on-the-job impressions during the first few days greatly influence and solidify attitudes toward the job and the company as a whole. **Orientation** is the formal means by which employees learn about their new employer, their jobs, and coworkers.[1]

Orientation accomplishes two major tasks: (1) **policy orientation (induction)**—informing employees of company policies and benefits and (2) **procedural orientation (process orientation)**—making employees aware of locations and procedures that affect their ability to do their jobs. Both tasks fall under the general concept of orientation—acquainting new employees with company policies and procedures and with their job environment.

POLICY ORIENTATION

A general area with which new employees must become acquainted is department and company policies and practices. These orientation subjects usually include personal days (vacation and sick days), holidays, disciplinary procedures, and how to fill out company forms. Employees need to study the options for medical and other fringe benefits, stock purchase plans, employee purchases and discounts, and retirement and insurance plans.

PROCEDURAL ORIENTATION

New employees must learn the locations of things that are pertinent to their working lives, for example: parking spaces, employee entrances and exits, time clocks, lockers, rest rooms, cafeteria, and work-related departments. Further orientation might include information about company procedures, safety equipment, rest breaks, and details about pay and benefits.

Sponsors for new employees.

Smart managers consider it good management practice for a veteran coworker to sponsor a new employee, at least during the first few days. In this way, a new employee can establish immediate rapport with a person in the same department and overcome feelings of shyness and strangeness. The coworker is available to answer questions and to introduce the new employee to others. In general, coworker orientation is a good method for easing the new employee into the company environment.

ORIENTATION IS KEY TO LONG-TERM PERFORMANCE AND MORALE

Orientation is a key to retention, morale, and performance. If employees are not properly oriented to the organization during the first few working days, both employees and the organization can suffer negative consequences for years to come. First impressions *are* lasting!

Turnover can be reduced by good orientation.

Studies confirm that turnover is relatively high in many organizations, but can be substantially reduced by effective orientation. Companies find that individuals who have been through several orientation sessions have a lower turnover rate than those with minimal orientation experience. Other benefits of effective employee orientation include greater loyalty, lower absenteeism, and higher job satisfaction.[2]

Orientation is a dual responsibility.

Orientation is the responsibility of both the employee's department and the human resource office. The department orientation is as important or more so than the personnel, paperwork orientation. The department should value (and celebrate!) employees from day one.

Joseph P. McCarthy, a human resources planner at Metropolitan Property and Casualty Insurance Company, says there are six key elements of an effective orientation program:

- **Supervisor.** The supervisor is the key contact for the new employee.
- **Mentor.** The mentor is a coworker who assists in a smooth transition into the job.
- **Partnership with peers.** Promotes teamwork.
- **Self-development.** Each employee is accountable for her or his self-development.
- **Feedback.** All involved need to provide both informal and formal feedback.
- **Orientation videos.** One video presents a brief history of the organization; another may feature themes that are valued by the organization, such as teamwork and creativity.[3]

Figure 8–1 shows an original orientation checklist to be used by a new employee's manager/leader. The human resource/personnel department would have a different list covering employee classification and records, safety, work rules, benefits, and other personnel-related activities.

During the orientation, it is beneficial to answer questions that the new employee, in general, will have. For example:

- What's your definition of a top producer?
- How will you let me know when my performance is unsatisfactory?
- How can I register a complaint?
- How formal should my communication be within the organization—e-mails or typed memos?
- What is the best time for me to talk with you?
- When, if ever, should I call you at home?
- How much social interaction is expected or appreciated in the organization? [4]

TRAINING AND DEVELOPMENT

Learning and development are fundamental for individual worker as well as organizational success. A person's success in an organization is determined in large part by the education, including orientation, training, and development received on and off the job. Because of its importance, organizations spend nearly $100 billion each year on training.[5]

WHAT IS TRAINING?

Training is the process of transmitting and receiving information related to solving a problem or doing a job better. Whether an employee comes to a job with previous experience or is trained by the company after being hired, job training of some kind, formal or informal, is crucial for optimal performance. Often the most difficult problem

FIGURE 8-1 ***MANAGER/LEADER'S ORIENTATION CHECKLIST FOR NEW EMPLOYEES***[a]

____1. A genuine, warm welcome from supervisors and coworkers (there should be room for fun and celebration)

____2. Preparation of coworkers (at least a telephone call in advance of introduction)

____3. Actual introduction to coworkers

____4. Introduction of employee to selected employees outside of the department

____5. Overview of job setting including tour of facility

____6. Assigning a volunteer mentor

____7. Providing an employee manual/handbook—enough information without overload:

  ____a. Brief history of organization

  ____b. Organizational overview

  ____c. Other items included by personnel department

____8. List of specific job requirements:

  ____a. Job responsibilities

  ____b. New employee's position in organization

  ____c. Work values

  ____d. Work expectations of the employee

  ____e. Emphasis on quantity and quality of work

____9. Critical facilities:

  ____a. Copy machine

  ____b. Restroom

  ____c. Telephone and norms for use

  ____d. Eating arrangements

  ____e. Parking

  ____f. Day care center

  ____g. Credit union

  ____h. Working hours

  ____i. Breaks

  ____j. Pay policies

  ____k. Performance appraisal policies

[a]This checklist is not intended to include personnel department items such as benefits. The personnel department should have its own checklist for orientation.

in job training is recognizing the need for it. Managers must be convinced to allocate time and money for training endeavors.

The training director or a training committee may develop training programs and select the best method (the medium) for delivering the training. Such a program might look like this:

1. New employee orientation—lecture in classroom
2. Stockroom orientation—videotape
3. Reservation desk orientation—computer-assisted instruction (CAI)
4. Orientation evaluation—survey participants and management

First select the training goals—then the medium.

It is important to select the most effective medium for each training program. For instance, listening to a lecture is not the most effective way to teach employees how to use a computer program; although, it may be the best way to help people learn how chose their benefits package. The content of a training program might not be learned adequately if the appropriate methods are not used.

Training is generally job specific with the outcome focused on improving an individual's ability to perform a job or organizational role. Most educational programs transmit information for its own sake, with no expectation of how and when the information will be used. The specific purpose of training is to communicate information that is immediately applicable to practical situations. After training, trainees should be able to demonstrate changes in behavior or performance that contribute to their abilities to deal skillfully with specific problems. Training, however, implies a formal commitment of time—be it 1 day or 6 months—to learn specific, directly applicable information.

Training can change behavior.

Training implies formal commitment of time.

Training takes two forms: traditional and emotional intelligence development. *Traditional training* is concerned with learning skills and theoretical concepts that can be applied in performing the mechanics of a job. Traditional skills are oriented to the "how to" aspects of work. *Emotional intelligence development* focuses on skills that enhance the ability to interact with others. Training is vital to today's working world. Without it, misunderstandings and mistakes are likely to occur, which usually result in wasted time, money, human energy, and emotion. Nowadays, employees are rarely expected to work at tasks for which they receive no training. A manager who does not know how to work with people is at as severe a disadvantage as a drill press operator who does not know how to run a drill press. Without job training, employees are put in the position of having to muddle through as best they can.

Training is a cyclical process involving at least four steps: (1) analyzing needs, (2) designing and developing training materials, (3) delivering training and development programs, assistance or counseling, and (4) evaluating results and conducting follow-up (see Figure 8–2). All four steps are important, but too often only step three is considered training. One of the reasons that so much training is ineffective is because it addresses only one point in the cycle. When the delivery system meets a need, is properly designed, and is evaluated, training is more effective.

DEVELOPMENT

Development emphasizes increasing participants' abilities.

Development falls between specific training and general education. There is an expected payoff to the sponsoring organization, but it is not always concerned with the participant's current job. **Development** activities put emphasis on increasing the participants' abilities to perform effectively in the organization.

FIGURE 8–2 *The Training and Development Process Cycle*

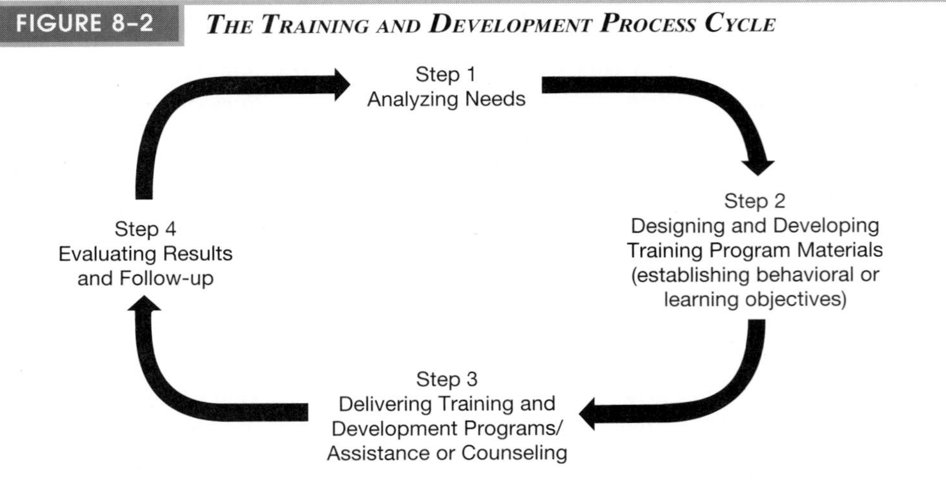

The focus of development is on the general needs of the organization, whereas the focus of training is on the present job and the almost immediate application of knowledge and skills to that job. Development is more oriented toward the future and is broader in scope than training.[6]

Who has the responsibility for development? Just as managers and trainers have the responsibility for seeing that employees are trained, both share the responsibility for development. Effort must be made to develop employees' capacities for and commitment to sharing responsibility for an organization's success. To be effective, the manager-as-developer must accomplish the following three major tasks:

1. Work with subordinates as a team to collectively share responsibility for managing the unit.
2. Determine and gain commitment to a common vision of the department's purpose and goals.
3. Work on the continuous development of individual subordinates' skills, especially in the managerial/emotional intelligence areas needed to be an effective member of the shared responsibility team.

The goal is to shape employees into powerful, cooperative, hardworking, dedicated, and responsible teams. Figure 8–3 shows the relationship between training, development, and education.

There are several reasons why managers fail to develop good subordinates:

1. Managers are chosen for their technical excellence, but they lack strong emotional intelligence.
2. Managers would rather avoid training and prefer to hire proven workers from other companies.
3. Managers are interested in enhancing their own status rather than empowering employees.
4. Managers know very little about their employees' potential, preferring to hire and promote people like themselves.

Managers can contribute much to the development of their subordinates by delegating small and large tasks, but it is sometimes difficult for managers to delegate.

FIGURE 8–3 *The Relationship of Training, Development, and Education*

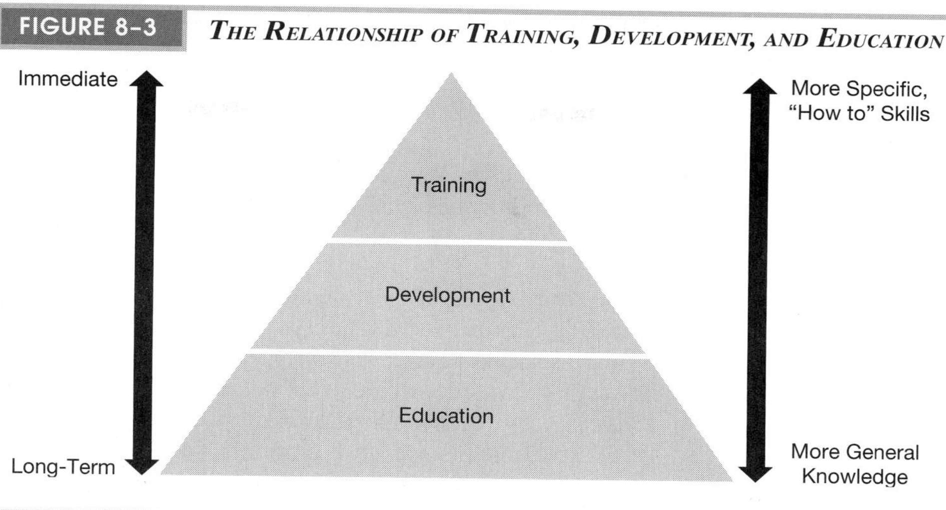

Learning means change.

One way to gauge whether a manager is delegating tasks effectively is to observe whether the department operates smoothly while the supervisor is on vacation; if it operates efficiently and effectively, people are being developed. This is important because to learn is to change. **Learning** is a relatively permanent change in knowledge or skill produced by experience. Good learning outcomes depend on the following:

- Training and development design
- Trainee characteristics
- Work environment
- Opportunity to perform
- Transfer of learning to the job
- Ability to perform, if motivated
- Occurrence and maintenance of knowledge transfer
- Positive work climate[7]

Positive attitudes from everyone involved in training and development help to make the learning process a worthwhile experience.

INSTRUCTIONAL METHODS

To instruct means to provide others with information, ideas, or skills. Instruction can be made available through many different media. On-the-job training, written material, lectures, programmed and computer-assisted instruction, videotape, and experiential exercises are a few mediums of instruction. The employees' participation in this process requires active listening and participation in order to learn the information that will make them more successful. Let us look more closely at some of the media available for training and development.

ON-THE-JOB TRAINING

Good OJT requires a good trainer.

On-the-job training (OJT) is achieved by assigning an experienced employee to mentor a new employee and train the employee in how to perform job duties.[8] This places the burden on the trainer. It is generally assumed that when a worker does not learn the job thoroughly, the teacher has not taught the job correctly. For an instructor to present material consistently, OJT should be preplanned. Information should be presented in manageable sections and in a logical sequence. To facilitate this process, the trainer should break down the job to be learned—either in writing or some other permanent record.

Regardless of what skill training is necessary to acquire a job, some on-the-job training is helpful. Without it, new employees learn only through trial and error. OJT can include informal comments and suggestions from others, but supervised OJT is more effective.

A person new to a job is nervous, which makes it difficult to concentrate. The trainee must be put at ease and not feel rushed. Impatience, irritation, or criticism tends to inhibit learning. The learner's accomplishments and efforts must be praised, helping to build self-confidence. A trainer should not interrupt when a trainee is performing correctly because it will break the concentration. However, when a trainer sees that an error is going to be made, the trainer should interrupt, thereby preventing the error from occurring. Doing a task incorrectly one time may cause a bad habit to form. To correct an error, the trainer should return to the step immediately preceding the error.

WRITTEN MATERIAL

Written material is good for details and easy access.

Probably the most popular way to disseminate general information is in written form. Businesses like to keep employees informed of fundamental company background and policy. Well-designed pamphlets about company activities and job manuals containing specific job data often help employees do their jobs more effectively.

One advantage of manuals is that job-relevant information can be accumulated so that maximum accessibility is ensured. Also, the mind is freed of learning and remembering many details when sources of information are available.

Written material, however, is often not read or is read superficially and soon forgotten. Writing is suitable for transmitting technical data, but it is not always useful for training and development that deals with emotions or attitudes.

LECTURES

Lectures can present a considerable amount of material to a large number of people. As with written material, the lecture method is best employed to convey ideas. Lectures are used in company training programs as the most reliable way in which to pass on information. However, lectures do not cater to individual needs and provide little opportunity for feedback. Question-and-answer periods, interspersed throughout or following a lecture, allow for some individual participation and should be used whenever possible.

Whether or not lectures are interesting depends on the material presented and the presentation. Lectures can be presented by anyone familiar with the information, but the listening rate often depends on the lecturer's speaking style. The most accomplished lecturers are able to sense the overall mood of the crowd, to which they respond spontaneously and appropriately.

PROGRAMMED AND COMPUTER-ASSISTED INSTRUCTION

Programmed instruction (PI), is a self-teaching method that is particularly useful for transmitting information and skills that need to be learned in a logical order. The "instructor" in this method is an instruction booklet, a computer, or both. It is possible to present PI entirely in written or computer form.

PI presents what is to be learned in a brief, logical sequence, one step at a time. The method is to present a small amount of information, followed by a simple question that requires an answer on the part of the learner. There is immediate feedback for each response so the learner knows whether he or she is on the right track. The main advantage to such an individualized program is that it is self-paced. For remedial instruction, enrichment material, or short segments, this method works well.

Immediate feedback.

Self-paced.

Computer-assisted instruction (CAI) has become the fastest-growing segment of the training industry. Although the costs of CAI are high, this method is more economical when compared to costs for formulating and delivering teacher-led courses over a period of several years.

Knowledge-based or expert computer systems, based on artificial intelligence, contain information on particular subjects and can give user-specific advice. Combined with interactive video, expert systems can be used as "intelligent" tutors to teach tasks and skills. The systems can also be used in the work environment as an aid to decision making on the job. Expert systems move training away from the pure transfer of knowledge to the application of goal-oriented tasks in the actual work environment.[9]

Advantages of PI and CAI include consistency, self-paced learning, and measurable outcomes. Both PI and CAI can reduce total training time appreciably and have the major advantage of immediate feedback. The major drawback is the cost of developing or purchasing materials.

VIDEOTAPE

Videotape is used to instruct new employees on how to perform their jobs. An assembly line can be filmed from several positions by a video camera, and the finished videocassette can be installed in a monitor or screen above the workstation. A well-timed tape describing a multistep job can create more job understanding than supervised, on-the-job training.

The new employee can watch the process on the screen several times before trying it. The employee can start or stop the videotape at any point desired, allowing the employee to learn at his or her own rate. Nervousness is minimized because the employee is not under the watchful eyes of a supervisor. In addition, supervisors can use their valuable time to attend to other duties. Videotapes can be made in-house with a limited staff and can be used immediately.

EXPERIENTIAL METHODS

There is an old saying, "Experience is the best teacher," but experience can also be very expensive if it is not conducted in a training and development environment. **Experiential methods** are any kind of training and development techniques in which the participants interact and express their thoughts and feelings as well as examine the rationale and consequences of their decisions. The core idea is for trainees to learn concepts through experience. Experiential training and development include simulations, in-basket exercises, case method, management games, role playing, sensitivity, and assertiveness development.

The **simulation** method is used (in a controlled environment) to develop a situation that is as near to real life as possible so that people can learn from their mistakes without those mistakes affecting their real jobs. Car and aircraft simulators re-create real-life situations. Astronauts work thousands of hours in the space shuttle simulator before taking their first flight. Other examples of organizational simulations include in-basket training, case study, and management games.

In-basket training is structured around the concept of a receptacle used for collecting incoming postal mail, e-mails, telephone messages, reports, and so forth. Materials that require problem solving are put into an in-basket, and the trainee plays the role of a manager who is responsible for solving the problems found in the basket. Trainees are given background information on the personalities and situations involved. Then, using their experience as a guide, trainees are asked to take the appropriate action within a short time period.

Problem solving under a time limit.

The in-basket method teaches planning and delegating.

The in-basket method has been used primarily to learn about effective management and supervision. The technique attempts to simulate real-life situations. Using a time limit helps to create the tension inherent in workday problem solving. The problems are organized to approximate work experience as closely as possible.

One typical in-basket approach is to ask trainees to assume the role of a manager who has just returned from a business trip and must leave again shortly on another trip. The trainee managers have 20 minutes in which to make decisions on materials that have accumulated in the in-basket. How well can the manager list priorities? What assumptions are made and are they warranted? Is the work distribution planned adequately? Is the work delegated appropriately? Action Project 8–1 gives several examples of in-basket exercises. Notice that there may be some "reverse delegation" (trying to get the boss to solve the subordinate's problem).

In the **case method**, a written problem or case is presented to an individual or group for analysis. Cases are intended to simulate real work situations and, therefore, include descriptions of the organizational structure and personalities involved. The individual or group studies the problem and recommends solutions. When it is a group activity, members are able to get immediate reactions to their ideas, as well as react to the ideas of others. A trainer facilitates the case study discussion sessions to insure that key points are emphasized. This experimental approach makes traditional management principles more meaningful to group participants.

Case study assumes that in business practice there is no one right way in which to accomplish an objective. It involves the ability to justify management decisions and to assign priorities to problems that are important to the company and its employees. For instance, a case study could involve an employee who was fired by a supervisor for using a company car for personal reasons. The employee has appealed to the grievance committee. As a member of the committee, each participant would receive pertinent information to decide whether to (1) uphold the firing, (2) suspend the employee for a period of time without pay, or (3) reinstate the employee with full rights.

Management games are games played by teams of employees that simulate competition engaged in by departments or other organizations. A management game is a form of problem solving. At least two teams, each representing an organization, make decisions concerning their company's operation. Decisions can be made about production, marketing, finance, human resource utilization, and other management challenges.

Good judgment is the key.

Simple management games emphasize making good judgments in a minimum amount of time, based on specific problems and limited rules. In simple games, effective strategies can be reached without making too many decisions and without having to use large amounts of managerial know-how.

When the model is complex, a computer must be used. The game can be continuous: Teams receive all or part of the results of their decisions on which they make new decisions, thus continuing the game. Figure 8–4 is a diagram of the steps in a management game.

Role playing is pretending to be someone else who has a specific role in the learning exercise. Role playing is an experiential exercise in problem solving; the exercise is

ACTION PROJECT 8–1

ABBREVIATED IN-BASKET EXERCISE (INDIVIDUAL EXERCISE)

Assume that you are Pedro Ramirez, manager of the Lakeview irrigation project. It is 2:30 P.M. on Tuesday, October 18. You have been in an executive committee meeting most of the morning making final arrangements for the annual project inspection that is to be conducted by a visiting group of government officials. Conferences with members of this team will occupy virtually all your time for the next 2 days. The team will be arriving at 5:20 P.M., and you must leave the office by 4:10 P.M. to meet them at the airport.

While you were in conference, the morning mail was placed on your desk along with interoffice memos and notices of phone calls. Your secretary has placed these at the top of the file of communications for immediate response. In addition, you have some e-mails that are marked urgent. Read all the correspondence carefully and then answer the question, "How would you dispose of each of the following communications?" Remember that you must leave for the airport by 4:10 P.M. and that you will be with the visiting team and away from your desk during the next 2 days.

INTERPLANT E-MAIL (1)

Date: Monday, October 18, 10:00 A.M.

To: Pedro Ramirez

From: Gonzalez, Maintenance Supt.

We have just received a call from the Lakeview Power Company telling us that all power to the project will be off from 7:00 A.M. to 9:00 A.M. Wednesday morning in order to make emergency repairs on the high-voltage transformer serving the project. I urged them to change the time, but they said this was the only time they could do it without causing an even longer shutdown. I tried to reach you by phone, but you were in a meeting. We need to get together as soon as possible to figure out how we are going to handle the power outage.

PHONE CALL

The Offset Printing Company called while you were out. They want you to call them back. Message: The page proofs for the Lakeview Irrigation Management Conference that is scheduled a week from Saturday are ready for checking. Because you are the conference chairperson, they would like you to take a look at the page proofs as soon as possible. They wanted me to be sure to remind you that printing must begin no later than tomorrow morning if the programs are to be printed in time for mailing.

INTERPLANT E-MAIL (2)

Date: October 18, 11:00 A.M.

To: Pedro Ramirez, Manager

From: Joan Rider, Personnel Director

Pedro, the approval came through for a facilities supervisor. Do you want to write up a formal job description for me? Do you want to have a panel interview candidates for the job or do you want to handle the interviews yourself?

(continued)

ACTION PROJECT 8-1

(CONTINUED)

TELEGRAM

October 18, 10:45 A.M.

Mr. Pedro Ramirez

Project Manager

Lakeview Irrigation Project

Too much water was sent down the Oasis lateral yesterday and all of our crops were flooded. We demand immediate reparations (monetary damages) for our farmers.

(Signed)

Y. Aguilar, President

Oasis Ditch Company

INTERPLANT E-MAIL (3)

Date: October 18, 11:10 A.M.

To: Pedro Ramirez

From: Lopez, Personnel Dept.

We received a call from the hotel saying that there has been a foul-up in reservations for our visitors arriving from the government headquarters. They could not provide the suite of rooms in the rear of the hotel that the government officials requested. The only thing available is a suite of rooms on the third floor, street side, which would be rather noisy. What shall I do?

INTERPLANT MEMO (4)

Date: October 17

To: Pedro Ramirez

From: Joel Peterson, Head Accountant

Sue Helga (the accounting clerk responsible for sending out bills) has not shown up for work the last 3 workdays. She cannot be reached by phone. There is a backlog in sending out customer statements. You know how anxious the president is to maximize income, and there is a large amount owed in the accounts receivable ledger. What shall we do?

designed primarily to aid in understanding human relations. Role playing works in small groups of two to eight people.

In a role play, a group is given a situation that requires a decision. Participants are then given descriptions of the attitudes of the people they are to represent, which they develop and dramatize as best they can, using their own personalities. This is not acting, contrary to the implication of the term role playing. It is putting one's self and emotions into a situation. There are no lines to memorize—all the characterizations are improvised.

Role playing is putting one's self into a situation.

The group works on the problem until they agree on a solution that satisfies most of the participants. Some members of the group may act as observers. After each role-

FIGURE 8-4 *Steps in a Management Game—An Important Aid in Teaching Production, Marketing, and Financial Concepts. Teamwork Is the Key in Arriving at Decisions*

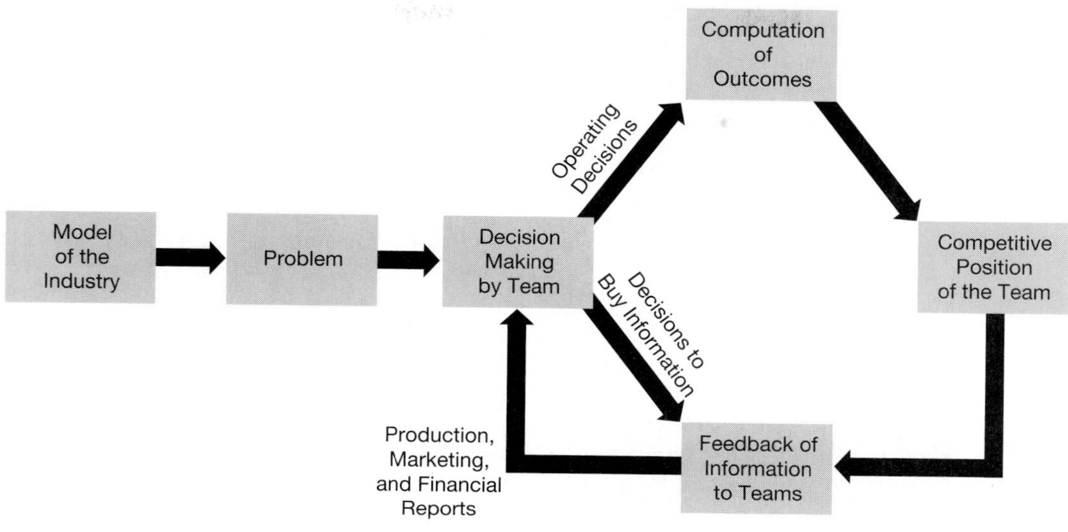

playing session, the observers comment on the process, giving feedback on communication skills, supervisory techniques, and attitudes expressed between supervisors and subordinates.

How we function in teams.

Sensitivity development is concerned with sensitivity to one's feelings and the feelings of others. The focus of sensitivity development is on observable "here and now" behavior rather than on assumptions about motives. Sensitivity development goals are increased confidence and team building and assist individuals in understanding (1) how they function in a group setting, (2) how a group functions, and (3) how to develop team skills.

The T-group, or training group, differs radically from more traditional forms of training because it lacks the demonstrable goal that exists in role playing. In this situation you play yourself. People who have been successful at getting things done find this experience frustrating and at first idiotic. With no problems to solve, participants are divested of their worldly status and authority. They are left to deal with other people without their formal relationships to back them up. Gradually, group members learn to be more honest in their communication. As they become more open with one another, they trust one another more and accept other points of view. They learn to give and take leadership and make group decisions without using formal authority as a crutch.

Trainers act as role models with whom T-group members can identify. Ideally, a trainer expresses feelings openly and honestly, is not defensive or withdrawn under criticism, and should exhibit acceptance and trust of others. Trainers display different leadership patterns, from very directive to virtually nondirective and from a high expectancy of participants to accept emotional risk to a low expectancy. These variables depend on the trainer's own preferences and on the constitution of the group itself. As a result, the styles and results of sensitivity groups vary greatly.

Assertiveness development emphasizes the approach.

Assertiveness development teaches people to stand up for their feelings without resorting to one-upmanship. It encourages development of a straightforward, deliberate way of handling emotions and developing a personal authenticity. The ultimate goal is to keep communications flowing back and forth between people—even in the face of strong feelings.

Assertiveness should not be confused with aggressiveness. Assertiveness allows you to express feelings constructively in a friendly manner. Straightforward, deliberate, and systematic rethinking is the first step toward a constructive change in our feelings and emotions,[10] and it provides a path toward higher emotional intelligence.

Overcoming the anxiety that prevents us from behaving assertively is the first step. It all comes down to your ability to size up a situation and tackle it without letting the other person's negative reactions sidetrack you. Here are a few rules.

1. **Say it directly.** It is natural to beat around the bush if you do not know how people will react. Recognize the other person's point of view, but be sure to get your own point across.
2. **Express how you feel.** If you have been asked to work overtime for at least 3 days a week for the last couple of months, express your feeling that you are tired of it. "I think I have done my part; perhaps it is time for others to put in their time."
3. **Be specific with a solution.** "I don't mind working 1 night a week, but 3 is just too much. Besides, I feel that if I work overtime just 1 night a week I can do a better job all around." Ending with a strong positive note makes that request more reasonable and understandable to the listener.

Only with improved performance brought about through education, training, and development can our individual employees and workforce teams be most committed, competent, and emotionally intelligent to do their jobs.

SUMMARY

Orientation to the job is a form of training that can greatly affect new employees' attitudes. Orientation familiarizes new employees with the organization and coworkers. New employees must also receive some on-the-job training (OJT). Even when they have previous job experience, no two jobs are the same. The success of OJT is up to the trainers, who should have a clear idea of training procedures.

Training is the practical side of education because it transmits information to improve problem solving and job performance abilities. Traditional training is concerned with mechanical and task knowledge; emotional intelligence development is concerned with emotions and attitudes. The main purpose of any kind of training is for learning to take place. Learning occurs when people change. Differences are demonstrated by changes in behavior.

Development, including management education, takes place when the learning activity puts emphasis on increasing the participants' abilities to learn other aspects of jobs and the organization. Both employees and management have responsibility for development.

The effectiveness of training and development is determined in part by the attitudes of the participants: employees, trainers, managers, and the company. To be successful, companies must be clear about training and development goals and then pick the methods most applicable to these goals. The success of training and development programs is usually measured from the company's viewpoint. Trainees may gain a lot personally, but if company goals are not met, the training and development has not paid off.

Instructional training methods include written material, correspondence courses, lectures, conferences, programmed instruction, and the many kinds of audio and visual aids. Well-known experiential techniques include the in-basket method, the case method, management games, and role playing. These methods share the goal of solving problems that are as close to real-life situations as possible.

ACTION PROJECT 8–2

ASSERTIVENESS DEVELOPMENT (GROUP EXERCISE)

This experiential exercise is designed to develop healthy assertiveness. Perhaps there are times you think, "I wish I had said . . . ." Often we are too shy, feel intimidated, or are not even conscious that we have not reacted more strongly and positively in a given situation. By actually taking an active role in a situation, we can become more confident and act more spontaneously.

Assertiveness development is very direct. By using group exercises, videotapes, and mirrors, one learns how to handle confrontations, honesty, disagreements, and questions of authority and how to develop a more assertive behavior in posture and gestures.

TERMS

Aggressive behavior—Such behavior does not take into account feelings or rights of others. Aggression is an attempt to get one's own way regardless of others. Assertion is firmness, not an attack.

Continued learning—When you rehearse or role-play assertive behavior, it is essential to continue practicing until responses become almost automatic. This helps prevent becoming flustered in an actual situation.

GUIDELINES

Keep in mind the following points about assertiveness development:

1. Be direct in your feelings. State specifically how you feel, but not in anger.
2. A good way to prevent assertion from becoming aggression is to simply restate your request as many times and in as many ways as possible.
3. Express a possible solution to your situation. It should be a reasonable request.

Avoid the following:

1. Do not start an argument. If there is a settlement in an argument, it more often appears as a win-lose situation. A calm discussion is more likely to end in a win-win situation where both parties feel like they have arrived at a justifiable conclusion.
2. Do not belittle the other party; avoid derogatory remarks.
3. Do not use one-upmanship by showing how much better you are in terms of words or actions. Don't demand certain action.

INSTRUCTIONS

Everyone in the class will be paired to practice this exercise. Find a partner within the classroom and together select one of the situations below, then decide who will play each part. Role-play the situation several times. After each attempt you and your partner should decide how it could be done better.

(continued)

ACTION PROJECT 8-2

(CONTINUED)

SITUATIONS

A. You were treated unfairly when the vacation schedule was made. The people with the greatest seniority have first selection on which week or weeks to take their vacations. You have seniority over four other people but you were sick the day vacations were scheduled. Your attendance has been excellent by company standards, and you wish to move two people who selected the vacation time you want. Roles: manager and employee.

B. You are returning a blouse or shirt with a seam that is coming loose and will ask for a cash refund. You do not have the sales slip, but the price and the name of the firm are listed on the sales tag attached to the item. The salesclerk states that company policy prohibits a cash refund without a sales slip. Roles: salesclerk and customer.

C. You question the restaurant bill of $58.43. You cannot read the individual charges, but you feel you were overcharged by about $10.50. It is an expensive place and the restaurant is very busy. Roles: cashier and customer.

D. You question your professor about a test grade. You believe you have not been given enough points on an essay question, and the total points for both the essay question and the objective questions were incorrectly added. The total points would affect your final exam grade. Roles: Professor and student.

PROCEDURES

After putting yourself into a situation several times, answer the following questions.

1. What problem did you select?______________________________
2. What was your most difficult action to overcome? Was it shyness, aggressiveness, or lack of confident voice tone and gestures? ______________________________
3. What more positive actions did you demonstrate by the time you did the last role playing session? Was it a calmer attitude? Was it a more confident, winning attitude? Did you state a solution in a clearer way? ______________________________

Emotional intelligence development advocates that learning about oneself is an effective tool in solving problems in human relations. Members of confidence-building or sensitivity-development groups learn to experience themselves and each other in an unstructured group context. Assertiveness development improves self-awareness and can result in behavior change as people see themselves from a new perspective.

CASE STUDY 8-1

TRAINING GARY FOR PROMOTION

Recently Don Taber, who is the supervisor of the auto repair department of a large domestic and imported car dealership, was informed that he would be promoted to a position in upper management—vice president of the dealership. He was told to select the most capable person in his department to prepare to take over Don's current supervisory position.

There is one person in particular whom Don would like to promote—Gary Kurtz. Gary has been the lead mechanic for the company for a number of years. He is a reliable employee and has always performed his work with the utmost competence. Don feels that Gary possesses the ability to become a good leader. Along with his knowledge of auto mechanics and friendly attitude toward helping and training the other mechanics, Gary is always willing to accept new responsibilities and enjoys working hard for the satisfaction of accomplishing goals that either he or others have set.

However, it will be necessary to work with Gary first before placing him in charge of the department. Although Gary has many good leadership qualities, he does have certain weaknesses that need to be strengthened. In the past, when Don has been on vacation or away on company business, Gary has been placed in charge. On these occasions, when he was actually put in a position of authority, he was nervous and high-strung. When deadlines on repairs were required, he had a difficult time scheduling his employees to finish the task. Under stress, Gary handled such situations poorly and vented his unreasonable frustration on employees and even customers. During these times he also tended not to listen to the ideas of the other employees and instead considered his own opinion as final and binding.

It is Don's opinion that these weaknesses can be overcome with proper training and that he will be able to develop Gary's good qualities so that the company and the employees will consider Gary an effective leader.

1. How should Don go about developing Gary's good qualities and aiding Gary in correcting his poor ones?
2. What training aids or techniques might Don use in developing Gary's leadership ability?
3. Give reasons why certain techniques might be best to develop certain leadership qualities.

DISCUSSION AND STUDY QUESTIONS—TO KEEP YOU THINKING

1. What items should be included in a new employee orientation?
2. Who has the responsibility for conducting the orientation?
3. What are the differences between training and development? What are the differences between training and education?
4. Describe the training and development process cycle.
5. Describe the differences between instructional methods and experiential techniques.
6. What are the differences between assertiveness and aggressiveness?

NOTES

1. Diane Arthur, *Recruiting, Interviewing, Selecting & Orienting New Employees* (New York: AMACOM, 1998).
2. Robert L. Mathis and John H. Jackson, *Human Resource Management*, 7th ed. (Minneapolis: West Publishing Co., 1994), 268.

3. Joseph McCarthy, "Focus from the Start," *HR Magazine* (September 1992): 81, 83.
4. "New People Need a Good Orientation," *Managers Magazine* (August 1991): 25.
5. Richard L. Daft and Dorothy Marcic, *Understanding Management*, 3rd ed. (New York: Harcourt College Publishers, 2001).
6. David E. Bartz, David Schwandt, and Larry Hillman, "Differences Between 'T' and 'D'," *Personnel Administrator* (June 1989): 164–170.
7. Irwin L. Goldstein, *Training in Organizations: Needs Assessment, Development and Evaluation*, 3rd ed. (Pacific Grove, CA: Brooks/Cole, 1993), 142–143.
8. Richard L. Daft and Dorothy Marcic, *Understanding Management*, 3rd ed. (New York: Harcourt College Publishers, 2001).
9. Peter R. Kirrane and Diane E. Kirrane, "What Artificial Intelligence Is Doing for Training," *Training: The Magazine of Human Resources Development* (July 1989): 37–43.
10. Ken Back, *Assertiveness at Work: A Practical Guide to Handling Awkward Situations,* 3rd ed. (Burr Ridge, IL: McGraw-Hill, 1999).

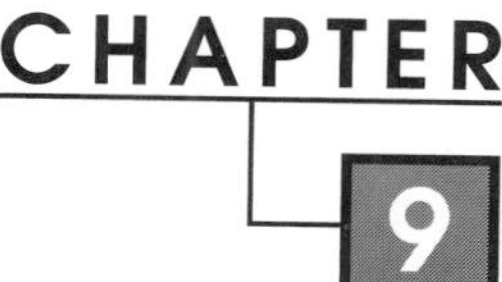

Appraisals, Promotions, and Dismissals

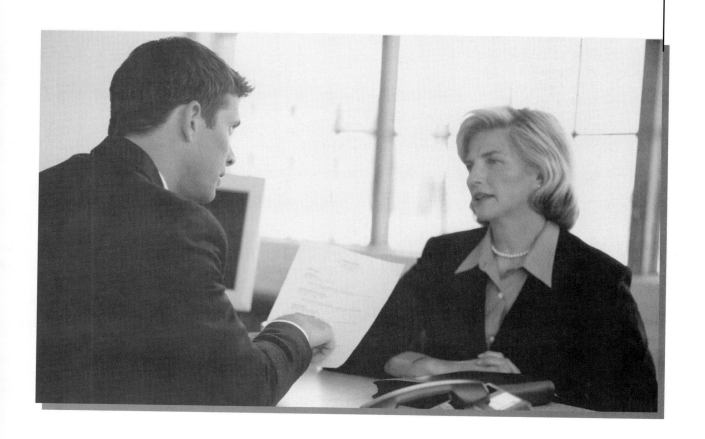

TO START YOU THINKING

Here are some questions to think about while reading the chapter. Take some time to form your opinions and discuss your answers with classmates.

- What, if any, are the differences between performance appraisal and performance evaluation?
- Why is a job description important?
- What type of appraisal is the most difficult to conduct?
- What is management by objectives (MBO)? What are behaviorally anchored rating scales (BARS)?
- What are some of the human errors in rating employees?
- What are the technological implications for paperless appraisals?
- How would you handle disciplinary action, demotions, and dismissals?
- What are some ethical and legal implications for appraisals, promotions, and dismissals?

LEARNING GOALS

After studying this chapter, you should be able to:

1. Discuss the importance of the three basic purposes of performance appraisals.
2. Describe how, ideally, an interviewer should prepare for and conduct an appraisal interview.
3. Define and give the advantages and disadvantages of the following types of appraisal methods:
   - Graphic rating scale
   - Critical incident behavior
   - Essay
   - Field review
   - Ranking
   - Management by objectives (MBO)
   - Self-evaluation
   - Behaviorally anchored rating scales (BARS)
4. Discuss the following errors that supervisors make when appraising employees:
   - Halo effect
   - Personal bias
   - Central tendency
   - Recency bias
5. Discuss the difference between merit and ability promotions.
6. Describe how to handle demotions and firings.

7. Discuss the increasing importance of benefits in establishing better employee—employer relationships.
8. Define and apply the following terms and concepts (in order of first occurrence):

KEYWORDS

- **performance evaluation**
- **performance appraisal**
- **administrative purpose**
- **informative purpose**
- **developmental purpose (of performance appraisals)**
- **graphic rating scale**
- **critical incident technique (CIT)**
- **360-degree feedback**
- **field review**
- **peer appraisal**
- **upward appraisal**
- **self-appraisal**
- **management by objectives**
- **behaviorally anchored rating scales**
- **halo effect**
- **central tendency bias**
- **recency bias**
- **merit promotion**
- **ability promotion**
- **disciplinary action**

APPRAISAL/EVALUATION OF PERFORMANCE

Employees need to know if they are doing a good job.

All workers need to know whether or not they are doing a good job. **Performance evaluation** is one way to measure performance and let workers know how they are doing. However, it is much more than a report card. The **performance appraisal** looks at potential promise for development as well as past performance. Tom Peters, management consultant, makes a plea to constantly measure the things that are important:

> Performance appraisals should be ongoing, based upon a simple, written "contract" between the person being appraised and his/her boss. . . . The following attributes can turn performance appraisal from a minus to a plus:

1. "Appraisal" must be constant, not focused principally on the big annual (or semi-annual) appraisal "event."
2. Appraisal is—and should be—very time consuming.
3. There should be a small number of performance categories, and no forced ranking.
4. Minimize the complexity of formal evaluation procedures and forms.
5. Performance appraisal goals ought to be straightforward, emphasizing what you want to happen.
6. Make the pay decisions public.
7. Make formal appraisal a small part of overall recognition.[1]

Throughout history, people have evaluated one another's performances, measuring actions against the codes of behavior, morals, and values that form the very fabric of society. Perhaps one of the earliest performance appraisals is found in the Bible, when God addressed the corrupt King Belshazzar. Written on Belshazzar's palace wall was this evaluation: "You have been weighed in the balance and found wanting" (Daniel 5:27). The poor rating so upset Belshazzar that "he turned pale, he became limp in every limb, and his knees knocked together." He was slain shortly thereafter.

The consequences of poor performance appraisals are clearly not so harsh today. In fact, the opposite may be true because of positive biases that enter into performance appraisal decisions. We will examine those biases later. First, let us look at the purposes of an appraisal.

PURPOSES OF AN APPRAISAL

Performance appraisals serve many functions and can be sorted roughly into three purposes: administrative, informative, and developmental. There is some well-founded criticism that all performance appraisals contain a subjective element and that one performance appraisal technique cannot meet all these purposes. One public administration expert notes:

> Developmental systems require employees to be open about their doubts and weaknesses. If they have any fear that these "confessions" might be used against them in any way, the developmental process collapses.[2]

Let's examine each purpose for rating employees.

Determine whether the employee should be transferred, promoted, or terminated.

The Administrative Purpose. From an administrative point of view, performance appraisals are useful because they provide a method of allocating the resources of the organization. Specifically, they are or should be the means of deciding who will be promoted, transferred, or terminated. In some companies, salaries are also determined by performance appraisals; other companies use a seniority system, which is easier to use, seems more objective, but can create resentment among employees. Effective performance appraisals compel supervisors to do some constructive thinking about both their subordinates and themselves.

Inform employees how they are doing.

The Informative Purpose. The **informative purpose** of a performance appraisal is to let the employee know whether or not management thinks that he or she is doing a good job. Management lets the employee know what the company expects, what the employee can expect from the company, and what aspects of the work his or her supervisor feels need improvement. Such appraisals can also show recognition for those aspects of the work that are outstanding. Finally, the informative purpose aims to help each employee perform his or her present job more efficiently and effectively and to help each employee prepare for possible promotion.

The developmental purpose is most important from the employee's viewpoint.

A Developmental Purpose. The **developmental purpose** of performance appraisal is the most important aspect from the employee's viewpoint. Individuals need—and want—to know how they are doing so they can continue to develop their strengths and work on their weaknesses. A developmental plan should be an integral part of any performance appraisal. How strengths and weaknesses are discovered is the subject of the methods section, which follows later in this chapter.

First, it is important to seek some assurance that people know on what bases their performance is being appraised. Performance appraisal is just that—appraisal of job performance, and, if it is to be successful for any of the purposes discussed here, the job must be defined.

JOB DESCRIPTION

Appraisals should be based on job descriptions.

An employee needs to know what is supposed to be done so that he or she can perform the job successfully. Similarly, the manager needs to know what an employee is supposed to be doing in order to make a meaningful appraisal. The best way—and the legal way—to evaluate an employee is to have a job description and decide how well the employee is carrying out his or her assigned duties.

Job descriptions are often written, describing in a general way the responsibilities and tasks of a position. The job description of a mail clerk might read: "Receives and opens the mail; stamps the date received on each item; distributes the mail to the proper department or individual; picks up the mail from each department; prepares and stamps the necessary envelopes; wraps, addresses, and stamps packages; delivers the mail to the post office." The job description must be clear to the employee and the manager, so that a meaningful performance appraisal can be made.

Behavioral dimensions—individual objectives and performance factors—are the basis for appraisal. To make the appraisal effective requires interaction between the employee, manager, and others, frequently in the form of an appraisal interview.

ADVANTAGES AND DISADVANTAGES OF PERFORMANCE APPRAISALS

Advantages of Appraisals

1. Provides a medium through which the employee knows that he or she will be evaluated.
2. Motivates the employee by providing feedback on how he or she is doing.
3. Gathers data for management decisions concerning merit increases, promotions, transfers, and dismissals.
4. Provides constructive information.
5. Allows for quicker discovery of good and bad performance.
6. Forces the manager to recognize and deal with poor performance.
7. Encourages superiors to communicate their judgments of employee performance to subordinates.

Disadvantages of Appraisals

1. A great deal of time and work is demanded.
2. Varying standards and ratings may be unfair.
3. Replacement of organizational standards with personal values and biases may occur.
4. Ratings may not be communicated to employees.
5. There may be resistance and avoidance of making formal appraisals, particularly when critical judgments are involved.

THE APPRAISAL INTERVIEW

Performance appraisals should not simply be handed to employees, put in their office mailboxes, or mailed to their homes because the appraisal serves as the formal basis for a discussion between the employee and the manager of the employee's performance. This discussion is known as the *appraisal interview.* In the job situation, the performance appraisal and interview are equally important to the employer and the employee.

The interview can be one of the most unpleasant tasks for a manager or one of the most satisfying, depending, to a great degree, on how good the employee's performance has been. It also depends on how well the manager is prepared and how successfully he or she conducts the interview.

PREPARING FOR THE INTERVIEW

The employee should be given advance notice and the opportunity to be involved in setting the time, place, and length of the interview. The manager should put down in writing as much detail as possible pertaining to the employee's performance. The appraisal forms should be filled out and the manager should be prepared to justify each item. The manager should spend time reviewing past performance reports and recalling what was covered in previous interviews. The manager should also remind the employee to prepare for the interview, to think about it ahead of time, and to jot down thoughts. A manager should consider what questions might be asked if he or she were in the employee's place and be prepared to answer those questions. The interview, however, should not be planned too rigidly. It should be flexible, for it is actually as much a discussion as it is an interview.

It is usually best not to have the interview immediately after a disciplinary action or a reprimand. The manager and employee should select a time when neither is likely to be under stress or tired; mornings are usually best. The manager should arrange not to be interrupted and should provide a private and comfortable place in which to meet. Comfort for both manager and employee may mean no barriers such as desks.

OPENING THE INTERVIEW

If an employee has been doing well, let it be known immediately.

If it is the employee's first appraisal interview, he or she should be told about the general purpose of the appraisal and the interview. If an employee's performance has been outstanding, it is often a good practice to make this known at once, because the employee will more readily accept any suggestion or constructive criticisms that the manager may want to make. However, if the performance is something less than outstanding, it may be best to avoid a discussion of the employee's overall rating at the beginning. Indeed, it is often best to avoid starting with the past at all.

Let the interview be future oriented.

It is very important to emphasize the future development needs of the employee. If the manager opens with a discussion of the employee's future goals and plans, the interview will naturally go on to areas of improvement in the worker's present performance, and from there it will return to and cover the past. However, if the appraisal interview opens with a discussion of the employee's past performance, the interview may stall in a detailed discussion of a particular item and never get beyond the past.

CODIRECTING THE INTERVIEW

An appraisal interview can be directive or permissive; that is, either the manager or the employee can direct its course. The ideal interview is neither of these, for both the manager and the employee have something to contribute. The whole discussion is about how the manager and the employee assess the performance of the employee; therefore, the participation of both is vital to a successful interview. The manager should encourage the employee to talk about himself or herself and the job. If possible, employees should self-analyze their performance; people tend to believe what they have determined for themselves more readily than what they are told. The manager should check his or her understanding of what the employee is saying by summarizing and clarifying the points in question.

The interview is partly a self-evaluation.

At times the manager does need to enter into the discussion in a more assertive way, letting the employee know how his or her performance is being viewed and whether it meets the job standards. It is crucial to let the employee know in what ways performance falls short and how it can be improved. In the final analysis, the appraisal interview is a joint problem-solving effort to which both the manager and the employee have something to contribute.

The interview is a joint effort.

ENDING THE INTERVIEW

The interview should close when the supervisor has clarified what he or she intended to cover and the employee has had a chance to review the issues of concern. Organization practices vary, but most supervisors give a copy of the performance appraisal to the employee immediately after the interview. However, if the appraisal and the interview have dealt with the employee's objectives and plans for achieving specific goals, that information is put into the report when the employee is given his or her copy. The employee should also be reassured as to the manager's interest and willingness to continue the discussion at another time.

APPRAISAL TECHNIQUES

A number of appraisal methods exist, each with advantages and drawbacks. Many people are beginning to question the effectiveness of performance appraisal systems—especially the forms. One expert writes that it is time to emphasize *performance planning* by encouraging employees to go beyond what they believe is achievable. Emphasis is on goal setting and is forward focused rather than backward oriented.[3] Some of the appraisal methods that are available include the graphic rating scale, central incident technique, essay appraisal, ranking, 360-degree feedback, management by objectives (MBO), and behaviorally anchored rating scales (BARS).

GRAPHIC RATING SCALE

The **graphic rating scale**, or profile rating sheet, usually lists the factors to be considered and the terms to be used. Figures 9–1 and 9–2 are abbreviated examples of forms that managers use.

When all managers are using the same form and all employees are being judged against the same criteria, comparisons can be made more easily and will probably be fairer. There is an important disadvantage, however. This method tends to be rigid and does not give a complete picture of the individual's past performance and future

FIGURE 9-1 *GRAPHIC RATING SCALE (OR PROFILE RATING SHEET) SHOWING VISUALLY HOW WELL AN EMPLOYEE IS PERFORMING ON THE JOB (PARTIAL RATING SHEET)*

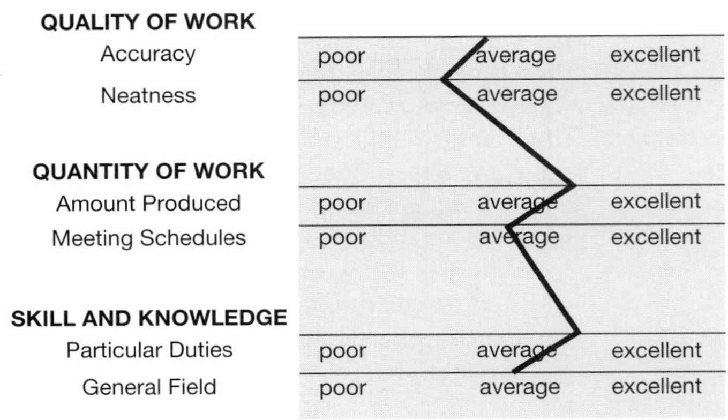

development potential. For this reason, the method is often employed in conjunction with the essay appraisal, which is discussed later.

CRITICAL INCIDENT TECHNIQUE

Record good and bad incidents that have happened.

When the **critical incident technique (CIT)** method is used, the manager records the actual behavior observed, noting examples when the employee used good or bad judgment. Keeping such records of all employees, however, demands a great deal of time.

A good discussion of the critical incident technique is provided in the following example:

> . . . a study of critical incidents in the life of a bank teller might focus on how that person would handle a situation where a customer is trying to cash a third-party check drawn on an account that has insufficient funds to cover it. The teller would be faced with the challenge of explaining to the customer that the bank could not honor the check, obviously a frustrating experience for the customer. Presumably, some tellers could handle the situation smoothly in a way that would not alienate the customer; others might be blunter and leave the customer angry at the bank in a situation in which it was merely an innocent bystander. A study of the ways in which "successful" versus "unsuccessful" tellers handle a specific bad-check incident might help in training future tellers. Thus, we see the value of studying critical incidents.[4]

ESSAY APPRAISAL

The essay appraisal requires the manager to write a paragraph or more about the employee's strengths and weaknesses, the quality and quantity of work, present skill and knowledge, and potential value to the company. Although this method may give a broader picture of the employee, it is likely to be more subjective than a simple graph or form and not of much value for the purposes of comparison. In addition, essay writing is difficult and time consuming for the average supervisor, and more emphasis may be put on writing ability than on the employee's performance characteristics.

FIGURE 9–2 **EXAMPLE PERFORMANCE APPRAISAL AND DEVELOPMENT FORM (ABBREVIATED)**

Part I Identifying Variables (names, department, SSN, dates, etc.) *(left blank in example)*

Part II Review Progress in Meeting Objectives/Standards of Performance Set Last Period

Objectives: (as agreed to and or modified during the period)	Performance Factors:	Weighting (total 100%):		Rating:		Score:
				5 = far exceeds standard 4 = exceeds standard 3 = meets standard 2 = does not meet standard 1 = way below standard		
(Each of the following is an example of items that would be tailored for each specific job):						
A. Improve customer service	1. Answers complaints promptly 2. Calls back within 30 minutes 3. Reduces callbacks	24%	×	4	=	.96
B. Take independent action	1. Shows initiative in work improvements 2. Identifies/corrects errors 3. Develops new work tasks 4. Solves problems	16%	×	3	=	.48
C. Improve people relations	1. Works cooperatively with others 2. Recognizes needs/desires of others 3. Treats others with courtesy and respect 4. Inspires respect and confidence	24%	×	3.5	=	.84
D. Improve effectiveness of supervision (over others, if applicable)	1. Leads/directs/utilizes subordinates 2. Conducts performance/ development reviews on schedule 3. Administers personnel policies effectively/fairly among subordinates	24%	×	4.5	=	1.08
E. Scheduling reports for management and customers		12%	×	3.8	=	.46
F. Any other specific objectives and performance factors	(weight and rate, if needed)	____	×	____	=	____

(continued)

FIGURE 9-2 *(CONTINUED)*

X. Quality of work (see note at right)* — 1. Completed work is accurate, neat, well organized, thorough and applicable

Y. Quantity of work (see note at right)* — 1. Completed work compares to (a) standards for job, and (b) quantity produced by coworkers.

*All jobs have a quality and quantity of work dimension so unless one is more important than the other, the remaining objectives should automatically take them into consideration. This example does not include quality and quantity dimensions.

TOTALS 100% 3.82

Part III Summary of Overall Performance (left blank but same scale as in Part II)

Part IV Development Plan

A. For areas of improvement in current job and/or if employee did not meet standard, the following actions/objectives have been agreed to:

1. ______________________
2. ______________________
3. ______________________

B. In preparation for possible advancements or career growth if employee is interested, the following actions/objectives are agreed to:

1. ______________________
2. ______________________
3. ______________________

C. For job enrichment, if advancement or career growth is *not* an option, or if employee is not interested, the following have been agreed to:

1. ______________________
2. ______________________

Part V Signatures *(left blank in example)*

The following examples from military officer efficiency reports illustrate how writing may detract from the appraisal:

- This officer has talents but has kept them well hidden.
- Can express a sentence in two paragraphs any time.
- A quiet, reticent, neat-appearing officer. Industrious, tenacious, diffident, careful, and neat. I do not wish to have this officer as a member of my command at any time.
- He has failed despite the opportunity to do so.
- His leadership is outstanding except for his lack of ability to get along with his subordinates.
- He hasn't any mental traits.
- Needs careful watching since he borders on the brilliant.
- Never makes the same mistake twice, but it seems he has made them all once.[5]

RANKING

Ranking compares the employee with other employees. This method is useful and justifiable in cases when several employees are being considered for promotion to a single position or when downsizing decisions must be made. For any purposes other than these, however, it is best if the appraisal compares the employee with job standards and not with fellow employees. Comparing a person with his or her peers will almost invariably create jealousy, rivalry, and low morale within the company's workforce.

360-DEGREE FEEDBACK

The 360-degree system solicits feedback from all stakeholders.

The **360-degree feedback** process is a performance appraisal system that solicits feedback from all stakeholders in an employee's performance. This may include superiors, peers, subordinates, customers, and others. Subsets of the 360-degree system are field review, peer appraisals, upward appraisals, and self-appraisals.

Field reviews involve appraisal by a group rather than by an individual. The group can consist of fellow employees, several managers, or a combination of these. Field reviews are sometimes used when there is reason to suspect prejudice or bias on the part of the manager or when an employee wishes to appeal an appraisal.

The judgment of the group is often more fair and valid than that of one individual, but field reviews are excessively time consuming. Further, it is not always easy to find a second manager who has any real firsthand knowledge of the employee. Some companies use the field method for all middle-management personnel on the grounds that it will arrive at a fairer evaluation and will overcome any personal bias. Peer evaluations are a type of group review and also contribute to the fairness and validity of the appraisal.

Peer appraisals solicit opinions and factual information from peers regarding an individual's performance. Peer systems are effective and gaining acceptance. Honeywell's commercial aviation division puts technicians, factory workers, and support staff through performance reviews by groups of their peers. Each person is rated on 14 measures such as how well the worker recognizes and solves problems and acts as a resource to others. One employee learned that he was average—his colleagues suggested "he keep them better informed about his whereabouts and his progress on projects." The advice struck a nerve: "If your manager says it, you might just say it's a personality conflict, . . . but when it comes from your peers, it's not real refutable."[6]

Upward appraisals obtain feedback from subordinates on the supervisor's performance. Upward appraisals empower employees and make appraisal decisions defensible against legal challenge because they are based on wider assessment data. However, there are drawbacks; managers may feel their position is being undermined or that subordinates will not be honest enough to make meaningful comments. If upward appraisal is to be effective, the manager and subordinates must have a sufficient degree of trust so that the manager supports the exercise[7] and subordinates are confident that responses will not cause retribution.

Self-appraisals of job performance allow employees to participate in their job reviews and create a dialog with the boss for performance evaluation. Self-appraisals provide timely, focused feedback, thereby eliminating the anxiety of performance ambiguity and motivating the individual to take more responsibility for performance and growth.[8] The experience gained from discussing job performance with a manager during a performance feedback interview helps an employee learn to accept constructive criticism as the basis for personal and professional growth. The experience in the developmental appraisal process will help employees overcome the apprehension associated with the formal evaluation process.[9]

Approximately 90 percent of *Fortune* 1,000 firms use some form of 360-degree feedback assessment. However, researchers Leanne Atwater and David Waldman recommend that this type of assessment be used initially for development to avoid grievances or lawsuits that may be filed when ratings are used for decisions about raises and promotions. Thorough research should be completed to assess organizational readiness before moving from multi-rater developmental appraisals to multi-rater appraisals for raises and promotions.[10]

MANAGEMENT BY OBJECTIVES

MBO has goals set by both supervisor and employee.

Management by objectives (MBO) is a widely used appraisal system. With this method, the employee and the manager set common goals, discuss what the employee can accomplish during the next evaluation period, and agree on what is expected of the employee. This method follows four rules:

1. The superior and the subordinate together set specific objectives to be accomplished for which the subordinate is held directly responsible.
2. Both decide how the performance will be measured.
3. Both develop short-term targets to be accomplished within a given time frame.
4. The appraisal focuses on the results that have been achieved in accomplishing these goals (see Figure 9–3).

MBO must be measurable.

The superior and the subordinate may have occasional progress reviews and reevaluation meetings, but at the end of the set period of time, the subordinate is evaluated on the accomplishment of the agreed-on goals. Employees may be rewarded for their success by promotion or salary increase. If they have failed, they may be fired, transferred, or given needed training or supervision. Whatever the outcome, it will be based on the employee's accomplishment of the goals that they had some part in setting and to which they had committed themselves.

FIGURE 9–3 ***The Path Taken to Establish and Follow a Management By Objectives Program***

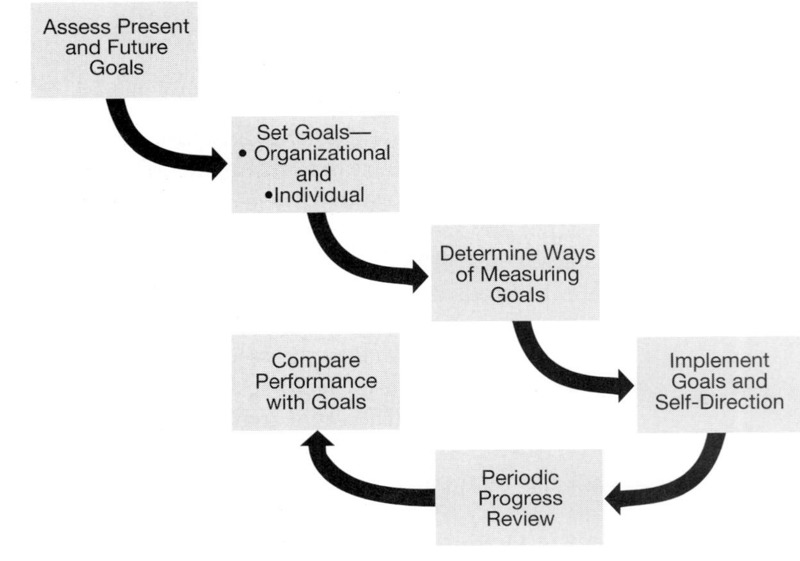

BEHAVIORALLY ANCHORED RATING SCALES

Behaviorally anchored rating scales (BARS) identify expectations of performance in specific behavioral terms. Rating specific behaviors rather than subjective ratings or rankings become the basis for the appraisal. Figure 9–4 is an example of BARS for an office support clerk. The possible outcomes of specific behaviors become part of a linear graphic scale where dimensions of job performance are the anchor points.

The BARS system is designed using a combination of the graphic rating scale and critical incident technique. To develop BARS scales, records are kept of critical incidents, and performance dimensions are developed and scaled to the incidents producing the final instrument.

PAPERLESS PERFORMANCE REVIEWS

Appraisal and employee development are now moving online, using software and Web-based delivery that provides users 24-hour availability of performance information. For example, PerformancePro.net, developed by Exxceed of Chicago, offers a user-friendly system for developing performance goals, objectives, and plans. It can log employee progress and evaluate performance over an established time frame.

In the planning section, the employee establishes goals, objectives, and plans for achievement. Tracking modules allow status reports at any point, so the manager can track performance and make adjustments when needed. Employees also have considerable participation and may submit requests to drop certain goals and submit revised goals with action steps for approval. All data is stored in the employee's performance history file; this information is accessible by the manager or the employee at any time. With electronic systems, performance management becomes a continuous improvement tool that is interactive and evolves over the course of the evaluation period.[11]

FIGURE 9–4 *Behaviorally Anchored Rating Scale*

Job: Office Support Clerk

Dimension: Interpersonal Relations

Performance	**Behavioral Anchor**
1. Unacceptable	Clerk is rude, sharp, and intolerant of others, their opinions, and questions.
2. Very poor	Talks aimlessly with clients; may argue with rude customer.
3. Poor	Exhibits poor follow-through when answering requests for information.
4. Average	Maintains communication with coworkers in a timely manner.
5. Good	Facilitates communications through effective questioning and listening.
6. Very good	Consistently provides high-quality treatment and acceptance of unusual clients and/or situations.
7. Outstanding	Always polite and courteous with others regardless of what difficulties arise.

EXPRESS YOUR OPINION

What kinds of performance appraisal techniques are used in the organization where you work or where someone you know works? How effective are these appraisal techniques? Your teacher uses performance appraisal techniques in this class—analyze their effectiveness and fairness. Discuss which type of appraisal you believe to be the most effective.

POINTS TO CONSIDER IN RATING EMPLOYEES

Managers draw from personal perceptions when they fill out performance appraisals. To be most objective, smart managers understand biases and adjust how they process the information for the most accurate results.[12] It is important to consider the halo effect, personal bias, central tendency, and recency bias to be an effective employee appraiser.

HALO EFFECT

One area of performance influences other areas.

The **halo effect** exists when a manager or other rater assumes that because an employee is above average in one area, he or she is above average in all areas. Many people attribute nonexistent virtues or accomplishments to people they like. Another term for this assumption is constant error—considering the employee to be excellent in one particular area, the supervisor rates that employee as excellent in all areas. It is similar to another natural tendency to rate a person as "excellent" rather than "above average" or to flatter a worker rather than leaving room for improvement. The halo effect can also work in reverse. If a person strikes us as unpleasant, we may assume that he or she is an inefficient worker.

PERSONAL BIAS

Favoritism to certain groups.

Personal bias is difficult to avoid. Every human being has prejudices of one sort or another. Preference may be given to employees of the same race or the same age or to workers who belong to the same club as the supervisor. Intelligent or good-looking persons may receive better ratings than their actual job performances deserve. On the other hand, managers are often aware of their prejudices and may attempt to compensate for them, giving individuals against whom they are negatively biased better performance appraisals than they really merit.

CENTRAL TENDENCY

Central tendency bias assumes all people are average.

When **central tendency bias** prevails, the manager uses similar ratings for all employees so that they all come out about average. In an attempt to be fair, the supervisor does not discriminate among different workers or among an individual's different areas of performance. Treating everyone as average is especially unfair to the outstanding performers. In the long run, it is also unfair to the substandard performer who needs constructive criticism in order to change performance behavior.

RECENCY BIAS

Recency bias occurs when an employee receives a higher or lower appraisal depending on his or her most recent performance. Managers have a tendency to judge an employee's performance for the whole rating period based on the employee's actions within the week just before the appraisal. The good or bad incidents of the last week are fresh in the mind; the achievements or failures of a year ago are forgotten.

For example, Mr. Smith is a manager for the Acme Concrete Company. The team he supervises consists of Nick, Pedro, and Donald. Nick is the outstanding employee on the team, but last week he and Mr. Smith had an argument. Donald, on the other hand, is only an average worker, but during the past week he has volunteered several times to stay a little late and help clean the machinery. Smith is about to submit his semiannual performance appraisal of his work team to top management. He wants to be a fair, but he will have a natural tendency to rate Donald higher than his overall performance during the past 6 months deserves and to rate Nick lower. If he had kept records of the actual performance of the men on the job through a critical incident or other technique and reviewed them prior to filling in the appraisals, his ratings might have been more accurate.

ACTION PROJECT 9–1

RATING EMPLOYEES (GROUP EXERCISE)

INSTRUCTIONS

A manager completed an employee's semiannual appraisal form yesterday and has scheduled a 30-minute interview period with the employee today to discuss the following ratings:

- Quality of work
- Quantity of work
- Work habits
- Work attitudes
- Relationships with others
- Dependability and initiative
- Ethics and standards of behavior
- Personal qualities
- Overall work performance

The manager tried to be honest in the appraisal, but is fearful that the employee will feel it is unfair. Thus, the manager is not looking forward to the interview. The employee feels that the rating is unfair in three areas (work attitudes, relationships with others, and overall work performance).

PROCEDURE

Divide the class into two groups. Everyone in Group 1 will play the role of the manager. Everyone in Group 2 will play the role of the employee. When the groups are segregated, each of the employees should choose the occupation they want to role-play. Some possibilities: assembly worker in a computer plant, accountant, or salesperson.

Next, break into pairs of one manager and one employee. Take a few minutes to get used to your role (the manager should review the important points of a good interview).

Now role-play the interview for 15 minutes. The manager should do his or her best to defend the appraisal and at the same time build up the employee so that the employee's next rating will be better.

After the role-playing sequence, the manager is to do a self-rating by completing Form A, and the employee is to rate the manager by completing Form B. When completed, get together and compare forms.

(continued)

ACTION PROJECT 9–1

(CONTINUED)

FORM A
MANAGER'S APPRAISAL OF OWN INTERVIEW TECHNIQUE

	Yes	More Or Less	No
1. Did I put the employee at ease?	____	____	____
2. Did I ask the employee's opinion about how he or she was doing on the job?	____	____	____
3. Did I make good points clear?	____	____	____
4. Did we clarify any disagreements over job performance?	____	____	____
5. Did I give the employee a chance to ask me questions about job performance?	____	____	____
6. Did I listen to any of the suggestions the employee raised and indicate that I cared about the input?	____	____	____
7. Did I establish job performance objectives for the future with the employee?	____	____	____
8. Do I know more about the employee's personal ambition as a result of this interview?	____	____	____
9. Did I leave the door open for future discussions on the subjects of mutual interest?	____	____	____
10. Did I make the employee feel he or she is important to our company?	____	____	____

After you have finished, your instructor may open a class discussion regarding the appraisal interview.

FORM B
EMPLOYEE'S APPRAISAL OF THE MANAGER'S INTERVIEW TECHNIQUE

	Yes	More Or Less	No
1. Did the manager make me feel comfortable?	____	____	____
2. Did he or she ask my opinion about my job performance?	____	____	____
3. Did he or she make any good points clear to me?	____	____	____
4. Did we clarify disagreements over my job performance?	____	____	____
5. Was I given a chance to ask questions about my job performance?	____	____	____

(continued)

ACTION PROJECT 9-1

(CONTINUED)

6. Did the manager listen to my suggestions and give me the feeling that he or she cared about my input? ____ ____ ____
7. Did the manager establish my job performance objectives for the future? ____ ____ ____
8. Does the manager know more about my ambitions as a result of this interview? ____ ____ ____
9. Did the manager leave the door open for future discussions on subjects of mutual interest? ____ ____ ____
10. Did the manager make me feel important to the company? ____ ____ ____

After you have finished, your instructor may again open a class discussion regarding the appraisal interview.

PROMOTIONS

Tradition, laws, and the availability of qualified candidates within a company influence whether a position becomes open to the general public or filled by an in-house promotion. First-level management positions are usually filled by in-house promotions, which are often determined by the immediate supervisor. For middle management positions, competition is generally opened to people outside the organization.

It is common practice for companies to check for internal talent before searching elsewhere. You should remember this when you are given expanded duties. It may be a method of testing you for a promotion.

Managers often need a way to determine who should be promoted and who should be terminated. A simple tool, known as a promotable people or replacement chart, can make it easier to identify and analyze employee potential. The first step is to sketch a chain of command with each job title in a separate box. Then color boxes blue for employees with excellent growth potential and use green for those with moderate growth potential. Questionable employees, those who are too new to evaluate, or marginal performers can be colored yellow. Poor producers and those due or overdue for termination would be colored red. At a glance, the completed chart will point out critical employee opportunities or problems.[13]

WHAT PROMOTION MEANS

To many people, job improvement or promotion means regular wage increases and more security. This is not always true; increased security is never guaranteed. As for wage increases, some people turn down promotions because the increase in pay does not seem to equal the increase in responsibilities. Promotion usually results in the following:

- More responsibility
- More authority
- More hours
- More communication
- More meetings

- More learning
- More development
- More management skills to acquire

Promotion does not always mean more money. Some individuals earn more than their boss and still keep their jobs by working on commissions and by other means. Most NFL quarterbacks and many other sports superstars make higher salaries than their coaches. Outstanding achievers, especially salespeople, in many industries may earn more than their managers.

PROMOTION BASED ON MERIT OR ABILITY

Merit is based on performance.

Merit promotions are based on past performance rather than on the ability to perform the duties of the advanced position. If a promotion is to be an incentive for an employee, the best performing employee should be advanced if that person wants to be promoted. However, differences in employee merit may not be readily measurable; when you make a promotion based on merit, the person who was not promoted may feel that favoritism was involved. Another difficulty with merit promotions is that it is hard to evaluate many on-the-job performances, such as that of the salesperson trying to sell a product that is in short supply.

Ability is based on potential.

Ability promotions are based on the potential that an employee has to hold an advanced position. In awarding promotions, it is important to look at the ability and the potential to perform well in advanced jobs. Consider this example: Larry is doing a good, even a great job in his present position, but on the surface he does not show the potential for additional responsibility. Charlie, however, is doing only adequate work, but he has poor supervision and the job is not challenging. A promotion to a more difficult assignment may allow him to blossom.

Walter Ulmer of the Center for Creative Leadership asks a penetrating question:

> Does your system of selecting the right people for promotion—as good as it is—do everything it should for your organization? The high percentage of managers who are promoted and then are seen to fail should be viewed as a national disgrace. Something is missing, including reliable definitions of "success" and "failure." Evaluation of candidates from multiple perspectives—not just from the perspective of the boss—might be a powerful part of the solution. Opportunities for monitored development on the job after structured feedback should help. But the true criteria for promotion remain unclear in almost all organizations.[14]

PROMOTION IS NOT FOR EVERYONE

Promotion is not appropriate for everyone.

In our culture it used to be unusual for an employee not to want to be promoted. Increasingly, people are choosing to concentrate on the quality of their current lifestyles, feel accomplishment in their current jobs, or prefer lateral transfers to different jobs, instead of being promoted. This is a positive development for employees and firms. It may be that some individuals are promoted to jobs they are not suited for or do not want, thereby putting the Peter Principle into practice. The *Peter Principle* is the act of promoting someone out of his or her area of competency into a position of incompetence. Unfortunately, doing so represents a high cost to the individual and to the organization. For these reasons, a clear recognition of each employee's skills and psychological needs is valuable to both the person and the company.

DISCIPLINARY ACTION

Disciplinary action may be punitive.

Disciplinary action is one method for achieving a desired state of order and readiness in an organization. Disciplinary action has traditionally been viewed as punishment for an infraction of rules or violation of an accepted group norm.

Disciplinary action usually involves several steps: an oral reprimand, written warnings, suspension, and eventually termination. Resorting to disciplinary action may be lessened by (1) *smart hiring* using background checks and extensive interviews, (2) *performance appraisals* with clear goals and objectives, (3) *training and development* to improve skills and increase performance, and (4) *rewarding* performance and goal achievement. In short, accentuate the positive in dealing with employees to avoid the negative consequences of disciplinary action.

Knowing when and how to use disciplinary action is frequently a tough call. One supervision expert lists the following four worst disciplinary mistakes of a supervisor:

- Being inconsistent
- Losing control of emotions; allowing temper to flare
- Avoiding any disciplinary action entirely
- Playing the role of buddy instead of leader[15]

Procedurally correct performance appraisals are important in court rulings.

The importance of having a procedurally correct performance appraisal system has recently been strengthened by court and administrative rulings. There is a need to adopt procedural due process for performance appraisal systems to rate employee job performance accurately because those ratings may be challenged. Legal problems can be prevented; make sure that employee disciplinary actions follow prescribed guidelines. Before imposing disciplinary actions, employers should ensure the following:

- Employees have been given advance notice of disciplinary action.
- Disciplinary rules are reasonable.
- Offenses have been properly investigated.
- Investigations are conducted objectively.
- Rules are enforced equally.
- Penalties are related to the severity of offenses.[16]

DEMOTIONS AND DISMISSALS

We have examined the positive aspects of appraisals, performance, and promotions. There is also a negative side when it is necessary to demote or dismiss an employee. Fortunately, there are actions that managers and others can take to make demotions and dismissals more humane and less vulnerable to litigation.

WARNINGS

Employees should be given written warnings of demotion or dismissal. In cases involving unsatisfactory performance, particularly for permanent employees, warnings in addition to the scheduled evaluation reports should be given before action is taken.

In most cases, permanent employees may not be dismissed for reasons of unsatisfactory performance unless documented evidence is available. Performance evaluation reports—scheduled and unscheduled—provide a written record of specific deficiencies. Employees' deficiencies affecting job performance that are not recorded on performance evaluation reports cannot be used as a basis for dismissal.

HOW TO HANDLE A DEMOTION

A demotion is required when an employee does not have the ability to perform specific tasks or when economic conditions within the company dictate staff changes. In the former case, an employee is usually aware that he or she is not performing to expectations. There is no need for the manager to be verbally abusive about the poor performance, especially if the employee has been given encouragement and alternatives such as retraining, and written warnings of the impending demotion. A manager's best approach is to be firm.

Make clear statements about the poor performance using actual incidents. If you are not clear, the employee may feel that the demotion is your fault and attribute the demotion to personality problems between the two of you. Remember, it is the performance that is unacceptable, not the employee. Giving the employee an assignment that is less taxing physically or emotionally, or one that requires less knowledge of current technology may be the answer. Remember, a demotion is not a dismissal.

The positive sandwich technique is bad news between slices of good feelings.

The *positive sandwich technique* is ideal in a demotion situation, as demonstrated by the following example:

> Charlie, you have been with us about 6 months now. You have adapted to the company and the employees seem to like you. You have a sincere desire to put in an honest day's work. That I like, Charlie!
>
> However, it wouldn't be fair if I told you that your performance has been up to par. We can't have so many mathematical errors in your docking and loading reports. As you have discovered, it has a domino effect all the way up to the accounting department.
>
> Now, we don't want to let you go because we feel you have potential, but not in your present position. I was thinking, Charlie, perhaps things would work out better for both you and the firm if we moved you to another position. Here is a description of the job I have in mind. I feel it is the type of job that is more suited to your nature and ability.
>
> Unfortunately, the pay is a little less, but if you can do the job well you can be making as much in 3 months as you are now. They have a good crew over there and you would still be reporting to me. I want you to know I have confidence in you, Charlie.

This approach leaves Charlie with self-respect and also gives him the alternative of either accepting the demotion or leaving the firm. Using this technique, you put Charlie in charge of his destiny because he has a choice, although you as the supervisor have decided that Charlie is no longer going to continue in the present position.

HOW DO YOU FIRE AN EMPLOYEE?

Place yourself in a typical managerial situation; when you analyze your department realistically and plan for its future goals, you come to the conclusion that loyal people in your department are shouldering the responsibility for one person who is not producing. You can see that it is unfair over a period of time for others to continually support the burden of the freeloader. In time, both morale and production will be lower if the problem continues. The solution to your problem is to "unhire" an employee.

Before you reach the decision to terminate a person's employment, ask yourself some questions:

1. Did I give ample warning? You are not being fair with the individual unless in performance reviews you have given constructive suggestions on how to improve his or her work or mend his or her ways.
2. Do I have a qualified replacement ready to step into the vacancy? You must be certain that the change will bring about a significant improvement. The potential for improvement must exist.
3. Is the primary responsibility for failure the employee's or mine? Did you pick the right person for the job? Did the person receive the necessary training and supervision? Perhaps all the person needs is a new manager, not a new employer.

The release of an employee should be handled delicately for the good of the employee, the company's image, and the morale of other employees. Recall the characteristics of positive, constructive feedback discussed in the communications chapters. Constructive feedback should have these characteristics, among others:

- Specific, not general
- Focused on behavior, not the person
- Considerate of the needs of the receiver
- Checked for accuracy

Care in firing can also head off a lawsuit that may charge discrimination because of age, sex, or race,[17] but don't sugarcoat the problem so that the fired employee is unaware that he or she has been fired.

Timing of the firing is very important; it should rarely be done near the employee's birthday or anniversary. Some experts suggest that a termination interview should be done at the beginning of the week; others suggest that Friday afternoon is ideal because the weekend provides adjustment time. Many organizations provide services to assist displaced employees in their job search.

Certainly the manager should do the firing personally and not rely on a stranger from personnel. Further, the bad news should be communicated in a conference room or the employee's office, so the boss can exit easily once the message is delivered. The location of the meeting room should also be off the beaten path in case the employee erupts when told that he or she is being let go.

Being fired can even be a positive experience for an employee, despite its initial pain. Let an employee go in a way that lets him or her maintain self-esteem. There may be other areas in which the individual can perform more effectively and be happier. Thus, on the positive side, managers may help an employee to recognize the opportunities involved in being fired and open new avenues to be explored.

Tell the employee that his or her ability and the job do not match.

Do recognize the importance of terminating an employee once other alternatives have been exhausted. Don't avoid the unpleasant because a bad situation will not get better by itself. A bad employee—especially a manager—can have very negative effects on the rest of the organization.

Harvey Gittler tells the story of an abusive manager (Jack) who was allowed to stay in the position of plant manager for 7 years because the "bottom line looked good." Gittler concludes:

> Never mind the human carnage [other employees who quit or were crucified]; the bottom line looked good. . . . It is not the Jacks of the world who should be indicted;

they are sick, pathetic men. It is their bosses who should be indicted for allowing abusive management to continue even for a day.[18]

LAYOFFS

With increasing economic uncertainties and technological advances, the number of layoffs is increasing. There is an uncertainty inherent in human resources forecasting that makes careful workforce reduction planning a necessity. A workforce can be reduced in several ways:

1. Attrition
2. Induced retirements
3. Selective dismissals
4. Layoffs

Attrition, the loss of employees in the normal course of events, may not reduce the workforce rapidly enough. Induced retirements such as (1) "the golden handshake," where an employee is given a financial inducement to retire, and (2) "window plans," where employees have a fixed period of time to resign, are costly. Layoffs, too, may be costly; however, managers can reduce negative impacts through contingency and outplacement planning. Layoffs assume the possibility of recall.

Organizations should have plans for reduction.

The organization should make plans for reductions and communicate the existence of those plans to employees, no matter how good business and economic times may seem. Sound human resources planning requires that personnel administrators always know not only what the job needs are, but also where the personnel surpluses are located. This information should be available at any given time in the form of some type of personnel database.

Reductions are determined by such factors as seniority, performance, and potential appraisal records. This reduction plan should be communicated to employees before the plan needs to be implemented. Finally, outplacement services provided by the company as an employee benefit can help soften the blow for the individual and the company. The survivors of a layoff may judge the company harshly and experience low morale if the cuts are made without an understandable plan.

ETHICAL AND LEGAL ISSUES

Employees want to be treated fairly. It is crucial for managers to establish guidelines that allow for fair treatment to avoid lawsuits alleging employment discrimination in appraisals, promotions, and dismissals. Gerald Maatman, an employment practices attorney with the law firm of Baker & McKenzie in Chicago, offers these guidelines to treat all employees fairly and with respect while making intentions clear throughout their tenure in the organization:

- Give clear instructions and warnings.
- Apply all personnel policies equally.
- Post job openings and thoughtfully consider every qualified employee for a promotion.
- Provide equal training opportunities and counseling.
- Take the employee's viewpoint into consideration.
- Promote an open door policy.[19]

When it is necessary to terminate an employee, proceed with great caution—avoid making terminations hastily and in heated circumstances. To reduce the legal

ACTION PROJECT 9-2

PROMOTIONS AND DISMISSALS (INDIVIDUAL OR GROUP EXERCISE)

The organization you work for has decided to reduce the size of the department that you manage. The decision has been made to promote one person to a supervisory position and to dismiss one employee. The decision as to who will be promoted and dismissed has been left up to you. A list of the employees in your department follows.

Rank each employee for promotion or dismissal. A "1" in the promotion column would be your preference for promotion. A "1" in the dismissal column would signify the employee you consider most eligible for dismissal.

Promote	Dismiss	
____	____	Brian: Eighteen years on the job, 7 years to retirement. Solid employee; but little potential for growth.
____	____	Laurie: Seven years of experience. Informal employee spokesperson and leader. Tends to create unrest and conflict among employees toward management.
____	____	Greg: Ten years on the job. Produces passable work. He is popular around office and is your close personal friend from college days. You hired him personally, shortly after gaining your current position.
____	____	Dale: Four years of experience. Most prolific producer. Quiet, prefers to work alone and never mixes socially with coworkers. Looked on suspiciously by coworkers.
____	____	Norm: Twenty-three years on the job, 2 years to retirement. Former productivity leader for most of his career but has lost enthusiasm lately—currently his productivity is poor.
____	____	Sally: Recently hired. Sally was highly recruited and considered an excellent prospect. Her productivity has been way below standards and expectations. She has had problems adjusting to coworkers.

On what basis did you make your rankings? Compare your individual rankings with others in your group.

Your Individual Ranking for			Group Ranking for	
Promotion	Dismissal		Promotion	Dismissal
____	____	Brian	____	____
____	____	Laurie	____	____
____	____	Greg	____	____
____	____	Dale	____	____
____	____	Norm	____	____
____	____	Sally	____	____

problems associated with firing a worker for poor performance, be sure you can provide adequate answers to the following questions:

- Do we have all the pertinent facts?
- Was the investigation fair and objective?
- Did the employee know the job expectations?
- Did the employee have a fair and reasonable opportunity to improve job performance?
- Is there any possible alternative to firing the employee that is more appropriate and fair?
- Have we treated other employees in similar situations in a consistent fashion?[20]

By taking these issues into consideration, managers can establish a climate of trust where employee perception of treatment is one of fairness.

SUMMARY

Performance is important in performance appraisal—personality idiosyncrasies are not. Performance appraisals serve many purposes. They let management know the quality of the company's personnel, they compel managers to think constructively about subordinates and about themselves, and they inform the employee of what management thinks about the job that he or she is doing.

There are several types of appraisal methods. The graphic rating scale is a form listing a number of performance factors; the supervisor states on the form whether the employee is poor, average, or excellent in a number of performance areas. In the critical incident technique, the manager keeps track of incidents and examples as they occur. The essay appraisal requires the manager to write a paragraph about the employee's performance. Ranking is a method whereby the employee is compared with fellow employees. The 360-degree feedback system solicits appraisals of an employee's performance from all stakeholders including bosses, peers, subordinates, customers, and suppliers. Management by objectives (MBO) places emphasis on the employee's goals and the methods whereby those goals can be achieved. An appraisal using behaviorally anchored rating scales (BARS) measures performance against predetermined standards that have been set mutually by manager and subordinate. Some organizations have gone to electronic, paperless appraisal systems that support a continuous improvement program.

When appraising employees, the supervisor must be careful to avoid biases. With the halo effect, a boss assumes that because an employee is outstanding in one particular field, the employee is outstanding in other ways too. Another bias involves placing too much emphasis on recent behavior.

Tradition, laws, and the availability of internal candidates influence whether a position is opened to the general public or someone is promoted from within the company. Some promotions are based on merit and ability; others are based on seniority.

Disciplinary action, demotions, and dismissals can usually be made only after oral and written warnings have been issued. Written warnings of substandard performance should be given before recommending a demotion or a dismissal. Before firing an employee, managers must think of the employee, the department, the company, and themselves as supervisors. If supervisors don't release an incompetent worker, they are failing themselves, their department, and the company. Planning for layoffs and employing outplacement counselors can reduce the trauma associated with cutbacks for both those who are dismissed and the "survivors."

CASE STUDY 9-1

PROMOTION BASED ON SUPERVISORY CHARACTERISTICS

You are asked by your superior to recommend someone in your department to supervise a staff of 10 salespersons. You think of three people in the department and you consider their backgrounds. Which person would you choose? What characteristics (either demonstrated or inferred) will help you make the choice?

John McVean has been a sales representative for 5 years and shows initiative and drive. He is friendly, loves to tell stories, and is basically easy to understand. He has exceeded his sales quota for the last 4 years. The major disadvantage is that he is overly aggressive. Fellow salespeople have recently complained about his aggressiveness or rudeness in front of customers, and customers have complained about John's inability to deliver what he promises.

Kathy Crevier, a sales representative for 3 years, is very personable and outgoing and tends to be the life of the party when she is in a group. However, when discussing business with you, she tends to become quiet and reserved. Her contribution to the discussion is often limited and you wonder if you are doing something wrong. Kathy's sales record is outstanding and her peers believe that she is a valuable member of the crew.

Bob Koyne has been with the company for 7 years. The last 6 years have been outstanding sales years. Bob, in contrast to John and Kathy, is a steady, quiet producer. He is a "team man" in his conversations with you, but he feels uncomfortable when the discussion turns to him as an individual.

1. How do you feel the new supervisor should relate to the employees?
2. Is it important for a first-line supervisor to have technical competence?
3. Does the fact that a first-line supervisor has initiative and drive have any effect on subordinates?
4. Is emotional stability important for a supervisor? Why?

DISCUSSION AND STUDY QUESTIONS—TO KEEP YOU THINKING

1. What are the purposes of performance appraisals? Can one instrument effectively serve more than one purpose? Explain.
2. Describe the various methods and types of performance appraisals.
3. Describe the types of biases that may occur in rating employees.
4. Explain why probationary employees should be evaluated frequently.
5. What are the best ways to be promoted in most organizations? Is it all right to earn more than the boss?
6. What are effective ways to demote and dismiss individuals?

NOTES

1. Tom Peters, *Thriving on Chaos: Handbook for a Management Revolution* (New York: Alfred A. Knopf, 1988), 494–498.
2. Dennis M. Daley, "Performance Appraisal as an Aid in Personnel Decisions: Linkages Between Techniques and Purposes in North Carolina Municipalities," *American Review of Public Administration* (September 1993): 211.
3. William Fitzgerald, "Forget the Form in Performance Appraisal," *HR Magazine* (December 1995): 134, 136.
4. David P. Campbell, "Inklings," *Issues & Observations*, published by the Center for Creative Leadership, Greensboro, NC (fourth quarter 1993): 10.
5. David P. Campbell, "Inklings," *Issues & Observations*, published by the Center for Creative Leadership, Greensboro, NC (fourth quarter 1992): 8.
6. Richard J. Newman, "Job Reviews Go Full Circle: It's No Longer Just the Boss Who Gets to Judge How Well You're Performing," *U.S. News & World Report* (November 1, 1993): 97.
7. Clive Fletcher, "Appraisal: An Idea Whose Time Has Gone?" *Personnel Management* (September 1993): 36–37.
8. John W. Lawrie, "Your Performance: Appraise It Yourself!" *Personnel* (January 1989): 21–23.
9. G. Stephen Taylor, Carol Lehman, and Connie Forde, "How Employee Self-Appraisals Can Help," *Supervisory Management* (August 1989): 32–41.
10. Leanne Atwater and David Waldman, "Accountability in 360 Degree Feedback," *HR Magazine* (May 1998): 96–98.
11. Gary Meyer, "Performance Reviews Made Easy, Paperless," *HR Magazine* (October 2000): 181–184.
12. Nancy Day, "Can Performance Raters Be More Accurate?" *Journal of Managerial Issues* (fall 1995): 323–342.
13. Charles H. Gray, "Charting Your Employees' Potential," *Management World* (May–June 1988): 11–12.
14. Walter F. Ulmer Jr., "Inside View," *Issues & Observations*, published by the Center for Creative Leadership, Greensboro, NC (fourth quarter 1992): 8.
15. Gary Bielous, "The Five Worst Discipline Mistakes," *Supervisory Management* (January 1995): 14–16.
16. Kenneth R. Gilberg, David McCarthy, and Jacqueline Shulman, "Disciplinary Guidelines," *Supervisory Management* (July 1989): 16–17.
17. Robert A. Mamis, "Employees from Hell," *Inc.* (January 1995): 50–57. Also, Cameron D. Reynolds and Morgan D. Reynolds, "State Court Restrictions on the Employment-at-Will Doctrine," *Regulation* (first quarter 1995): 57–66.
18. Harvey Gittler, "Free at Last, Free at Last," *The Wall Street Journal,* March 1, 1993, A14.
19. Timothy Paul, "Avoiding a Leading D&O Claim: Employee Termination Disputes," *American Society of Association Executives, Association Management* (1999): 61–63, web.lexis-nexis.com/.
20. Ibid.

CHAPTER

10

Conflict Management and Negotiations

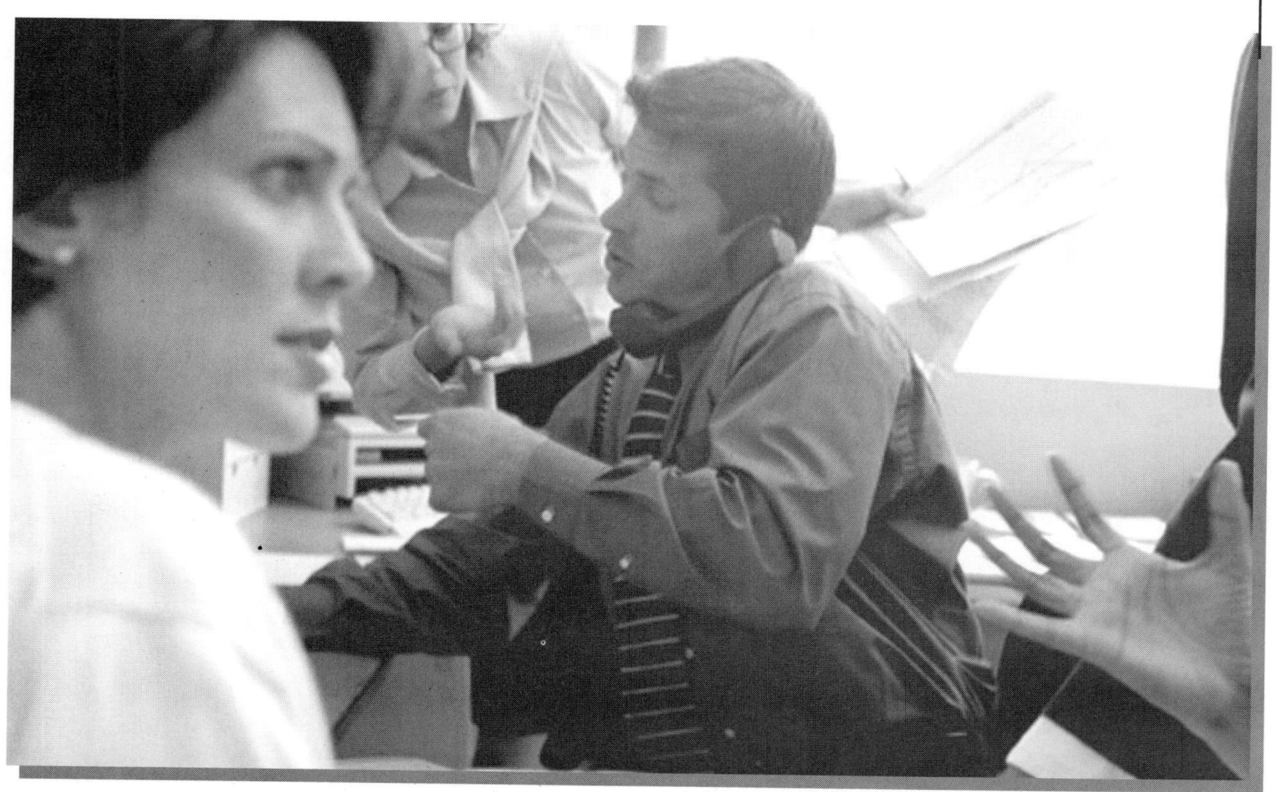

TO START YOU THINKING

Here are some questions that may stimulate your thinking about conflict management and conflict resolution in organizations and in your own life. The answers will be found in the readings and from your personal experiences and opinions.

- What is conflict?
- Is conflict always part of personal and business relationships?
- When I win, does it mean that someone else has to lose?
- What causes conflict? Can it be avoided or just managed?
- Is conflict always bad?

LEARNING GOALS

After studying this chapter, you should be able to:

1. Identify the three levels of conflict exploration.
2. Distinguish between cognitive and affective conflict.
3. Explain the conflict paradox.
4. Discuss what causes conflict in organizations.
5. Identify the role of goals in conflict management.
6. Articulate strategies for effective conflict management.
7. Identify key principles of effective negotiations.
8. Discuss when conflict is good for an organization. When is it bad?
9. Define and apply the following terms and concepts (in order of first occurrence):

KEYWORDS

- **intrapersonal conflict**
- **interpersonal conflict**
- **environmental context**
- **cooperative conflict theory**
- **functional conflict**
- **dysfunctional conflict**
- **C-type conflict**
- **A-type conflict**
- **conflict paradox**
- **principled negotiation**

CONFLICT MANAGEMENT AND NEGOTIATIONS

No organization runs so smoothly that disagreements don't occasionally come into play. Conflict can occur over work unit goals, job assignments, strategy to achieve goals, compensation, and a myriad of other factors. When this happens, what is the manager's role in helping to resolve the issues and get the unit moving ahead? What are some underlying principles of conflict, conflict management, and negotiation? What are some specific strategies for moving individuals past the problem and toward a more productive work environment?

This chapter will consider the essential elements of conflict in organizations, focusing particularly on the causes of conflict, the impact of conflict in organizations, and the distinction between cognitive and affective conflict. In addition, it discusses negotiation and conflict resolution strategies that improve work unit performance and interpersonal relationships. The discussion of the key principles of conflict will focus students' attention on the complex interdependencies associated with understanding and managing conflict in the work environment. We will explore the multiple roles that both managers and employees may assume in their efforts to address conflict.

WHAT IS CONFLICT?

INTRAPERSONAL CONFLICT

A common definition of *conflict* is that it is a process, involving two or more parties, in which one party perceives that its interests are being opposed or negatively affected by another party. The study of conflict may be undertaken at several different levels. The first level of consideration is at the intrapersonal or within-self level. It is easy to see that individuals may have internally competing values, interests, priorities, and roles as they go about their daily activities. Each of us may be, at any moment, an employee, a friend, a sibling, a parent, a child, a spouse, or an employer. Each of these different roles have their own sets of expectations. Each role may produce competing demands that have significant potential to create conflict within an individual as he or she attempts to reconcile those demands.

For example, many people want to improve their lives by advancing their careers or getting a different job that has a better schedule, better location, more opportunity for advancement, or more money and benefits. These individuals feel the need to engage in activities that will lead to accomplishing their goals. Strategies that can help the individual achieve a better job include working harder, working longer hours, or getting additional education (at night, on weekends, or online) while continuing to work. At the same, however, the individual may feel pressure to spend more time with friends and family, or to pursue hobbies and favorite recreational activities. These competing demands and expectations can frequently lead to significant internal conflict. This issue of work-life balance is one that is receiving increased attention in organizations today.

INTERPERSONAL CONFLICT

Conflict may also be considered from the standpoint of relationships between individuals, between groups, and between an individual and a group. This **interpersonal conflict** is common within organizations and is often a function of the degree of interdependence between individuals or work units. *Interdependence,* in this context, refers to the extent to which two or more entities depend on one another for assistance, compliance, or coordination in the performance of their respective organizational tasks.

Interpersonal conflict can result from several factors, including competition for scarce resources or rewards, different goals, desire for autonomy, and differences in value structures between individuals and/or work units in and between organizations. In some cases, conflict is precipitated by the desire of one individual or group to dominate another individual or group. The more that performance criteria and performance rewards are evaluated on a micro, rather than a macro level, the greater the likelihood that conflict between departments will occur. Perceptions of uneven distribution of resources (e.g., raw materials, manpower, facilities, support personnel, etc.) can also contribute to conflict between individuals as well as conflict between organizational units.[1]

CAUSES OF CONFLICT

INDIVIDUAL CHARACTERISTICS

Our consideration of the causes of conflict begins with a look at how individual differences generate conflict. Individuals have different personalities, different values and goals, varying levels of commitment to reach those goals, different cultural backgrounds, and different problem-solving strategies/approaches. It should not be surprising, then, that when people with these differences come into contact with each other, one or more of them will view their objectives as being frustrated by the position taken by the other. In addition, the relative strength of the commitment of individuals to their positions vary, resulting in differential responses to suggestions for compromise and negotiation. Certainly, too, the extent to which an individual is under stress, is angry, or has varying degrees of authority to act autonomously in the decision circumstance can lead to conflict.

INTERPERSONAL FACTORS

To the extent the situation is perceived negatively or where there exists renewed hostility because of previous interactions or dislikes, the potential for conflict to appear is made more likely. In addition, the nature and extent of interpersonal communication, insults, and even the nature of the organizational structure can lead to conflict in the situation.

NATURE OF THE ISSUES

The nature of the issue may itself precipitate conflict among the parties. If, for example, the issue is particularly complex (e.g., deciding to close down a company facility and relocate the employees), the potential for disagreements on methods, timing, and a host of other factors related to that decision are substantial. Conversely, if the issue is relatively simple (e.g., whether to purchase a new copy machine for the human resources office), the likelihood of conflict of the same scope as in the previous example is clearly less.

Another issue that may contribute to conflict between individuals or groups in the organization is the relative importance of the issue to the individuals and to the organization. Exploring to what extent the issue is closely related to core company or individual values will provide insight into the potential for conflict. To the extent the issue threatens to change any aspect of those core value positions, the likelihood of experiencing conflict in the decision process is enhanced.

ENVIRONMENTAL CONTEXT

Because conflict is embedded within a larger **environmental context**—for example, a department, an organization, a nation—the historical and/or current nature of that environmental context can have a significant impact on if, when, and how conflict occurs. For example, the negotiations that occurred early in this decade to resolve the conflicts in the Middle East took place within the larger historical religious and political context that has been part of that region for centuries.

EFFECTS OF CONFLICT

The conflicts that occur between individuals, work units, departments, organizations, and even nations are not without costs. Conflict impacts individuals in multiple ways. First, people involved in conflict usually become upset and expend considerable emotional capital as they struggle to resolve, or in some cases maintain, the level of conflict intensity. In addition, they can experience social and emotional separation from a group or other individuals. Third, their motivation levels are reduced, which leads to decreased individual and organizational performance.

Individual behavior is influenced in several ways. For example, who hasn't seen someone lose his or her temper at work? Emotional outbursts are common behavioral manifestations of conflict. In addition, individuals who are in conflict with organizational decisions tend to have a lower commitment to implementing those decisions. Consequently, they may perform at a lower level or withdraw entirely.

Conflict in organizations may influence the structure of the organization or department. For example, leadership may be changed, reporting relationships may shift, and resources may be reallocated. On some occasions the organization may tend to increase its focus on its core activities, withdrawing from more complex and conflict-generating activities. The opposite also may occur—the organization may choose to extend its activities into new and different arenas resulting in a change in the status quo, precipitating resistance and increasing conflict within the organization.

As conflict progresses, issues tend to become more complex. Additional issues are often drawn into the conflict situation. These outcomes cloud the original focus and may even result in the initial issue being overshadowed by later ones, creating even more difficulty for conflict resolution.

COOPERATIVE CONFLICT THEORY

Goals are important in conflict management.

One way to understand what impacts how people work (or fail to work) together is explained by **cooperative conflict theory**. This theory focuses on individuals' perceptions of how their goals may be related to others with whom they are interacting.[2] Research confirms that when people believe their goals are compatible, they believe that when one of them succeeds, the others succeed. These compatible beliefs result in increased cooperation because when one person is successful, others are helped in reaching their goals. This fosters a win-win climate and team collaboration.

On the other hand, if people believe their goals are competitive, they also tend to believe that if one wins, others must lose. For a competitive employee who needs to prove that he or she is the most capable and that his or her ideas are superior, other people's successes are frustrating. Competitive goal strategy fosters a win-lose climate.[3]

Employees' views of professional and organizational goals as either cooperative or competitive affects their orientation and intentions toward one another, as illustrated in Figure 10–1. Those viewing goals in a cooperative climate want others to be effective and view others as wanting them to be effective, because doing so is in everyone's best interests. They believe that their risk and effort will be supported and reciprocated. Consequently, they trust that they can rely on coworkers.

Cooperative employees know others' views.

When employees cooperate they share information, know each other's points of view, exchange resources, assist and support each other, and use higher-quality reasoning. This helps all those involved to complete tasks quicker, reach high-quality solutions together, reduce stress, strengthen work relationships, and foster future collaboration.

In this climate of trust, cooperative employees manage their conflicts productively—freely speaking their minds, revealing their frustrations, and talking out their anger. In working for win-win solutions that strengthen the cooperative relationship, they explore alternative perspectives, creatively integrate differing views, and feel confident that they will continue to work together cooperatively.

Competitive employees foster suspicion.

Those who view goals as competitive, on the other hand, foster the suspicion that people only want to look out for their own interests, even at the expense of others. This mistrust halts the flow of information and resources and creates unproductive conflict that deters productivity, increases stress, and decreases morale. Confrontations are often harsh because of a win-lose attitude.

Discuss how to handle conflict with your antagonist.

Discussing competitive and cooperative conflict in a team setting is a useful way for people to manage conflict more productively.[4]

When—not if—conflicts arise, it is important to work through them to mutual understanding. The conflict may not always be resolved, but it ought to be communicated and managed.

There ain't no good guys
There ain't no bad guys
There's only you and me,
And we just disagree.

Dave Mason, in James A. Wall Jr. and Ronda Roberts Callister, "Conflict and Its Management," *Journal of Management* (May–June 1995): 44–46.

FIGURE 10-1 ***Cooperative Conflict Theory***

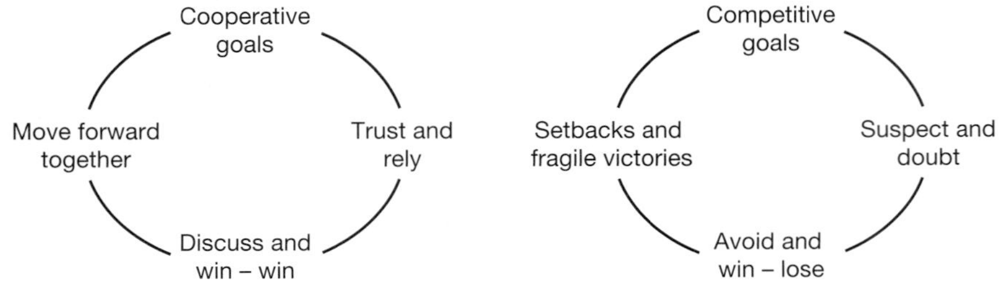

Source: Dean Tjosvold, *Learning to Manage Conflict: Getting People to Work Together Productively* (1993), 45. First published by Lexington Books [now Jossey-Bass Inc., San Francisco]. Reprinted with permission of author.

TEAMS AND CONFLICT MANAGEMENT

Organizations depend on teams, from top management teams to self-directed work teams. The underlying assumption in the movement to team-based management is that teams will increase organizational productivity because teams foster higher creativity, energy, and performance.[5]

In the 1990s, cross-functional teams were promoted by academics, practitioners, and the business press as a miracle cure for companies. Indeed, the increased autonomy and open communication fostered by teams create an atmosphere in which innovative ideas can be developed into products and services that are more responsive to customers' needs than ever before.[6]

Being a team member provides the employee with the opportunity to reach beyond the job being performed and become involved with achieving organizational goals. In addition, team involvement enhances decision making, builds consensus, increases support for action, and provides a cooperative, goal-oriented culture—critical factors when the coordinated efforts of employees are essential to reaching organizational goals.

Conflict can improve team effectiveness.

Conflict *can* improve team effectiveness. The problem is that, once aroused, conflict is difficult to control. Sometimes it remains task focused, facilitating creativity, open communication, and team integration. In other instances, it loses its focus and undermines creativity, open communication, and integrated effort.[7]

CONFLICT IN THE ORGANIZATION

Conflict is a natural, healthy part of any organization. However, all teams are not effective; the reality of teams and their effectiveness is often different from the promise. It can be painful when not managed productively. Carrying a grudge has no positive benefits and can have negative consequences.

> I've had a few arguments with people, but I never carry a grudge. You know why? While you're carrying a grudge, they're out dancing.
>
> Buddy Hackett quoted in Richard J. Mayer, *Conflict Management: The Courage to Confront* (Columbus, OH: Batelle Press, 1995), 3.

As a result, while offering the potential of major breakthroughs, ineffective teams increase the amount of time needed to make a decision. This is largely due to the ineffective use of conflict management in teamwork.

Dean Tjosvold provides the following guides for action and pitfalls to avoid in conflict management.

Action Guides for Conflict Management:

- Distinguish between the conflict over the issue and the conflict over how conflicts are being managed.
- Recognize that characterizing the other person as arrogant and closed-minded grows out of competitive conflict.
- Take the first steps toward discussing openly how conflicts are being managed.

- Check assumptions that the other is unwilling to improve conflict management.
- Deal with competitive, negative attitudes.
- Try to remain open-minded and fair.
- Focus on working together to improve conflict management.
- Discuss the costs of the destructive conflict and the mutual benefits of productive conflict.
- Signal that the conflict can be constructively resolved.
- Avoid blaming or shaming others in public.
- Demonstrate that you are trying to understand the other's perspective.
- Counter the negative perceptions your antagonist has of you by changing behaviors.
- Empower your antagonist by offering options to choose.
- Know and be prepared to use alternatives to a negotiated agreement.

Avoid These Pitfalls in Conflict Management:

- Don't assume you alone must manage conflict.
- Don't assume your opponent alone must change.
- Don't believe that conflict means the other person intends to be frustrating and mean.
- Don't convince yourself that your antagonist does not want to manage conflict based on indirect evidence.
- Don't wait for the other person to make the first move to prove good intentions.[8]

Individual Conflicts. Jimmy Calano and Jeff Salzman of CareerTrack offer strategies for managing conflict successfully by harnessing the power in conflict and transforming it to achieve personal success. Some points they recommend are:

1. *Choose the time and place carefully when addressing conflict.* Avoid initiating conflict in public or in front of uninvolved people. Remember to "praise in public and criticize in private."
2. *Change behaviors not people.* Fix the problem instead of fixing the blame on another. Instead of wasting energy trying to convince a coworker that he or she is to blame, concentrate on a win-win solution.
3. *Agree on something.* Establish basic goals that are common to all involved. This creates a positive foundation, minimizing defensiveness and fostering cooperation and problem solving, by looking at different ways common goals can be achieved.
4. *Use "I" language.* State your case in relation to how you feel instead of attacking another person. For example, "I'm not happy with the progress of our project" is more effective in approaching problem solving than "You don't have the report done on time!"
5. *Figure out where you went wrong or how you may have contributed to the conflict and admit it.* Perhaps you were late in providing information. If so, start the confrontation with, "I know that I was late getting the data to you initially."
6. *Criticize concretely.* Don't be vague by saying, "You are unprofessional." Be concrete by stating, "The report is 3 days late and in the wrong format." Being concrete provides guidelines for improvement.
7. *Bow out for a while.* When emotions are high, take some time—a few hours or a day—to allow both parties to move from the blame stage to the solution stage.
8. *Embrace conflicts.* Bring up problems and annoyances as they happen to build honest relationships.
9. *Find the win-win solution.* When emotions are high, it is human nature to lock into your position. Break out of your resolve to win and defeat your coworker and consider new possibilities that provide a win-win solution.[9]

Thomas Capozzoli describes the nature of conflict as neither good nor bad:

> Conflict is not something that is a tangible product but it lies in the minds of the people who are parties to it. However, it does become tangible when it manifests itself in arguing, brooding, or fighting. The problem lies with the inability for people to manage and resolve it effectively. If managed effectively, conflict can be constructive. If not, conflict can be a destructive force in people and organizations.[10]

Conflict is constructive (i.e., **functional conflict**) when:

- People grow and change positively as a result of the conflict.
- The conflict provides a win-win solution.
- Involvement is increased for everyone affected by the conflict.
- Team cohesiveness is increased.

Conflict is destructive (i.e., **dysfunctional conflict**) when:

- The problem is not resolved.
- It drains energy from more important issues.
- It destroys the team spirit.
- The team or individuals become divided.

TEAM CONFLICTS

Conflict in teams serves a productive purpose when it is focused on the differing perspectives and judgments of how to reach an organizational goal. Conflict becomes unproductive and harmful to team effectiveness when it focuses on a team member rather than an issue. Personal attacks often diminish team cohesion.[11] On the other hand, conflict is a natural, healthy occurrence when people work together. Finally, conflict prevents complacency in teams, which deters growth.

MAKING CONFLICT A SUCCESSFUL COMPONENT OF TEAM INTERACTIONS

Effective team members view conflict positively; ineffective team members view conflict as a burden.

Effective teams use conflict as an advantage to build discussion and foster creative thinking, thereby improving decision making and acceptance of decisions by team members. Ineffective teams do a less successful job of managing and resolving their differences. Ineffective team members view conflict as a burden—something to avoid. Avoiding conflict leads to weak decisions and underutilized teams.

TYPES OF TEAM CONFLICT

Differences of opinion will always happen among team members. Amason, et al. identified two types of conflict that teams experience: *cognitive* or *C-type* conflict and *affective* or *A-type* conflict. Whether the outcomes of team conflict are positive or negative is generally dependent on whether the conflict is C-type or A-type.

C-TYPE CONFLICT

C-type conflict focuses on substantive, issue-related differences of opinion. Amason found this type of disagreement is a natural part of a properly functioning team. Natural, because as team members gather to make important decisions, they bring different ideas, opinions, and perspectives to the table. C-type conflict occurs as team members examine, compare, and reconcile these differences. Attention is focused on the assumptions underlying the particular issue rather than on the emotion associated with either its causes or its impacts. Because assumptions are challenged, the groupthink mentality that can sometimes develop is diminished and the degree of acceptance of the ultimate decision is increased. This process is key to the team's ability to reach high-quality solutions.[12] Managers generally agree that C-type conflict improves overall team effectiveness because team members participate in frank communication and broad consideration of different alternatives. This facilitates creative problem solving with innovative thinking, thereby improving the quality of decision making.

A-TYPE CONFLICT

The downside of conflict is that when used ineffectively, it can harm the team and create hostility among a team's members. Affective conflict (**A-type conflict**) emerges when C-type conflicts are corrupted—when there is too much pushing or disagreeing on cognitive conflict issues. As a result, the quality of decision making actually declines along with the commitment and understanding necessary for the decision to be successfully implemented. In a team context, affect is comprised of both nonverbal behaviors (body language, facial expressions) as well as verbal behaviors (voice tone, emotional outbursts) exhibited by team members during their interactions with one another. Unlike disagreements over substantive issue-oriented matters, which are largely beneficial, disagreements over personalized, individually oriented matters are largely detrimental to team performance.

A-type conflict lowers team effectiveness by provoking hostility, distrust, cynicism, and apathy among team members. A-type conflict in organizational teams focuses on personalized anger, resentment, or hostility, usually pinpointing certain individuals instead of organizational goals. This anger, when directed at individuals, may span team boundaries and spread to other areas of the organization. Remember that:

> Unlike C-type conflict, A-type conflict undermines team effectiveness by preventing teams from engaging in the kinds of activities that are critical to team effectiveness. A-type conflict fosters cynicism, distrust, and avoidance, thereby obstructing open communication and integration. When that happens, not only does the quality of solutions decline, but also commitment to the team itself erodes because team members no longer associate themselves with the team's actions.[13]

Effective teams learn to combine the diverse capabilities of their members. In contrast, team members who are distrustful of or apathetic toward one another are not willing to engage in the types of discussions necessary to synthesize their different perspectives. As a consequence, the creativity and quality of the team's decisions suffer. Similarly, team members who are hostile or cynical are not likely to understand, much less commit to, decisions that are made largely without their participation. Thus, in the best case, these members are unable to carry out the decision because they do not understand it. In the worst case, these disgruntled team members are unwilling to work to implement the decision as intended, or, in fact, work against it. A-type conflict also undermines a team's ability to function effectively in the future. Team members who have been burned by A-type conflicts are less likely to participate fully in future meetings.[14]

THE CONFLICT PARADOX[15]

While a number of studies have found that conflict is important to a team's effectiveness, many others have found that conflict can be harmful. On one hand, conflict appears to improve decision quality, while on the other it may weaken the ability of the group to work together. The impact of this **conflict paradox**, if left unresolved, may cause managers to be unsure of what actions to take because of the apparently competing outcomes of conflict episodes. Resolving the paradox becomes a significant challenge for the leaders of today's organizations.

One place to begin is in examining the *interaction processes* the team uses to reach decisions. Managers can use several techniques to creatively stimulate constructive conflict, including devil's advocacy and dialectical inquiry. Devil's advocacy is the process of assigning a group member to raise contrary arguments about a topic under consideration. Such an assignment helps ensure that discussion on a topic will occur. Dialectical inquiry goes a step further by actually structuring a debate on two different courses of action regarding the same issue, forcing opposing views and the assumptions underlying them to be thoroughly explored. These processes enable team members to identify, extract, and synthesize their perspectives to reach a decision in a productive and timely manner.

Because research suggests that conflict can be both beneficial and detrimental to team effectiveness, it is important to foster C-type conflict and discourage A-type conflict in groups, as illustrated in Figure 10–2.

C-type conflict enhances team effectiveness by improving the quality of decisions as well as increasing the chances that decisions will be successfully implemented. Conversely, A-type conflict reduces team effectiveness by decreasing decision quality and undermining the decision's implementation.

MANAGING C-TYPE CONFLICT WHILE AVOIDING A-TYPE CONFLICT

Amason et al. points out several strategies to help manage "C" while avoiding "A."

Awareness. Effective teams are intuitively aware of the two types of conflict and develop attributes for using "C" without invoking "A."

FIGURE 10–2 *Outcomes of C-Type and A-Type Conflict*

DECISION-MAKING INTERACTION FLOW

A-TYPE CONFLICT	C-TYPE CONFLICT
Destructive conflict	Better decisions
Reduced progress	Increased commitment
Poorer decisions	Increased cohesiveness
Decreased commitment	Increased empathy
Decreased cohesiveness	Increased understanding
Decreased empathy	

Source: Adapted from Allen C. Amason, Kenneth R. Thompson, Wayne A. Hockwarter, and Allison W. Harrison, "Conflict: An Important Dimension in Successful Management Teams," *Organizational Dynamics* (autumn 1995): 27.

Focused Activity. Effective teams focus on the problem and stay close to the task, reaching decisions quickly and efficiently. Less effective teams stray from the central task, dwelling over insignificant points, and losing sight of their primary task. As a result, less focused groups take longer to define problems and have to develop solutions more quickly than groups that are more focused.

Creativity. Effective teams develop a climate that fosters creativity by encouraging members to consider problems from different angles and discover new and diverse solutions to the problems. C-type conflict is a central force for team creativity. By fostering open communication that encourages differing opinions and creative suggestions, a team is cultivating C-type conflict.

Open Communication. Teams are more effective when they have more open communication and operate in a culture that promotes free speech and open disagreement with others' viewpoints, free from the threat of hostility, animosity, or retribution. Open communication is the key to achieving genuine team member participation, increased decision quality, and strengthened team commitment and acceptance. Teams which lack open communication tend to be less effective, with members offering only guarded responses and being fearful of expressing their true opinions.

Outspoken, honest, and sincere communication may produce some disagreement and conflict. However, when team members view the conflict as task oriented, or C-type conflict that is meant to enrich the team's overall effectiveness, they tend to react positively. Only when the conflict seems to be A-type does communication start to undermine team effectiveness by starting self-serving disagreements, by promoting the interests of one team member at the expense of another, and by adopting a defensive stance.

Integration. All team members are utilized in effective teams. Effective teams using C-type conflict are aware of how crucial it is to include and get the best from all team members. When teams fail to make the fullest possible use of all team members, there is often a disproportionate contribution by only a few members. Why go to the trouble to form a team when the benefit is lost because only a few team members participate in the decision-making process?

Leaders can make their teams more effective by asking for opinions of less active team members and moderating the input from members who overpower the discussion. Integration and participation are crucial for obtaining a commitment to the decisions that are made.

Build a Conflict-Tolerant Culture for Meetings and Other Interactions. Teams that encourage discussion, debate, and integration can gain higher levels of satisfaction from their members than teams that ignore their differences. The ability to manage conflict so that team members feel free to state their concerns or opinions, even when those concerns or opinions counter the majority, is key to achieving integration of the team members. Obviously, the role of the team leader is central in getting each member of the team involved, as well as building the sort of culture that will improve the team's effectiveness. The responsibility for managing conflict lies disproportionately on the team leader.[16]

CONFLICT AND TOP MANAGEMENT TEAMS

It is often the case that among senior management teams, conflict fails to occur. Research supports that this lack of conflict is a result of several seemingly inherent attributes of some top management teams (TMTs):

- Senior executives crush dissension
- "Groupthink"—camaraderie of senior team is more valued than critical thinking, resulting in self-censorship and a "veneer of harmony"
- Lack of conviction about one's own opinions
- Ignorance of others' viewpoints
- Implicit assumption that everyone agrees
- Executives find conflict "unpleasant" and become personal
- Fear of endless debate[17]

There are several suggestions about how TMTs can generate and use conflict to improve effectiveness. For example, the commitment to build a heterogeneous team—one with deliberate diversity—can create the expectation of conflict in the team setting. Additionally, creating frequent interactions among team members, cultivating different (and even competing) roles for various executives, and structuring the process to require that multiple alternatives and multiple strategies to resolve issues be developed are ways to precipitate "C-type conflict" among TMTs.

The team leader has the responsibility for managing conflict within the team. Because effective teams are increasingly valuable to organizations, people who are successful at leading or facilitating team interactions play an increasingly important role in organizations. Effective team leaders and coaches perfect their conflict management skills, including diagnosis, by these means:

- Determine when members are suppressing their ideas to avoid conflict.
- Determine if divergent or unpopular ideas are being rejected or ignored.
- Keep tabs on whether conflict is constructive and task related.
- Recognize when members try to smooth over conflict rather than confront it.

In addition, leaders and coaches can intervene in conflict using these tools:

- Draw out and summarize opposing positions.
- Steer conflict away from personalities and toward task-related issues.
- Tolerate and sustain task-related conflict even when it makes some members (including the leader) uncomfortable.
- Help the team recognize that task-related conflict encourages innovation and creativity.[18]

NEGOTIATION FUNDAMENTALS

"Negotiation is a fact of life. In business, government, or the family, people reach most decisions through negotiation."[19] It is an inescapable element of most things that we do—from buying a car or a house to deciding on where to go for dinner with friends or family. A discussion of conflict management would not be complete without some introductory comments about the process of negotiation as a means of conflict resolution. In this section we highlight some of the basic components of negotiations and outline some of the key principles of negotiation practice.

There are several basic elements associated with most negotiation processes that, if understood, can help anyone more successfully navigate disagreements with another individual or group.

According to Fisher and Ury, recognized authorities in negotiation strategy and practice, most people view a negotiation situation in one of two ways. One perspective, referred to as *soft negotiation,* is characterized by a desire to avoid personal conflict and often results with the negotiator feeling exploited and bitter at the outcome of the process. The other perspective, known as *hard negotiation,* is characterized by viewing the situation as a contest of wills in which one person must lose in order for the other person to win. Extreme positions are staked out and compromise is difficult to achieve. Usually the long-term relationship between the parties is damaged. While there are degrees of difference along this negotiation continuum, all of these perspectives typically involve trade-offs between what one wants and getting along with people.

The Harvard Negotiation Project identified a third negotiation strategy, known as **principled negotiation**, in which the focus of the negotiations is on the merits of specific issues, rather than on what either of the sides claim they will or won't do. This attempt to objectify the decision-making criteria is designed to make the outcome of the negotiations based more on issues than on emotions and self-interests.[20]

Fisher and Ury identified five key elements for achieving success in the process of principled negotiation. The first of these elements is the prescription to avoid bargaining over positions. A position is a statement of issues by one party in the negotiations. Each individual or group in the negotiation may have positions or issues to be addressed. Because people can see the same circumstance differently, arguing from the basis of one's position usually results in positions becoming more, rather than less, firm. Less time is spent attempting to meet underlying concerns as more time is spent clarifying one's position. Positional bargaining often becomes a contest of wills and can be very damaging to long-term relationships.

The second element of principled negotiation is that people must be separated from the problem. As human beings, we are subject to our own perceptual biases with respect to individuals and circumstances. These biases lead us away from focusing on the merits of the issue and toward a contest of wills with the opposing party.

The third element of principled negotiation is the prescription to focus on interests, not positions. It is important to understand in a negotiation situation that the objective must be to satisfy the underlying interests of the other party. If they are not satisfied, the likelihood of an agreement being reached is substantially reduced. Not infrequently, positions individuals take are not fully representative of their real interests; instead they are usually more extreme. Compromise between positions is not likely to produce an agreement that will effectively meet the needs that originally led people to adopt those positions in the first place.

The fourth element of principled negotiation is generating options for mutual gain before deciding what to do. In negotiation situations, it is difficult to come up with and effectively think through creative solutions that meet the needs of both parties. Remember, if both parties' needs aren't met, a negotiated solution is unlikely. Spending time outside of the negotiation to address a number of possible options that might be acceptable to both sides is time well spent.

Finally, negotiators should agree to objective standards at the outset. In any negotiation, there is little reason to agree to an option that does not meet your interests. The same is true for the other party. It is essential, therefore, that both parties agree to a standard or standards that both parties consider fair and independent of the will of the other party. Discussion about what both parties would consider fair, without discussing what either party would do, can set the groundwork for a subsequent agreement.[21]

ACTION PROJECT 10–1

FORCED-LADDER CHOICES (INDIVIDUAL AND GROUP EXERCISE)

For this exercise your instructor will ask you to rank the following statements in order of personal feelings, putting the most distasteful one at the top of the ladder. Note: Use the parentheticals to write on the numbered rungs of the ladder. It is important that you distribute your choices among all the lines. What matters most is how strong your feelings are. When you are finished, your instructor will break the class into groups of five to discuss your decisions. The groups will then be asked to arrive at a group conclusion. You may cross out, draw arrows, or make changes, but you must arrive at a final group decision.

1. A man reports his neighbor to the IRS because he heard him mention how he falsified his deductions on his income tax forms (income tax).
2. A family man with two children and a concern for the population explosion has a vasectomy without consulting his wife. She wants more children and he doesn't (father).
3. A man believes one should have complete freedom of personal choice. He feels that he should be able to play golf where he pleases and with whom he pleases. He builds a golf course and operates a segregated club to keep out minorities (golf club).
4. Two men get their kicks by harassing gays and lesbians. (two men).
5. A son criticizes his dad for working in a plant that makes munitions to sell to foreign governments. His father tells him to be quiet because the money he makes helps send the boy to college (blue-collar worker).
6. A cop turns his son in for smoking pot (cop).

Complete your individual feelings rankings first; then wait for your group to work out its rankings.

Individual Feelings	Group Feelings
1. ________	1. ________
2. ________	2. ________
3. ________	3. ________
4. ________	4. ________
5. ________	5. ________
6. ________	6. ________

1. Does personal ego interfere with making logical deductions? Please explain.
2. When someone in the group challenged you on your opinion, did you lash back, withdraw, or simply refuse to listen to them? Please explain.
3. Did the most aggressive and talkative person win over most of the group? How about the most reserved member; was he or she in control? Please explain.

SUMMARY

Conflict is common in all organizations. It may be studied from several different perspectives, including intrapersonal and interpersonal ones. Conflict is better understood as a process rather than an episode. It typically will have multiple causes, including differences in personalities, objectives, resources, and historical relationships. Similarly, conflict can have both functional and dysfunctional impacts on the organization and on individuals within it.

The challenges managers and nonmanagers alike face in achieving effective conflict management are significant. There are numerous pitfalls to avoid as one attempts to navigate the emotional minefield of conflict circumstances. Developing the skills to optimize cognitive conflict (C-type conflict) in team interactions while minimizing the affective impacts of A-type conflict is the key to effective conflict resolution.

Principled negotiation is a particular form of conflict resolution that focuses on five important dimensions of the conflict circumstance. These include not bargaining over positions, separating the people from the problem, focusing on the interests of the parties rather than their positions, seeking options for mutual gain, and selecting objective standards on which to evaluate the criteria.

CASE STUDY 10-1

CHARLIE HAS A CHANCE TO GET AHEAD

Charlie is employed as an accountant in a small assembly plant in the Midwest. In his 7 years at Astro-Technology, he has become acquainted with most of the 200 employees and enjoys the atmosphere of his office and the company attitude toward him. However, in the past 3 years he has not received a promotion, and there is little chance for one in the near future. The raises he has received have not kept up with inflation. He has discussed the situation frequently with his wife, Rita, who is working as a personnel officer at a research firm in town. Although Rita has never told Charlie, she feels that her job has more status than his. Even though Charlie earns slightly more income, she has more flexible hours, more holidays with pay, better company fringe benefits, and apparently more status when the two companies' organizational charts are compared. Rita enjoys her present position and the salary she receives. Their two daughters are doing well in grammar school and are active in the Girl Scouts and their local swim team.

A month ago Charlie heard of a new position for an accountant in his company's home office in Dallas. He knows that his company has a practice of promoting from within, and his supervisor feels that he would have a good chance of getting the position. It would mean an immediate 15 percent raise in pay; more prestige, because he would have a private office; and more opportunities for promotion. He applied for the position, but was afraid to tell his wife. When the interview was scheduled, he informed Rita that he had to go to Dallas for a seminar.

Charlie was impressed with Dallas and the possible neighborhoods from which his family could select to make their home. The home office was impressive! Dark walnut and chrome were everywhere, and the personnel in the office were very friendly. After a tour of the facility he had an interview with five managers. A week later he was informed that he was one of the three finalists. He was excited and eager to accept the position if it was offered to him. That night, when he told Rita, she was upset. The move would mean they would have to leave the lovely home they had been remodeling during the last 7 years. The girls would have to find new friends.

Finally, and most important, could Rita find a job as good as the one she has? It seemed unfair to force her to move and give up a good job just so Charlie could satisfy his own ego. It turned into a real argument. Charlie wants to move and Rita does not. Charlie wants to achieve more in his career and Rita is happy with her current job and their present lifestyle.

1. What points can Charlie use to justify the move and his attitudes about advancing in his career?

2. What points can Rita use to justify staying where they are? What points can she make to say that the status quo is satisfactory for them?

DISCUSSION AND STUDY QUESTIONS—TO KEEP YOU THINKING

1. What is the difference in cooperative and competitive goal conflicts?

2. Discuss some points for dealing effectively with individual conflict.

3. Compare and contrast C-type and A-type conflict.

4. What aspects of the negotiation process make achieving agreement particularly difficult?

NOTES

1. E. Frank Harrison, *The Managerial Decision-Making Process* (Boston: Houghton-Mifflin Company, 1995), 261–295.
2. M. Deutsch, "Sixty Years of Conflict," *The International Journal of Conflict Management* (January 1990): 237–263.
3. Dean Tjosvold, *Learning to Manage Conflict: Getting People to Work Together Productively* (New York: MacMillan, 1993), 44–46.
4. Ibid.
5. Valerie I. Sessa, "Using Perspective Taking to Manage Conflict and Affect in Teams," *Journal of Applied Behavioral Science* (March 1996): 101–115.
6. Katherine Zoe Andrews, "Cross-Functional Teams: Are They Always the Right Move?" *Harvard Business Review* (November–December 1995): 12–13.
7. Allen C. Amason, Kenneth R. Thompson, Wayne A. Hochwarter, and Allison W. Harrison, "Conflict: An Important Dimension in Successful Management Teams," *Organizational Dynamics* (autumn 1995): 29.
8. Tjosvold, *Learning to Manage Conflict*, 48–49.
9. Jimmy Calano and Jeff Salzman, "How to Turn HEAT into Light," *Working Woman* (March 1988): 122–123.
10. Thomas K. Capozzoli, "Conflict Resolution—A Key Ingredient in Successful Teams," *Supervision* (December 1995): 3–5.
11. Erich Brockmann, "Removing the Paradox of Conflict from Group Decisions," *Academy of Management Executive* (May 1996): 51–62.
12. Amason, et al., "Conflict: An Important Dimension . . .", 22.
13. Ibid., 25.
14. Ibid., 29
15. Brockman, "Removing the Paradox . . .", 51
16. Amason, et al., "Conflict: An Important Dimension . . .", 29–30.
17. K. M. Eisenhardt, M. Kahwajy, and J. L. Bourgeois III, "Conflict and Strategic Choice: How Top Management Teams Disagree," *California Management Review* 39 no. 2 (winter 1997): 42–61.
18. Greg Burns, "The Secrets of Team Facilitation," *Training & Development* (June 1995): 49.
19. Roger Fisher, William Ury, and Roger Patton. *Getting to Yes: Negotiating Agreement Without Giving In*, 2nd ed. (New York: Penguin Books 1991), xvii.
20. Ibid., xviii–xix.
21. Ibid., 3–94.

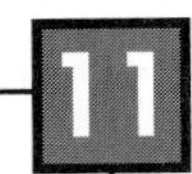

Leadership

TO START YOU THINKING

Consider these questions as you begin to read the chapter. Some answers may be found in the chapter; others may be answered through outside reading, exploring relevant Web sites, or talking to people in leadership roles.

- What makes a leader effective?
- Is there an ideal leader for all situations?
- Can leadership be learned?
- Are men or women better leaders? Why?
- What roles do followers play in leadership?
- What is the function of a leader in a group?
- What is the impact of changing technology, globalization, and the changing workforce on leadership?
- How can we measure leader behavior?
- What type of leader are you?

LEARNING GOALS

After studying this chapter, you should be able to:

1. Distinguish between leadership and management.
2. Explain various leadership models, including the trait, behavior, and contingency theories, leadership substitutes, and transformational leadership.
3. Explain leadership as an influence process.
4. Explain the role of followers in the leadership process.
5. Characterize the differential impacts of gender roles in defining leadership effectiveness.
6. Identify key influences on leadership entering the twenty-first century.
7. Define and apply the following terms and concepts (in order of first occurrence):

KEYWORDS

- **unconscious incompetence**
- **conscious incompetence**
- **conscious competence**
- **unconscious competence**
- **leadership**
- **managerial roles**
- **value-added competence**
- **job-centeredness**
- **employee-centeredness**
- **consideration**
- **initiating structure**
- **autocratic or Theory X leader**
- **participative or Theory Y leader**
- **consultive leaders**
- **democratic leaders**
- **managerial grid**
- **contingency model**
- **path-goal approach**
- **situational leadership**
- **transformational leader**
- **substitutes for leadership**

The scarcest resource in the world today is leadership talent capable of continuously transforming organizations to win in tomorrow's world.

Noel M. Tichy, author of *The Leadership Engine*

Forty-one-year-old Andrea Jung, looking more like a movie star than the CEO of Avon, the $5.3 billion women's consumer products company, walked onto the stage at the Thomas and Mack Center in Las Vegas to greet 13,000 sales reps from across the United States. Jung was named CEO in November 1999, and her challenge at this annual convention was to invigorate this group of middle-America moms about the future of their company.

Avon is confronted with the need to reconcile the explosive growth of the Internet, the fact that three-quarters of American women work, and the company's old economy direct sales business model. Avon's sales growth has been modest—only 5 percent per year during the past decade—and profits grew less at 4 percent per year.

Jung's history is that of a marketer who became second in command at I. Magnin & Company before she was 30. By the time she was 32, Jung was in charge of all women's apparel for Neiman Marcus. She joined Avon in 1994 with the task of unifying Avon's regional brands into one powerful global label.

Jung joins one of corporate America's most elite groups: women who, like Carly Fiorina of HP and Marjorie Scardino of Pearson Media Group, are leading complex and problem-ridden corporations.

What distinguishes Jung, Fiorina, and Scardino as leaders in the first decade of the new century? In Jung's case, one element is a clear vision of what she wants the company to become: "the ultimate relationship marketer of products and services for women . . . the source for anything and everything a woman wants to buy." More than that, she wants to give busy women a choice in how they do their buying: through an Avon rep, in a store, or online. Furthermore, Jung is pushing radical change (e.g., going into retail to lure younger customers), and she is very ambitious. "We will change the future of women around the world!" Jung exclaimed at the Las Vegas convention.

Her initiatives in the Internet arena are bold—she has committed $60 million to build a Web site focused on the Avon reps and the company's catalog—and she acts swiftly. In the short time she has been CEO, she has polled reps about how technology could help them as well as conducted focus groups comprised of Web-savvy and Web-illiterate customers to ensure the site is what everyone can use. She has visited over 20 countries during the last year. Jung is cautious about trying to do too much at once, and to that end, is emphasizing open communication, including setting up a CEO advisory council of 10 top performers from every level of the company and from around the globe.

When Jung graduated from Princeton University in 1979, magna cum laude with a degree in English literature, she joined an executive training program at Bloomingdale's. Once described as "shy and aloof," she is now described as "a leader who's willing to tell her story."

She looked at Avon differently than old economy management. Her no-nonsense views about whether or not the company should move into retail (in 1994, her answer was "No, we're not ready") drew the attention of senior management. She proved that she was decisive. Jung is described as charismatic—a quality some say will be essential as she begins to move the company into uncharted waters of new products and services.

Jung recognizes she is under intense pressure to perform. Since being named CEO, Jung has overseen an increase in Avon's stock of 23 percent, sales of 9 percent and profits by 40 percent.[1]

Andrea Jung offers us a valuable introduction to the study of leadership. Consider what qualities or traits have helped her be successful to this point. Would you expect a young woman of Chinese ancestry with a bachelor's degree in English literature to become the CEO of a $5.3 billion corporation? Would you expect that a former Bloomingdale's management trainee would today spend her time jetting off to countries all over the world touting her company's products and exploring new marketing and distribution venues? Can she be successful if the Avon representatives don't support her efforts to change the company's business model? What steps does she need to take to convince them that her ideas make sense for tomorrow's success? These are core questions about leaders and leadership in the new century.

What behaviors does she display that you might conclude are those that all leaders display—decisiveness, risk taking, vision? How much of her success (and therefore her leadership effectiveness) can or will be attributed to the unique point in her company's history that she came on the stage? How much do you suppose Jung knows about the details of the chemistry of her company's products or the technology that goes into packaging and shipping them? How much does she need to know in order to be effective? And what about her efforts to balance her professional and personal life—she has a 3-year-old son and an 11-year-old daughter—how can those roles be reconciled? Does it take a woman to lead Avon? Would a man do a better job?

INTERNET ACTION PROJECT 11–1

To learn more about Andrea Jung and Avon Corporation, go to www.avon.com.

Our goal in this chapter is to help you, as a student of leadership, broaden your understanding of important leadership concepts. In addition, it is our hope that you will continue to develop your leadership skills and abilities and be able to apply these concepts in your everyday experience. Be aware, however, that this process is an evolutionary one—it takes some time and considerable effort to become a truly effective leader. Author Richard Daft suggests that people typically progress through a series of stages as they develop their understanding of and ability to apply leadership concepts successfully in their everyday experience. Those four stages are:

Unconscious incompetence—individuals have no or minimal leadership competence or experience and are unaware they lack competence or what competencies they lack.

Conscious incompetence—individuals become conscious of what they do not know and aware of what's required to do well, but still do not possess those requisite skills. One can begin to visualize a desired future, influence others to engage in that future, and have the courage to take on real change.

Conscious competence—In this stage of leadership development, the leader becomes aware of what he or she is doing well and where continued development is essential. Feedback is received about how well the leader is doing.

Unconscious competence—Once an individual develops his or her leadership skills to the point they are applied naturally, in appropriate settings, one can be said to have achieved Stage 4 in leadership development.[2]

As you begin this chapter, think about which of these stages characterizes your current level of knowledge and experience. Think, too, about what stage of leadership development you would like to be in as you finish this course.

WHAT IS LEADERSHIP?

Andrea Jung's experiences provide an excellent working definition of leadership—the efforts of one member of an organization over other members to help that group or organization achieve its goals.[3] In Avon, as well as in most other organizations, leadership is multidimensional in nature; it involves many components and requires the individual involved in the leadership role to engage in a variety of tasks and activities.

Leadership involves several important and distinct, yet interrelated, constructs, including influence, intention, personal responsibility, shared purpose or vision, followers, and change.[4] See if you can identify how each element is illustrated by CEO Jung. *Influence* refers to the deliberate, multidirectional and noncoercive efforts of one individual to change the behavior of another individual or group. Such actions have *intent;* that is, they are deliberately designed to achieve a specific set of objectives or vision. Leadership is a reciprocal process that occurs between an individual and followers, who play a key role in helping the leader to attain his or her vision. Indeed, effective leadership cannot occur without the cooperation of followers. Finally, leadership is about changing the status quo. As described in the Avon case, without Jung aggressively pursuing strategies to change how the company does business (e.g., markets its products), the future of Avon is cast in doubt.

MANAGEMENT VERSUS LEADERSHIP

The words *management* and *leadership* are often used interchangeably. It is important to make clear the distinction between these two concepts and to discuss how they are related. Kotter characterized his views of management and leadership in the following way:

> Leadership is different from management, but not for the reasons most people think. Leadership is not mystical or mysterious . . . it is not the province of a chosen few. Nor is leadership necessarily better than management or a replacement for it. Rather, leadership and management are two distinctive and complementary systems of action.[5]

Managing is not the same as leading.

Management is not the same thing as leadership. In the context of how organizations function, managers are typically individuals who hold formal positions of authority in the organization's hierarchy. They typically plan, organize, direct, monitor, and control the actions and activities of individuals (nonmanagers/subordinates) who report to them. Leaders, on the other hand, may be either managers or nonmanagerial employees. By virtue of their personal attributes, leaders exert influence on other employees toward the achievement of some end.

Leaders tend to focus on their own personal vision for the organization and explore what can be done to make that vision a reality. Their view is longer term than that of their managerial counterparts and is directed toward larger goals than the typical short-run objectives that command the bulk of managers' attentions and energy.

Organizations need both sets of skills for them to become and remain successful in the dynamic, rapidly changing environment of the twenty-first century. Managers are essential in keeping the organization on task to accomplish its agreed-upon objectives. Leaders are critical to inspiring the organization to define its future and what steps should be taken to get it there. Warren Bennis, noted leadership researcher, says, "Organizations are under led and over managed. They do not pay enough attention to doing the right thing, while paying too much attention to doing things right."[6]

Additional real-world insights regarding the distinction between management and leadership are found in Lewan and Associates, a 450-person, $100 million gross sales (1998) office technology company based in Denver, Colorado. Lloyd and Paul Lewan characterize management as being concerned primarily with staffing, planning, and organizing. They view leadership as "bringing out the entrepreneurial spirit in all employees by empowering them."[7] Further, they believe that how a company treats its customers is one way to determine the individual's orientation. "There are some leaders who have good management skills," says Lloyd Lewan, "However, it is somewhat more difficult to find a manager with good leadership skills."

Leaders empower others.

Attributes of leadership, according to the Lewans, include: vision—a passionate and realistic belief in the company's future; focus—providing a context within which the organization's work is accomplished and problems can be solved; and influence—consistently treating employees and customers with respect and dignity, and recognizing that modeling behavior will be motivating to employees. Being a good manager does not necessarily mean you are a good leader. Many companies pretend that management is the same as leadership—it is not.[8]

LEADERSHIP MANAGERIAL ROLES

For students of leadership to have a clear understanding of the complexity of the leadership function in organizations, they should have an appreciation for the true nature of managerial work. Henry Mintzberg studied what managers do by following them through their day. He identified 10 **managerial roles** grouped into three categories: interpersonal, informational, and decisional. Earlier conceptualizations of managerial activities held that managers planned, organized, staffed, directed, and controlled individuals and activities in the organization. Mintzberg's insights, described below, provide a more realistic portrayal of the nature of managerial leadership in today's organizations.

Three role categories: interpersonal, informational and decisional.

INTERPERSONAL ROLES

In the figurehead role, the manager/leader represents the organization in legal, ceremonial, symbolic, and social activities. In the leader role, the manager/leader performs all those activities typically associated with "being in charge"—hiring, training, terminating, setting the organization's direction. This critically important role pervades all other aspects of the manager's activities. In the liaison role, the manager/leader acts as a linking pin between the organization or work unit and the outside world. This networking activity keeps the organization in touch with what is happening beyond its boundaries and establishes important contacts that may prove valuable in the future.

INFORMATIONAL ROLES

Informational roles include the monitor, disseminator, and spokesperson. Each of these roles serves the organization by gathering critical information from the organization's internal and external environments (monitor), sending information to others in the organization or work unit (disseminator), and sending information to others outside the organization's or work unit's boundaries (spokesperson).

DECISIONAL ROLES

The final set of roles includes the entrepreneur, disturbance handler, resource allocator, and negotiator. The entrepreneur role is characterized by the proactive steps performed by managers when they are initiating improvements in work processes or developing new products or services. The disturbance-handler role tends to be reactive, involving behaviors undertaken in response to emergency situations (equipment malfunctions, labor strife, time-dependent delivery), when organization processes have been (or have the potential to be) disrupted in a meaningful way.

Resource allocators make key decisions regarding the allocation of the organization's financial, human, and technological resources. The negotiator role involves working to achieve the organization's or the work unit's objectives when specific guidelines or parameters are not yet established that would prescribe a definitive course of action to take.[9] How successful a leader is in fulfilling any one or all of these various roles will influence how effective he or she is perceived by subordinates, peers, superiors, and by those inside and outside the company with whom he or she deals.

MOST ADMIRED LEADER CHARACTERISTICS

We have discussed the distinctions between leadership and management and the different roles that managers perform. Now we turn our attention to the qualities that individuals seek in their leaders.

James B. Kouzes and Barry M. Posner argue that four characteristics stand out in the lengthy list of qualities followers most admire (the full list appears as Figure 11-1.) These attributes are honesty, forward-looking, inspiring, and competent. Leader honesty is the single most important ingredient in the leader-follower relationship. Followers form their judgments about leader honesty from observing how that leader behaves across different situations, and from the leader acting from a basis of strongly held beliefs and values. In addition, followers expect their leaders to have a sense of direction—a vision for the future of the organization, as well as for how to lead it there. Constituents see this clear sense of a true north for the organization as critical.

Honesty is the most important characteristic.

Not only do followers expect their leader to have a sense of the future, but they also want and expect that person to communicate it energetically and enthusiastically.

Individuals expect their leaders to be competent—to have the requisite knowledge and skills to be able to accomplish goals. Competence doesn't always mean being technically competent in the business's core technology, but varies as a function of the particular position. For example, a customer service team leader in a software enterprise should be technically competent in the analysis of product application problems, but not necessarily skilled at strategic planning for the entire enterprise.

On the other hand, those same core technology competency skills would likely not be as necessary for the chief financial officer to effectively lead his or her area of responsibility. Instead, strategic abilities that enable the organization to achieve its objectives are more critical. Thus, effective leaders have **value-added competence**—that unique blend of personal skills that contribute meaningfully to helping the organization achieve its objectives.

Credibility results from honesty, vision, and competence.

Taken together, these attributes comprise what is commonly referred to as credibility. Effective leaders must have credibility in order for us to believe they are worthy of our time and talents to follow into tomorrow.[10]

FIGURE 11-1 *CHARACTERISTICS OF ADMIRED LEADERS*

Characteristics	1995 Respondents: Percentage of People Selecting	1987 Respondents: Percentage of People Selecting
HONEST	88	83
FORWARD-LOOKING	75	62
INSPIRING	68	58
COMPETENT	63	67
Fair-minded	49	40
Supportive	41	32
Broad-minded	40	37
Intelligent	40	43
Straightforward	33	34
Dependable	32	32
Courageous	29	27
Cooperative	28	25
Imaginative	28	34
Caring	23	26
Determined	17	20
Mature	13	23
Ambitious	13	21
Loyal	11	11
Self-Controlled	5	13
Independent	5	10

Source: James B. Kouzes and Barry M. Posner, *The Leadership Challenge* (San Francisco: Jossey-Bass, Inc., Publishers, 1997), 21

A CLOSER LOOK AT LEADERSHIP THEORIES

Leadership has been studied from a number of theoretical perspectives. In this section we look at a sample of those perspectives. In this way, you can gain a basic understanding of where the current thinking about leadership has come from and how it has influenced our modern views of leadership theory and practice. Why so many approaches to studying leadership? As one author says:

> We all see leadership differently, depending on . . . our current paradigm, our current virtual environment. We all live everyday in . . . *realities defined* [italics added] . . . by our ideas and our experiences. Viewpoints other than those descriptive of our current reality will be seen as wrong, incorrect, perhaps inconceivable to us.[11]

As you develop your understanding of leadership, keep this insight in mind and remember that leadership may be understood in several different ways. It may be defined by describing attributes that leaders possess in the form of traits or qualities. It may also be defined by examining what leaders do (i.e., their behaviors). It may incorporate consideration of the specific situation as a major factor influencing leadership effectiveness and style. Finally, it may be concerned with the nature of the relationship between the leader and followers.

First, we examine the trait theory of leadership, followed by a discussion of several behavioral theories and the contingency approach. We conclude with a look at transformational leadership.

LEADERSHIP TRAITS

The search for a finite list of individual traits that distinguish leaders from non-leaders has been an ongoing one. Traits refer to people's general characteristics or capacities. Early in the twentieth century, social scientists attempted unsuccessfully to isolate and analyze the characteristics necessary for effective leadership. Trait theories, once widely accepted, fell into disfavor when research demonstrated that no traits were universally associated with effective leadership.

During the latter half of the twentieth century, however, trait theory made a comeback, leading Kirkpatrick and Locke to conclude that certain core leadership traits significantly contribute to business leaders' success. These six traits are:

Six traits contribute to success.

Drive: traits that reflect a high energy level, including striving to succeed, ambition, energy, tenacity, and initiative.

Motivation: the desire to influence and lead others, including the need for power, sometimes described as "the leader's currency."

Honesty and Integrity: without these qualities, leadership is undermined, while together, they build trust in the credibility of the leader.

Self-Confidence: personal conviction in the correctness of one's course of action and skills as well as the ability to convince others that those actions are correct. Impression management is a key element of effective leadership because it bolsters followers' self-confidence. Emotional stability is another important component of self-confidence. The ability to remain composed and confident in the face of a crisis is an important trait of an effective leader.

Knowledge of the Business: Effective leaders know a great deal about their company, industry, and technical matters. Successful managers tend to spend their careers in the same industry, while less successful ones often lacked industry-specific experiences. Some researchers also argue that technical expertise is more important than education in determining leader success.

Cognitive Ability: Effective leaders need above-average intelligence to enable them to integrate large amounts of complex information, develop successful strategies, and make correct decisions. Having strong analytical ability, good judgment, and the capacity to think strategically and multidimensionally are seen as essential leadership attributes. Another important dimension is the followers' perception of the leader's intelligence, which forms the basis of authority in the leadership relationship.[12]

CAN LEADERSHIP TRAITS BE DEVELOPED?

Of these six traits, cognitive ability is the most difficult to develop. The other five traits can be influenced through training and work experiences. Honesty is a virtue that one chooses, and can be reinforced by appropriate modeling behavior by the organization's senior management group.[13]

EMOTIONAL INTELLIGENCE AND LEADERSHIP

Effective leaders have high EI.

Many authors believe that emotional intelligence also distinguishes the truly successful leaders from those who are merely technically competent and have a high IQ. The individual leader who has well-developed emotional intelligence skills (i.e., self-awareness, self-regulation, motivation, empathy, and social skills) has a greater potential for being successful. Emotional intelligence skills are very similar to the attributes of effective leadership discussed in earlier sections (see Chapter 2).[14]

GENDER DIFFERENCES AND LEADERSHIP

Gender consistently receives attention among those who study leadership. With increasing numbers of women in the workforce, and increasing numbers of women moving into key leadership roles, the question of the impact of gender differences among leaders in organizations is frequently raised. Ibarra and Daly identified two perspectives that characterize the gender and leadership discussion: psychological and situational.

Psychological perspective holds that men and women differ in their leadership approach.

The psychological perspective suggests that women, on average, differ from men in their approach to managerial jobs. Those differences stem from variations in the socialization processes experienced by both sexes as they were growing up. Men seem to demonstrate more independent, instrumentally oriented, and competitive behaviors, while women seem to demonstrate greater affiliation, attachment, cooperation, and nurturance behaviors.

The psychological perspective argues that traditional organization management is characterized by "tough-mindedness and emotional detachment."[15] For women to succeed in business, women need to adopt the "male" model of successful managerial behavior.

The situational perspective holds that differences in power, status, and opportunity have more impact than gender.

The alternate perspective is known as the situational perspective. It assumes that men and women, when placed in a similar situation with similar expectations, will respond in similar ways. Further, behavior and attitudinal differences are better explained by differences in power, status, and opportunity than by gender. Ibarra and Daly's research concluded that, in general, women do not differ from men in the ways they administer the management process.

However, other researchers have concluded there is evidence that men and women managers tend to differ in their choice of influence strategies: men tend to rely on power strategies for influence, while women tend to use personal relationships and indirect influence strategies to accomplish their leadership objectives.[16,17]

These two perspectives suggest the following strategies for further understanding the gender/leadership relationship:

- Leadership research should expand the definition of effective leadership to include those methods and orientations used by women.
- Leadership initiatives should expand the behavioral repertoire for both men and women to increase the capability of both to respond to and survive in a competitive and increasingly diverse economic environment, and
- Women must have equal access to jobs with opportunity and power, as well as career paths that lead there.[18]

How this can be accomplished remains as a major stumbling block to removing actual or perceived gender differences in business.

Male leaders are task oriented.

Female leaders are interactive.

Roesner provides an additional perspective on gender issues in leadership. Whereas men tended to describe their leadership style as transactional (i.e., task oriented and quid pro quo), women describe their leadership with attributes that could best be characterized as transformational or interactive (i.e., getting their subordinates to transform their own self-interest into the interest of the group through concern for a broader goal). Interactive leaders:

Interactive leadership encourages participation.

- encourage participation—inclusion is at the core of interactive leadership; creating mechanisms that get people to participate;
- share power and information—encourage two-way communication and avoid information hoarding;
- enhance the self-worth of others—sharing information and power with others helps them feel important, valued, and more committed;
- energize others—performing their jobs with enthusiasm for their work and making others a part of it.[19]

The discussion on leadership traits can be summarized as follows:

- There are some traits that distinguish effective leaders from those who fall short. These include drive, motivation, self-confidence, honesty and integrity, knowledge of the business, and cognitive ability.
- Most of the critical leadership traits can be developed through training and strong leadership modeling.
- Emotional intelligence, as a leadership trait, is receiving considerable attention as an important new component of effective leadership behavior.
- Two perspectives on gender differences suggest that the definition of leadership ought to be expanded to enable both men and women to incorporate those characteristics necessary to help them lead more effectively.

WHAT LEADERS DO: BEHAVIORAL APPROACHES TO UNDERSTANDING LEADERSHIP

A different approach toward understanding and identifying effective leadership considers how leaders interact with those with whom they work. Research undertaken at the University of Michigan and The Ohio State University during the 1930s through the 1950s focused on behavioral approaches. From the behavioral perspective, leadership is a unique combination of knowledge, skills, and behaviors that leaders use as they work with their associates.

The most significant results of these efforts affirmed two different approaches that leaders take toward the accomplishment of their responsibilities. One focus is on getting the task accomplished, while the other is on recognizing and supporting the needs of the people accomplishing the task.

UNIVERSITY OF MICHIGAN STUDIES

The University of Michigan studies, under the direction of Rensis Likert, resulted in the development of a one-dimensional leadership model that was characterized by two distinct behavioral styles: job-centered leader behaviors at one end of the continuum and employee-centered leader behaviors at the other.

Job-centeredness refers to the extent to which the leader takes charge to get the job done. At this end of the continuum, the leader focuses on task accomplishment, often with little or no regard for the needs of the employees who are actually doing the tasks. **Employee-centeredness** means that leaders engage in behaviors aimed at building trust, support, and respect among employees, while at the same time working to meet individual employee needs. Leaders whose efforts tend more toward this end of the leadership continuum place more emphasis on building relationships than on getting the task accomplished. According to this view of leader behavior, if a person is low on job-centeredness, then he must be high on employee-centeredness.

THE OHIO STATE UNIVERSITY STUDIES

The Ohio State studies characterized leadership as having two dimensions with four leadership styles. The two dimensions are **consideration** (essentially employee centeredness) and **initiating structure** (essentially the same as job centeredness). A leader can be high or low on each dimension, resulting in the potential for four distinct leader styles (see Figure 11–2).

Both of these leadership models have had a significant influence on how organizations interact with their employees. One impact has been the conclusion that there is no one best style of leadership. Another conclusion is that employees tend to be more satisfied with a leader who is high in consideration.[20] As a result of these studies, organizations began to place more emphasis on the "people" side of the business. The popular phrase, "A happy worker is a productive worker," came from this period of behavioral research in leadership.[21]

FIGURE 11–2 *THE OSU MODEL*

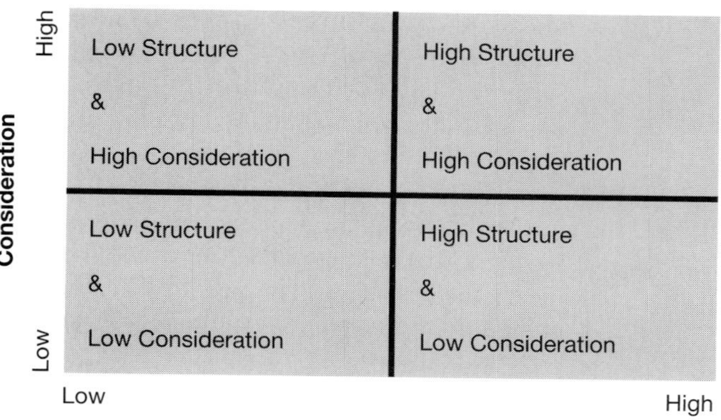

Source: Paul Hersey and Kenneth Blanchard, *Management of Organizational Behavior*, 6th edition, Upper Saddle River, NJ: Prentice Hall, 1993, 102.

THEORY X AND THEORY Y LEADERS

McGregor's X and Y theories.

Douglas McGregor, the management consultant discussed in Chapter 1, developed a different leadership perspective. His efforts to explain and predict a leader's behavior were based upon the leader's attitudes about followers. This framework is known popularly as the X and Y theories of leadership.

During the period of sweatshop labor in the early twentieth century, the leadership style demonstrated by supervisors was primarily that of an **autocratic** or **Theory X leader**. Some still hold this view—that people work mostly for money and status rewards.

However, McGregor believed that leaders are capable of focusing on employees as well as on the accomplishment of the company goal. The **participative** or **Theory Y leader** believes that many people naturally aspire to independent responsibility and self-fulfillment and, further, that people need to feel respected as being capable of assuming responsibility and correcting mistakes on their own.

AUTOCRATIC LEADERS

Theory X leaders leave no doubt about who is in charge. They use the power they have acquired by their rank, knowledge, or skills to reward or punish workers. Their ability to command is the major or sole method by which things get done. This posture does not imply hostility or negativity, but rather sureness of will. Authoritarian leaders give orders and assume that people will respond obediently.

PARTICIPATIVE LEADERS

Theory Y leaders invite decision sharing. Their style calls for subordinates to exercise a high degree of responsibility and freedom. They use as little authoritarian control as possible and are concerned with group interrelationships as well as with getting the job done.

Participative leaders decide after group input.

Democratic leaders confer final authority to the group.

The two types of participative leaders are consultive and democratic. **Consultive leaders** encourage a high degree of involvement from employees, but make it clear that the decision rests with the leader. **Democratic leaders** confer final authority to the group and abide by whatever the group decides, with no exceptions.

Participative leaders request and expect constant feedback, a practice that provides them with the best available information, ideas, suggestions, talent, and experience. When people participate in making the decisions that affect their lives, they support those decisions more enthusiastically.

Participative leadership does not mean that one considers the employee first and the company second. The employee-centered supervisor who gets the best results tends to recognize that high production is also among his or her responsibilities. The major difference between participative leadership and autocratic leadership is that participative leaders give their subordinates a share in decision making and communicate more openly with employees than the autocrat.[22] Figure 11–3 compares the two leadership styles. Which one is more comfortable for you?

MANAGERIAL (LEADERSHIP) GRID

Another approach to measuring and depicting leader behavior is the **managerial grid** (Figure 11–4) developed by Robert Blake and Jane Mouton. This model is based on a matrix of values 1 through 9 for two primary dimensions: a manager's concern for

FIGURE 11-3 *Traits of Autocratic and Participative Leaders*

AUTOCRATIC STYLE: X THEORY TRAITS	PARTICIPATIVE STYLE: Y THEORY TRAITS
Task oriented	Employee oriented
Interested in details	Interested in generalizing
Efficiency minded	Democratic to very permissive
Time and motion studies	Sensitive to individual's needs
Product oriented	People oriented
Interested in promoting oneself	Aware of morale
Fast decision maker	Slow decision maker
Somewhat extroverted	Somewhat introverted
Self-appointed or company appointed	Group appointed
Close supervision	General supervision
Task specialist	Maintenance specialist
Paternalistic	Democratic

FIGURE 11-4 *The Blake and Mouton Managerial Grid*

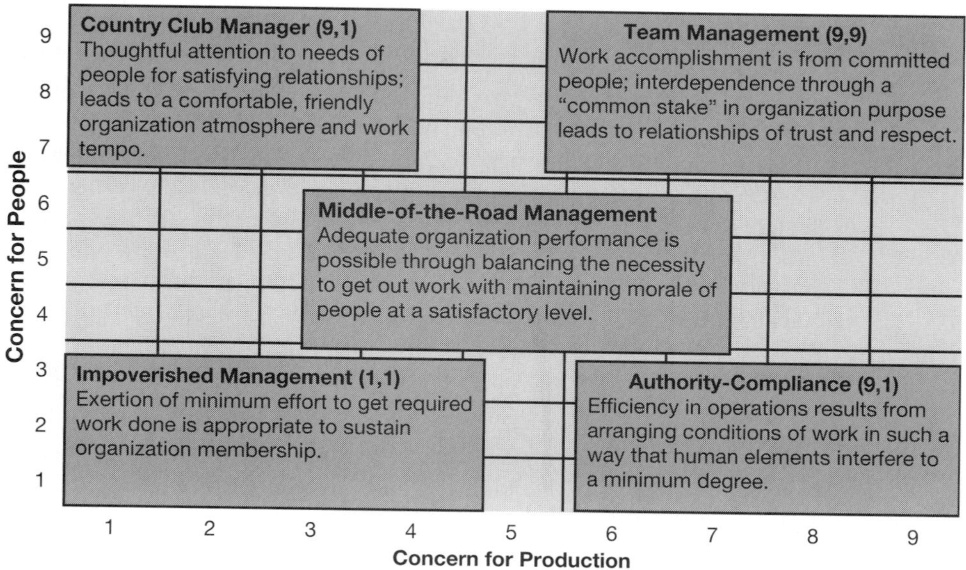

Source: Stephen P. Robbins. *Essentials of Organizational Behavior*, 4th edition, Upper Saddle River, NJ: Prentice Hall, 1994, 139.

people and management's concern for production. A nine by nine matrix yields 81 possible combinations, but the most important styles fall into five categories:

- 1,1 ("What's the Use?") Management has low concern for both people and production.
- 9,1 ("Get-the-Job-Done"—at people cost) Management has high concern for production but low concern for people.
- 5,5 ("Status Quo"—organization) Management has a balanced concern for both people and production.
- 1,9 ("Keep Everybody Happy"—at the cost of production) Management has low concern for production, but high concern for people.
- 9,9 ("Pinnacle"—team) Management has high concern for both people and production.[23]

The managerial grid concept has been widely used in management development programs as a tool to help managers diagnose their relative strength of orientation toward either task- or people-focused activities.

In summary, behavioral theories focus on the need for both production and people orientations. In addition, they illustrate the fact that one does not need to be a "formal" leader to engage in these key production or people leadership activities. These orientations are essential dimensions of the leadership function across organizations, industries, and cultures.

Critics of the behavioral theories argue that the models are too simplistic. They point out that there are occasions where styles other than the 9,9 or the employee-centered style may be most appropriate. They believe that the appropriate style depends on (i.e., is contingent on) the situation. The fact that leadership research professionals and practitioners recognized this point is, in itself, a significant contribution of the behavioral theory movement. It paved the way for a closer look at the contingency theories of leadership effectiveness, which we examine in the next section.

CONTINGENCY MODELS

Researchers interested in providing more complete explanations of leader behavior looked beyond both the trait and behavioral models. These researchers created **contingency models**, which sought to explain how effective leadership behavior differed by the specific leadership context. In essence, these models argued that the most effective leadership behavior depended upon the nature of the specific situation. In other words, there is no one best way to lead. For example, in one circumstance, the most appropriate leader behavior might be highly autocratic and in another, highly participative.

DETERMINING THE SITUATION—MATCHING THE STYLE

Fred E. Fiedler, business and management psychologist at the University of Washington, developed the first significant contingency model. According to Fiedler, anyone can become a good leader, given the right circumstances. Effective leadership is not the function of any one particular management style but, rather, of matching the right style to the right job at the right time.

To use the contingency model, one must first identify a manager's leadership orientation. Fiedler developed a method for identifying the extent to which leaders

The relationship-motivated leader is interested in people.

were either relationship oriented or task oriented. The relationship leader is motivated primarily by relating to people. These leaders are stimulated by forming and maintaining good work relationships with their subordinates and in doing this can get jobs done very well—in certain situations.

Task-oriented leaders are focused on task accomplishment, with little regard for relationship building along the way. They, too, can get jobs done very well, in certain situations.

After determining the leader orientation, Fiedler examined the specific characteristics of the leadership situation, focusing particularly on how favorable or unfavorable the situation was for a task-oriented or relationship-oriented leader. He argued the situation is determined by three factors:

1. Leader-member relations: the nature of the interpersonal relationship between the leader and follower, expressed in terms of good through poor;
2. Task structure: the nature of the subordinate's task, described as "structured" or "unstructured," in terms of the amount of creative freedom allowed the subordinate to accomplish the task; and
3. Position power: the degree to which the leader's position itself enables the leader to get group members to comply with and accept his or her direction.

He concluded that relationship-oriented leaders do best in situations that are either very difficult or very easy to lead[24] (see Table 11–1).

THE PATH-GOAL APPROACH

Another contingency approach to understanding leadership is the **path-goal approach**. In the path-goal approach, the leader clarifies a path by which subordinates will be able to achieve organizational goals. The leader's behavior is based on his or her perception of subordinate characteristics and of the work environment. The relevant

Table 11–1

Matching the Leader to the Situation, According to Fiedler's Contingency Model

SITUATION			**LEADER STYLE NEEDED**
Leader-Member Relations	**Task Structure**	**Leader Position Power**	
Good	Structured	Strong	Task
Good	Structured	Weak	Task
Good	Unstructured	Strong	Task
Good	Unstructured	Weak	Relationship
Poor	Structured	Strong	Relationship
Poor	Structured	Weak	Relationship
Poor	Unstructured	Strong	Can be either
Poor	Unstructured	Weak	Task

subordinate characteristics include their ability to do the job, the extent of training and experience, and other factors.

Work characteristics include the subordinate's task, the primary work group, and the formal authority systems. Specific leader actions are determined by the leader's assessment of the subordinate's readiness to undertake the work, given the nature of the specific situation. Effective leadership behavior is behavior that impacts a subordinate's perception of the goals and the paths to those goals. Figure 11–5 illustrates the path-goal process.

Here are some of the findings of path-goal studies:

1. When the task or work situation is ambiguous, a directive style of leadership is desirable. When task demands are clear, directiveness is a hindrance.
2. Supportive leadership has its most positive effect on satisfaction for subordinates who work on stressful, frustrating, or dissatisfying tasks.
3. In non-repetitive, ego-involved tasks, employees are more satisfied under a participative style of leadership than a non-participative style.[25]

FIGURE 11-5 ***A Path/Goal Spiral with Emphasis on Both Leader and Employee Effectiveness***

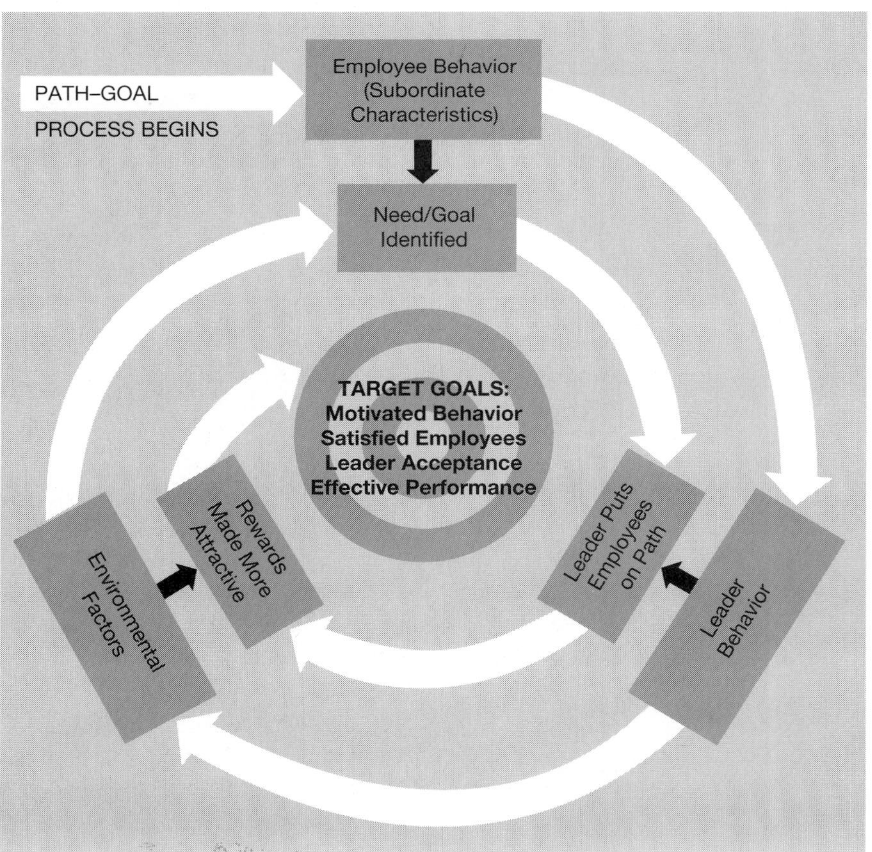

FIGURE 11–6 *SITUATIONAL LEADERSHIP BEHAVIOR MODEL*

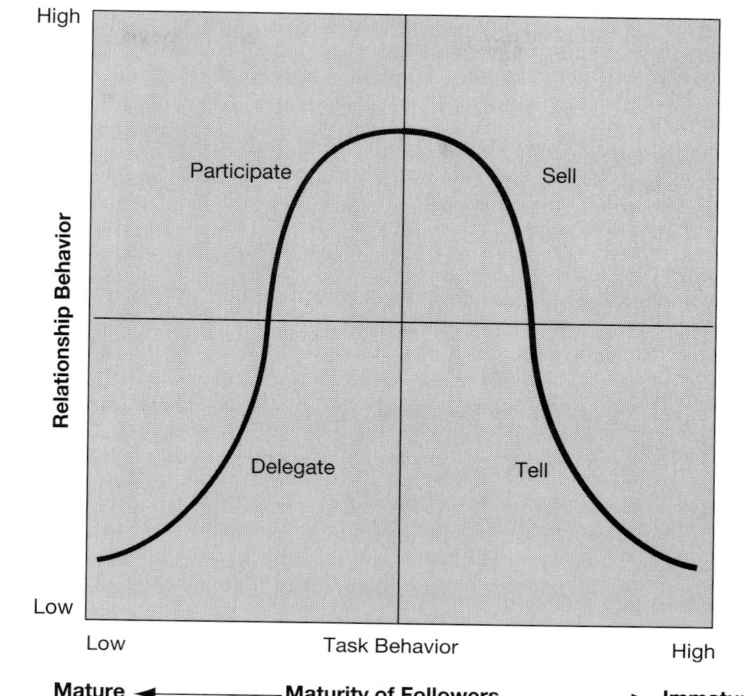

Source: Paul Hersey and Kenneth H. Blanchard. *Management of Organizational Behavior,* 5th ed. (Upper Saddle River, NJ: Prentice Hall, 1988), 182.

SITUATIONAL APPROACH

The **situational leadership** approach, developed by Hersey and Blanchard, suggests the leader match styles to followers' readiness levels. This contingency approach states that there are two dimensions to leadership: task behavior and relationship behavior. These two dimensions form a four-quadrant matrix such as that shown in Figure 11–6.

The bell-shaped curve becomes a "development cycle" indicating growth in follower readiness. Note that the readiness curve is read from right to left. As a follower's readiness level increases, and as the relationship and task levels change, the style of the leader changes. For example, if the follower is new, the leader's task behavior is high and relationship behavior is low; thus, the leader is in a "tell" mode.

As the individual progresses and the relationship behavior increases, the leader moves to "sell" mode, then through the "participate" stage, where the task is low but relationship is high. Finally, with a fully developed follower, the leadership style can shift to one of "delegate," low relationship and low task behavior.[26]

TRANSFORMATIONAL LEADERSHIP

Yet another approach characterizing leader behavior is transformational leadership. Just as the name implies, **transformational leaders** are capable of effecting major changes in their organizations because of their compelling vision, their willingness to change the status quo of the organization, and their effectiveness in enlisting the support of followers in working toward achieving their vision by aligning it with the followers' value systems and priorities. Effective transformational leaders are said to possess certain attributes:

- They see themselves as change agents.
- They are visionaries who have a high level of trust in their intuition.
- They are risk takers, but not reckless.
- They are capable of articulating a set of core values that tend to guide their own behavior.
- They possess exceptional cognitive skills and believe in careful deliberation before taking action.
- They believe in people and show sensitivity to their needs.
- They are flexible and open to learning from experience.[27]

There are many examples of good transformational leaders: Jack Welch transformed General Electric and Herb Kellerher achieved wonderful success at Southwest Airlines. Carly Fiorina at Hewlett-Packard and Andrea Jung at Avon are trying to achieve similar successes in very different industries.

An interesting observation about the concept and the examples given is that transformational leaders inspire others to empower their subordinates to be transformational as well. One of the main benefits of the approach is that it is quickly demonstrated that leadership is not a one-person show.

Transformational leaders are concerned about both the long-term goals of the organization and the developmental needs of individuals in those organizations. They change individuals' awareness of issues by helping them look at old issues in new ways and by rising to the challenges of new problems. Walter Ulmer, past president and CEO of the Center for Creative Leadership, said:

> I think we have a significant flaw in much of the recent literature and training on leadership. That flaw is the failure to distinguish between two fundamental dimensions of organizational leadership: "operating" and "building." In the former, the leader is concerned with making the organization as efficient and immediately productive as it can be; in the latter, the leader is concerned with the continuing capacity of the organization to be efficient and productive.[28]

FIVE PRACTICES OF EFFECTIVE LEADERSHIP

Leadership practices can be learned.

In *The Leadership Challenge*, Kouzes and Posner discuss the development of a leadership model that today has become widely recognized as a useful and practical conceptualization of leadership practices. They define leadership as "the art of mobilizing others to want to struggle for shared aspirations."[29] Kouzes and Posner argue that effective leadership practices can be learned (and therefore taught), that effective leadership is not the province of a selected few, and that effective leadership and its essential components are easily recognized and agreed upon by individuals in diverse situations.

Their leadership model focuses on effective leadership behavior and consists of five practices, including:

- Challenging the process—leaders search for opportunities to change the status quo, and by doing so, experiment and take risks.
- Inspiring a shared vision—leaders passionately believe they can make a difference and envision the future, enlisting others to see the same future.

- Enabling others to act—leaders foster collaboration and build spirited teams, strengthening others in the process by creating trust and fostering human dignity.
- Modeling the way—leaders create standards of excellence, set the example for their constituents, and help them achieve small wins as they work toward larger objectives.
- Encouraging the heart—leaders recognize contributions individuals make and celebrate their accomplishments, making people feel like heroes.

The model has significant and widespread empirical support and is widely used in leadership development programs.[30]

SUBSTITUTES FOR LEADERSHIP

Kerr and Jermier suggest that in some circumstances, characteristics of the followers, the task itself, or the organization may reduce the need for formal leaders or may neutralize the leadership function. Those attributes act as **substitutes for leadership** by providing the necessary direction and support that a leader would typically provide. For example, follower characteristics such as the level of followers' ability to perform a work task, their knowledge about the task, their level of training, and their level of experience in accomplishing the task can reduce or eliminate the need for task-oriented leadership. As pointed out by Yukl, "in effect, substitutes (for leadership) are aspects of the situation that cause intervening variables (e.g., subordinate experience, structured tasks, or a cohesive work group) to be at optimal levels, whereas neutralizers are constraints that prevent or discourage the leader from doing anything to improve existing deficiencies in intervening variables (e.g., a labor contract that neutralizes management's use of certain rewards as incentives)."[31]

In circumstances where specific work tasks are routine, relatively simple and straightforward, and provide intrinsic satisfaction to those completing the tasks, the need for active, task-oriented leadership is reduced. The nature of the task may be said to be substituting for or neutralizing the need for explicit leadership tasks. Finally, the organization itself may be structured in such a way as to minimize or remove the need for direct leadership. For example, in organizations characterized by closely-knit work groups, highly formalized procedures, limited flexibility, and organizational rewards outside of the leader's control, formal leadership may be neutralized.[32]

EMERGING ISSUES IN LEADERSHIP

The dramatic changes occurring in nearly every facet of society as we enter the twenty-first century bring on many exciting challenges and opportunities for organizations. Three of those challenges have specific implications for leadership effectiveness: technology, globalization, and workforce demographics.

Technology. Technology is about making more information more available to more people throughout the organization faster than ever before. While many bemoan the pace of technological change, technology enhances every person's capacity to achieve far more than they otherwise might have been able to do. Witness the development of e-business solutions across every industry. Each of these advances in product design and development, marketing, manufacturing, and human resources has obvious implications for how leaders will manage their organizations to achieve optimal performance. Leading in an environment that is increasingly virtual, as organizations continue to develop their e-business capabilities, presents significant challenges.

E-business creates leadership challenges.

For example, how does one evaluate performance when there is little or no face-to-face contact with employees? What leader behaviors or traits are called for in such an environment? How does one lead a company that exists essentially in cyberspace, rather than as bricks and mortar?

Peter Yip, cofounder and CEO of China.com, points out that in e-businesses, the work style and corporate culture is vastly different than in a traditional company. Differences in rank are de-emphasized and the ability to make something happen is elevated.

> Leadership must be able to handle a demanding pace, because the changes dictated by the marketplace are more sudden and more severe. Leadership in an e-business is more comfortable with a much higher level of overall risk than a traditional bricks and mortar establishment. Get it done now. In today's business world, time waits for no one.[33]

With easy access to so much information comes increased responsibility to use technology appropriately. Leaders of tomorrow must become well versed in the ethical dimensions of technology. They must be prepared to deal with the challenges of protecting customers' and employees' rights to privacy on the one hand, and appropriate disclosure on the other.

Globalization. The communication revolution has redefined how business is being done around the world. With advances in communication technologies and dramatic reduction in communication costs, businesses and their customers are able to be in nearly instantaneous contact. These developments have raised customer expectations to a level unsurpassed at any time in history and have opened markets to competitive forces from literally anywhere. The ability to customize products for niche markets anywhere in the world and to meet customer expectations requires leadership that has the perspective to take full advantage of the global opportunities. Today's new business models have dramatically increased in complexity as a result of their global focus.

Leaders need to focus on global opportunities.

Continuing new technology developments and intense global competition and exchange will combine to create unprecedented volatility in the world of work. Firms and entire industries will rise and fall with surprising rapidity.[34]

Successful leaders in this new environment will need to develop the skills to deal with the diversity, speed, and complexity of a global business community. Knowing one's own core strengths, having a clear vision of what business the organization wants to be in, and being able to obtain the necessary resources to compete effectively are key attributes of tomorrow's effective global leader.

Workforce Demographics. The third challenge facing leaders in the new century is that of changing workforce demographics. These changes are typified by two important trends, both of which have sometimes contradictory implications for organizations and their leadership. Those two trends are: (1) the graying of the workforce and (2) the increased diversity of the workforce.

In the United States, there are unmistakable changes occurring in the makeup of the workforce. The beginning retirement of the baby boom generation, combined with a slowed population growth, will result in organizations continuing to have trouble finding qualified workers to meet their demands. At the same time, social security benefits are almost certain to be reduced by the time the boomers begin to turn 65, resulting in some boomers electing to stay in the workforce longer than they otherwise would. The workforce is getting older.

The implications for leadership are significant. For example, how can a leader keep workers motivated when senior positions do not open up as rapidly as might otherwise be expected and younger individuals are forced to remain in less senior positions longer than would typically be the case? How should benefit packages be changed to accommodate the changing needs of a significantly older workforce?

Workforce diversity.

The second unmistakable trend relates to the increasing diversity of the nation's population and workforce. It is estimated that white, non-Hispanics will account for 68 percent of the workforce in 2020. In western states, particularly in California, diversity will be more significant, as the Hispanic and Asian shares of the population and workforce rise rapidly. Specifically in California, white non-Hispanics will comprise a minority of every age group under the age of 50 by the year 2010. The gender diversification of the workplace will also proceed, with women comprising half of the 2020 workforce.

In the 1990s, immigration accounted for fully half of the increase in the labor force. If immigration policy remains unchanged, immigrants will constitute an increasing share of workers in the early years of the twenty-first century. Unless these immigrants acquire more schooling in the United States than they did in their native countries, recent immigrants will account for rising share of an otherwise dwindling number of Americans who do not have at least a high school education. The leadership challenges will be difficult in this arena as well, as organizations struggle to accommodate issues of language, culture, and skill development, as well as different expectations of such a diverse workforce.

Again, the implications for leadership are dramatic. Leaders must become more culturally aware and their organizations must undertake more extensive recruitment and training programs to find individuals to meet the skill demands of an evolving workplace. They will need to become more creative in developing employee–friendly benefit programs, including child care, mentoring, more creative job design to keep employees motivated (because people are staying longer). Pressure for different types of employee benefits will mount, as the benefit needs and preferences of a demographically different workforce are acknowledged.[35]

INTERNET ACTION PROJECT 11–2

To read more about current issues in leadership, go to the Web site for the Center for Creative Leadership at www.ccl.org, the Leadership Digest at www.leadership.wharton.upenn.edu/digest, or to Leaders Online at www.leadersonline.com.

INTERNET ACTION PROJECT 11–3

To learn more about current workforce diversity issues, go to the Web site for Diversity, Inc. at www.diversityinc.com.

SUMMARY

Leadership involves several important and distinct yet interrelated constructs, including influence, intention, personal responsibility, shared purpose or vision, followers, and change. Management and leadership are two distinctive and complementary systems of action. In the context of how organizations function, managers are typically individuals who hold formal positions of authority in the organization's hierarchy. They typically plan, organize, direct and monitor, and control the actions and activities of individuals who report to them. Leaders, on the other hand, may be either managers or nonmanagerial employees. By virtue of their personal attributes, leaders exert influence on other employees toward the achievement of organizational goals.

Leaders are often called upon to play a variety of roles in the course of meeting their organizational responsibilities. These may include informational, interpersonal, and decisional roles.

Recent leadership research concludes that there are differences between leaders and non-leaders on a few traits. Those traits are drive, leadership motivation, honesty and integrity, self-confidence, knowledge of the business, and cognitive ability. Other research has concluded that all situations do not require the same type of leader and some groups may not require a formal leader at all. Contingency models identify a manager's leadership style, analyze the job situation, and match the best leader for the job at that particular moment in time.

Many other approaches are available for selecting the appropriate leadership style: the managerial grid, the path-goal, situational, and transformational approaches.

Effective leadership is determined by the nature of the relationship between the leader and those being led in the context of the specific leadership situation. All agree that without that relationship being characterized by trust, openness, and credibility, organizations will have a difficult time achieving and maintaining effective leadership.

CASE STUDY 11-1

CAUGHT IN THE MIDDLE—A LEADER'S DILEMMA

Fire Claims Group Four (FCG-4) is led by Julie Collings, a 10-year veteran at Acme Insurance. She has been in charge of the 18-person team for about 6 months, following her promotion and transfer from another Acme region. It is responsible for inspecting damage and determining insurance reimbursement amounts for all personal and commercial fire damage claims in the remote western region of the state.

Julie sought out this leadership opportunity after having served as an FCG team leader for 3 years. She felt she was ready for more responsibility and eagerly anticipated the move. However, in the last month or so, Julie and her division manager, Aaron Shannan, a 28-year company veteran, have not been seeing eye-to-eye on a number of issues. Her team wants her to go in one direction and her boss wants to go in a different direction. Julie feels caught in a real leadership dilemma.

MR. SHANNAN: I don't care, Julie, what the reasons are. You've been in the company long enough to know how things are done. There are rules and regulations that must be followed. As long as I am the division manager, it is my job to see that all eight FCGs in this region perform properly, and that means these rules and regulations will be followed.

JULIE: In my view, Aaron, and with all due respect, your insistence on following these regs to the letter is hindering my team members in their job performance and hurting their morale. I can't help but feel that, in this case, the regulations should be eased or modified for the team's benefit. We are not in the regional office, and my team dresses similarly to the people with whom they come in contact. We're not hurting the company's image at all by our casual dress standards. We don't want to be seen as stuffed shirts! Aren't we trying to appeal to a younger clientele? Other companies are pressing us on this seemingly minor issue. Several of my people have been contacted by competitors promising them great benefits, including relaxed dress standards and more flexible work schedules. Besides, we always make it a point to "clean up" when anyone of us goes to the regional office.

MR. SHANNAN: We are having a lot of success and enjoy a good company image as a result of our doing the right things. We are seen by our executive office as productive—our numbers tell that story—and that's what's really important. Our numbers may be down a little bit, but we're still number one. Turnover in the FCGs in this region is the lowest in the company. Our claim settlements are within company parameters, our error rates are low, and our customer satisfaction ratings are high. I think we are doing a lot of things right. Why should we change? Besides, if I make exceptions for your FCG, then I've got to do the same for the other seven. That I won't do!

JULIE: But Aaron, ours is the only group that is so widely dispersed! Our use of the new wireless technologies makes it almost unnecessary for us to come into the FCG office at all. I can't help but feel that you're being too strict with the team about enforcing dress codes standards way out here. I agree that appearance is important, but I don't think your reprimanding Wes this afternoon about how he looked was appropriate. I would prefer that you talk to me, and I'll work with my team members. How can I gain their confidence and respect if I'm overruled in their presence?

We should all be treated as the professionals we are. I sometimes wonder if all that empowerment stuff isn't just words, with no real intent to give people a say.

MR. SHANNAN: "Julie, I'll say this only once more: I intend that the Fire Claims Division—all of it—will continue to be successful. I know you're fairly new here, but if you find the situation unbearable, a transfer can be arranged.

CASE QUESTIONS

1. If you are Julie, what specific actions would you consider taking at this point? What leadership issues are you likely to encounter, given the actions you may take?
2. Discuss what you would say to your team. Does this circumstance create a leadership dilemma for you?
3. Discuss the implications of disobeying the division manager's instructions—for you, for your team members, for your fellow FCG managers, for your relationship with Aaron, and for the rest of the company.
4. If you are Aaron, how would you resolve the problem with Julie? What leadership issues are you likely to encounter?

DISCUSSION AND STUDY QUESTIONS—TO KEEP YOU THINKING

1. What is leadership?
2. Distinguish between leadership and management.

3. Describe interpersonal, informational, and decisional managerial roles.
4. What are the four stages that one typically progresses through in developing understanding of and ability to apply leadership concepts?
5. Define the six traits that contribute to leadership success.
6. Compare and contrast the leadership theories between the University of Michigan studies and The Ohio State Universities studies.
7. What are the different characteristics of the Theory X and Theory Y leader?
8. Describe the five practices of effective leadership.
9. Discuss the contingency theory of leadership, using several examples.
10. What are three emerging issues in leadership? Explain how these issues impact leadership.
11. Identify some specific examples of leadership substitutes or leadership neutralizers that you have encountered. Did they impact the leader's traditional role?

NOTES

1. Based on "Avon: The New Calling," *Business Week* (September 18, 2000): 137–140.
2. Richard L. Daft. *Leadership: Theory and Practice* (Orlando, FL: The Dryden Press, 1999), 23–24).
3. G. Yukl, 1989, as quoted in J. M. George & G. R. Jones. *Understanding and Managing Organizational Behavior*, 2nd ed. (Boston: Addison-Wesley Publishers, 1999), 404.
4. Daft, *Leadership*, 5–6.
5. John Kotter, "What Leaders Really Do," *Harvard Business Review* (May–June 1990): 103.
6. Warren Bennis, "Why Leaders Can't Lead," *Training and Development Journal* 43, no. 4 (1989): 34–39.
7. "Profit from Leadership," *Business Systems Magazine* (July 1998): 2.
8. Ibid., 2–3.
9. Henry Mintzberg. *The Nature of Managerial Work* (New York: Harper & Row, 1973), 92–93.
10. James M. Kouzes and Barry Z. Posner. *The Leadership Challenge* (San Francisco: Jossey-Bass Publishers, 1995), 20–29.
11. Gilbert W. Fairholm. *Perspectives on Leadership* (Westport, CT: Praeger Publishing, 2001), xviii.
12. S. A. Kirkpatrick and E. A. Locke, "Leadership: Do Traits Matter," in *Leaders and the Leadership Process*, 2nd ed., eds. Jon L. Pierce and John W. Newstrom. (Boston: Irwin McGraw Hill, 2000), 35–39.
13. Ibid., 39.
14. D. Goleman, "What Makes a Leader?" *Harvard Business Review* (November–December 1998): 93–102.
15. Herminia Ibarra and Kristin Daly. "Gender Differences in Managerial Behavior: The Ongoing Debate," *Harvard Business School Note 9-495-038*, March 12, 1995): 1–2.
16. G. N. Powell, "One More Time: Do Female and Male Managers Differ?" *Academy of Management Executive* 4, no. 3 (1990): 68–75.
17. S. Donnell and J. Hall, "Men and Women as Managers: A Significant Case of No Significant Differences," *Organizational Dynamics* (spring 1980): 60–77.
18. Ibarra and Daly, "Gender Differences . . ." 3–4.
19. Rosener, Judy B. "Ways Women Lead," *Harvard Business Review* (November–December 1990): 3–10.
20. B. M. Bass. *Handbook of Leadership: A Survey of Theory and Research* (New York: Free Press, 1990).
21. Robert N. Lussier and Christopher F. Achua. *Leadership: Theory, Application, Skill Building* (Cincinnati, OH: South-Western Publishing Co., 2001), 74.
22. Douglas MacGregor. *The Human Side of Enterprise* (New York: McGraw-Hill, 1960).
23. Robert Blake and Jane Mouton. *The Managerial Grid III* (Houston, TX: Gulf Publishing, 1985).
24. Fred E. Fiedler, "When to Lead, When to Stand Back: If You Want to Be a Directive Leader You'd Better Be Smart. Otherwise, Get Your Employees Involved," *Psychology Today* (September 1987): 26.
25. Robert J. House and Terence C. Mitchell, "Path-Goal Theory of Leadership," *Journal of Contemporary Business* (autumn 1974): 81–99; see also R. J. House, "Retrospective Comment," *The Great Writing in*

Management and Organizational Behavior, 2nd ed., ed. L. E. Boone and D. D. Bowen. (New York: Random House, 1987), 354–364.

26. Paul Hersey and Kenneth H. Blanchard. *Management of Organizational Behavior* (Upper Saddle River, NJ: Prentice Hall, 1988) and personal communication with Ken Blanchard, August 1994.
27. Lussier and Achua, *Leadership*, 382–384.
28. F. Ulmer, Jr., "Inside View," *Issues and Observations* (Greensboro, NC: Center for Creative Leadership, 1993), 6.
29. James B. Kouzes and Barry M. Posner. *The Leadership Challenge* (San Francisco: Jossey-Bass, Inc., 1995), 30.
30. Ibid., 8–14.
31. G. Yukl. *Leadership in Organizations*, 5th ed. (Upper Saddle River, NJ: Prentice Hall, 2002), 217.
32. S. Kerr and J. Jermier, "Substitutes for Leadership: The Meaning and Measurement," *Organizational Behavior and Human Performance* 22 (1978): 375–403.
33. Shannon Copeland. "E-Commerce Leadership: Interview with Peter Yip, Co-Founder and CEO, China.com," *Wharton Leadership Digest* 5, no. 3 (December, 2000): 6–8.
34. Richard W. Judy and Carol D'Amico. *Workforce 2020: Work and Workers in the 21st Century* (Indianapolis, IN: The Hudson Institute, 1999), 121.
35. Ibid., 118.

CHAPTER

12

Group and Team Dynamics

TO START YOU THINKING

Here are some questions to stimulate your thinking and open avenues of discussion before you read the chapter.

- What is a group? What determines if it is effective?
- What is the difference between a group and a team?
- What attracts you to another person or group of people?
- How do you obtain consensus in group behavior and decision making?
- Are there major differences in behavior, power, and control between formal and informal groups?
- What is groupthink and why should it be avoided?

LEARNING GOALS

After studying this chapter, you should be able to:

1. Understand groups and their characteristics.
2. Describe a common perspective on the process of group evolution.
3. Distinguish between groups and effective teams.
4. Appreciate propositions about group dynamics, including group cohesiveness, risky shift, and social loafing.
5. Understand consensus building, its advantages, and disadvantages.
6. Understand and differentiate task, maintenance, and individual roles.
7. Understand role prescriptions and role behaviors.
8. Identify types of nonfunctional group or team behaviors.
9. Articulate the manager's role in the group process.
10. Consider alternative views of team effectiveness.
11. Define self-managed work teams, including the forces leading to their increased presence in the workplace and the consequences of that increased presence.
12. Explain the role of groupthink and risky shift in decision making.
13. Define and apply the following terms and concepts (in order of first occurrence):

KEYWORDS

- **group dynamics**
- **group**
- **primary group**
- **secondary group**
- **formal group**
- **informal group**
- **homogeneous group**
- **norms**
- **group cohesiveness**
- **consensus**
- **task-related roles**
- **maintenance-related roles**
- **individual roles**
- **role prescriptions**

- **heterogeneous group**
- **nominal group**
- **temporary group**
- **permanent group**
- **teams**
- **group development**
- **role behaviors**
- **role ambiguity**
- **role conflict**
- **nonfunctional group behaviors**
- **concertive control**
- **risky shift**

GROUP DYNAMICS

The demands of meeting individual challenges are minuscule compared to being effective in groups or teams. Sheer numbers and the accompanying arithmetic or geometric interactions possible among groups make the task of managing groups challenging. Groups, like individuals, have and develop their own personalities.

Group dynamics are the social processes by which small groups interact. The term also refers to the collective effect that individuals have on each other. The sense of belonging, prestige, and shared perceptions can dramatically affect one's individual behavior.

Interaction, interdependence, and communication are the keys to group activity. There must be some commonality of objectives and interdependency of individuals to accomplish those objectives. Thus, communication among those individuals is imperative to successful fulfillment of group goals.

WHAT IS A GROUP?

A group is a collection of people.

A **group** is a collection of two or more people who are psychologically aware of each other and who interact to fulfill a common goal.[1] Note that the definition of a group does not require that they meet face-to-face; only that they be psychologically aware of each other and share a common goal.

Groups are usually involved in meetings, task forces, or teams. All these activities are affected by many variables, including the size of the group and the predisposition to work together to accomplish an objective. Figure 12–1 shows the various factors that influence group task accomplishment.

Five dimensions of groups.

In the study of group or team dynamics, researchers typically distinguish among groups along five dimensions: (1) primary and secondary; (2) formal and informal; (3) heterogeneous and homogeneous; (4) interacting and nominal; and (5) temporary and permanent.

The distinction between primary and secondary groups relates to the type of relationship that exists between members. **Primary groups** are those groups whose member interactions tend to be based on personal relationships, such as families and friendship groups. **Secondary groups** are groups whose member relationships are more work-based or task focused. Clearly both types of groups exist in organizations.

Formal groups are those explicitly created by the organization to accomplish a task or set of tasks. Project teams, task forces, and organizational departments are representative of formal groups in the work environment. These groups are usually comprised of supervisors, managers or leaders, and other employees.

FIGURE 12–1 *Factors Influencing Group Task Accomplishment*

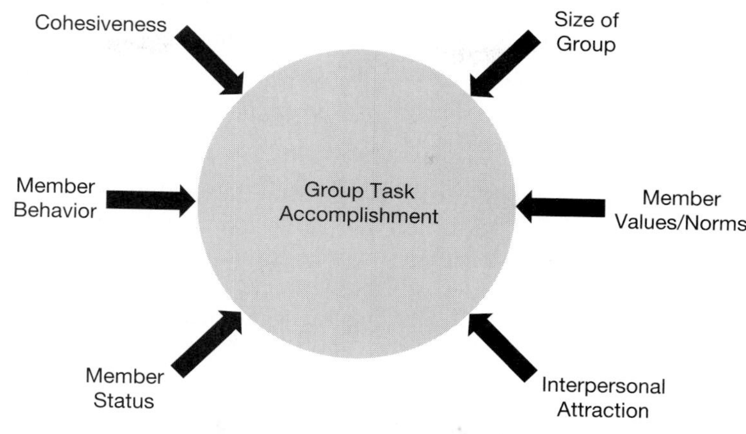

Informal groups are those associations that arise out of interaction among the organization's members. Informal groups tend to be more relationship oriented than task oriented. These groups concentrate on sentiments derived from activities and interaction of the group members. They are more directed by group rules derived by consensus rather than by formal regulations established by the organization. Informal groups typically do not have formally stated objectives, but it is clear they do serve a number of implicit goals. These goals may include meeting social needs of the members that are distinct from the more task-oriented and organizational-sanctioned goals of the formal group. Figure 12–2 compares formal and informal groups.

Another way to compare groups is by the degree of similarity (homogeneity) or dissimilarity (heterogeneity) among group members. In a **homogenous group** the members have a number of key attributes in common (for example, values, gender, age, attitudes), whereas a **heterogeneous group** is characterized by diversity along similar dimensions. Understanding the extent to which the degree of similarity or dissimilarity influences how the group may perform is an important aspect of optimizing organizational performance and employee satisfaction. It will continue to be important because of the increasing cultural, gender, and racial diversity prevalent in today's organizations.

FIGURE 12–2 *Comparisons of Formal and Informal Groups*

Concept	Formal Group	Informal Group
General Orientation	Official, formal	Unofficial, informal
Primary Comparison	Formal, delegated authority	Political prowess
Behavior Guidelines	Rules and regulations	Norms and privileges
Power Source	From management	From group members
Control Source	Rewards and punishment	Group entitlements

A fourth way to examine groups is with respect to the nature and extent of interaction that occurs among the group members. Historically, groups have interacted in face-to-face meetings for the most part. These group meetings are characterized by active and direct interactions among the members. **Nominal groups**, in contrast, have less direct interaction, achieving their goals via a third party or in computer-mediated environments. It is increasingly common to have nominal group meetings or other interactions with individuals separated by thousands of miles.

Nominal groups communicate via a third party or electronic media.

Finally, groups are often differentiated on the basis of their expected duration. A **temporary group** is formed to achieve a specific task or project goal. Once the goal is accomplished, the group is disbanded. A **permanent group** is formed with the expectation that it will continue indefinitely, addressing a variety of task or project goals. Interestingly, with the increasing tendency in business to utilize temporary workers, the management implications of working with these short-duration groups will likely become more important.[2]

GROUPS VERSUS TEAMS

Groups are not necessarily teams.

Many individuals use the terms *group* and *team* interchangeably. The distinctions between a group and a team are important, although sometimes they are not easily observed. Groups may evolve into teams over time or as a result of conscious efforts to do so. It is incorrect to assume that just because a collection of people has been brought together and declared a team, that, in fact, an effective team has suddenly been created.

Effective **teams** are characterized as having members who share the same goals, are interdependent, and are mutually accountable to each other and to the organization. In addition, team members often share leadership roles—that is, leadership responsibility often moves to the person in the team who has the expertise needed for a particular aspect of the team's task. In the course of accomplishing the team's task, leadership responsibility may move through several team members.

The work products produced by a team tend to be collaborative ones, rather than individually based, as is typically found in a work group. Team members provide each other with feedback on how they are doing. The team is acknowledged (both by team members and external parties) as the appropriate and legitimate body to enforce sanctions on those individuals in the team who are not fulfilling legitimate role expectations. In contrast, sanctions levied in groups tend to be administered by the group's supervisor or manager. Teams typically have a defined set of goals that include productivity, team member satisfaction, and personal growth. Criteria that are used to assess team effectiveness include the ability to achieve specified performance outcomes, the speed of innovation/adaptation to changes in the environment, efficiency (i.e., resource utilization optimization), quality, employee satisfaction, and customer satisfaction. When a team is able to achieve these goals with high quality and high team member satisfaction, team effectiveness is the result.

GROUP DEVELOPMENT

Groups or teams do not become effective simply because a manager wishes they would. The process of **group development** takes time and effort on the part of the group members. Tuckman suggests that this process be viewed as a five-stage model through which a group evolves in order to achieve its optimum effectiveness.

Forming.

In the first stage, forming, group members attempt to get to each other and to find out what the group's goals and working arrangements will be. This stage is completed when most of the members feel that they are actually part of the group.

Storming.

In the next stage, storming, group members struggle to establish their positions in the group, identify who will lead and who will follow, and determine how much power any one individual will have. Additional efforts at clarifying the group's task and methods to accomplish the task also occur in stage two.

Norming.

Stage three of the Tuckman model is called norming, which refers to the developing sense of commonly understood purpose and methods of operation that the group achieves. Feelings of friendship and camaraderie are typical as this stage ends with agreement on how to undertake the task at hand.

Performing.

It is in stage four, performing, that the actual work of the group is undertaken. Group members engage in their respective tasks to get the goal of the group accomplished. This stage is completed when the group's task is done. At that point, the group moves to stage five, adjourning, in which the group disbands. Of course, in many organizations, the tasks of a particular work group are ongoing, and it does not disband. In such instances, the group does not enter stage five.[3]

When observing groups and group processes, managers should keep in mind the stage of group development and what impact that might have on group member behavior. In addition, managers should always be aware of group deadlines and the propensity of most groups to avoid coming to grips with the core task until the pressure is on (i.e., the last half of the available time).[4] These insights will provide managers with a greater understanding about how and why a group is functioning in the manner that it is.

NORMS

Norms are values that a group develops regarding expected behaviors of individuals in the group or team. Once developed, they become the rules the groups use to operate.

Norms are usually unwritten but powerful.

Norms are usually unwritten but powerful devices for assuring group conformity. Feelings often run strong within the group about what qualifies as right and wrong conduct. In one sense, group norms are summations of the individual members' values, but more than the sum. Group norms can become, in some instances, powerful controlling forces of member behavior, even to the extent of defining group members' values.[5]

Consider the example of a group that assembles aircraft or automotive products. The values that individuals attach to money, human life, and congeniality of a group all affect the speed and quality of production output. If the members are on a pay-for-piecework basis, their output may be guided primarily by the amount they can produce. If the product is safety related and might endanger its end user if not properly produced, their output may be more balanced with concern for quality and safety. Perhaps most importantly, if an individual wants to be a part of the group, he or she must cooperate with the group members and adopt the value set of the group and their work standards.

GROUP COMPOSITION

Why are we attracted to some individuals? Certainly sharing common task goals in the workplace may facilitate attachment, if not attraction. In addition, we are often attracted to work with others because of similar attitudes, opinions, behavior, goals, age, education, and personality. Continued exposure and frequent interaction are also reasons for interpersonal attraction in group and team settings.

Another factor influencing group composition is the group's perceived attractiveness or desirability of association. If we perceive an association with a person as having desirable traits, then we anticipate that a relationship will be rewarding. If we grow to like an individual through association and interaction, the relationship becomes mutually rewarding.

SIZE OF GROUP

Group size impacts group process.

The overall effectiveness of a group is influenced significantly by its size. Groups of two can be very effective depending on their interpersonal relationship and task goals. But groups are more commonly thought of as having more than two people. Group size minimums are not as important as maximums. Five to seven individuals may function very effectively as a group. In groups over seven, the low participators tend to stop talking to each other and speak more to the leader. Subconsciously this situation becomes more formal and real interaction generally declines. The tendency for individual members to put forth less effort increases as the size of the group grows. In addition, group effectiveness and group size may also be impacted by whether the group meets face-to-face or virtually.

There is a greater tendency for stronger directive leaders to emerge as size increases. Communication difficulties arise as the size of the group grows. Figure 12–3 compares communication and complexity of interaction in small groups (6 members) and large groups (16 members). As group size increases, consensus becomes increasingly difficult to achieve. If the group becomes too large, a false consensus (nominal agreement only) may be obtained.

There is an inverse relationship between group size and the ability of the group to function efficiently and effectively. Factors influencing the optimal size of a group include the group's purpose and the individuals' needs for influence, interaction, and interdependency.

GROUP COHESIVENESS

Group cohesiveness, the degree to which members are attracted to each other and are motivated to stay in the group,[6] is determined primarily by three factors—the amount of interaction the members have with one another, the extent to which the members of the group share the same mission and goals, and the degree of personal attraction members share for one another. How well an individual is perceived as contributing to cohesiveness depends on the factors discussed earlier: norms, social class, interpersonal attraction, and group size.

Highly cohesive groups reach consensus more easily.

A highly consensual group exhibits high group cohesiveness. Similarly, a highly cohesive group (where group members' desires to remain a part of the group are high) can reach consensus more readily because of their mutuality. Highly cohesive groups, relative to groups that are not as cohesive, tend to experience better morale and increased satisfaction with the group's activities and outputs.

Group cohesiveness may be impacted by how emotions affect the group's decision making. Emotional conflict in the group can lead to consensus being reached due primarily to members' avoidance or withdrawal from group processes—the "I don't care" and "Do anything, just get this over with" syndromes—can occur even in

FIGURE 12-3 COMPLEXITY OF INTERACTION IN SMALL AND LARGE GROUPS

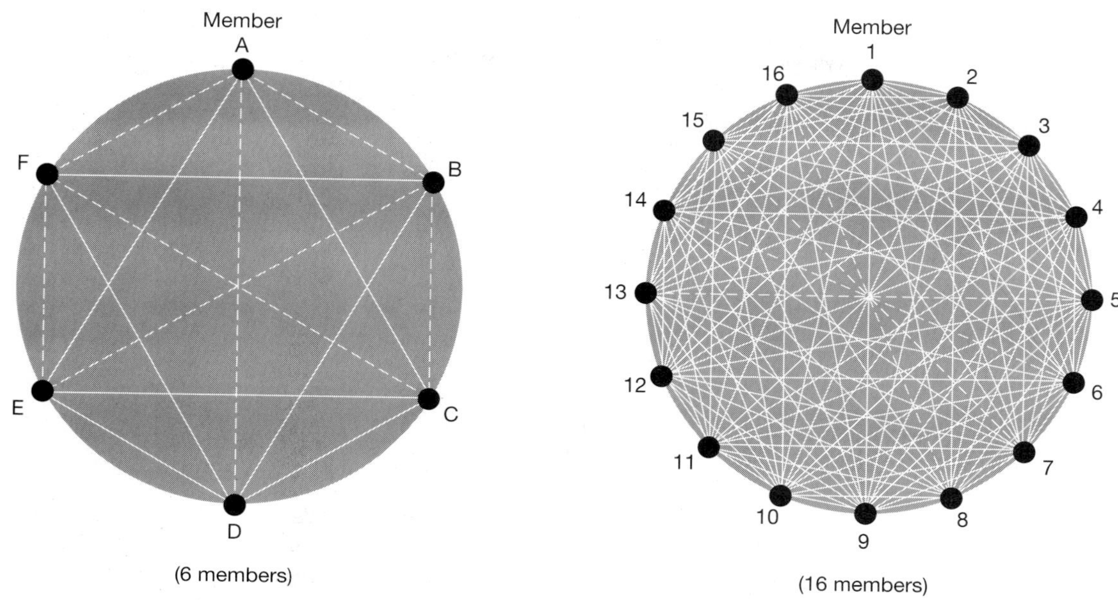

important decisions affecting group members. Difficult or particularly troublesome decisions in such instances are handled on an ad hoc basis rather than as part of a cohesive, well-functioning group. Figure 12–4 lists several characteristics of group dynamics and consensus building.

GROUP CONSENSUS

Consensus is an attempt to arrive at a solution acceptable to most group members. How is consensus among members obtained? Communication and hard work. Consensus requires extensive communication, especially, but not limited to, interpersonal dialogue either between two people or a small number of individuals or within a group.

The communication behaviors of group members can either facilitate or hinder group consensus. If communication is group oriented, it will have a positive effect on group consensus. Highly opinionated or "me" statements such as "This is my area of expertise—if you don't agree with me, you're wrong!" have a negative effect on the group.

Even the terminology employed can affect the group's behavior. Efforts need to be made to secure agreement, adaptation, and compromise, instead of getting "locked in" or becoming defensive about one's position (e.g., see the earlier discussion on principled negotiations in Chapter 10). A very practical approach to achieving consensus is to work with group members to focus on their underlying objectives, rather than forcing them into a position that must be defended.

As noted in the section on cohesiveness, decisions can become emotional, ad hoc, and hurried. When discussions and differences of opinion take place on a more rational

FIGURE 12-4 *How Do You Obtain Consensus?*

Building a group into a cohesive, consensual team requires the following:

1. Recognition that groups are everywhere—in all kinds of settings.
2. Recognition that groups have power in numbers.
3. Recognition that groups have positive and negative outcomes:
   a. Positive outcomes may include better (more thought-through) decisions, acceptance, and actions.
   b. Negative outcomes may include unnecessary group conformity and groupthink.
4. Hard work—especially among professionals.
5. Leadership guidance and facilitation.
6. Extensive communication, including interpersonal dialogue.
7. Give and take—giving and taking of advice, and giving and taking of constructive criticism.
8. Group-oriented communications—not highly opinionated or "me" statements.
9. Restatement of decision-making processes—not final solutions, in which individuals become locked onto a position and therefore put into a defensive posture.
10. Limiting group size to a workable number (maybe five to seven) of affected individuals in order to avoid a false consensus (nominal agreement only to get the group process completed).

Group rapport and trust develop morale.

basis, it is more likely that the group will achieve true consensus for a decision. When that occurs, group rapport and trust also usually develop.

GROUP ROLES

Group roles are shared expectations of how group members are to perform in their positions. We develop roles based on our understanding of the activities, interactions, and beliefs of others in the group about how we will participate in the group.

Group member roles may be divided into task-related, maintenance-related, and individual roles. Task-related roles are those behavioral expectations that directly aid in the accomplishment of group objectives. **Task-related roles** include helping define problems, acquiring and providing facts, and summarizing group deliberations. **Maintenance-related roles** are those behavioral expectations that are directly related to the well-being and development of the group. Examples of maintenance-related roles are consensus-seeker, facilitator, and reconciliator. Figure 12–5 lists examples of task, maintenance and individual roles in a group.

Task and maintenance-related roles help the group become more productive and cohesive. However, individual roles are typically counterproductive for the group and may lead to the group becoming nonfunctional. **Individual roles** focus attention away from the group and its goal. Group members may perform these behaviors consciously

ACTION PROJECT 12–1

CAN YOU COME TO A CONSENSUS? (GROUP EXERCISE)

Wayout University, like other institutions of higher learning, is experiencing grade inflation: steadily increasing grade levels in its seven colleges. Students and faculty alike are continually concerned with the grading systems employed. The topic of grades is frequently broached in both formal and informal settings. Today, Harry Benedict, a student government representative, convened a problem-solving conference on grades. Note: Harry doesn't show up for the meeting, but all the other invitees do. Can you reach some consensus regarding what, if anything, to do about grade inflation? In groups of five, each individual should assume one of the roles described and participate in the group meeting. After the meeting, discuss the communication challenges and conflicts group members experience as they atempt to achieve consensus.

ROLE FOR AARON SHANNAN

You have been associate dean of students at Wayout for the past 5 years. You are becoming increasingly alarmed at the number of student problems and dropouts. You feel strongly that the grading system has something to do with these rates.

ROLE FOR PAT FOSTER

You are the assistant dean in the College of Physical Sciences. Your responsibilities include ensuring that undergraduate instruction in your college meets the standards of accrediting associations of various disciplines and screening applicants for graduate study in your college. You are concerned about the grading systems, but need some measure of student performance in order to carry out your responsibilities, and grades seem to be the best thing you've got right now.

ROLE FOR LYNN SAMSON

You are a professor of mathematics. You are dissatisfied with the grading system because you believe it imposes artificial barriers among students. You do realize that all students are not born with bachelor's degrees stamped on their birth certificates and that some students do unsatisfactory work for various reasons. You are particularly interested in having a system in place that rewards the exceptional student and appropriately evaluates those students who do not perform as well.

ROLE FOR MARION JOHNSON

As an average student, you get easily discouraged when your grades are not as high as your expectations. Consequently, you are suffering some physiological and psychological health problems.

ROLE FOR FRANCIS ALBRIGHT

You are an exceptionally good student in that you study hard, get excellent grades, and get involved in class and out-of-class discussions. You are well respected by your peers and professors. You expect to be rewarded for your efforts and achievements.

or unconsciously. Examples of individual roles include aggressor, player, and recognition seeker. Group roles are also a function of role prescriptions and role behaviors.

ROLE PRESCRIPTIONS AND ROLE BEHAVIORS

What we say and do are largely matters of expectations, role prescriptions, and role behaviors. The things that people are expected to do are known as **role prescriptions**; the things that they actually do are known as **role behaviors**. To the extent that role

FIGURE 12-5 *Task, Maintenance, and Individual Roles of Group Members*

Examples of Task-Related Roles	Examples of Maintenance-Related Roles	Examples of Individual-Related Roles
Objective(s) clarifier	Consensus seeker; mutual support	Aggressor
Planner	Encourager; facilitator	Blocker
Organizer	Mediator	Dominator
Seeker of information (acquire & provide facts)	Gatekeeper (relevant to group norms)	Evader; self-confessor
Leader	Compromiser	Help seeker
Coordinator	Communicator	Player
Energizer	Standard setter	Recognition seeker
Evaluator	Observer	Special-interest pleader
Summarizer	Evaluator	
	Reconciliator; tension reducer	

behaviors match the appropriate role prescriptions, an individual is said to be effective or successful. It is assumed that the individual is contributing to company goal achievement.

Doing as other's expect you to do is playing the role.

The role prescription is the set of expectations that affect a particular role, such as a manager's position. All the different people with whom the employee comes into contact collectively form the basis for the employee's multiple roles.

Performance evaluation is essentially a matter of determining the degree to which the role prescription and role behavior match. It is an attempt to equate organizational goal attainment with the individual contribution. What is really important as far as an organization is concerned is not how much an individual does, but how much of what he or she does is organizationally relevant as determined by his or her role.

Roles are the sum of expectations.

The role is thus the sum total of expectations placed on the employee by his or her supervisors, subordinates, peers, customers, vendors, and others.

ROLE AMBIGUITY AND ROLE CONFLICT

When self-expectations and others' expectations differ, role conflict develops.

Employees must be able to integrate these expectations, as well as their own expectations, into a coherent pattern if they expect to perform successfully. **Role ambiguity** occurs when the employee lacks a clear understanding of these expectations. **Role conflict** occurs when the expectations conflict with each other or with the employee's own expectations. Employees are unable to satisfy some of these expectations when role conflict develops.

Research suggests that when there is a sizable discrepancy between a manager's concept of his or her role and the employees' role expectations of that job, motivation and efficiency tend to be poor. For example, if managers see themselves as mediators and developers of compromises between management and labor, but both management and the union expect them to be hard-nosed negotiators, role conflict develops. Many employees find their function in a company much easier when their role prescription is defined clearly than when it is not.

TYPES OF NONFUNCTIONAL GROUP/TEAM BEHAVIOR

Not every person who becomes part of a group or a team views his or her relationship to the team or the team's task in the same way. Not infrequently, individuals will engage in behaviors that are dysfunctional; that is, they tend to work in ways that limit the team's effectiveness. Examples of **nonfunctional group behaviors** and a brief description of each appear below. Remember that in some circumstances, these behaviors may be helpful to the group's activities. They are nonfunctional when they become the focus of the team's attention and disrupt team operations.

- *Being aggressive:* dominating the team setting in an attempt to take it over
- *Blocking:* using tactics that prevent the group from reaching decisions
- *Self-confessing:* continually explaining one's personal inadequacies
- *Competing:* competing against another team member rather than working productively for task accomplishment—in a way that is detrimental to the team's effectiveness
- *Seeking sympathy:* drawing attention specifically to the one's unique circumstance as a reason for not taking action or getting an assignment accomplished
- *Special pleading:* Asking for special favors that detract from task accomplishment
- *Horsing around:* refusing to settle into the task
- *Seeking recognition:* Saying, "Look at me!" rather than "How can we get the task done?"
- *Withdrawal:* refusing to participate in a meaningful way in the group's activities.

SELF-MANAGED WORK TEAMS

During the last decades of the twentieth century and into the twenty-first century, there have been significant efforts to involve employees to a greater extent than ever before in the decision-making processes of organizations. This increased participation and empowerment has had major impacts on how work gets done and who accepts responsibility for ensuring that it is completed.

While the forces driving the trend toward more participation by employees in organizational decision-making groups and teams have been widely discussed elsewhere (e.g., technology, expanding global marketplace, increasing education level of the workforce and the growing diversity of the workforce), the consequences of more participation from the standpoint of team members have not been as widely discussed. Among those consequences are the recognition that extensive team involvement takes more time and more energy on the part of employees, as well as an expanded skill mix that includes increased collaborative skills. Increased participation also tends to result in increased commitment to the organization.

Self-managed work teams empower employees.

One example of how empowerment is being manifested in the workplace is through self-managed work teams. A self-managed work team is a structural form in which employees make many of the decisions managers once made and supervise their own work behavior. Using such teams in the workplace results in a work environment that is more participative, less hierarchical, and often without external super vision. In such circumstances, the team itself is responsible for hiring and disciplining team members, coordinating workflow, training employees, and coordinating within the company.

Those who are ardent supporters of self-managed work teams say that companies benefit because employee commitment is enhanced and productivity is increased. In addition, self-managed work teams tend to be more responsive and more flexible to changing demands within the company.

James Barker, a leading teams researcher, cautioned about group norms, roles, and values becoming so entrenched in the self-managed work team and so powerful that team members complied with team decisions out of fear of sanction by the rest of the group. He referred to this phenomenon as **concertive control**, which he defined as team members acting in concert with one another to create a mechanism for controlling their own behavior. When concertive control occurs, individual team members subordinate their own desires to the collective will of the organization.[7]

Concertive control.

With the increased organizational emphasis on full participation in teams, along with a shift toward team management, some have raised the question of whether or not managers are still needed. What roles can managers possibly fulfill when teams complete all the work? Several authors have suggested there are a number of important roles that managers can fulfill as the use of teams continues to expand. For example, managers frequently are the ones most familiar with the organization's strategic objectives and resources, and as such, can make meaningful contributions to team processes by sharing those insights and obtaining resources for the team.

Managers are still needed in a self-managed work team environment.

In addition, and because of their historical position in the organization, managers can often serve as linking pins between the team and various other parts of the department and organization. They frequently have strong change management skills and can be used to help move the self-managed work team along in its development process. Managers often can serve as the ideological pillar in the team because of their central role in the organization's operations. Finally, managers typically have communication skills that the team can use as it relates to other parts of the organization or to external constituencies.

GROUP PHENOMENA

Two important group phenomena that have received a considerable amount of attention by those who study group processes are groupthink and risky shift. Their impact on group decision making and ultimately on group performance can be significant.

GROUPTHINK

The downside to group cohesiveness is the risk that everyone in the group will start to think alike. Groupthink sets in. As introduced in Chapter 7, groupthink is a deterioration of the decision-making processes because of in-group pressures to think alike. Characteristics of groupthink include strong group unity, self-censorship, shared stereotypes of true opposition, and overconfidence.

Groupthink may inhibit alternative points of view.

A strong sense of group unity and a feeling that "we" are on the right track can lead to finding the quickest, but not the best, answer. Closely knit groups sometimes suffer from the illusion of unanimity—that is, no one wants to break up the cohesiveness of the group. Group leaders may also assume, incorrectly, that silence on the part of a member means consent or agreement.

Illusion of unanimity.

Members of a group may engage in self-censorship, failing to mention a legitimate idea when it is contrary to the group's direction. They believe that the idea is

Self-censorship.

not really what the group wants to hear. Many of us want so much to be a member of the team that we will not oppose the group's conclusion.

Shared stereotypes.

Shared stereotypes of the opposition are another aspect of groupthink. Typical of the comments one might hear in a conversation where groupthink is occurring are the following: "Well, all those people feel the same way, but what do they know?" "They really aren't that important. Actually, their opinions are not worth consideration." Such group behavior can even lead people to think that, "If I think differently from the group, I will be seen as the opposition or that I don't want to be part of the team."

Groupthink creates a sense of infallibility.

Groupthink can also generate the illusion of invulnerability. Typical of such comments reflecting that invulnerability is: "After all, we have been a leader in the field for many years; why shouldn't people accept our results?" Successful companies are likely to find that their committees fall into the groupthink syndrome. Overconfidence results when group members think alike and encourage each other in their opinions. Do you have a strong leader of your committee who states an opinion before others? Such group leaders frequently bring about groupthink.[8]

RISKY SHIFT

Risky shift may result from diffused responsibility.

Another interesting phenomenon in group decision making is known as risky shift. **Risky shift** is the term used to describe the process whereby a group becomes more extreme than individual group members in its willingness to endorse risky decisions. When risky shift occurs group members end up agreeing with decisions that they would not normally make as individuals.

One reason proposed for the phenomenon is that responsibility for the decision is diffused across all group members, making the decision less risky from an individual's standpoint. Another, and perhaps more widely accepted reason, is that the shift is actually an effort by members holding a minority position in the group to accede to the majority's wishes, thereby enabling the majority to have its position become the group's position. While not necessarily changing their views, the minority members of the team do enable the majority's views to be the "sense of the team."[9]

EXPRESS YOUR OPINION

Think of a national issue, a company decision, or a well-known local situation in which a group or committee has fallen into the trap of groupthink. Review the four aspects of groupthink.

1. Illusion of unanimity
2. Self-censorship
3. Shared stereotypes of the opposition
4. Illusion of invulnerability

Give reasons for each point listed as to why the group, committee, or company has succumbed to groupthink.

SUMMARY

Groups and teams have a powerful influence on the success or failure of our organizations. They exert significant influence (not always positive) on the behavior of individuals in those organizations. In this chapter, multiple types of groups were identified and their relevance to group performance highlighted. Not all groups become teams, but those that do tend to exhibit several characteristics that distinguish them from traditional work groups. Those characteristics include such attributes as interdependence, mutual accountability, and high commitment to the task.

The success of groups and teams is influenced by factors such as size, cohesiveness, interpersonal attraction, as well as individual behavior, status, values, or norms of members.

A key to effective group behavior is the ability of the group to reach consensus and the key to obtaining consensus is keeping discussions focused on task-related, rather than personal, issues. Concerted effort by the group leader and group members to be fair, open, and trusting will help achieve consensus. In addition, efforts to maximize participation and contribution by all group members will enhance the quality of the process and the decisions. Groups communicate more easily and are more cohesive when they are smaller in size.

How people in a group, team, or organization believe their goals are related is important in understanding how effectively they work together. When group members believe their goals and values are compatible, group cohesiveness is strengthened. Some individuals engage in behaviors in the team setting that can be characterized as nonfunctional, that is, the behaviors detract from, rather than contribute to, successful team accomplishment of tasks.

One strategy that reflects management's recognition of employee desires to have greater control over their work life is the creation of self-managed work teams. While significantly empowering to the members of the team, such efforts do have a downside. In some cases, these efforts can lead to a team placing a disproportionate emphasis on the objectives of the team, often at the expense of individual members' own identity and good judgment. Team members need to continually be on guard against the potential influence of at least two very common and very powerful group phenomena: groupthink and risky shift.

Even with the dramatic increase in empowerment in today's organizations, there are still significant opportunities for managers to play a critical role in team success.

CASE STUDY 12–1

THE NEW AIRBAG

Pat, Tara, Chris, and Liu are all recent engineering graduates assigned to a newly created work team at Alpha Electronics. The group is in charge of designing a new vehicle airbag sensor and mechanism that is less harmful to children and small adults when deployed. The new airbag has the potential to save lives and add substantially to the success of Alpha Electronics.

The team has no assigned leader. Pat, as the oldest member, and the member with the most applied engineering experience, has begun to act as the leader of the group by assigning individual component design tasks to Tara, Chris, and Liu. Pat usually provides justification for his decisions but appears frustrated with any resistance from team members.

Chris was a strong performer in engineering school and resents the fact that Pat has taken over the group. Chris has attempted to bring Pat's decisions to the group in order to decide issues more democratically, usually by suggesting that the team hold another meeting to discuss the issues. Pat sees these efforts as a challenge to his authority. Tara and Liu have also not responded as Chris had hoped, adding to the difficulty in the team's functioning. Liu is visibly uncomfortable with conflict in the team and would like to see one leader emerge to make decisions—for better or for worse. Tara appears to welcome dissension in the group and uses the opportunity to air problems she sees with the company in general and problems she is having with her boyfriend. The prototype design for the new airbag is due in less than 3 weeks. Team members want to do a good job on the project, but so far have been unable to make much progress in completing their design task. If something does not change soon, the team will miss its deadline.

CASE QUESTIONS

1. What developmental stage is the team in? What tasks confront the team in order for it to move into the next stage?
2. What roles have individual team members begun to take?
3. What nonfunctional group behaviors are occurring? Who is responsible and what would an appropriate reaction be from other team members?
4. What problems might the team encounter later because of lost time early in the team's formation?
5. Should the team be disbanded and members reassigned? Under what conditions would such a drastic solution be warranted?

DISCUSSION AND STUDY QUESTIONS—TO KEEP YOU THINKING

1. What determines group effectiveness?
2. What are the major differences in behavior, power, and control between formal and informal groups?
3. What are some examples of task-related, maintenance-related, and individual roles you play in groups?
4. Discuss the growing impact of technology on group performance and effectiveness, particularly as it relates to "virtual groups."
5. Consider Barker's concept of concertive control. Can organizations place too much emphasis on teamwork? Discuss.
6. What can be done to minimize the effects of groupthink and risky shift?

NOTES

1. James L. Bowditch and Anthony F. Buono. *A Primer on Organizational Behavior*, 5th ed. (New York: John Wiley & Sons, 2001), 131.
2. Ibid., 132–135.
3. B. W. Tuckman, "Developmental Sequences in Small Groups," *Psychological Bulletin* (June 1965): 384–399.
4. C. J. Gersick, "Time and Transition in Work Teams: Toward a New Model of Group Development," *Academy of Management Journal* 31, no. 1 (1988): 9–41.
5. James R. Barker, *The Discipline of Teamwork* (Thousand Oaks, CA: Sage Publications, 1999), 38–50.

6. Stephen P. Robbins. *Organizational Behavior* (Upper Saddle River, NJ: Prentice Hall, 2001), 237.
7. Barker, *The Discipline of Teamwork,* 162–164.
8. Lee Roy Beach. *The Psychology of Decision-Making: People in Organizations* (Thousand Oaks, CA: Sage Publications, 1997), 137; Jennifer R. George and Gareth R. Jones. *Understanding and Managing Organizational Behavior*, 2nd ed. (Reading, MA: Addison-Wesley Publishing Co., Inc., 1999), 506–507.
9. Robbins, *Organizational Behavior*, 242.

PART 4

Contemporary Issues

CHAPTER

13

Intercultural Relations

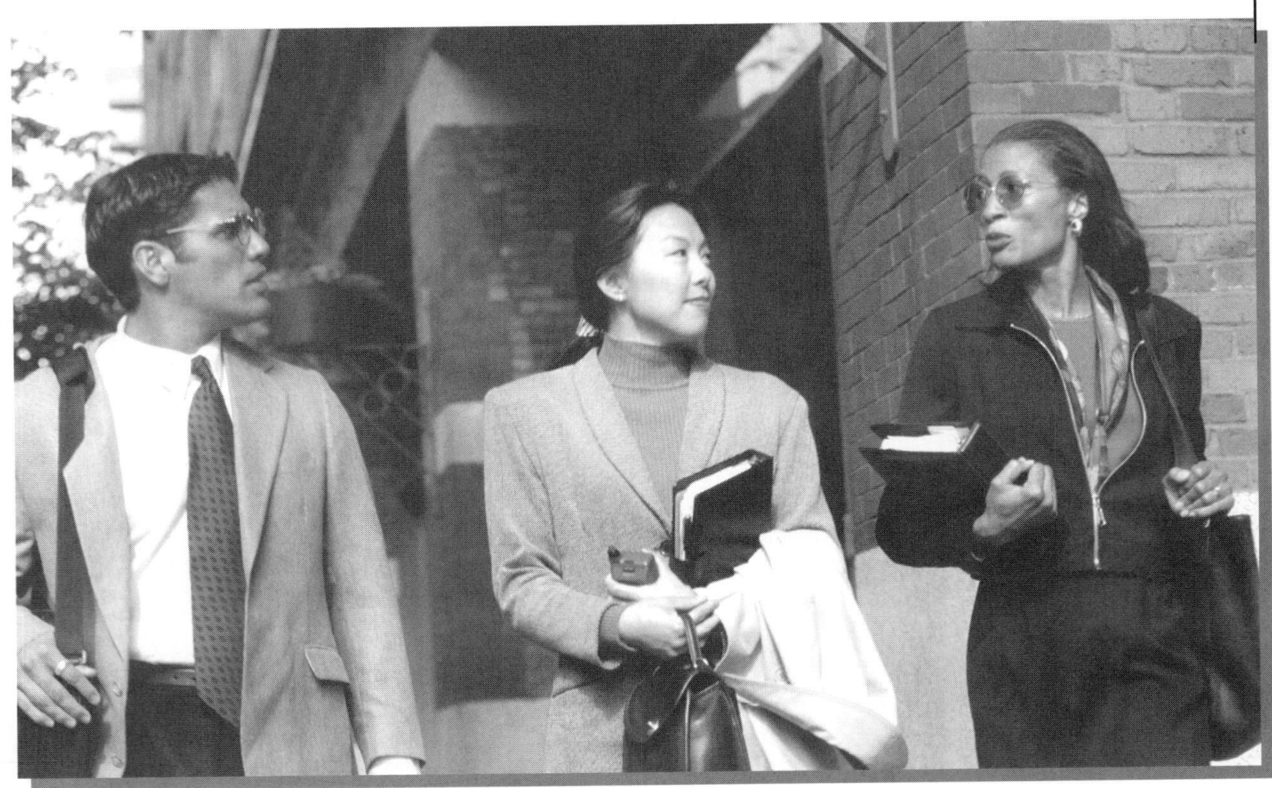

TO START YOU THINKING

Again, it is time to ask ourselves questions. This time our topic is the field of intercultural relations—how do you feel about individuals from diverse ethnic groups and those with cultural backgrounds that differ from yours? How can we work effectively with diverse people?

- Do you feel uncomfortable with foreign visitors in this country—even if they speak English?
- Is time more important in American culture than it is in other cultures? Is physical space more important to us or to others?
- What nonverbal actions have you observed in a particular foreign group that are different from your group of friends?
- What are some of the acceptable mores in our culture that are "off limits" elsewhere in the world?
- Are there standards by which we should judge all cultures?

LEARNING GOALS

After studying this chapter, you should be able to:

1. Discuss the importance of establishing good intercultural relations before embarking on an international venture.
2. Describe the meaning of ethnocentrism and cultural relativity as these topics relate to intercultural relations.
3. Discuss why intercultural relations are more important in today's organizations.
4. Discuss the importance of the following:
   a. Vertical and horizontal space in terms of intercultural business relationships.
   b. Hidden language of time difference between the United States and other cultures.
   c. The relationship of touch and friendship as it differs from one culture to another.
   d. Language of agreements in relation to each of the three basic types of rules that usually apply to business contracts.
5. Discuss what is meant by high- and low-context cultures and give an example.
6. Compare intercultural managerial differences, individual characteristics, and values.
7. Describe what individuals can do to improve their effectiveness in global settings.
8. Describe what organizations can do to improve their effectiveness in global settings.
9. Define and apply the following terms and concepts (in order of first occurrence):

KEYWORDS

- **culture**
- **intercultural relations**
- **isolationism**
- **ethnocentrism**
- **parochialism**
- **cultural relativity**
- **intercultural socialization**
- **ugly American**
- **multinational corporations**

- **nationalization**
- **comparative management**
- **maquiladoras**
- **elasticity of time**
- **inner circle**
- **language of context**
- **repatriation**

INTERCULTURAL RELATIONSHIPS IN A SHRINKING WORLD

A **culture** is comprised of the values, beliefs, customs, and norms shared by people in a society. In today's globalized economy, cooperation among diverse cultures is imperative for company success.

All cultures are tied together by information.

Technology has truly made the world a smaller place. All cultures are now tied together by information.[1] Technology has made communication and travel easier and has increased the amount and speed of global interaction. As our world continues to shrink, the importance of intercultural relations increases. **Intercultural relations** require people of different cultures to value diversity and work in harmony.

Business is often the first link between countries.

Managers and workers across different cultures are likely to have differing, and sometimes conflicting, perspectives. Business is often the first link established between societies. For example, business was one of the first links between the United States and Japan after World War II. Also, it is one of the first links between the United States and China, after years of isolation. Today, American organizations have established economic relationships with most countries around the globe.

We must learn how to deal with other cultures.

Business ties have far-reaching effects on relations between Americans and other peoples by permitting the parties to offer each other material goods not available through other channels. The fuel and precious metals crises that have plagued the United States have reminded people in this country that we have needs that can only be met by cooperation with other countries. For this reason, if business is to fulfill its job of providing material needs, it must learn how to deal with other cultures in a way that satisfies the material and social needs of both parties.

For companies to be successful in international markets, their managers' "repertoire of people-handling skills must expand to include employees of culturally diverse backgrounds. Managers are challenged to demonstrate greater finesse in communicating with people who speak English as a second language."[2] This requires managers to try to truly understand and be sensitive to divergent perspectives.

CULTURAL ATTITUDES TOWARD MULTICULTURAL DIVERSITY

Ethnocentrism.

Historically, some Americans adopted an attitude of **isolationism**—a policy of seclusion from international economics and politics. Events during the twentieth century toppled our policy of isolationism, but have not necessarily changed our **ethnocentrism**, that is, the belief that our way of doing things and looking at the world is the only way, the natural, normal way (Figure 13–1). It is also the case that people from other cultures may be ethnocentric. Thus it is important for managers to be aware of their own and other's ethnocentrism.

Enculturation, the process of learning cultural values and norms within one's society, can lead to ethnocentric attitudes, which are found all over the world in all cultures. As long as we are taught just one way, and know no other, we tend to accept that way as the right way. Because of this feeling of superiority of one's own culture,

FIGURE 13-1 ***Attitudes Toward Foreign Cultures. Where Do You Stand on Your Attitudes Toward Individuals from Foreign Cultures?***

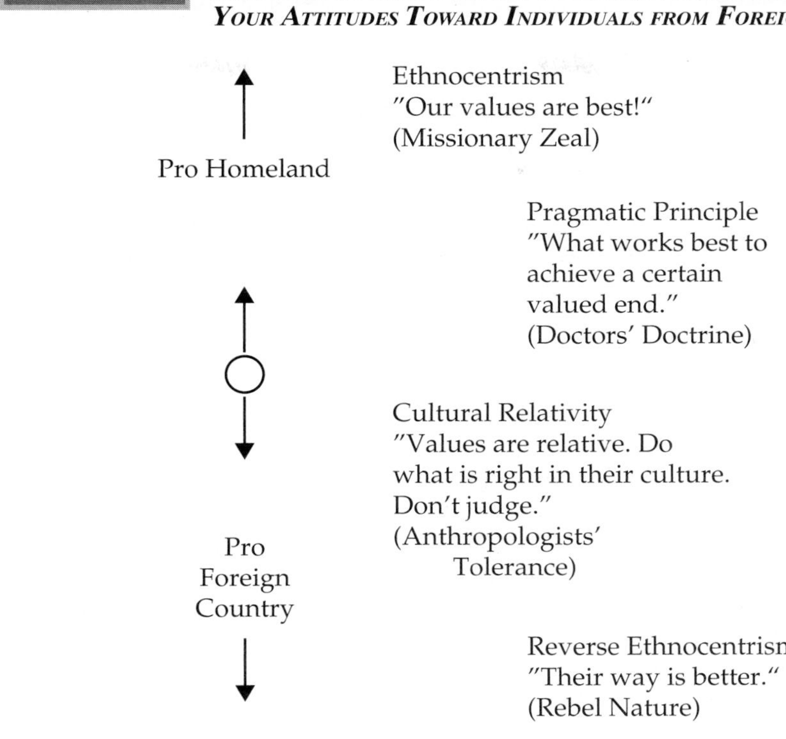
Ethnocentrism
"Our values are best!"
(Missionary Zeal)
Pro Homeland
Pragmatic Principle
"What works best to
achieve a certain
valued end."
(Doctors' Doctrine)
Cultural Relativity
"Values are relative. Do
what is right in their culture.
Don't judge."
(Anthropologists'
Tolerance)
Pro
Foreign
Country
Reverse Ethnocentrism
"Their way is better."
(Rebel Nature)

global companies are implementing international human resource management programs to sensitize employees to other cultures, including overseas deployment of home-country expatriates.[3]

Ethnocentric attitudes usually surface in the form of patronization, superiority, or stereotyping. "If a manager adopts a sincere attitude by patiently accepting a subordinate from another culture, that empathy will normally be received in a trusting, positive manner."[4]

Parochialism is the characteristic of having a narrow perspective. In terms of intercultural relations, parochial people are unable to appreciate cultural differences in others. The concept of **cultural relativity** holds that there are no absolute standards for judging customs, and that a society's customs and ideas should be viewed in the context of that society's culture. People advocating cultural relativity draw the conclusion that all cultures and cultural practices are equally valid. Can we have tolerance and respect for other cultures and cultural practices, even when those cultures happen to differ from ours, without agreeing that all cultural norms are equally valid?

Cultural relativity.

Intercultural socialization involves becoming aware of another culture's habits, actions, and reasons behind behaviors. "Americans presume they are the safest, most sanitary culture in the world, but a large majority of the automobiles in the United States would not pass inspection in Germany. The Japanese (and other cultures) think Americans are unhygienic for locating the toilet and bathing facility in the same area."[5]

One of the major lessons to be learned is that "reaching a level of comfort with colleagues in an intercultural collaboration takes a long time. A necessary part of the

Americans must modify their intolerance of others.

process is allowing yourself the time you need to expose underlying assumptions that drive culturally determined behaviors you may not understand."[6]

DEVELOPING CULTURAL SENSITIVITY

The image of the impolite, ill-mannered, and patronizing "**ugly American**" barging through foreign countries like a barbarian is legendary, and it is both false and true to some extent. In the past, and sometimes in the present, some Americans have acted this way, leading people from other cultures to react negatively. Right or wrong, the image does tell us something about the problems associated with attempting to establish good business and human relations with the people of other countries.

Growth of multinational corporations.

The recent growth of **multinational corporations**, companies that operate in several countries, points to the need to prepare the manager to deal with foreign cultures and business practices.

To a degree, the United States enjoys a "respected society image," but it can backfire. Consider the following true story:

> A man attending an international relations banquet was seated across from another man who possessed Asian physical characteristics. Wishing to advance international relations, he asked the Asian, "Likee foodee?" The man politely nodded his head. During the program, the Asian was introduced as an award-winning professor of economics at a prestigious university and was asked to make a few projections about world trade imbalances. After a brief discussion in perfect English, the Asian professor sat down, glanced across at his astonished neighbor, and asked, "Likee talkee?"

To avoid similar embarrassing situations, managers should not make assumptions from physical appearances, attributes, or superficial characteristics.[7] This is good advice—domestically and internationally.

Additional advice comes from Doug Ready, founder and CEO of the International Consortium for Executive Development Research:

> Don't believe your own press releases. It's too easy to think that you're a global company because you keep saying you're a global company. Search for measurable indicators that your organization is behaving more globally than it was last year and the year before. Believe in behaviors, not rhetoric. Celebrate your progress, but never allow yourself to become fully satisfied that you have made it.[8]

Don't be ugly; don't be arrogant.

What can American companies, other organizations, and individuals do to increase cultural sensitivity? The first and best answer is: "Don't be ugly; don't be arrogant or portray a 'we-are-better-than-you' attitude." If indeed we have a unique technology or skill, then we can export/market it, but remember our foreign host is our customer—deserving the respect any other customer, domestic or global, would receive.

SUBTLE DIFFERENCES

Cultural differences go deep but are subtle.

A gesture that is friendly in one culture may be interpreted as hostile in another; an innocent gesture can be an insult. Subtle cues can complicate the problems of international business relations in a way that cannot be deduced from business experience in the United States.

The business manager who is faced with such subtle cultural differences as gestures and tone of voice is participating in a frame of reference that is different from his or her own. Because communication always takes place within a frame of reference, international business managers must make sure they can communicate in one that is not their own. The broad outlines of a culture are marked by the political and economic frames of reference.

THE POLITICAL FRAME OF REFERENCE

Close relationships between business and political well-being.

When we watch the stock market fluctuate with every major or minor crisis in our political lives, we are aware of the close relationship between politics and business. The political climate of our nation is determined largely by its economic well-being. Major decisions in business and industry can affect political movements and vice versa. This is also true on an international scale.

For example, in the aftermath of the fall of the Berlin Wall, American managers have established trade agreements with the new nations that once were part of the former Soviet Union. One lesson we have learned is that the political structure of those nations is far more bureaucratic than managers are accustomed to in the United States. Trade agreements must be passed through dozens of government bureaus and may take three times as long to complete as similar transactions here.

Another politically related problem facing the multinational corporation has been the risk of **nationalization**, the taking over of private companies, owned by foreign firms, by the host country. Some companies have sought to counter this problem by hiring local managers in the country where the corporation is operating. When local nationals head up the branches of a multinational corporation, the company may be more immune from political expropriation or nationalization. Even if hiring local managers does not reduce the risk of nationalization, it does increase the likelihood that the firm will better understand local customers, employees, and competitors.

THE ECONOMIC FRAME OF REFERENCE

Standards of living vary greatly.

One of the first things that American business managers traveling abroad may recognize is the difference between the standard of living to which they are accustomed and those that exist in the host country. Americans enjoy a higher standard of living and productivity than many countries, and the difference affects relations there.

Countries with low income but high inflation encourage spending now.

The low level of economic development in many emerging nations is aggravated by high birth rates and high inflation. Both factors discourage saving, which is one of the prerequisites for capital accumulation necessary for investment and expansion. The workers in such countries are essentially trapped by the cycle of low income, large families, and inflation that encourages spending rather than saving.

The multinational corporation, however, has both the resources and the responsibility to help break the vicious circle in which such workers find themselves. In return for business profits realized from cheap labor and easy access to local natural resources, the multinational corporation can and should help develop the human resources of its host nation.

THE CULTURAL FRAME OF REFERENCE

When "the American way" of doing business is transplanted to foreign soil, it must bend and twist, give and take, absorb and develop, according to local expectations and traditions. In the process, a third way of doing business will be formed; one that borrows from both cultures and aims at filling the needs of both. This process requires that the American business manager become versed not only in the economics and politics of a country, but also in its culture and in its manners. We must learn to understand and respect others' way of life, because we naturally view the world based upon the culture in which we were raised.[9] We must also be aware that others will view the world based on their cultural beliefs. Thus, effective human relations means overcoming our biases and helping others to overcome theirs.

Language is a major barrier.

Language is the foremost barrier to good international relations. Although English is commonly accepted as the international business language, foreign business managers usually frown on the inability of Americans to converse in the native language. Americans tend not to study second languages in school, which has made people of other countries feel that Americans do not make an effort to communicate.

Europeans, on the other hand, are in close and constant contact with people who speak other languages. Switzerland, for example, has four national languages: French, German, Italian, and Romansch. It is helpful if American managers try to communicate in the language of their host countries, both for necessity and as a mark of goodwill.

EXPRESS YOUR OPINION

Are American work values changing? Do we still value the importance of work? Is work the central purpose of our lives? Is work an end in itself or a means to an end? Do we put more emphasis on leisure time than on work? As we mature, do we put more emphasis on both quality work and leisure time?

COMPARATIVE MANAGEMENT

Comparative management is the study of how management and leadership practices vary across different cultures. Both the Kluckhohn-Strodtbeck and the Hofstede models provide good frames of reference for analyzing differences.

THE KLUCKHOHN-STRODTBECK MODEL

The Kluckhohn-Strodtbeck framework is a model that is used for analyzing differences among cultures. It is based on six cultural dimensions:[10]

1. Relationship to the environment. Are people dominating of, in harmony with, or dominated by the environment?
2. Time orientation. Does the culture focus on the past, present, or future?
3. Nature of people. Does the culture view people as good, evil, or a mix of the two?
4. Activity orientation. Does the culture emphasize being, doing, or controlling?
5. Focus of responsibility. Is the focus of the culture individualistic, hierarchical, or group oriented?
6. Concept of space. Does the culture conduct business in private, in public, or a mix of the two?

Table 13–1 shows the six dimensions and the combinations of variations within each.

THE HOFSTEDE MODEL

Geert Hofstede, at the University of Limburg in the Netherlands, is responsible for what is probably the most widely used typology and assessment vehicle for intercultural differences among different cultures. His excellent article in the *Academy*

TABLE 13–1

Variations in Value Dimensions

VALUE DIMENSION	VARIATIONS		
Relationship to the environment	Domination	Harmony	Subjugation
Time orientation	Past	Present	Future
Nature of people	Good	Mixed	Evil
Activity orientation	Being	Controlling	Doing
Focus of responsibility	Individualistic	Group	Hierarchical
Conception of space	Private	Mixed	Public

Note: The jagged line identifies where the United States tends to fall along these dimensions.

Source: Stephen P. Robbins, *Organizational Behavior: Concepts, Controversies, and Applications,* 6th ed. (Upper Saddle River, N.J.: Prentice Hall, 1993), 75.

The meaning of management differs around the world.

of Management Executive is equally as provocative as some of his earlier works. He asserts:

> Management as the word is presently used is an American invention. In other parts of the world not only the practices but the entire concept of management may differ, and the theories needed to understand it may deviate considerably from what is considered normal and desirable in the USA.[11]

Another point he makes is that one of the shortcomings of American management research is that we concentrate our research on managers rather than workers: "Managers are much more involved in maintaining networks: if anything, it is the rank-and-file worker who can really make decisions on his or her own." Originally, Hofstede developed four dimensions for his assessments:

1. Power distance. The degree of inequality in power distribution among people in a national culture.
2. Individualism/collectivism. The degree to which people in a country prefer to act as individuals rather than collectively as members of groups in caring for themselves.
3. Masculinity/femininity. The degree to which tough values such as assertiveness, performance, success, and competition, which in most societies are associated with masculinity, dominate over tender values like the quality of life, maintaining warm personal relationships, service, care for others, and the environment.
4. Uncertainty avoidance. The degree to which people in a culture prefer structured over unstructured situations and feel threatened by uncertainties and ambiguities.

More recently, he has added a fifth dimension from a Chinese value survey:

5. Long-term versus short-term orientation. On the long-term side are values oriented toward the future, such as thrift and persistence. On the short-term side are values such as respect for tradition and fulfilling social obligation.[12]

These dimensions serve as guides to effective leadership styles, control characteristics, and ways of delegating authority. Table 13–2 shows cultural value dimension scores for selected countries.

TABLE 13–2

Cultural Value Dimension Scores for 10 Selected Countries

COUNTRY:	PD	ID	MA	UA	LT
United States	40	91	62	46	29
Germany	35	67	66	65	31
Japan	54	46	95	92	80
France	68	71	43	86	30[a]
The Netherlands	38	80	14	53	44
Hong Kong	68	25	57	29	96
Indonesia	78	14	46	48	25[a]
West Africa	77	20	46	54	16
Russia	95[a]	50[a]	40[a]	90[a]	10[a]
China	80[a]	20[a]	50[a]	60[a]	118
Range	35–95	14–91	14–95	29–90	10–118[a]

[a]Estimated.

Key: PD = power distance, ID = individualism, MA = masculinity, UA = uncertainty avoidance, LT = long-term orientation.

Source: Geert Hofstede, "Cultural Constraints in Management Theories," *Academy of Management Executive*, February 1993, 91.

THE CHANGING WORLD COMMUNITIES

Let us take a look at a few other cultures with which we have had considerable intercultural work relationships.

JAPAN, ANOTHER LOOK AT THEORY Z

In 1981, William Ouchi created a stir in the management field by writing *Theory Z: How American Business Can Meet the Japanese Challenge.* Theory Z encompasses mutual trust and benefits among employers, workers, and the organization. It stresses team effort over individual drive. The qualities admired in American managers—ambition, risk taking, and independence—are handicaps in Japanese companies where group cooperation and a strict decision-making hierarchy prevail.

> Japanese managers generally choose a company for life, and they move up the corporate ladder very slowly and according to seniority rather than ability. Regimented in a multi-layered management structure, they are known for working long hours and piling up years of unused vacation time. Japanese companies have been described as Machiavellian bureaucracies where absolute loyalty is demanded and where one wrong political move can ruin a career—dumping a promising manager into what the Japanese call the madogiwa-zoka (the by-the-window tribe).[13]

A good company image attracts good workers.

Because of the lifetime employment concept, great care is taken in the selection of a company for employment. Likewise, great care is taken among Japanese business concerns to maintain a strong company image. If the image is poor, it will be difficult for the company to attract good young people.

Although there is a movement in Japan toward adopting some of the more Western approaches, there are fundamental cultural differences between Japan and the United States.

Who are the "party animals"?

One practicing anthropologist, a vice president of a multinational pharmaceutical firm, examined several cultural databases, including social knowledge and cultural logic. One example of the importance of these databases can be seen in their drinking habits. Drinking (not always alcoholic drinking) provides the foreigner with a chance to mingle socially with Japanese hosts. The social values attached to this event allow freedom of speech; it is a place to get things "off the chest."[14]

> Business is usually not done at the bar, where drinking offers the Japanese an opportunity to express *honne* [insider] opinions about . . . relationships with colleagues, both foreign and Japanese. . . . Everyone is in the same social circle. For this reason, one must constantly be alert for signals that might indicate something is on a colleague's mind. [At one session, a manager] felt that something was bothering his Japanese counterpart, but as the evening wore on, nothing was said. Just before it ended, the Japanese manager put his face down on the table and muttered that he had something important to say. The American leaned forward and asked what it was. All the Japanese said was "Your Johns-san is an (expletive)." Nothing more was said and the subject was never raised again. The American assumed that just stating the opinion was enough to relieve the tension the Japanese had. The opinion was not reported to Johns. The next business day discussions with the Japanese gentleman were more relaxed than had been previously experienced.[15]

MIDDLE EAST

We should not consider every country in the Arab world as having similar attitudes, philosophies, or political ambitions, just as foreigners should not think all North Americans are the same. Certainly the attitudes of Canadians, Americans, and Mexicans are not always similar. However, most people from the Middle East are similar in one respect—they are all profoundly influenced by their religion.

In dealing with people from the Middle East, we must recognize the influence of their basic religious beliefs, which may be totally alien to Americans. For example, most Moslems strongly believe in the teachings of the Koran, which says that society must come before the individual.

EUROPE

The European Union represents a major economic market.

The European Union (EU) evolved from the European Economic Community, which was formed in 1992 to permit the free movement of goods and services as well as human and financial capital. The EU is a single economic market, a commonwealth of nations without economic borders that allows more than 350 million consumers, capital, goods, and services to move freely across borders.

Perhaps the EU changes will not have a direct impact on human relations in the United States, but indirectly, American managers should take care not to treat all the cultures of Europe in the same way, even though their economic markets are unified. The EU will open many markets to U.S. business, and how we respond to these opportunities will determine how successful we are.

CHINA, KOREA, AND OTHER PACIFIC RIM NATIONS

Demographically, Asia is the greatest economic market for the United States. Many U.S. companies and other multinational conglomerates are charging into China: AT&T, Motorola, Nissan (Japan), Volkswagen (Germany), and Total (France) are just a few. China has been described as the "emerging economic powerhouse of the twenty-first century," but there are problems (opportunities) both domestically and globally. For example, peasants searching for jobs far from their homes are creating growing social problems.[16] Truck transportation remains a significant problem, although their rail systems are quite good.

China and Korea and Japan are major markets.

Coming out of the Asian economic crisis, Korea is well on its way to becoming an economic power, not only in Asia, but globally. Further, South Korea is making progress in improving relations with North Korea, a development that should help both nations. On the road to recovery are the other Pacific Rim nations—Taiwan, Thailand, Singapore, Malaysia, and Indonesia. American firms are increasing their involvement in these countries through trade and direct foreign investment.

NORTH AMERICA

Quality economic markets close to home.

Experience with the North American Free Trade Agreement (NAFTA) has led to many positive relationships with Canada and Mexico. Canada remains a major trading partner of the United States in agriculture, automobiles, and other industries.

Even before NAFTA, we had good working relationships with Mexico because of the **maquiladoras**, domestic Mexican firms that manufacture or assemble products for U.S. companies, for example, toys for Mattel and appliances and electronic products for Zenith and other manufacturers.

HIDDEN NORMS

Language and religion are only two of the more obvious frames of reference in which business takes place. A basic understanding of them allows American business managers to negotiate on roughly equal footing with their foreign associates. People communicate in hidden "languages" or norms of time, space, agreements, touch, and friendship. These languages vary from culture to culture, are often incredibly complex, and are usually as important as the spoken language in establishing good communication and human relations abroad.

THE LANGUAGE OF TIME

In the United States, people become impatient when the person they are meeting is 5 to 10 minutes late. Such lateness can signal that the meeting is of low priority on the part of the person who is late. In Europe, people will wait 30 minutes for the other party to arrive before becoming impatient or being insulted.

> Northern Europeans, Americans, and Latins all share the belief that they can manage their time in the best possible way. In some Eastern cultures, however, the adaptation of man to time is seen as a viable alternative. Time is viewed neither as linear or subjective, but as cyclical. The evidence, they reason, is everywhere; each day the sun rises and sets, people grow old, die and are succeeded by their children. It has been this way for 100,000 years. Cyclical time is not a scarce commodity. As they say in the East, when God made time, he made plenty of it.[17]

Business decisions in Asia are arrived at quite differently than in the West. An Asian thinks long term and does not see time wasting away but as coming around again in a circle, where the same opportunity will present itself later—when the decision maker is several days, weeks, months, or even years wiser.

In the Arab world, close relatives take absolute priority in time; non-relatives are kept waiting. Foreigners may be kept waiting for a long time. In the Middle East, assigning a deadline is a cultural trap because a deadline in this part of the world is viewed as rude, pushy, and demanding.

Deadlines can appear rude and pushy.

In the language of time, most cultures other than ours may seem to be tied to antiquity. The Indians of South Asia have an elastic view of time; indefiniteness does not mean they are evasive—just deliberate. The **elasticity of time** is the length of time it takes to accomplish a task. The less important time is and the longer it takes to accomplish the task, the greater the elasticity of time.

THE LANGUAGE OF SPACE

Space speaks.

When business managers arrive in a foreign country, they must try to be sensitive to what space tells them. Some useful advice to a newcomer: Try to be aware of where people stand in relation to you and don't back up. This, in itself, can greatly enhance people's attitudes toward you. If employees are deemed more important, they are given more space and their offices are walled in completely. A person from another culture may wonder how managers can supervise when they are unable to see their subordinates.

In the United States, the executive suites are usually on the top floor and the relative ranks of vice presidents are placed along "executive row." The top floor in Japan is frequently seen as the place for the average worker. Why must the executive spend his time going to the top floor? The privilege of class is for the first and second floors. Likewise, the top floor in a Japanese department store is not reserved for furniture, but the "bargain roof." Similarly, in Rio De Janeiro, Brazil, the higher one lives up on Sugarloaf Mountain, the poorer one is. The poverty stricken may have the view, but the aristocrats have the conveniences of the beaches and living downtown.

Sociologists have also found that different cultures keep different social distances—the distance between people corresponds to the degree of comfort they feel in each other's presence. The distance we keep between others and ourselves is known as our **inner circle** or our personal space. Americans normally keep a distance of about 4 to 6 feet during business conversations, but other cultures are more inclined to reduce the distance, sometimes to 3 or 4 inches!

THE LANGUAGE OF TOUCH

We also communicate by the frequency and manner in which we touch each other. These customs differ radically from culture to culture. American men rarely go beyond a formal handshake. If they happen to be old friends, they may slap each other on the back. Infractions of these rules are fraught with tension; if someone refuses to shake a hand that is offered, he or she implies a serious insult or rejection. The person who is an indiscriminate back-slapper is usually viewed with either distaste or some fear because the act implies intimacy without consent.

The relationships between men and women in other cultures are also sensitive to touching. The ease with which American women enter into touch may be interpreted as promiscuous by some cultures; yet in other cultures, American women may be seen as cold and unfriendly.

THE LANGUAGE OF CONTEXT

The cultures of the world can be placed on a language-of-context continuum. The **language of context** is based on the amount of communication contained in the nonverbal context and chitchat compared with the amount in the formal message. In a

Low context: You start business quickly.

low-context culture you get down to business very quickly. The high-context culture requires considerably more time, simply because the people need to know more about you before a relationship can develop.

High context takes longer; learn to chitchat.

In India, for example, merchants and others are more comfortable doing business with you if they get to know you personally. In the Middle East, if you aren't willing to take the time to sit down and have coffee or tea, you will have a problem doing business.

The challenge with high-context cultures is that it is hard to get an American to take each step seriously and to be coached. In terms of high and low context, the United States tends toward the middle of the scale. The low-context Swiss around Zurich don't even know their neighbors. The Swiss value their privacy so much that they may not develop a large circle of friends. The privacy of Swiss bank accounts is legendary. Look at Figure 13–2. Where would you place other cultures on the context line of the continuum?

THE LANGUAGE OF FRIENDSHIP

Many Americans have offended others by refusing or offering to pay for items tendered as tokens of friendship. These types of encounters abroad have made some foreigners feel that Americans approach all human relations with the cynical and cold feeling that "everything has a price." Americans must be careful to distinguish between friendship and business relations and to find out what gestures are significant in matters of friendship and hospitality. The offering of food, for example, is a universal gesture of friendship. To protest that one is on a diet may be interpreted as an unwillingness to "break bread together," a rejection of friendship and good relations.

THE LANGUAGE OF AGREEMENTS

"Unwritten" rules for contracts.

For any society to produce goods and services on a commercial level, a set of rules must be developed and accepted on which agreements can be reached. The language of agreements may be absolute or flexible, sophisticated or informal; in every case,

FIGURE 13–2 *Cultural Language of Context Placed on a Continuum*

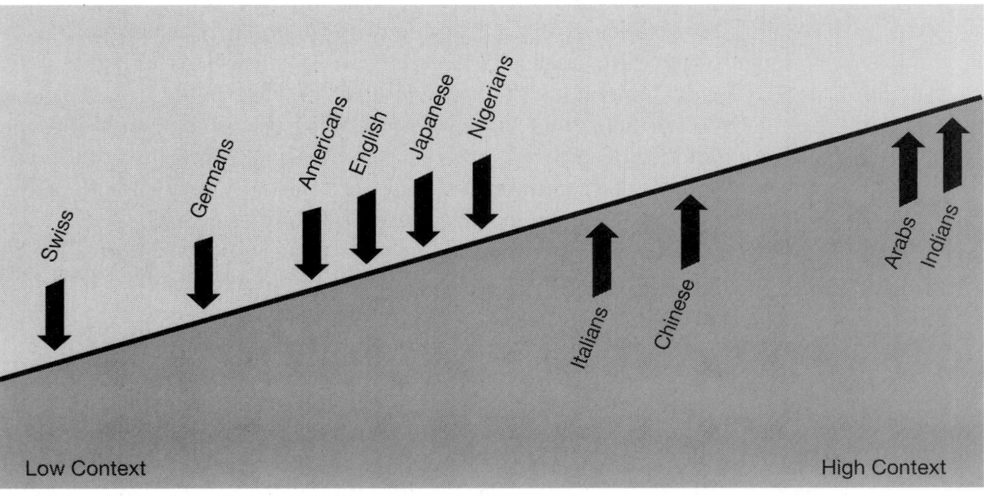

A verbal contract may be just as binding as a written contract.

both parties must understand what the rules are of the agreement. For example, in the Arab world, a man's word is considered as binding as his legal signature (a woman may not have certain legal rights in business). To require a Moslem to sign a formal contract runs the risk of violating his sense of honor.

Build good international human relations.

On the other hand, to a Greek, a contract may only represent a sort of way station along the route of negotiations to be modified periodically until the work is completed. If an American complains about such a procedure, the Greek may exclaim, "Take me to court." Mutual satisfaction is reached only through mutual respect and understanding of the various meanings of the agreement.

ACTION PROJECT 13–1

THE INTERNATIONAL CULTURE QUIZ

How knowledgeable are you about customs, practices, and facts regarding different countries? The following multiple-choice quiz will provide you with some feedback on this question. The correct answers can be found at the end of the chapter.

1. In which country would Ramadan (a month of fasting) be celebrated by the majority of people?
   a. Saudi Arabia
   b. India
   c. Singapore
   d. Korea
   e. All of the above
2. Upon first meeting your prospective Korean business partner, Lo Kim Chee, it would be best to address him as
   a. Mr. Kim
   b. Mr. Lo
   c. Mr. Chee
   d. Bud
   e. Any of the above are readily accepted
3. In Brazil, your promotional material should be translated into what language?
   a. French
   b. Italian
   c. Spanish
   d. No need to translate it
   e. None of the above
4. In Japan it is important to
   a. Present your business card only after you have developed a relationship with your Japanese host
   b. Present your business card with both hands
   c. Put your company name on the card, but never your position or title
   d. All of the above
   e. None of the above
5. Which of the following sports is the most popular worldwide?
   a. Basketball
   b. Baseball
   c. Tennis
   d. Futbol
   e. Golf

(continued)

ACTION PROJECT 13–1

(CONTINUED)

6. For an American businessperson, touching a foreign businessperson would be least acceptable in which of the following countries?
   a. Japan
   b. Italy
   c. Slovenia
   d. Venezuela
   e. France
7. Which of the following would be an appropriate gift?
   a. A clock in China
   b. A bottle of liquor in Egypt
   c. A set of knives in Argentina
   d. A banquet in China
   e. None of the above would be appropriate
8. Which one of the following countries has the most rigid social hierarchy?
   a. United Kingdom
   b. United States
   c. Japan
   d. India
   e. Germany
9. Traditional Western banking is difficult in which one of the following countries because their law forbids both the giving and taking of interest payments?
   a. Brazil
   b. Saudi Arabia
   c. Mongolia
   d. India
   e. Greece
10. As an American businessperson, in which of the following countries would you be expected to be on time for a business meeting?
   a. Peru
   b. Hong Kong
   c. Japan
   d. Morocco
   e. All of the above

Source: Professor David M. Hopkins, University of Denver, 1991. Reprinted with permission.

TIPS FOR THE WORLD TRAVELER

First and foremost, "do your homework" before leaving for a foreign assignment. Know what to expect regarding social engagements, schools when necessary, and living conditions. Study the culture, customs, religions, and taboos to avoid cultural blunders and embarrassments discussed earlier.

CULTURE SHOCK

Culture shock is a normal phenomenon:

> Culture shock can go far deeper than the everyday hassles of learning how to use chopsticks, adjusting to hot weather, and getting locked in a traffic jam. Culture shock may also include an adjustment to loss of status and pay which normally comes with a job. The overseas assignment in a new culture may affect the state of a marriage; frustration with life in an overseas posting can definitely lead to anger and resentment toward the working partner.[18]

Spouses and children must be considered—or their early return to their home country can be very expensive. Robin Pascoe writes that: "Corporations lose money when they post a family overseas and, after 6 months, the wife turns to her husband and says she is getting out. A wife who has been properly prepared for the experience is not as likely to want to run away."[19]

Many people around the world know more about Americans than most of us know about any other country. This is because our television shows, movies, music, and music videos are distributed worldwide. Sometimes, we have to pay attention to overcoming misconceptions about our own culture: Not all Americans have two cars or carry guns.

INTERCULTURAL TRAINING

Americans need to avail themselves of education and training opportunities to help become culturally sensitive. What should global training courses include? Sylvia Odenwald recommends that the menu of global training programs be arranged in six overlapping categories:

1. Cultural awareness
2. Multicultural communication
3. Country-specific training
4. Executive development
5. Language courses
6. Host-country workforce training[20]

REPATRIATION

Often, upon returning to the United States, Americans find that things have changed while they were away, depending on the length of stay. **Repatriation** is the process of transferring employees back to their home country—economically, socially, and organizationally.

> In addition to losing most or all of the generous company-provided benefits they enjoyed overseas, expatriates are likely to feel that their assignment has small value in the eyes of management, either because the company had no formal plans for

repositioning them within the organization or because no one in the organization seems to care about what they learned while doing business overseas. Moreover, repatriates return home feeling personally changed by their overseas experiences, but find that everyone else has more or less stayed the same.[21]

It is as important to concentrate on the repatriation process as it is on the initial orientation for foreign assignment. Too often, when repatriates return "after a stint abroad (during which time they have typically been autonomous, well-compensated and celebrated as a big fish in a little pond), they face an organization that does not know what they have done for the past several years, does not know how to use their new knowledge, and, worse yet, does not care."[22]

WHAT ORGANIZATIONS CAN DO TO IMPROVE IN GLOBAL SETTINGS

Remember that many small businesses benefit from improved intercultural relations when doing business abroad. Businesses and other organizations need to follow these suggestions:

1. Capitalize on our strengths as individuals; domestically, we advocate teamwork that is more prevalent in other cultures, but they also admire our individualism. The key to effectiveness is putting the two dimensions together and using our individualism in a non-arrogant manner to work more closely with others—including other cultures—as a team.
2. Tap one of our major resources—our higher education system, including technical and community colleges. Our 4-year institutions' abilities to deliver undergraduate, graduate, and continuing education are admired and unsurpassed as a group throughout the world. Universities need to work more closely with industry to provide even better fundamental education and tailor relevant training programs.
3. American and other countries' companies doing business abroad should capitalize on U.S.-educated, in-country nationals. The numbers of students—particularly graduate students—have increased dramatically in the last few decades, yet multinational companies do not always capture their newly acquired skills.
4. Improve the political and social awareness of all Americans working in other cultures. The social blunders of one unprepared representative can tear down many months—maybe even years—of preparation for cross-cultural commerce and other exchanges. Host countries may be very forgiving, but they also may not be; intercultural preparation is indispensable.
5. Learn the language. Again, this may vary from culture to culture. In some countries, you may not need to understand the language in detail, but knowing the greetings and certain key phrases is essential. Having a skilled interpreter when conducting business is important. The best interpreters understand economic terms and the language of business as well as culture. Consulates and bank correspondents are good sources for interpreters.

Finally, coming full circle regarding our individualism, we need to maintain our identity but participate in other cultures. Businesspeople should consider the national culture, the general business culture, and the specific corporate culture, as well as the individual communication style. Effective intercultural relations are dependent on effective communication because "cultures don't communicate, individuals do."[23]

SUMMARY

The first unofficial ambassadors to other countries are frequently business managers, and the multinational corporation is becoming so common that it bears the task of establishing good intercultural relations. American business managers must learn how to relate successfully to people from other cultures to fulfill the role of business in our economy.

Our attitudes toward foreigners can be ethnocentric. Ethnocentricity is the view that our way of doing things is the only correct way. Another attitude is that of cultural relativity, which holds that a society's customs should be viewed in the context of that society's culture. We find that Americans have varying attitudes about foreigners and how to do business globally.

Theory Z tells us that Japanese culture reflects a great deal of mutual trust between the employee and the employer, and after an appropriate breaking-in period, even foreigners. The company works hard at developing a strong company image to attract the best workers. Where Americans believe in individualism, the Japanese believe in the group effort.

The Middle Eastern world is composed of countries that are principally of the Moslem faith. Arabs also have a strong belief in the power of society over the individual; therefore, individual status improvement is very difficult, if not impossible. Authority is not to be questioned, be it religious or governmental. Arabs can be strongly goal oriented and use a closer "inner circle" than Americans.

The European Union, based on an economic alliance formed in 1992, presents challenges and opportunities for U.S. human relationships. Job security and powerful European labor unions may dictate the relative success of the European Union in world markets. Perhaps the greatest challenges are the Pacific Rim countries. The Chinese market is developing rapidly, but different values—especially long-term orientation—make doing business in China and related cultures different from anywhere else.

The languages of time, space, touch, and context are sources of important cultural differences. They can be worked out if we keep in mind the fundamental concepts of human dignity, empathy, and individual differences, among other things. Also keep in mind the basic common bond of humanity; understand that one's own values are not universal, but come from one's own culture, and make a serious effort to respect and understand cultural differences.

CASE STUDY 13-1

INTERNATIONAL BRIBERY

Henry Cordero works for Maytax Industries, a large multinational corporation with production and research facilities in several foreign countries. Henry is in charge of one of the facilities in a South American country. A member of the country's government recently informed Henry that if Maytax wished to remain operating in the country, the corporation should begin contributing to that country's medical research association.

Somewhat shocked, Henry asked if the order was official. The individual told him that although the order did not come officially from the government, it could easily be enforced. Well aware that bribery payments were being demanded, Henry returned to the corporation's home office to discuss the matter with vice president, Mr. Charles Manoushek.

After filling in Mr. Manoushek on the details of the demand, Henry was asked what should be done concerning the matter. "It is my opinion," stated Henry, "that we should not become involved in making bribery payments. Aside from the fact that such payments are against our moral ethics and our system of free enterprise, the American public and our government take a pretty dim view of such matters."

"I agree with you there, Henry," stated Mr. Manoushek, "but I don't think you understand the realities of the problem. In countries such as this one, bribery has been an accepted custom for years and years. Although our country is against this type of thing, many countries abroad are not. We are a corporation that does the majority of our business abroad and we must deal with these countries on their own terms. If we don't, some other company will."

"But if we begin paying these bribery payments every time someone suggests it, where will the demands end?" retorted Henry. "On the other hand, when we begin offering these payments on our own initiative and the public finds out, we will be no better off for it. I know company image suffers when the American public finds out about companies doing this sort of thing. If it was my choice, I'd back out of the country if necessary."

"Our duty, Henry, is to our shareholders first, and that duty is protecting our investments abroad. If we must contribute to a country's medical research association to protect our investment, then that is what we must do."

CASE QUESTIONS

1. Whose side do you favor—Henry Cordero's or Charles Manoushek's? Give reasons for your stand.
2. Is giving small gifts acceptable? When does it stop being a gift and become a bribery payment? At what point do you make the distinction? Is there a dollar value?
3. If codes should be established, who will say what is ethical?
4. Companies have stated that there will be no "unusual payments." What is considered unusual?

CASE STUDY 13-2

A PROBLEM OF CULTURAL COMMUNICATION

Harold Underhill walked into the office of the Latin American country's commercial attaché for help. Harold had arrived 2 weeks earlier from the United States for the purpose of securing a several-million-dollar production order. Harold is the sales manager of a corporation that produces communications systems. When Harold first arrived in the country he had been under the impression that his business would take no more than a few days, and then he could take a few days vacation before returning within his allotted 7-day period.

Upon arriving in the country, Harold immediately contacted the minister of communications, who he needed to have sign the production order. He was then instructed that Minister Muñoz would see him that afternoon. When Harold arrived he was forced to wait in the outer office for a considerable amount of time and then only to be greeted briefly, but politely, by the minister before being ushered out without any business being discussed. Harold was informed that the minister would see him the following Wednesday for lunch. Although the delay was upsetting, Harold accepted the invitation.

When Harold and Señor Muñoz did meet the following week for lunch, Harold soon realized that the minister had no intention of talking business. Somewhat in a panic he tried pressing the fact that he needed the order signed. As a result of this, the minister politely cut short the business conversation and invited Harold to meet him again in a few days.

As a result of these events Harold asked the commercial attaché for his advice. "You must understand," stated the attaché, "that business relations are not the same here as they are in the United States. Things are not always done overnight here. Latin Americans feel a need to know with whom they are doing business. You should not rush things—let them take the initiative. When you are in another country you must follow their rules of behavior."

When Harold again met with the minister of communications they took a walk in a memorial park near the minister's office. As Señor Muñoz commented on the beauties of the park, Harold failed to recognize the statue of Simon Bolivar, and then compounded his error by stating that he had never heard of this man. Insulted, the minister decided that the pushy, rude American was not the person with whom he wanted to do business and informed both Harold and his employer that he didn't wish to continue negotiations.

CASE QUESTIONS

1. Identify Harold's problem.
2. Name several error's in Harold's approach.
3. How could Harold's company have prepared him better for the business transaction?

DISCUSSION AND STUDY QUESTIONS—TO KEEP YOU THINKING

1. What are the differences between ethnocentrism and cultural relativity?
2. Relate the differences between space and touch in your culture and a culture of another country.
3. Relate the differences between context and friendship in your culture and a culture of another country.
4. Why is the Theory Z approach so successful in Japan? What are its advantages and pitfalls in both Japan and other countries including the United States?
5. Where are the greatest trading opportunities for the United States? What are the pitfalls of each?
6. Are Americans more similar or different than people from other cultures?
7. What can organizations do to improve their effectiveness in global settings?

THE INTERNATIONAL CULTURE QUIZ ANSWERS

The correct answers are:

1. a
2. b
3. e (Portuguese)
4. b
5. d
6. a
7. d
8. d
9. b
10. e

NOTES

1. William Van Dusen Wishard, "Humanity as a Single Entity?" *The Futurist* (March–April 1996): 60.
2. Phil Van Auken, "International Business Realities That Affect Supervisors," *Supervision* (April 1996): 8.
3. Rochelle Kopp, "International Human Resource Policies and Practices in Japanese, European, and United States Multinationals," *Human Resource Management* (winter 1994): 594.
4. Rose Knotts, "Intercultural Management: Transformations and Adaptations," *Business Horizons* (January–February 1989): 32–33.
5. Ibid., 33.
6. Joan Tavares, "Building a Leadership Development Program: A Intercultural Collaboration." In *Issues & Observations*, Greensboro, NC: Center for Creative Leadership, Fourth Quarter 1995, 9.
7. Knotts, "Intercultural Management," 32.
8. "Don't Be an Ugly American Manager," *Fortune* (October 16, 1995): 225.
9. Bruce C. McKinney, "Intercultural Communication Differences Between the United States and Vietnam with Implications for Future Relations," *Canadian Business and Current Affairs* (August 2000): 23–33.
10. F. Kluckhohn and F. L. Strodbeck, *Variations in Value Orientations* (Evanston, IL: Row, Peterson, 1961).
11. Geert Hofstede, "Cultural Constraints in Management Theories," *Academy of Management Executive* (February 1993): 81.
12. Ibid., 90.
13. Leah Nathans, "A Matter of Control," *Business Month* (September 1988): 46.
14. Richard H. Reeves-Ellington, "Using Cultural Skills for Cooperative Advantage in Japan," *Human Organization* (summer 1993): 206–207, 212.
15. Ibid., 213.
16. Special Report, "China: The Making of an Economic Giant," *Business Week* (May 17, 1993): 58.
17. Richard D. Lewis, "Where Time Moves in Mysterious Ways," *Management Today* (January 1996): 77.
18. Robin Pascoe, "Employers Ignore Expatriate Wives at Their Own Peril," *The Wall Street Journal* (March 2, 1992): A10.
19. Ibid.
20. Sylvia Odenwald, "A Guide for Global Training," *Training & Development* (July 1993): 24–29.
21. J. Paul Tom, "Abroad at Home," *Across the Board* (September 1992): 36.
22. Charlene Marmer Solomon, "Repatriation: Up, Down or Out," *Personnel Journal* (January 1995): 29.
23. Iris I. Varner, "The Theoretical Foundation for Intercultural Business Communication," *The Journal of Business Communication* (January 2000): 39–57.

CHAPTER

Workplace Issues

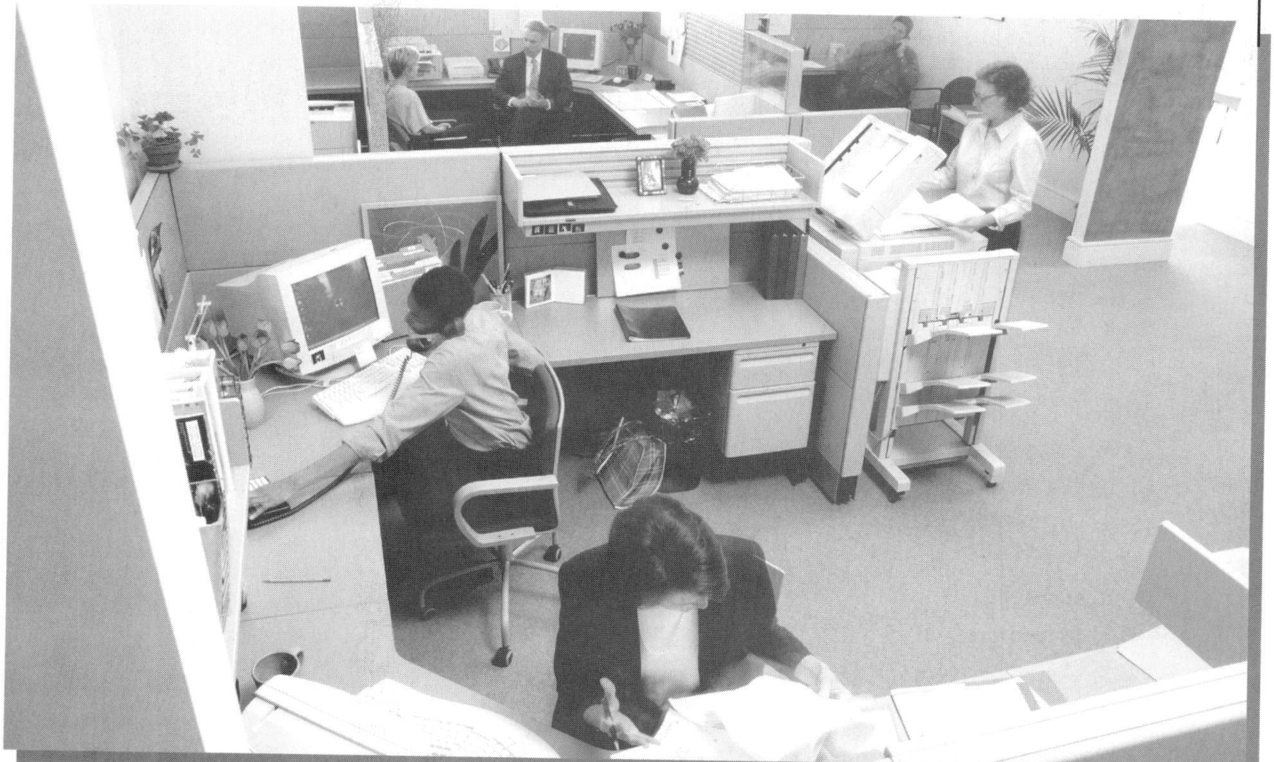

TO START YOU THINKING

Again, here are some questions to start you thinking about topics in the chapter. You may want to discuss some of these questions with others before you read the chapter.

- Which is better—to let problem employees go or try to help them?
- What can you do for the employee who is an alcoholic or drug abuser?
- Is drug testing fair in the workplace?
- What is meant by discrimination?
- How do we discriminate against older workers and workers with disabilities? (How do you define *older* and *disabled?*)
- What is sexual harassment?
- Are you worried about workplace violence? Do you know of anyone who has been impacted by workplace violence?

LEARNING GOALS

After studying this chapter, you should be able to:

1. Discuss the problems of alcoholism and drug abuse at work and develop some background in how to deal with employees with these problems.
2. Identify what employee assistance programs can do to help employees.
3. Define and discuss the meaning of prejudice and discrimination.
4. Discuss some of the ways in which it is possible to see and measure discrimination in the business world.
5. Describe and give examples of the ways in which discrimination can be overcome.
6. Understand the protections for the aging, disabled, and other legally protected groups.
7. Discuss affirmative action.
8. Recognize the legal aspects of sexual harassment.
9. Discuss steps to prevent workplace violence.
10. Define and apply the following terms and concepts (in order of first occurrence):

KEYWORDS

- **substance abuse**
- **employee assistance programs**
- **biases**
- **prejudice**
- **stereotypes**
- **discrimination**
- **disparate treatment**
- **Americans with Disabilities Act (ADA)**
- **individual with disability**
- **undue hardship**
- **glass ceiling**
- **affirmative action**

- **disparate impact**
- **Equal Employment Opportunity Commission (EEOC)**
- **older worker**
- **sexual harassment**
- **quid pro quo**
- **hostile work environment**
- **workplace violence**

TYPES OF WORKPLACE ISSUES

This chapter addresses legal workplace issues that impact managers and employees. First we discuss alcohol and drug abuse in the workplace and employee assistance programs. The chapter goes on to present issues related to employment discrimination and discusses types of sexual harassment and the responsibility of employers to prevent it. Finally, the increasing prevalence of workplace violence is noted. Throughout the chapter, emphasis is given to the organization's response.

The magnitude of these issues and what, if anything, to do about them are challenges for management. Substance abuse, discrimination, sexual harassment, and workplace violence are important in that each can keep members of the workforce from being as productive as they can be.

SUBSTANCE ABUSE

The increased complexities of modern life have added to nearly everyone's stress, tension, and anxiety. Some people seek relief from their stress by drinking alcohol or using drugs. **Substance abuse**—defined as excessive alcohol or drug consumption—reduces efficiency, effectiveness, and reliability, three essential qualities for good job performance. Substance abuse, whether of alcohol or drugs, has become an issue for managers.

In the workplace, an alcoholic employee is a person whose repeated overindulgence in alcohol sharply reduces job performance and dependability. Drug abuse occurs when individuals use drugs to the point that they cannot function without them. Substance abuse in the workplace cuts across all socioeconomic groups, geographic boundaries, and industries.

HOW WIDESPREAD IS THE PROBLEM?

The National Council on Alcoholism estimates that 10 percent of the 110 million people who drink alcohol in the United States suffer from alcoholism. Of that 11 million, only about 700,000 to one million are undergoing treatment. In addition, although the rate of drug use is higher among the unemployed, most drug users are employed. Of the 12.3 million adult illicit drug users, 9.4 million (77 percent) were employed either full time or part time.[1]

Over 75 percent of all current adult drug users are employed.

COSTS ASSOCIATED WITH SUBSTANCE ABUSE

The job costs associated with excessive drinking and drug use are immense whether we measure them on an employee or societal level. On an individual level, increased costs include absenteeism, accidents, turnover, medical benefits, and worker's compensation claims.

The alcoholic employee is absent approximately three times as often as a nonalcoholic employee, while drug-using employees are absent 1.5 times as often.[2] A 1997 survey by the Substance Abuse and Mental Health Administration found that workers who report heavy alcohol use are more likely than others to have skipped 1 or more days of work in the past month. The same study found that workers who report drug use are also likely to have skipped 1 or more days of work in the past month.[3]

Turnover among employees who reported heavy alcohol use is also greater. Such employees are more likely than others to have worked for three or more employers in the past year. Workers who use drugs are more likely than those non-drug users to have worked for three or more employers as well as to have changed employers in the past year.[4]

Medical benefits for alcoholic and drug-using employees are three times greater than for nonalcoholic employees. In addition, on-the-job accidents for alcoholic employees are two to four times more frequent than among nonalcoholic employees. This is one reason why drug users are five times more likely to file a worker's compensation claim.[5] Finally, according to the U.S. Chamber of Commerce, employed drug users are 33 percent less productive than their colleagues who do not use drugs.[6]

The effects of substance abuse can spill over to employees who are related to substance abusers. Nonalcoholic members of alcoholics' families use ten times as much sick leave as members of families in which alcoholism is not present.[7]

On the societal level, alcohol and drug use cost American businesses over $100 billion every year in lost productivity, accidents, employee turnover, and related problems. Up to 40 percent of industrial fatalities and 47 percent of industrial injuries can be linked to alcohol consumption and alcoholism. Shortfalls in productivity and employment among individuals with alcohol or other drug-related problems cost the American economy $80.9 billion in 1992, of which $66.7 billion is attributed to alcohol and $14.2 billion to other drugs.[8]

Firms face reduced revenue and productivity, theft, and increased insurance costs as a result of alcohol and drug abuse. To these costs we must add intangibles such as loss of experienced employees, job friction, lower morale, waste of supervisory time, bad decisions, and damaged customer and public relations.

Managers have a responsibility to protect the firm and other employees and to reach out to help the employee in question. Firms have taken many steps from developing drug training seminars for managers to using preemployment and random drug testing as well as offering employee assistance programs.

As popular as preemployment drug testing has become, it only screens out potential new hires who exercise poor judgement by using drugs or alcohol within a day or so (depending on the substance) prior to the test.[9] Further, such foods as poppy seed muffins (poppy seeds are used to create heroin) can create a false positive result. Companies are supplementing preemployment tests with post-accident and random drug testing.

RECOGNIZING SUBSTANCE ABUSERS

Supervisors should be suspicious if there is a decline in the quality or amount of work produced by a usually competent individual. Figure 14–1 outlines several signs that will indicate if the problem is due to alcoholism.

Supervisors should keep records of absenteeism and investigate causes of on-the-job accidents, including post-accident drug tests. Figure 14–2 shows drugs that are commonly detected in workplace testing.

FIGURE 14–1 *Signs of Alcoholism and Stages the Alcoholic Passes Through from Inconsistent Performance to the Time of Termination*

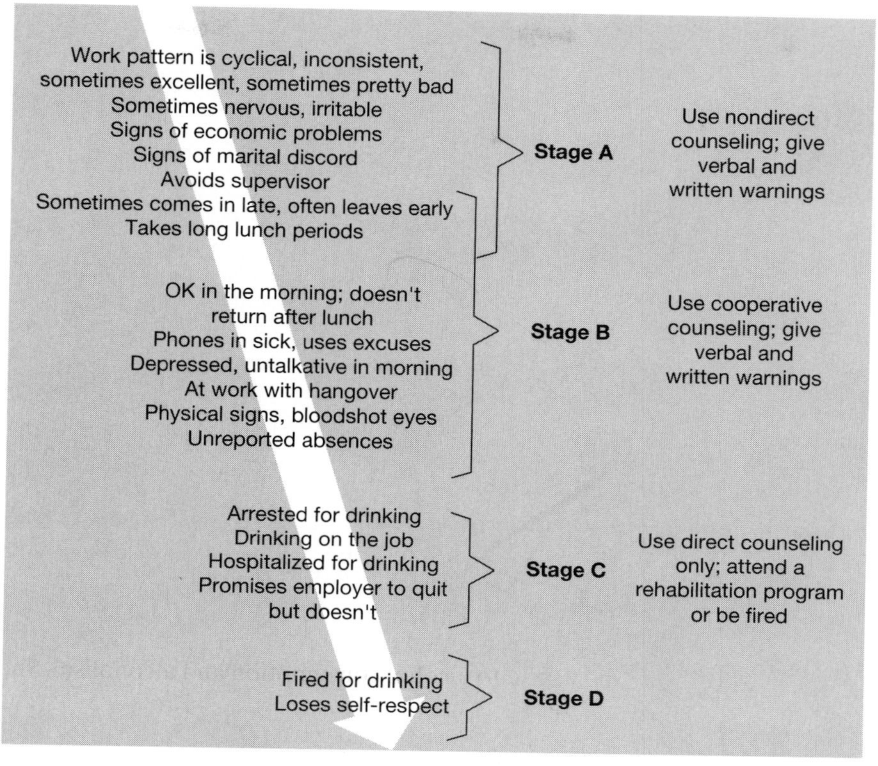

Don't be surprised if the employee gives a wide variety of excuses when asked by a supervisor about unusual behavior. Major excuses include fatigue caused by family problems, anxiety, night school, or having a rare hangover.

DEALING WITH SUBSTANCE ABUSERS

The manager becomes concerned when employee drinking or drug use interferes with doing a good job.

It cannot be stated too strongly that it is only when the use of alcohol or drugs interferes with work that the supervisor is obligated to recognize and deal with the problem. Employee drinking or drug habits that do not create problems at work are of no concern to managers. The sensible managerial view is the following: "What my employees do during their leisure time is not my business. It becomes my business when it prevents them from doing their jobs properly." Companies offering medical treatment options to substance abusers find that people usually recover.

INTERNET ACTION PROJECT 14–1

Surf the Web to find information about prevention programs, try www.ncadd.org/facts/workplac.html as a starting point.

FIGURE 14-2 **Commonly Detected Drugs in General Workplace Testing**

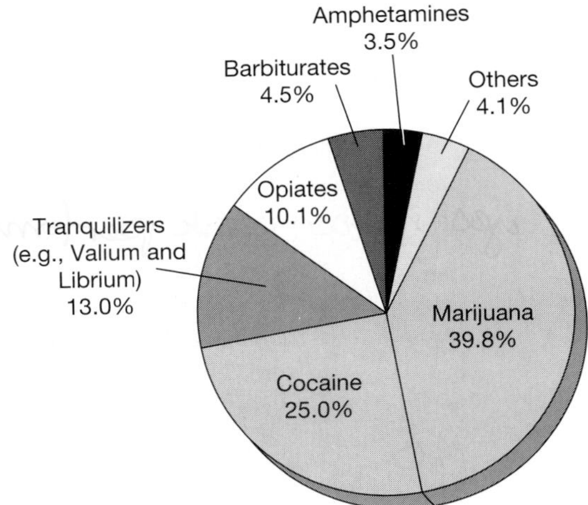

Source: Based on more than nine million tests conducted by SmithKline Beecham Clinical Laboratories, news release, October 12, 1993, 3.

ACTION PLAN FOR PREVENTING SUBSTANCE ABUSE

It is best if the company is proactive in its approach to dealing with potential substance abuse. Some steps to take include:

1. Education. Consider establishing programs for managers and employees to arm them with the facts and heighten their consciousness of substance abuse.
2. Programs. Establish a program and develop a company policy. Include members of security, the legal department, the human resource department, the union, supervisory personnel, the workforce, medical specialists, and top management. If the problem is perceived as the sole responsibility of a single group to solve, then policy and program implementation will be difficult.
3. Follow-up. Stay current with the needs of your employees and understand the legal and ethical consequences of substance abuse in the workplace.

Drug abuse and alcoholism in the workplace can be counteracted. Job applications and drug testing can help screen job applicants. Workers who abuse drugs or alcohol may be detected through drug testing, but these activities must be handled carefully to avoid legal action. In a 1991 survey, 63 percent of responding firms were using some sort of drug testing, a 200 percent increase since 1987.[10]

A GUIDE FOR MANAGERS AND SUPERVISORS

Be alert to changes in the work and behavioral patterns of all personnel under your supervision. Document particular instances in which an employee's job performance fails to meet minimum established standards. Do not attempt to diagnose medical or behavioral causes for work deterioration.

Early identification is important, and the earliest cause for action is poor work performance. Supervisors who suspect that an employee's work difficulties may be

EXPRESS YOUR OPINION

Many companies are now using urinalysis to detect traces of drugs including alcohol. Abstinence for a period of time before the test will throw off the results of the test.

Some companies use random or unannounced tests. What do you think? Are these tests an invasion of privacy? What are the arguments for and against corporate prohibition of drug usage even off the job? Does it make a difference if the job is in a sensitive industry such as nuclear power generation, air traffic control, or law enforcement?

due to problem drinking or drug use should discuss the poor performance with the employee, and seek to determine the cause without making accusations. The matter should be treated confidentially and discussed with no one else, except perhaps counseling or medical personnel if appropriate.

Conduct an interview with the employee when the documented record of his or her unsatisfactory performance warrants. At the end of the interview, inform the employee that the services of the Employee Assistance Program (EAP) are available. If there is no company program, it will be necessary to work out some kind of personal rehabilitation plan. Advice on how to do this can be obtained from doctors, counseling experts, government agencies, or Alcoholics or Narcotics Anonymous. There is no one best way in which to handle an employee with a drinking problem, but there are some general rules worth observing with which these professionals can help.

If the employee's performance continues to deteriorate, conduct a second interview and take whatever first-step disciplinary action is warranted. Inform the employee that failure to improve job performance will result in further disciplinary action up to and including termination. Conclude with a strong recommendation that the individual use the services of the EAP on a confidential basis. If deterioration of performance continues, conduct a third interview.

Conclude by offering the employee the choice between accepting the services of the EAP or being terminated because of unsatisfactory job performance. Avoid diagnosing a problem or confronting the employee with what you suspect might be the problem. Termination should always be related to job performance standards.

Give complete documentation of the employee's job performance problems and arrange for referral to the EAP representative as soon as possible if the employee chooses that alternative. If the employee refuses help or if his or her performance remains unsatisfactory, the manager will need to take the appropriate disciplinary action or dismiss the individual from employment.

Use firm, consistent procedures.

Any deviation from firm and consistent administration of these procedures because of misguided feelings of sympathy or other reasons is not in the interest of the firm or the employee. It is important that managers not focus their attention on the cause of the problem. The only criterion used for referral to the EAP is deteriorating job performance. The program places the responsibility for needed diagnosis, counseling, and treatment in the hands of qualified professionals.

EMPLOYEE ASSISTANCE PROGRAMS

A California study estimates that every dollar spent on treatment programs saves seven dollars in crime, health care, and welfare costs. **Employee assistance programs** provide counseling and other remedies to employees having substance abuse, emotional, or other personal problems as well as some work-related problems such as downsizing. "Although EAPs used to focus mainly on alcohol and drug abuse, today they address stress management, family and marital problems, workplace violence and the emotional disruption that can accompany downsizing."[11] According to one survey, utilization of EAPs has increased 10 to 15 percent over the past few years, and EAP counselors are frequently called on to help with corporate downsizing and reorganization. Of 198 companies surveyed, 73 percent said their EAPs cover these workplace concerns.[12]

The first step in an EAP involves the maintenance of performance records and the application of corrective measures when performance falls below standard. The second phase constitutes the link between the work context and community treatment resources. Two experts recommend that management should address (1) the effect of program participation on disciplinary procedures, (2) the disposition of information about employees' participation in the program, and (3) the evaluation of results over time.[13]

Employee assistance programs can help employers cope with the effects that substance abuse has on job performance. Because poor employee performance can mean substantial economic losses, companies have turned increasingly to various forms of EAPs in an effort to reduce costs.

FOLLOW-UP

The employee must be assured that job security will not be jeopardized if he or she obtains the recommended treatment, progresses toward control of the illness, and job performance improves. The employee should also be advised not to expect any special privileges or exemptions from standard personnel administration practices. If a relapse occurs, close follow-up and coordination between the supervisor and the company medical director is of utmost importance. In spite of relapses, many people ultimately control their disease.

It is important to remember that substance abuse is usually a symptom of deeper social and psychological problems, and that for rehabilitation to actually work, these problems must be taken into account. However, if the employee refuses help or accepts treatment but makes no progress toward rehabilitation, and job performance remains poor or deteriorates further, supervisors must take the action they would normally take in cases of unsatisfactory job performance, usually dismissal.

DISCRIMINATION

Discrimination is by no means a resolved issue. Progress has been made through better management practices and antidiscrimination laws, but there are still opportunities for better business and government practices with or without executive, legislative, or judicial intervention.

Discrimination is a continuing human relations problem for both management and workers. Most people are familiar with the overt, violent acts of racial discrimination that are reported by the media. Other kinds of discrimination, however, are often much less recognizable and, for this reason, difficult to overcome. Because it affects so many people in the job market, and because people need to work to live, discrimination deserves serious attention.

PREJUDGMENTS AND BIASES

Making a prejudgment is normal because we cannot handle every event freshly in its own right. If we did, what good would our past experience be? Although prejudgments help to give order to our daily living, our mind has a habit of assimilating as much as it can into categories by which it prejudges a person or event. However, by over-categorizing, we tend to form irrational rather than rational categories, and this may lead us to biases, prejudices, and stereotyping.

Prejudice is an attitude, not an act.

Biases are predispositions to act and decide on preconceived notions rather than rational analysis. **Prejudice** is an attitude, not an act; it is a habit of mind, an opinion based partially on experience and partially on ignorance, fear, and cultural patterns of group formation, none of which has a rational basis.

A person usually learns to be prejudiced because of his or her socialization (learned attitudes through family, school, community, and society). It is in one's environment that one's attitudes are shaped and can be reshaped.

A prejudiced person tends to think of members of a group of people as all being the same, without considering individual differences. This kind of thinking gives rise to stereotypes. **Stereotypes** are generalized beliefs about groups of people based partially on observation and partially on ignorance and tradition.

> In an ideal workplace, people would accept co-workers on the basis of merit. Yet even among the most sincerely open-minded, stereotypes and subtle prejudices can create difficulties. Managers can't change others' opinions—but they can work to ensure that all workers are treated fairly.[14]

WHAT IS DISCRIMINATION?

Discrimination is the actual behavior resulting from prejudice. Thus, we can think of prejudice as an attitude, and discrimination as an overt act demonstrating our prejudice.

Discrimination is an act; prejudice is an attitude.

In a legal sense, discrimination manifests in two forms: disparate treatment and disparate impact. **Disparate treatment** occurs when different standards are used to treat different classes of employees. One group is exempted in some way from the standards that are applied to another group. **Disparate impact** occurs when standards appear to be neutral but there is an underrepresentation of a group in hiring, promotions, compensation, or other personnel decisions.

Almost 13 percent of the population is African American.

Over 11 percent of the population is Hispanic.

Underrepresentation is determined by comparing the percentage of minorities in a given profession with the equivalent percentage in the population. According to the U.S. Census,[15] African Americans number over 35 million, or 12.8 percent of the total U.S. population (see Figure 14–3). More than 11.9 percent of the total U.S. population, or over 32 million Americans, classify themselves as nonwhite Hispanic. Asian Americans comprise 4.1 percent of the U.S. population.

TYPES OF DISCRIMINATION AND PROTECTED CLASSES

The review of legislation affecting discrimination in Table 14–1 shows that our society is moving to overcome discrimination. The Civil Rights Act of 1964, as amended, is the vanguard of civil rights legislation. It established the **Equal Employment Opportunity Commission**, a federal government agency that establishes guidelines for hiring, recruiting, and promoting minority groups. It is the responsibility of the EEOC to enforce our laws against discrimination.

FIGURE 14-3 ***RESIDENT POPULATION ESTIMATES OF THE UNITED STATES BY SEX, RACE, AND HISPANIC ORIGIN: APRIL 1, 1990 TO JULY 1, 1999, WITH SHORT-TERM PROJECTION TO NOVEMBER 1, 2000***

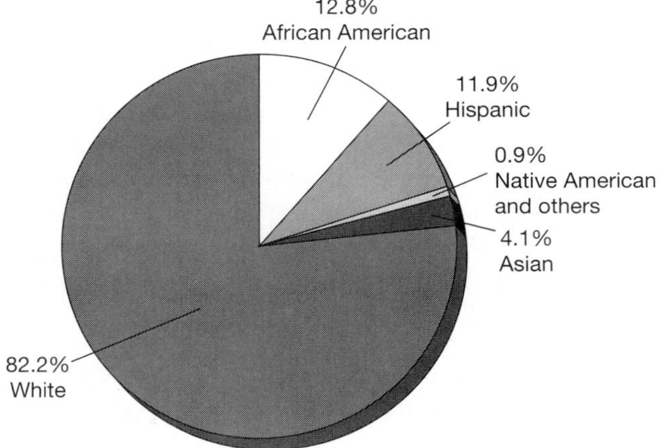

Source: Population estimates program, Population Division, U.S. Census Bureau, Washington, DC, retrieved from www.census.gov. Respondents may indicate more than one ethnic origin.

TABLE 14-1

Legislation Affecting Job Discrimination

1896	U.S. Supreme Court establishes "separate, but equal" doctrine.
1938	Congress passes Fair Labor Standards Act, including Child Labor Laws, which have been amended several times.
1954	Supreme Court rules that "separate education facilities are inherently unequal" and orders schools desegregated.
1963	Equal Pay Act passed.
1964	Civil Rights Act of 1964 passed, establishing the Equal Employment Opportunity Commission (EEOC).
1967	Age Discrimination in Employment Act passed.
1968	Architectural Barriers Act (handicapped accessible) passed.
1973	Vocational Rehabilitation Act (for the handicapped) passed.
1974	Vietnam-Era Veterans Readjustment Act passed.
1974	Congress passes Employee Retirement Income Security Act.
1978	Amendment to the 1967 Age Discrimination Act banning mandatory retirement at 65 years of age.
1978	Pregnancy Discrimination Act passed.
1985	Consolidated Omnibus Reconciliation Act (COBRA).
1986	Age Discrimination in Employment amendments removing upper limit of any age to retirement.
1990	Fair Labor Standards minimum wage amendments.
1990	Americans with Disabilities Act (ADA).
1991	Civil Rights Act of 1991 (punitive damages for victims of discrimination).
1993	Family and Medical Leave Act of 1993.

Racial and Religious Discrimination. Title VII of the Civil Rights Act of 1964 prohibits employment discrimination based on race, color, religion, sex, or national origin. In recent years, there has been an increase in the number of complaints of discrimination based on religious beliefs.[16]

Sex Discrimination. The broad prohibitions against discrimination based on a person's sex specifically cover sexual harassment and pregnancy-based discrimination. We will discuss types of sexual harassment in a later section. As a manager, you should treat pregnancy, childbirth, and any related medical conditions in the same way as other temporary conditions or illness according to the law.

Age Discrimination. The Age Discrimination in Employment Act (ADEA) protects people over 40 years of age (**older workers**). Today there are more than 34 million Americans, or 13 percent of the total population, over age 40 and the size of that age group is increasing as baby boomers age.[17] Historically, this legislation applied to retirement, promotion, and layoff decisions, but now applies to all human resource decisions and its use is increasing. Employers should be advised "that a blanket refusal to consider experienced or highly paid applicants for employment may operate to exclude older employees from job opportunities, in violation of the ADEA."[18]

Discrimination Against People with Disabilities. The **Americans with Disabilities Act (ADA)** applies to employers with 15 or more employees and prohibits employment discrimination against qualified individuals with disabilities. An **individual with disability** is someone who has a physical or mental condition that substantially impairs a major life activity, has a record of such impairment, or is regarded as having such impairment. Major life activities are activities that an average person can perform with little or no difficulty such as walking, breathing, seeing, hearing, speaking, learning, and working.

A qualified individual with a disability is someone who satisfies skill, experience, education, and other job-related requirements of the job, and who with or without reasonable accommodation, can perform the essential functions of that position. Categories of reasonable accommodation are listed in Table 14–2.

Employers are not required to lower production standards to make an accommodation, nor are employers required to make reasonable accommodations if doing so would impose an undue hardship on the operation of the business. **Undue hardship**

TABLE 14–2

Reasonable Accommodation

- Making existing facilities readily accessible to and usable by individual with disabilities
- Restructuring the job
- Modifying work schedules
- Providing additional unpaid leave
- Reassigning the person to a vacant position
- Acquiring or modifying equipment or devices
- Adjusting or modifying examinations, training materials, or policies
- Providing qualified readers or interpreters

Source: The Americans with Disabilities Act of 1990, Titles I and V.

means an action that requires significant difficulty or expense when considered in relation to such factors as the size, financial resources, and nature of the business.

Job engineering and job reassignment.

Job engineering and job reassignments are two things that companies can do to help older workers and employees with disabilities. Job engineering is the process of redesigning the workstation so that work can be done in a way that is less taxing for the employee. It may be planning the work so that it can be done sitting down, providing different power equipment, reducing body movement, or changing the flow of work. Job reassignment is moving the person into a different position in which the task does not demand so much in terms of dexterity or speed, but the job itself is just as rewarding.

JOB ISSUES INVOLVED IN DISCRIMINATION

What activities are made illegal by antidiscrimination laws? These laws prohibit discriminatory behavior in:

- hiring and firing;
- compensating, assigning, or classifying employees;
- transferring, promoting, laying off, or recalling;
- advertising job positions;
- testing;
- allocating fringe benefits (e.g., retirement plans or disability leaves);
- providing other terms and conditions of employment.

Employers are required to post notices advising employees of their rights under the law. Such notices must be accessible, as needed, to people with visual or other disabilities that affect reading.

It is important to note that hiring minorities is not enough—they must be retained. That means effort on the part of employers, leaders, and peers. It is especially difficult for a minority employee who doesn't have very many, or any, minority colleagues who share his or her cultural heritage and preferences in food, clothing, and entertainment.[19] A basic issue for many groups is how to integrate with the majority of society, but still maintain their unique individual cultures.

Equal pay and promotion opportunities are important.

The representation of minorities and women in upper management in American business is not nearly the same percentage as in the general population. The term **glass ceiling** is used to refer to a see-through barrier that prevents advancement for women and other protected groups to higher level jobs. Part of the Civil Rights Act of 1991 was a glass ceiling initiative to establish a commission to study and make recommendations on how to eliminate those barriers. In addition to promotion opportunities, equal pay for equal work is an important issue. Women are paid approximately 70 percent of what men are paid for comparable jobs. African American men earn 24 to 27 percent less than their white counterparts.[20]

One way for women and minorities to succeed is to work long hours and continually exceed performance standards.[21] Another way to break the glass ceiling is for women to start their own firms. According to the Small Business Administration, American women own 9.1 million businesses that employ 27.5 million Americans, contributing $3.6 trillion to the U.S. economy.[22]

COUNTERING DISCRIMINATION THROUGH EDUCATION

Education helps break down our prejudices about one another. More importantly, education helps to level the playing field by giving everyone the skills and knowledge required for a successful career.

Unfortunately, the rate of college-bound African Americans and Hispanic Americans has been declining, especially among young men. For African Americans, only 37 percent of men continue on to college from high school compared to 63 percent of women.[23] Similarly, Hispanic college attendance is 46 percent for young men compared to 54 percent for young women.[24]

LEGAL AND LEGISLATIVE ACTION AGAINST DISCRIMINATION

Civil Rights Act of 1964 prohibits discrimination.

EEOC enforces antidiscrimination laws.

The battle against discrimination is also being waged in the legislature and the courts. As noted already, the most important antidiscrimination bill is the Civil Rights Act of 1964. Under this law and its amendments, the Equal Employment Opportunity Commission has brought discrimination cases to court.

These cases define the areas in which the federal law applies and serve to rectify situations in which discrimination is being practiced. Because the law is being clarified and modified continuously by the court decisions, employers need to be alert to changes brought about by recent court rulings.

For example, the concept of reasonable accommodation for religious preferences has been the source of some confusion between the courts and the EEOC. Reasonable accommodation of religious preferences means employers are expected to consider religious beliefs in assigning work. The EEOC assigns the primary responsibility to the employer to reasonably accommodate religious preferences. However, the courts have put the primary responsibility on the individual. The challenge is for managers and employees to work out agreements that treat everyone fairly and with respect.

Treat all individuals with dignity and respect.

One area clarified by the courts has been the testing of job applicants. In *Griggs v. Duke Power Company*, the Court decision stated that (1) if any employment test or practice has a disparate effect on individuals due to race, sex, religion, or national origin, for example, a test with a higher percentage of black failures than white failures; and (2) such a test is not job related and an accurate predictor of job performance, then the test is discriminatory and illegal.

WHAT IS AFFIRMATIVE ACTION?

Affirmative action is a federal mandate requiring an employer to make efforts to employ qualified members of minority groups. Affirmative action requires more than employment neutrality. An employer is required to make additional efforts to recruit, employ, and promote qualified members of groups formerly excluded. It recognizes the necessity for positive action to overcome the effects of systematic exclusion and discrimination, where neutrality in employment practices would tend to perpetuate the status quo. Originally, affirmative action initiatives included the use of quotas to rectify disparate impact discrimination.

In 1987 the Equal Employment Opportunity Commission directed government agencies to focus on removing barriers to the advancement of women and minorities. Managers of government agencies were not required to meet quotas, but they were directed to take race, national origin, and gender into account when choosing among qualified applicants.[25]

Reverse discrimination argument.

There has been a movement to eliminate affirmative action. The first lawsuit against affirmative action was the reverse discrimination case involving *Bakke v. University of California* in 1978. Bakke argued against the quota system used by the school that resulted in the acceptance of a lesser-qualified minority applicant over a more qualified nonminority candidate. He asserted that his rights had been violated because the school set aside 16 of 100 positions specifically for minorities. Thus, he was able to compete for only 84 of the 100 positions, whereas minorities could compete for all 100. The Supreme Court agreed with Bakke's arguments and issued a ruling that struck down the use of racial quotas in school admissions, but still allowed schools to consider race in deciding which students to accept.

The Supreme Court again cut back on affirmative action quota systems in 1989 when, in *City of Richmond v. J. A. Croson,* it held that a plan to set aside 30 percent of construction contracts for minority business enterprises was constitutionally suspect. They said there is no such thing as benign racial classification—even if it is used as a tool to remedy past discrimination.

Currently, there are cases on appeal in Washington, Texas, and Florida that many observers believe will cause the Supreme Court to directly rule on affirmative action initiatives in higher education after 20 years of silence. The central issue in these cases is whether race can be considered in college admission decisions to achieve the goal of student diversity.[26]

In summary, the Court allows the use of race as a component in making a decision about an individual candidate, but prohibits the use of quotas.

As the debate over affirmative action continues, many companies have decided to address the issue in a different way and use diversity initiatives to ensure equal opportunity for employees in recruitment, selection, and hiring; training and promotion; termination and layoff; salary and benefits; and job classification.

EXPRESS YOUR OPINION

1. Do you know persons (including yourself) who are underpaid because of an ethnic, religious, gender, or other discriminatory reason?
2. Do you know persons (including yourself) who have been sexually harassed at work?
3. Do you know persons (including yourself) who have been otherwise discriminated against on the job, in their living community, or in social settings?

If you answer "No" to these questions, you are probably living in a protected, unique environment. If your answer is "Yes" to any of these questions, answer the following:

4. What is being done to diminish the effects of the acknowledged discrimination?

As noted earlier, sexual harassment is a specific case of sex discrimination, and is discussed in the next section.

SEXUAL HARASSMENT

Sexual harassment is defined as unwelcome sexual conduct that is sufficiently severe or pervasive and which the employer or its managers knew, or should have known, was occurring and failed to take prompt remedial action. There are basically two types of sexual harassment: quid pro quo and hostile work environment. Section 703 of Title VII of the Civil Rights Act of 1964 makes sexual harassment illegal.

Quid pro quo ("something for something") sexual harassment occurs when a person (1) makes unwelcome sexual advances or requests for sexual favors, and (2) indicates, implicitly or explicitly, that submission to, or refusal of, such conduct is a condition of the person's employment. **Hostile work environment,** which is the more common type of sexual harassment, includes unwelcome sexual conduct that has the purpose or effect of unreasonably interfering with an individual's work performance or creating an intimidating, hostile, or offensive work environment.

The following verbal and physical behaviors are considered to be sexual harassment:

- Continued or repeated sexual jokes, language, or flirtation.
- Verbal abuse of a sexual nature.
- Overly repetitive or suggestive compliments about a person's appearance.
- The display in the workplace of sexually suggestive objects, pictures, posters, cartoons, or graffiti.
- Asking questions about sexual conduct.
- Whistling, leering, or stalking.

The supervisor* is *the company.

In determining whether a behavior constitutes sexual harassment, the EEOC and the courts look at the record as a whole. Sexual harassment includes acts by employees as well as outsiders, such as customers and suppliers.

Sexual harassment victims are not always women. Physical, visual, comments, and unwelcome advances can be aimed at men as well as women.

PREVENTING SEXUAL HARASSMENT

According to a survey conducted by *Personnel* magazine, the majority of medium and large companies have a formal policy on sexual harassment. The survey found that confidentiality is a major concern of employees who are hesitant to report an incident of sexual harassment. Companies use surveys, hot lines, and complaint boxes to encourage employees to report harassment.[27]

The key to eliminating or at least reducing sexual harassment is prevention. The EEOC guidelines make a strong claim that prevention is the best tool for controlling sexual harassment. Guidelines suggest that the employer should:

1. Be familiar with the varying forms of sexual harassment.
2. Use EEOC guidelines and case law to clearly define sexual harassment and explain the various types to employees.
3. Establish a written sexual harassment policy.
4. Communicate this policy to all employees on a regular basis.
5. Strongly denounce sexual harassment, confirm that it will not be tolerated, and connect sexual harassment violations to disciplinary remedies.
6. Inform all employees of their legal rights to complain about sexual harassment under Title VII of the Civil Rights Act of 1964.[28]

To avoid aggravating sexual harassment, it is important that employers:

- Do **not** ignore complaints just because they are not formally filed.
- Do **not** ignore complaints because they allegedly happened several years ago.
- Do **not** try to convince an employee not to complain and do **not** defend the offensive behavior as "only joking."
- Do **not** dismiss the employee who complains as a way to remove the problem.
- Do **not** put off taking action, because the harassed employee asks that no action be taken.[29]

Prevention requires active management support.

For a sexual harassment prevention program to be effective, it must have the full support of management. Written policies that are distributed throughout the organization are also important preventive measures. Sanctions and mechanisms for complaint procedures should be a part of those policies. Finally, counseling should be available to individuals who have been victims of harassment.

WORKPLACE VIOLENCE

According to the National Institute of Occupational Safety and Health (NIOSH), one million American workers are assaulted and more than 1,000 workers are murdered annually because of workplace violence.[30] Homicide is the second most frequent cause of fatal injuries in the workplace, with firearms responsible for three-fourths of all work-related homicides. **Workplace violence** is usually caused by one of the following: a disgruntled or former worker; a person intent on robbing the business; a person with a romantic obsession or a stalker, a disgruntled former spouse or ex-boyfriend; or a random incident.

According to some experts, an individual who becomes violent in the workplace is often experiencing:

- a life crisis, such as divorce or death,
- drug or alcohol abuse,
- depression,
- job insecurity,
- an obsession with guns, or
- paranoia.[31]

Often the individual has a history of violence and has made previous threats or pleas for help.

Experts think that, in many situations, there are three escalating levels of workplace violence of which managers should be aware. In the beginning, the person verbally attacks his or her coworker(s). Such attacks can include excessive arguing, acting belligerent, spreading rumors or gossip, or using excessive profanity. The next level starts when the person intensifies his or her behavior. For example, the employee may steal property for revenge, refuse to obey company procedures, or sabotage company property. In the final stage, the person begins to see him- or herself as the victim, makes verbal or written threats, displays intense anger, engages in recurrent fights, or openly destroys property.[32]

SUMMARY

There are increasingly complex issues facing managers these days. While you cannot be an expert on all of them, to be effective in your career, you should be aware of these issues and where to go for help when you need it.

Alcoholism is a major disease and drug addiction is increasing throughout the population. Both do great damage to our national productivity and result in a waste of human resources. Companies are responding with employee assistance programs to help their employees overcome these disabling problems.

Prejudice is an attitude and discrimination is an action. According to the 2000 U.S. census, almost 13 percent of the population is African American, almost 12 percent is

SOME STEPS EMPLOYERS CAN TAKE TO PREVENT WORKPLACE VIOLENCE

1. Preemployment screening: Check applicant backgrounds, including references, criminal records, work history, and so forth.
2. Train managers and workers how to resolve conflicts: Develop skills in communicating effectively, team building, and resolving disputes and encourage respect for diversity.
3. Develop policies to protect employees: Develop a policy defining harassment, how employees are to report complaints, and how complaints will be investigated.
4. Train supervisors to recognize signs of a troubled employee: Supervisors should be trained to intervene before an incident escalates.
5. Treat employees with dignity and respect, especially when they are discharged: Think and plan beforehand to keep the situation from escalating.

Hispanic, and over 4 percent is Asian. Discrimination is clear when we find that those percentages are not well represented in managerial and other professional areas.

Since the Civil Rights Act was passed in 1964, several laws have been enacted to aid in overcoming discrimination; primary emphases have been on antidiscrimination measures for the aging, individuals with disabilities, and family and medical leave provisions, as well as changes in minimum wage laws.

Affirmative action programs should be based on a thorough analysis of minority and female representation in various levels of the company. Disparities should be remedied by the achievement of a set of specific goals and objectives over a given period of time. Pay equity remains an area in need of improvement for women and minorities.

Sexual harassment is a significant workplace problem that employers are responsible for preventing and responding to quickly. Managers should be aware of both quid pro quo and hostile work environment types of harassment, especially the latter because it is more common.

Workplace violence is becoming increasingly common in our high-stress world. Companies need to educate managers and employees on the symptoms and effective responses in order to prevent workplace tension from escalating into violence.

CASE STUDY 14-1

THE SWEET SMELL OF GRASS

Tom Nowak walked to his office on Monday morning to find Dan Porter waiting for him at his door. "Tom, I would like to see you right away in my office." Tom was surprised at the sudden approach that his boss had used the first thing on a Monday morning. It must be serious, he thought, as they walked down the hall together. He thought that they had always had an amicable relationship.

"What's up?" asked Tom, trying to keep from sounding too apprehensive as they arrived at Dan's office.

"Sit down, Tom, it's important. It involves some of the people in your department." Dan was obviously disturbed. "You have been responsible for the shipping room for several years, and I haven't had any serious reason to doubt how you handle your staff or the decisions you make in that department, but this new development upsets me. I've heard, and occasionally seen, a group of your employees seem to take their breaks surreptitiously in out-of-the-way places—the restroom and behind the loading dock. I've heard the reason is because they're smoking marijuana. Is that true, Tom?"

"You might be right, Dan. I really don't know, but I suspect it."

"Have you ever confronted them with the idea? Have you asked them outright?"

"No," said Tom quietly, "and I am not sure it's a good idea."

"Why not," replied Dan, "do you have a better idea?"

"The first reason is that they would probably lie if I asked them outright if they were smoking pot. They would lie for fear of losing their jobs. Another is that I am not their father or guardian of their morals. Their break time is strictly their own. Oh, I know it's illegal, and the company could get into trouble even though we don't control their breaks, but we might be opening 'Pandora's box' if we approach it head on."

"What do you mean by a comment like that, Tom?" inquired Dan.

"You know as well as I do," said Tom, "that there are some guys under you that have openly discussed the effects of pot and who have admitted trying it. I don't have to name them, you know them."

Dan looked perplexed. "You're right, but they haven't stepped out of line at work to my knowledge. If we condone its use at work we have a problem. It is illegal, you know. We just can't take the risk that it is being done on company time."

CASE QUESTIONS

1. What would be your approach to solve the immediate problem?
2. If you were to counsel any of the employees, which counseling approach would you use?
3. Should Tom and Dan try to solve the problem between them or should they confer with others?
4. There is no company policy on the matter; should they develop one?

CASE STUDY 14-2

LOVE IN BLOOM OR . . . ?

Fran is a good-looking, 19-year-old student who works full time at a small fast-food restaurant. Fran is working to accumulate enough money for college and a new car. The manager of the restaurant, Pat, is also a college student and about 4 years older than Fran. There is an assistant manager for each of the work shifts, and Fran would like to be promoted to that position for the extra pay and status. Pat likes Fran and has made no secret about it. In fact, several times Pat has asked Fran out to movies after work and suggested that they take their breaks in Pat's car. Pat has openly commented on Fran's attractive qualities. Fran has rejected Pat's advances. Pat appears to be hurt and has told Fran that unless they can take breaks together and date, Fran doesn't stand a chance of becoming an assistant manager.

CASE QUESTIONS

1. What do you think—is this sexual harassment or just "love in bloom"?
2. What can Fran do?
3. Would it make a difference to know that Fran is a young man and Pat a young woman? Go back through the case and see if there are any differences.

CASE STUDY 14-3

DISCRIMINATION AGAINST A WOMAN ACCOUNT EXECUTIVE

Diane Patterson is employed as a registered representative by Johnson and Hunt, a large metropolitan brokerage firm. Diane was promoted to this position 5 months ago when the company lost a few of its brokers to a competing firm. Diane had worked previously for a number of years as a secretary to Scott Pitts, one of the partners in the firm, and he recommended her for a promotion when a vacancy arose.

Although Diane assumed her duties with enthusiasm, Cliff Stevenson, the office manager, soon felt it necessary to question Diane on her deteriorating performance. Cliff suspected the reason for Diane's poor performance. When Diane assumed her duties as a registered rep, Cliff had heard some of the men speak against her, as if they resented her taking on the job. He also knew that Diane was losing customers for no apparent reason other than the fact that she was female.

When Cliff questioned Diane on this, she replied, "I don't like being the only female in the department. I feel as if everyone is against me here." She added, "Many of my male clients seem to think that because I'm a woman, I'm not qualified to be an account executive." Diane also mentioned that perhaps a new start in another department would enable her to carry out her duties more effectively.

Cliff knows that Diane is capable of performing her duties, even though she has few clients, and with the shortage of account executives in Cliff's department, he does not want to lose her. Cliff decides to ask Scott's opinion on the problem.

"The men feel threatened by Diane," Scott replied. "They feel that being an account executive is a demanding job and should belong to men only. One of the men said that she has no right to fill a position that may be needed by a man to support his family."

"I find that a bit hard to believe," replied Cliff.

"Believe it, Cliff. Even Harry Morgan mentioned something about not only having to worry about younger men taking over his job, but now he'd have to worry about his secretary."

Now, understanding the problem that exists, Cliff must decide what course of action to take. If you were Cliff, what would you do?

CASE QUESTIONS

1. Would you let Diane go?
2. Would you discuss the problem with the men separately?
3. Would you discuss the problem with Diane present?
4. How could you, as a manager, enhance Diane's status?
5. What is the best course of action for all concerned?

DISCUSSION AND STUDY QUESTIONS—TO KEEP YOU THINKING

1. How can you recognize substance abuse?
2. Explain how discrimination is influenced by prejudice.
3. What are at least three ways in which discrimination can be overcome?
4. What, if anything, should the organization do to help the older worker?
5. What are some of the actions that are being urged to lessen sex discrimination?
6. How do you define "individuals with disabilities" on the employment scene?
7. What is management's obligation to current and prospective employees regarding discrimination, irrespective of the law?
8. Are education and training playing any part in overcoming specific discriminatory practices?
9. What are appropriate steps for preventing sexual harassment?
10. What behaviors would make you suspect that workplace tension is escalating into violence? What steps would you take to deal with your suspicions?

NOTES

1. U.S. Department of Health and Human Services, Substance Abuse and Mental Health Services Administration, Office of Applied Studies, *Summary of Findings from the 1999 National Household Survey on Drug Abuse*, www.samhsa.gov/oas/NHSDA/2kNHSDA/chapter2.htm, accessed February 28, 2002.
2. Kevin Murphy, "Why Pre-Employment Alcohol Testing Is Such a Bad Idea", *Business Horizons* (September–October 1995): 69–74.
3. Substance Abuse and Mental Health Administration, Office of Applied Studies, *Worker Drug Use and Workplace Policies and Programs: Results from the 1997 National Household Survey on Drug Abuse*, www.samhsa.gov/oas/NHSDA/A-11/, accessed January 23, 2002.
4. Ibid.
5. T. E. Backer, *Strategic Planning for Workplace Drug Abuse Programs.* Washington, DC: National Institute on Drug Abuse, 1987, 4.
6. "Drug Abuse Costing America Billions," *Ledger-Enquirer* (Columbus, Georgia), February 4, 1996, A7–A8.
7. M. Bernstein and J. J. Mahoney, "Management Perspectives on Alcoholism: The Employer's Stake in Alcoholism Treatment," *Occupational Medicine* 4, no. 2 (1989): 223–232.
8. National Institute on Drug Abuse and National Institute on Alcoholism and Alcohol Abuse, "The Economic Cost of Alcohol and Drug Abuse," 1992 (preprint copy) 5/98, 5-1, www.nida.hin.gov/EconomicCosts/Index.html, accessed January 28, 2002.
9. Kevin Murphy, "Why Pre-Employment Alcohol Testing Is Such a Bad Idea," *Business Horizons* (September–October 1995): 69–74.
10. E. Greenberg, ed. American Management Association (AMA) Research Reports. "1991 AMA Survey on Workplace Drug Testing and Drug Abuse Policies," 1.
11. Christina Many, "Beyond Drug and Alcohol Abuse," *Business Insurance* (June 26, 1995): 3.
12. Ibid., 3–4.
13. Steven H. Appelbaum and Barbara T. Shapiro, "The ABCs of EAPs," *Personnel* (July 1989): 39–46.
14. "Diversity: Getting Past Stereotypes," *Supervisory Management* (August 1995): 1, 6.
15. Resident Population Estimates of the United States, Population Estimates Program, Population Division, U.S. Census Bureau, retrieved from www.census.gov/population/estimates/nation/intfile2-1.txt.
16. Janine S. Pouliot, "Rising Complaints of Religious Bias," *Nation's Business* (February 1996): 36–37.
17. Resident Population Estimates of the United States, Population Estimates Program, Population Division, U.S. Census Bureau, retrieved from www.census.gov/population/estimates/nation/intfile2-1.txt.
18. Betty Southard Murphy, Wayne E. Barlow, and D. Diane Hatch, "Manager's Newsfront: Salary Test

May Be a Proxy for Age Bias," *Personnel Journal* (October 1993): 26–27.

19. E. K. Daugin, "Minority Faculty Retention: What It Takes—The Hire Is Only the Beginning," *Black Issues in Higher Education* (October 21, 1993): 43–44.
20. U.S. Department of Commerce, Bureau of the Census, *Population Profile of the United States 1995*, July 1995.
21. Bill Leonard, "Long Hours, Hard Work Can Break the Glass Ceiling," *HR Magazine* (April 1996): 4.
22. Statistics on Women Business Ownership, Small Business Administration, retrieved from www.sba.gov/womeninbusiness/welcome.html.&hbsp, accessed January 28, 2002.
23. Daren Fonda, "The Male Minority," *Time* (December 2, 2000): 35.
24. Ibid.
25. "What Is Affirmative Action?" *Government Executive* (April 1996): 14.
26. Kenneth Cooper, "U.S. Courts Differ on Preference: Affirmative Action Gets Mixed Results," *The Washington Post*, December 7, 2000, A10.
27. Diane Feldman, "Sexual Harassment: Policies and Prevention," *Personnel* (September 1987): 12–17.
28. Ruth Ann Strickland, "Sexual Harassment: A Legal Perspective for Public Administrators," *Public Personnel Management* (winter 1995): 504.
29. Ibid.
30. "Violence in the Workplace," National Institute for Occupational Safety and Health, www.cdc.gov/niosh/violpr.html, accessed April 24, 2002.
31. Jurg W. Mattman, "Preventing Violence in the Workplace," Workplace Violence Research Institute, www.noworkviolence.com/articles/preventing_violence.htm, accessed April 24, 2002.
32. Ibid.

CHAPTER

15

Organized Employee Relations

TO START YOU THINKING

Again, here are some questions that you might think about and discuss before you read this chapter.

- Do you think that unions are as beneficial to society now as they were 10, 20, or 30 years ago?
- Are there more strikes now than 10 years ago? Why?
- What types of strikes are illegal?
- What is the difference between a mediator and an arbitrator?
- Do you think that public employees should be members of a union and be allowed to strike?
- What is the difference between a union shop and a closed shop?
- What is a yellow-dog contract? A boycott? A lockout?
- Why don't more people join unions?
- How does a grievance get resolved in a unionized workplace?
- What are some ethical and technological implications surrounding unions?

LEARNING GOALS

After studying this chapter, you should be able to:

1. Appreciate the historical origins and purposes of unions.
2. Explain the different approaches that management might take toward unions.
3. Give some of the major reasons why people join or do not join unions.
4. Relate the functions and difficulties of the shop steward and the company supervisor in the labor-management relationship.
5. Compare the basic negotiating procedures in collective bargaining from the union and management points of view.
6. Explain the various tactics that unions and management can use to achieve their goals.
7. Discuss grievance procedures and the process of arbitration that is used when no decision can be reached.
8. Describe the impact of the global economy on unions.
9. Define and apply the following terms and concepts (in order of first appearance):

KEYWORDS

- **organized employee representation**
- **collective bargaining**
- **National Labor Relations Act (NLRA; the Wagner Act) of 1935**
- **National Labor Relations Board (NLRB)**
- **Fair Labor Standards Act**
- **labor union**
- **American Federation of Labor and Congress of Industrial Organizations (AFL-CIO)**
- **density**
- **containment**

- **unfair labor practices (management)**
- **Taft-Hartley Act of 1947**
- **unfair labor practices (labor)**
- **right-to-work laws**
- **closed shop**
- **union shops**
- **Landrum-Griffin Act of 1959**
- **cooperation**
- **dual loyalty**
- **certification**
- **shop steward**
- **grievance**
- **mediator**
- **arbitrator**
- **conciliation**

A HISTORICAL PERSPECTIVE

The history of organized employee representation is colorful—and sometimes violent. **Organized employee representation** involves an independent labor union that employees choose to represent their interests in management. During the late nineteenth and early twentieth centuries, employers resisted unionization through such means as private security forces like Pinkertons and occasionally U.S. Army and National Guard units. At times, the "labor wars" became extremely violent and destructive, leading to various attempts at legal control. Until the 1930s, courts developed most labor law using common law principles.

During the first 2 decades of the last century, union membership increased rapidly. At the end of World War I in 1919, employers moved to reduce union strength and penetration. The employer strategy was so successful that membership dropped from over 20 percent of the workforce in 1920 to less than 14 percent in 1930. Then, with the coming of the Depression and the election of Franklin Delano Roosevelt in 1932, Congress began to enact laws favorable to collective bargaining. A more positive legal environment and militant workers' organizations created the groundwork for the modern labor movement.

Collective bargaining is the process by which representatives of employees and management convene to negotiate a working agreement or other work rules. Collective bargaining first became part of statutory law with the passage of the **National Labor Relations Act (NLRA)** of 1935. The NLRA, commonly called the Wagner Act, guaranteed workers' rights to form unions to represent them to management. It also set up the **National Labor Relations Board (NLRB)** to investigate cases of unfair labor practices committed by employers or unions. The NLRB is responsible for holding elections to determine whether a firm's employees want a union and, if so, which one.

NLRA controls organized employee relations.

The act specifically listed **unfair labor practices (management)** on the part of the employer. It is an unfair labor practice for an employer to:

- interfere with, restrain, or coerce employees in exercising their legally sanctioned right of self-organization
- dominate or interfere with either the formation or administration of a labor organization
- discriminate with regard to hiring or tenure of employment in order to encourage or discourage membership in any labor organization
- discharge or otherwise discriminate against employees simply because the latter files unfair practice charges against the company
- refuse to bargain collectively with the employees' duly chosen representatives

Amendments to the NLRA include the Taft-Hartley Act of 1947 and the Landrum-Griffin Act of 1959. Essentially the **Taft-Hartley Act** amendments provided a list of unfair labor practices on the part of unions. **Unfair labor practices (labor)** include:

- Coercing or restraining employees in the exercise of the rights guaranteed to them for purposes of collective bargaining or processing of employee grievances
- Coercing or attempting to coerce an employer to discriminate in any way against an employee to encourage or discourage membership in a labor organization
- Refusing to bargain in "good faith" with an employer about wages, hours, and other employment conditions
- Engaging in certain strikes, boycotts, or other types of coercion
- Exacting excessive or discriminatory employee fees or dues
- Causing or attempting to cause an employer to pay or deliver any money or other thing of value for services not performed ("featherbedding") and certain other discriminatory practices that will be defined later

A special part of the Taft-Hartley Act is the **right-to-work** provisions outlawing the **closed shop**, under which only union members are hired, and enabling the states to prohibit **union shops** from requiring individuals to join a union after they have been hired. Right-to-work states include the following:

- Alabama
- Arizona
- Arkansas
- Colorado (modified)
- Florida
- Georgia
- Idaho
- Iowa
- Kansas
  Louisiana
- Mississippi
- Nebraska
- Nevada
- North Carolina
- North Dakota
- South Carolina
- South Dakota
- Tennessee
- Texas
- Utah
- Virginia
- Wyoming

The **Landrum-Griffin Act of 1959** is a bill of rights for union members designed to protect employees from abuses by their own unions. Corruption and misuse of union funds, racketeering, and other practices prompted passage of the amendments. Even recently, rank-and-file union members continue to accuse their leadership of improprieties. In early 1994, a North Carolina teamster accused Teamster President Ron Carey of "excesses that drain the union's coffers."[1] Carey was proposing boosting dues by 25 percent to replenish depleted funds.

Executive orders brought collective bargaining to the public sector.

Executive orders by Presidents Kennedy in 1961, Nixon in 1971, and others, brought to the public sector collective bargaining similar to that in the private sector. Many states as well as the federal government now authorize bargaining by government employees.[2]

The **Fair Labor Standards Act**, as amended, regulates the minimum wage, limits the number of hours that employees can work without being paid overtime, and discourages use of child labor. The law defines the normal working week and requires time-and-a-half pay for all hours over 40 worked by an employee during a week, although there are some exceptions and exemptions.

WHERE ARE UNIONS GOING?

Some would argue that labor unions as we know them are quickly becoming a thing of the past. Indeed the rough-and-tumble and sometimes violent unions of the mid-twentieth century are, for the most part, changing. Some violence remains in isolated strikes and other actions, but is the labor union movement dead or simply changing?

Some would mandate more union involvement and power. The Dunlop Commission (named for one of the members of the Commission on the Future of Worker-Management Relations) advocated active participation on the part of the government to increase the number of employees represented by unions. One of the fundamental principles of the NLRA, however, is that employees—not employers, not unions, not a government commission or agency—should decide whether they will be represented by a union.[3]

Strikes have always been the major weapon of most unions. Some public employees, like police and firefighters in some jurisdictions, are prohibited from striking. More fundamental than the right to strike is the welfare of employees for which unions have fought. Today, many of the economic provisions employees desired have been obtained; thus, unions must change strategy and tactics to a more conciliatory and cooperative stance if they are to survive.

Unions have several options.

According to Peter Drucker, the single most important factor in the decline of labor unions is "the shift of gravity of the workforce from the blue-collar worker in manufacturing industry to the knowledge worker."[4] Drucker believes that unions have three choices: (1) do nothing and disappear, (2) maintain themselves by influencing the political power structure, or (3) rethink their function. Some suggestions for alternative three are as follows.

> The union might reinvent itself as the organ of society—and of the employing institution—concerned with human potential and human achievement, and with optimizing the human resource altogether. The union would still have a role as the representative of the employees against management stupidity, management arbitrariness, and management abuse of power. . . . The union would work with management on productivity and quality, on keeping the enterprise competitive, and thus maintaining the members' jobs and their incomes.[5]

Unions can have positive influences.

Unions and their influence are not dead, but they must be restructured if they are to survive and serve a useful purpose. Certainly their impact and membership have declined, but new horizons and opportunities for cooperative action remain and, in some sectors, are growing. Peter Seybold of Indiana University's Division of Labor Studies says:

> The face of the labor movement is changing as women and minorities play an increasingly important role in the labor movement and in organizing drives. . . . Unions are focusing increasingly on issues that affect these newer members, such as child care, affirmative action, and sexual harassment. Other issues gaining prominence include national health-care reform, health and safety on the job, worker training and education, and rights of the disabled.[6]

ARE UNIONS A PART OF A PROBLEM OR A PART OF A SOLUTION?

Question: First, what problem? Answer: The productivity problem. Are unions contributing to productivity problems? In other words, are we better off with or without unions?

Fortunately, a reevaluation of earlier research on the role of unions answers these questions. Richard Freeman, one of the outstanding authorities on unionization in recent decades, confirms the following:[7]

1. Unionism reduces the probability that workers will quit their jobs and increases the workers' tenure with firms.
2. Unions alter the composition of the compensation package toward fringe benefits.

3. Unions reduce the inequality of wages among workers with measurably similar skills.
4. Union workplaces operate under more explicit rules than do nonunion workplaces.
5. Most unions are highly democratic, especially at the local level . . . far from being the corrupt institutions that union-baiters often allege.
6. The view that unions harm productivity is erroneous. In many sectors, unionism is associated with higher productivity. In only a few sectors is unionism associated with lower productivity.
7. It is erroneous to blame unionism for national macroeconomic problems, such as wage inflation or aggregate unemployment.
8. Union wage gains reduce the rate of profit of unionized firms, motivating considerable antiunion activity by employers.
9. The decline in union density is due in large part to employer opposition to union organizing in National Labor Relations Board representation election campaigns.

Unions can also have negative effects.

As positive as Freeman's analysis is, there are some negative aspects of union behavior today as well. Freeman concludes that the research and labor market developments of the 1980s clearly indicate that the unionism of the 1990s and into the twenty-first century will have to differ in major ways from the unionism that developed under the Wagner Act:[8]

Unions will have to change to survive.

> To succeed, unions will have to enhance their voice role in defending workers, providing democracy at the workplace, and improving workplace conditions. . . . The evidence from the 1980s suggests that these changes are necessary, not only for society to obtain the greatest benefit from the union institution, but also for unions to rejuvenate themselves.

Because of human nature, people tend to:

1. Protect the status quo.
2. Resist making changes because of habit, fear of the unknown, security, and loss of power and control.

Union development today is a classic example of this resistance to change. Today's wage earners often fear that the company holds all the keys to their well-being and, rather than lose what they have, will accept what the company offers on any grounds to protect what they have won for themselves in the past.

Employees don't own what they produce.

The only thing employees can claim is ownership of their labor. If they sell their labor to a company, most laborers feel that they have the right to bargain over the price of their labor, just as the company has the right to haggle with the buyers of their product over its wholesale cost.

Currently, there exists a positive challenge: both employers (management) and employees (labor in general as perhaps represented by labor organizations) must be more flexible in the future. Flexibility here means attitude and "heart" as much as specific job assignment. To summarize:

> The power to reassign work and workers, the flexibility so envied by managers in union companies, is not a productivity panacea because it sets in motion protective human behavior. Indeed, in some nonunion settings, the company may choose to "buy" individual worker cooperation in ways that are ultimately counterproductive. . . . The very fact that employee participation programs have been introduced so widely in the nonunion sector is evidence for . . . our view in this regard. In part, nonunion employers are recognizing that the top-down exercise of managerial power may not maximize productivity, both because managers do not know everything and because workers can react to "managerial flexibility" in ways inhibiting productivity.

WHO ARE UNION MEMBERS?

A **labor union** is an organization of employees formed for the purpose of furthering the interests of its members. Most people think of unions in terms of the blue-collar movement, because most union members have been in such fields. The **American Federation of Labor and Congress of Industrial Organization (AFL-CIO)** is a national federation of many of the craft and industrial unions. One of the largest unions within the AFL-CIO today, however, is the American Federation of State, County, and Municipal Employees, which includes white-collar as well as blue-collar workers.

Other large unions include the Teamsters, the Food and Commercial Workers, and the National Education Association, an employee representation organization. The United Auto Workers is one of the largest unions affiliated with the AFL-CIO. It rejoined the AFL-CIO in June 1981, ending a 13-year separation. The Teamsters also affiliated with the AFL-CIO in the late 1980s. Recently the United Steel Workers and the United Rubber Workers merged on July 1, 1995.

Table 15–1 shows the percentage of union members in various employment sectors. Note that the membership in almost all sectors is declining. The greatest potential for union development is in the retail, services, and financial sectors, as well as among the medical and legal professions. Public employee unions have been the fastest growing of any segment of unionism. This sector includes teachers, police officers, firefighters, and county employees.

Even middle-class workers have sought to join unions. More than 4 million white-collar workers are now union members. Despite their growth, however, labor organizations have not kept up with the growth of the labor force (see Figure 15–1). This is due in part to management's decision to offer the same benefits to nonunion employees that union members receive. Membership in unions has been steadily declining from more than 30 percent of the civilian labor force prior to 1960. Yet **density**, the percentage of civilians in the workforce who are union members or otherwise represented, is high in some sections of the country.

TABLE 15–1

Union Membership: Percentage of All Workers in an Employment Sector of the United States

	1980	1985	1995	1998
Transportation and public utilities	48.4%	37.0%	27.3%	25.5%
Government	35.9	35.8	37.8	37.3
Manufacturing	32.3	24.8	17.6	15.6
Construction	30.9	22.3	17.7	19.1
Mining	32.0	17.3	13.8	10.6
Wholesale and retail trade	10.1	7.2	6.1	5.2
Services	8.9	6.6	5.7	5.5
Finance, insurance, and real estate	3.2	2.9	2.1	2.1

Source: U.S. Department of Labor, Bureau of Labor Statistics. *Summary of Union Membership; U.S. Department of Labor*, Bureau of International Labor Affairs. *The American Workforce* (Washington, DC, September 1992), 23; and U.S. Census Bureau. *Statistical Abstract of the United States*, 116th ed. (Washington, DC, 1996), 438.

FIGURE 15-1 *The Percentage of Union Members Relative to the Total Workforce*

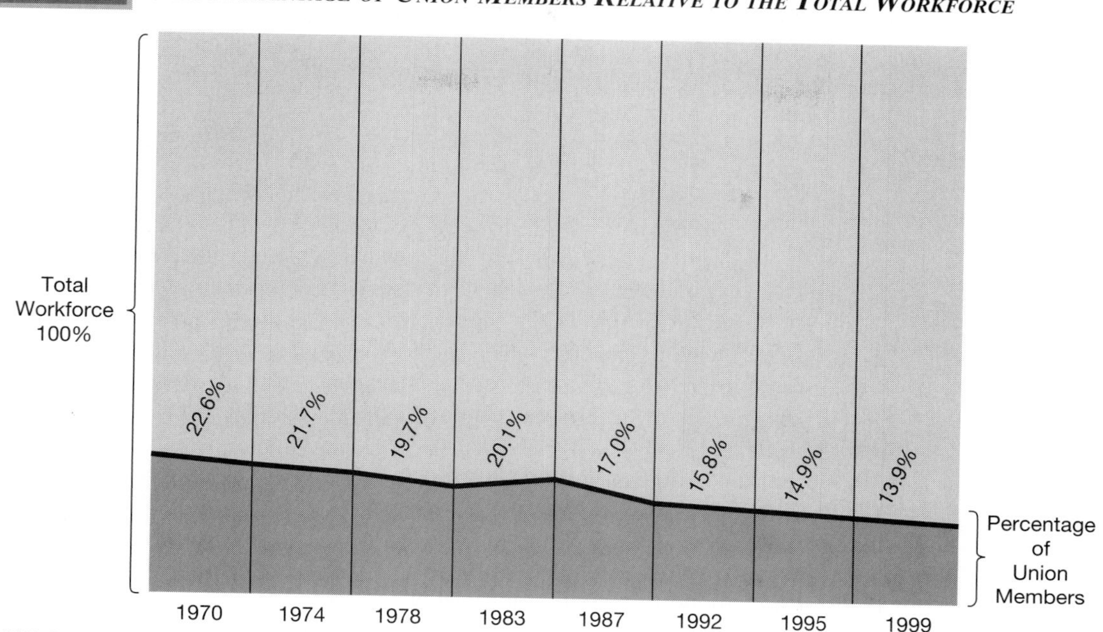

Source: U.S. Census Bureau. *Statistical Abstract of the United States*, 116th ed. (Washington, DC, 1996), 437–438; U.S. Department of Labor, Bureau of Labor Statistics. *Union Membership Summary*, Washington, DC, 2000.

A CLASH OF GOALS

There is a hand-in-glove relationship between labor and management. One cannot survive without the other, but a struggle between the two has been going on for years. Many companies in the United States have been faced with the fact that attempts at union organizing are here to stay. There are no precise formulas to make dealing with unions easy and no directions on the back of union contracts to help management come to an understanding of how a union works or why it is necessary in the first place.

Management versus unions.

Too often, both the company management and the union forget that the other is made up of people and that working with and understanding people takes more time and effort than does mastering a complicated computer language. Computer languages are logical and always consistent; people rarely are. Management sees the union as a corporate body that is in opposition to management goals. Unions see management as a profit monster that does not willingly undertake the time or expense necessary to attend to the needs of the workers who feed it. A good example of this clash of goals is in the major league baseball and football owners and players' associations.

MANAGEMENT'S ATTITUDES TOWARD UNIONS

The goals of management, which are varied, include profit making, market development, and corporate efficiency. By concentrating on efficiency and profit, the managements of many American companies have neglected personnel problems for a long time, leaving such problems to the supervisors and shop superintendents. Faced with unions challenging their authority, employers have generally been opposed to unions in the past.

Some U.S. employers have now come to accept unionism and forms of collective bargaining, but a few remain bitterly opposed to the principles of unionism. The typical attitudes of employers can be classified from *exclusion* to *cooperation,* with intermediate steps of *containment, acceptance,* and *accommodation.*

Exclusion.

When the employer's policy is that of union exclusion, management tries to discourage workers from joining unions by coercion or by trying to provide the wage and fringe benefits that their competitors grant through collective bargaining.

Containment.

Faced with a law compelling them to deal with unions, employers usually act accordingly, but do everything possible to direct the loyalty of the workers away from the union and back to the company. Under **containment**, all relations with the union are kept on a strictly legal basis, and the scope of collective bargaining is kept as narrow as possible. By doing so, the company hopes to rid itself eventually of collective bargaining.

Acceptance and accommodation.

Acceptance and accommodation mean that the employer recognizes the union as part of the industrial scene and tries to use collective bargaining to improve its employee relations.

Cooperation.

Finally, in conditions of **cooperation**, management seeks the assistance of the union in production problems that are not usually the subject matter of collective bargaining. Acceptance and accommodation are more prevalent than are exclusion or cooperation (see Figure 15–2).

DUAL LOYALTY

Dual loyalty or divided loyalty.

Dual loyalty is loyalty felt by the employee for both employer and union. Sometimes the employee must decide between the two just before a contract vote. With employment and union membership comes a problem unique to workers. Their wages come directly from their employer, but they perceive that the protection of their

FIGURE 15–2 Attitudes of Employers toward Unions and How They Deal with Them

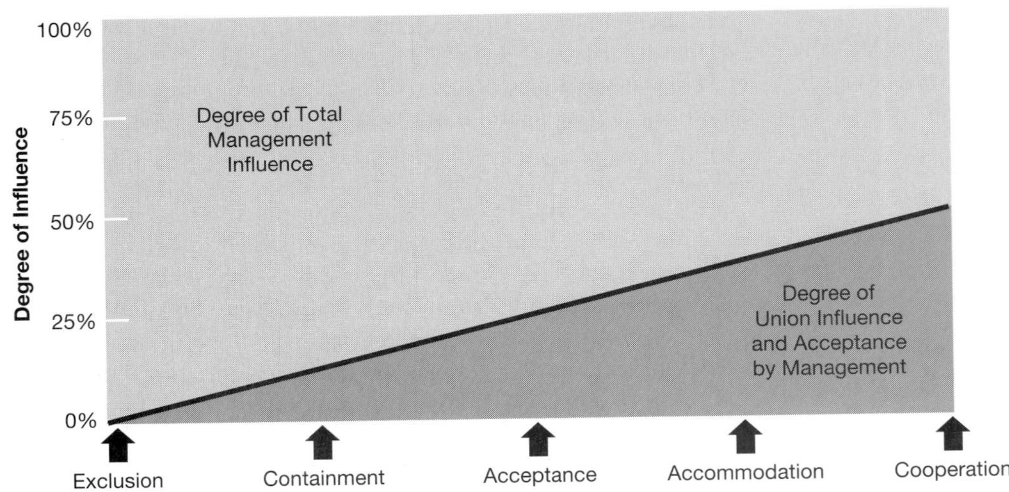

rights and privileges as employees comes from their union. Some personnel managers and union officials believe that employees will give their loyalties to the side that benefits the individual most, without considering the overall impact of their actions on society or on the economy.

No longer can unions or management count on blind support from their members or employees. So many aspects of labor problems have been brought to public attention that union employees cannot help but know the effects of their proposed actions even before they are taken. Workers are forced to take public reaction into account now because the public, through television, may know about the strike or walk-out, even before some of the workers do. Public sympathy for a strike for higher wages or increased fringe benefits cannot be gained by simply making the facts known, no more than management can get the public on its side by claiming low profits and increased costs.

Public reaction can give support to one side.

WHY DO PEOPLE JOIN UNIONS?

Poor morale rather than wages encourages employees to join unions.

On the surface, people join unions for economic advantage and security. In other settings, nonwork benefits, political ideology, and social values may be reasons for unionization.[9] Workers also gain some protection through grievance procedures. However, both unions and employers often agree that it is not wages but inhumane treatment that leads employees to join unions.

Job satisfaction, job security, and positive attitudes toward unions are among major reasons why people join unions. If an individual does not receive job satisfaction on the job from management, then the union becomes more attractive. Similarly, if an individual has no assurance of continued employment, he or she may find job security by belonging to a union.

Faced with the threat of unemployment in the 1990s, union members have shifted their priorities from compensation to job security issues.[10] It is more difficult for management to get rid of a union employee than a nonunion employee because of formalized grievance procedures and other mechanisms built into a collectively bargained agreement.

Lack of worker participation and complaint systems encourage union entry.

When a company becomes highly structured and bureaucratic, it can create a breeding ground for unions. When all the rules are written by the employer with no representation on the part of the employees, look out nonunion companies! Many large companies in such industries as banking, insurance, and finance cultivate bureaucratic systems, partly due to size. If there is no effective open-door or complaint and grievance policy, the firm is encouraging unionization.

WHAT CAN UNIONS PROMISE?

1. Unions can reveal working conditions that are not equal to those for other employees in similar situations, but they cannot promise better wages, working conditions, or benefits.
2. Unions can usually deliver a job posting system that provides employees with the opportunity for upward mobility. Every vacancy should be posted with a job description, salary range, and necessary qualifications.
3. Unions can usually develop a complaint system that can be monitored to protect employees against jeopardy.
4. Usually, unions contracts contain requirements for promotion by seniority where skills are equal, eliminating cutthroat competition and affording a feeling of regularity and justice.

ACTION PROJECT 15–1

YOUR UNION ATTITUDE (INDIVIDUAL EXERCISE)

The following test will judge your attitude toward unions. Select one of three answers for each question. Your choices are as follows: "I agree with the statement" (Agree), "I am not sure how I feel" (?), or "I disagree with the statement" (Disagree).

	Agree	?	Disagree
1. As an employee, I would discourage other workers from joining a union by encouraging better wages without unionization.	A	?	D
2. Collective bargaining is a strong union tool but not a good way to solve problems.	A	?	D
3. Union negotiations should be kept strictly to the letter of the law.	A	?	D
4. Employees would be better off without collective bargaining.	A	?	D
5. The unions are part of the American scene and must be accepted as an integral part of business today.	A	?	D
6. More people today accept the idea of unionism than they did 10 years ago.	A	?	D
7. Employers today more readily recognize unions and meet with them on a continuing basis.	A	?	D
8. Collective bargaining is a constructive way to improve relations between employees and employers.	A	?	D
9. Smart managers actually seek assistance from the unions in production problems that are not the subject of collective bargaining.	A	?	D
10. The wise supervisor considers the shop steward as an ally rather than as an adversary (an enemy).	A	?	D

This test was constructed from the typical attitudes of employers toward unions. The first four questions relate to exclusion and containment, and the remaining six questions relate to acceptance, accommodation, and cooperation.

If you answered "I agree" to the first four questions and "I disagree" to most of the last six, you are probably a strong management person. If you disagreed with the first four questions and agreed with most of the last six questions, you are probably a union person. Rate yourself based on the test:

Management person ____ Union person ____ Not sure ____

AN ELECTION CAN VOTE A UNION IN OR OUT

A **certification** is an election used by the NLRB to determine whether an identified union will represent the employees. Unions can also be decertified—removed as the representative of the employees. Both elections require a simple majority, 50 percent plus one, of those voting.

EXPRESS YOUR OPINION

Analyze your own community in terms of union activity. Would you say that your community is becoming more union or more management oriented? For example, do you see evidence of union activity around company plants, on main street, or in the local newspaper? Have you seen pro- or antiunion activity on bulletin boards, on local television, or at street rallies? What main points are used by union or management to gain supporters? Are the political issues really clear? Can you relate to a particular company in town and identify which attitude it is using with the unions? Is it exclusion, containment, acceptance, accommodation, or cooperation?

UNION ELECTION TERMINOLOGY

Recognition. If the employees of a company wish to be represented by a union and more than 30 percent of the workers sign recognition cards, the cards will be submitted to the National Labor Relations Board. Once the NLRB certifies the list, an election will follow.

Certification (Election). Once an election is called, the union can request a list of all employees and their addresses. The union can contact employees at home, but not on company grounds. A simple majority, 50 percent plus one, of a substantial or representative number of eligible employees, can vote union representation into a company.

Decertification. At the end of a union contract, if the union members wish to terminate their relationship with the union, a simple majority of the union members must vote for decertification.

Deauthorization. Except in right-to-work states, a union can negotiate a union security agreement with the employer that requires all employees to pay union dues. Employees may petition the NLRB for a withdrawal of the union's authority to enforce compulsory dues payments. Typically, dissatisfied employees will seek to end the relationship altogether by means of decertification.

THE TWO PERSONALITIES IN THE MIDDLE

The supervisor and shop steward are caught in the middle.

There are two positions within the structure of the typical company whose occupants are answerable to more officials, managers, workers, and boards than most of the other positions (Figure 15–3). These two are the shop steward and the company supervisor. Although on opposing sides, their functions are similar, and each is situated in the hierarchy of either the union or the management, so that each is one step above any worker on the line. Each has the unenviable position of being answerable to superiors who sometimes have no practical knowledge of the work.

SHOP STEWARD

The shop steward represents the employee.

On the union side, the **shop steward** is a representative for a specific group of workers and is generally elected by the workers in his or her department. The steward is an employee of the company and works side by side with the men and women represented.

FIGURE 15-3 *The Union Adds an Additional Formal Organization to the Employment Relationship*

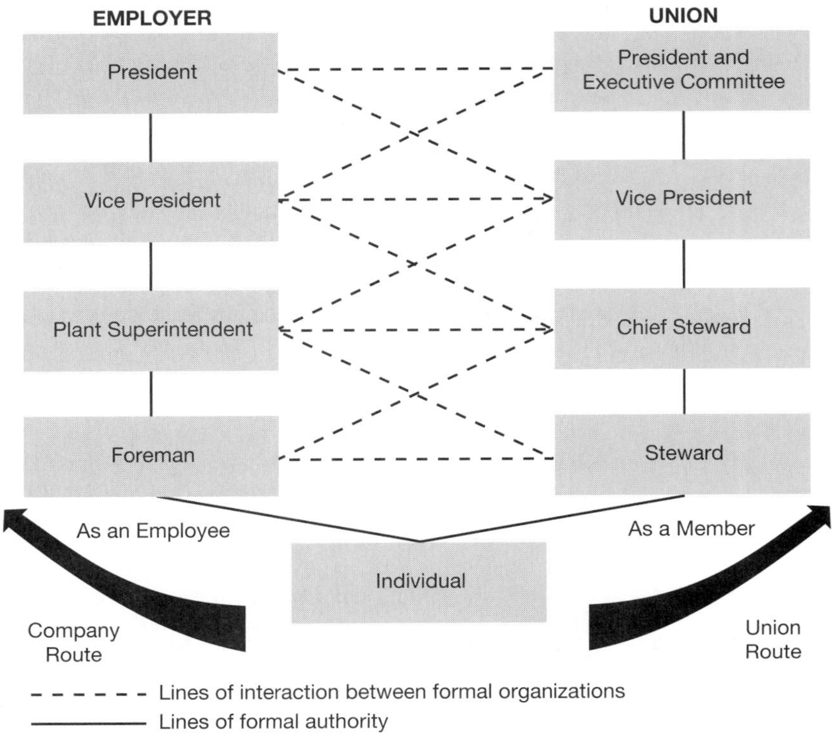

EMPLOYER
President
Vice President
Plant Superintendent
Foreman

UNION
President and Executive Committee
Vice President
Chief Steward
Steward

As an Employee
As a Member
Individual
Company Route
Union Route

- - - - - - Lines of interaction between formal organizations
———— Lines of formal authority

The steward's attitude reflects the attitude of the employees.

Provisions are usually made in the union contract that allow the shop steward time off to conduct union affairs. The steward's attitude toward management is a reflection of the attitude of the workers.

If the union is new and the members are militant, they may elect a person whose main quality is expertise in rallying support against the company. This antagonism, if recognized by management, can be dealt with by establishing management credibility. Many of the problems coming from the growth of a new union are related to the workers' general suspicion of management.

The steward hears employee complaints.

The shop steward functions as a safety valve in most cases. He or she represents individual employees in grievance hearings with management. The steward listens to employee complaints and gives advice on whether the employee is justified in taking the complaint to management. On occasion, the supervisor may bring a problem to the shop steward that the steward forwards to the individual involved. Generally, stewards are more satisfied with procedures that permit oral presentation of grievances at the first step and include screening by grievance committee or other union officials.[11]

COMPANY SUPERVISOR

A realization of the importance of the supervisor in labor-management relations has brought about critical changes in the selection and training of supervisors by American management. Some time ago, supervisors were selected primarily for their ability to do their jobs well. The emergence of the union as a force in business has caused a reduction in the power of the supervisor, making leadership and interpersonal skills more important in the selection of new supervisors.

Training programs for supervisors are needed.

An increasing number of companies have instituted training programs to teach their supervisors basic psychology, leadership skills, and group dynamics. However, training programs sometimes fail to change the supervisor's belief in a system of unquestioned authority. Still, the supervisor must learn to satisfy the needs of management and to cope with the workers' new status as a bargaining force.

Union strength can undermine the supervisor's authority.

Union power is, in many cases, so strong—involving discipline, work assignments, seniority, transfers, and so forth—that frequently supervisors feel they don't have the authority to deal properly with subordinates. As they become better acquainted with the union and its functions, supervisors may realize that shop stewards, once regarded as uncooperative antagonists, can be useful in maintaining discipline, screening unwarranted complaints, counseling employees on personal problems and work habits, and communicating with management about employee problems.

Developing mutually beneficial communication can result in a supervisor-steward relationship that would alleviate many of the difficulties inherent in the labor-management conflict. The shop steward is also a leader and is often influential in determining the opinion of the employee with regard to management. A mutual understanding and open lines of communication between the steward and the supervisor are desirable.

COLLECTIVE BARGAINING AND GRIEVANCES

The bargaining agreement is legal, has time limits, and is complete.

Although considered by some to be a legal contract, the collective bargaining agreement is much more flexible than a contract. It does have some of the properties of a contract, in that: (1) it can be enforced by law, (2) it has a time limit, and (3) it is complete in itself. However, provisions for change built into the agreement allow one or the other of the parties to interpret and apply the clauses on a continuing basis. It is a working document of conflict resolution and, as such, is subject to renewed debate if conditions not covered by the agreement arise at a later date. Because the collective bargaining agreement is flexible, it is also interpreted in many different ways. In the opinion of some, it merely controls day-to-day union-management relations. This is a limited interpretation and covers only a small portion of the intended purpose of the agreement.

The collective agreement can be divided into three sections: (1) binding provisions, which include clauses in which little or no change is anticipated by either party (e.g., wages, union security, and the duration of the contract itself); (2) contingent clauses governing actions taken by union or management concerning new conditions not present at the time of agreement (e.g., promotion, transfer, change in operation techniques, governmental legislation); and (3) grievance procedures for use when disputes arise concerning interpretation of the agreement.

MANAGEMENT AND UNION PREPARATION

Understand the issues.

1. A clear understanding of the issues is necessary. Issues can include wages, severance, conditions of work, the criteria for promotion, seniority rules, discipline, delays in the settlement of grievances, or disputes over interpretation.
2. If the dispute involves procedures, it should be made clear that the disagreement concerns the manner in which goals are attained. Formulating criteria and agreeing on how to evaluate procedures must be spelled out clearly in operational terms.

3. Management should be acquainted with the unions, their leaders, structure, policies, and style of negotiation. The basic attitudes of union leaders or managers in accepting or rejecting ideas, and their trust or suspicions of each other, will directly determine the degree of success at the bargaining table.
4. Negotiators should estimate, as part of their preparation, which outcomes are critical and which are less critical or of no importance. What they will concede, cannot concede, and could possibly concede are important tools of compromise. Negotiators should also be aware of the alternatives available to them in case an agreement cannot be reached. They should be prepared to negotiate at a future time for employee benefits or changes that cannot be made at the time. It is best when the negotiating process is approached with the goal of achieving a win-win solution.

Negotiators must know what to obtain and what to concede.

A COMPLAINT CAN BECOME A GRIEVANCE

The company's handling of worker complaints is the same whether or not unions are involved. The essential difference in a unionized shop is that a dissatisfied worker may appeal the supervisor's decision by filing a formal charge, or grievance, against the company for a violation of one or more of the articles of the labor agreement. A **grievance** is a complaint about an alleged violation of a collective bargaining agreement or the law as it applies to a worker. A complaint handled improperly can, and often does, become a grievance.

Consider each complaint a potential grievance.

The contract between union and management spells out workers' rights involving wages, hours, and working conditions. The contract is a formal, written document that limits the union's authority, as well as management's, because all parties to the contract must operate within the guidelines contained in the contract.

HOW TO PREVENT GRIEVANCES

The only way to prevent grievances is to understand the reasons behind complaints. Discontent among employees often stems from an accumulation of small, unresolved problems. Remember, supervisors get results through people.

1. Let each employee know how he or she is doing. Be honest and let people know what you expect. Help by pointing out how an employee can improve.
2. Give credit when credit is due. Look for the employee's extra performance and reward the person verbally during or shortly after the job.
3. If you think that a policy is unfair, express that opinion to your supervisor, not to your subordinates, and suggest changes to improve the policy.
4. Tell employees in advance about policy changes that will affect them and explain the reasons for each change. If possible, get employees to participate in the change.
5. Make the best possible use of each person's ability. Instead of standing in a person's way, give him or her the opportunity for more responsibility and growth.
6. Solicit ideas from your employees. Employees often have great ideas for jobs or products that they should be encouraged to develop. Ask what can be done to eliminate bottlenecks and friction.

THE GRIEVANCE PROCEDURE

Where unions exist, a formal procedure for the processing of grievances will be spelled out in the union contract. A typical procedure follows. Some procedures may have more or fewer steps.

Step 1. If the supervisor cannot solve the complaint, it then becomes a grievance. The supervisor meets with the shop steward or grievance committee, while the employee files a written grievance. If the problem cannot be resolved at this level, it then moves to the second step (Figure 15–4).

Step 2. The supervisor's immediate superior and a representative from the labor relations department meet with the union grievance committee. At this point, the problem usually involves more than one person and may relate to the individual rights of many people. For example, a safety practice in the plant may have serious implications for all who work in the area. If the problem cannot be solved at this level, it moves to top management.

Step 3. Top management from both the company and the local union are now involved. The labor relations director and the plant or division manager meet with the union grievance committee. A representative from the local union may now represent

FIGURE 15–4 *THE FIVE STEPS THROUGH WHICH A COMPLAINT INVOLVING UNION AND MANAGEMENT CAN PASS*

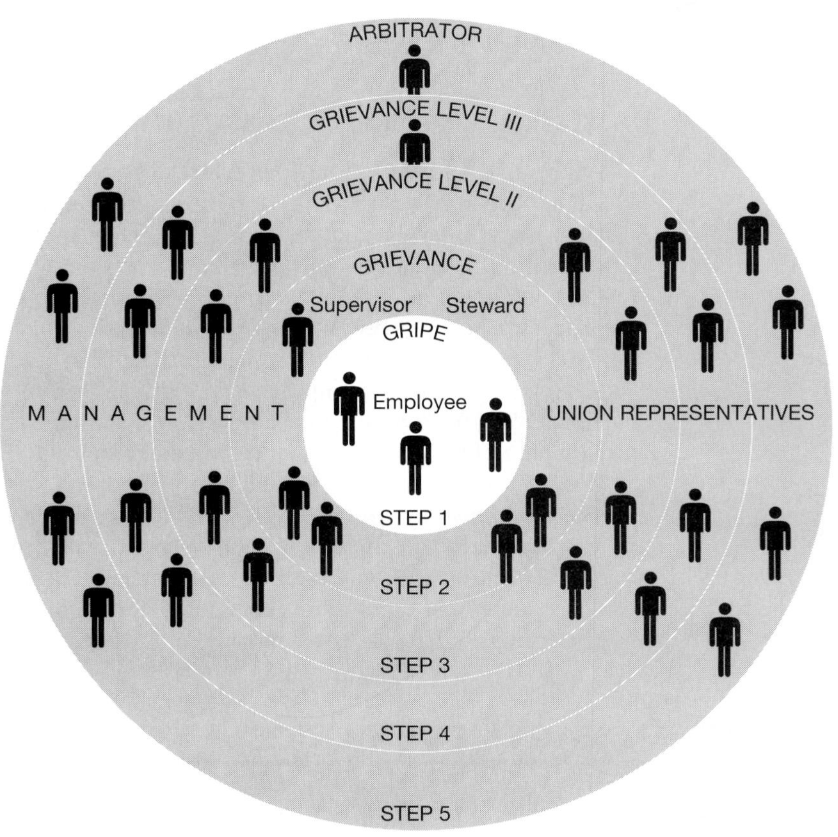

the union's own grievance committee. Time and money begin to mount, and both sides usually want to solve the issue as quickly as possible.

Step 4. Members of top management discuss the issues with a group from the national union. If the local union has no affiliation with a national union, an attorney or business agent meets with management representatives. At this point, both parties can select a mediator. A **mediator** is a neutral third party who is called to review both sides of the issue. The mediator is often a public official—for example, an attorney or college professor—who is respected by both sides. After hearing both points of view, the mediator recommends a solution. However, his or her decision is not binding on either party.

Step 5. At this point an arbitrator is usually called in on the dispute. The **arbitrator** is a neutral third party who conducts fact-finding and mandates binding resolution. He or she is usually a professional arbitrator, recommended by the American Arbitration Association, the Federal Mediation and Conciliation Service, or one of the various state agencies. **Conciliation** means making peace among the parties by soothing anger and conflict. At this level, both sides have usually become polarized and the arbitrator often spends most of his or her time working with the disputing parties.

The arbitrator will conduct hearings that are similar to legal proceedings. Witnesses are called, and testimony is recorded. The hearing may be quite informal, however, depending on the arbitrator's style. The important difference between a mediator and arbitrator is that the decision announced by the arbitrator is binding on both the company and the union.[12]

The arbitrator's decision is binding on management and union.

ALTERNATIVE DISPUTE RESOLUTION

Alternative dispute resolution (ADR) is becoming a popular method to avoid the legal hassles inherent in mandatory arbitration and government involvement. The Society for Human Resources Management encourages the establishment of dispute resolution procedures that allow employers and employees to resolve disputes in a fair, balanced, and timely manner without expensive government administrative processes or the need to resort to private litigation.

In 1995 McGraw-Hill announced its Fast and Impartial Resolution (FAIR) ADR program for its employees in publishing. The three-step program is voluntary and starts with bringing in a supervisor or human resource representative to resolve a dispute. If that does not work, the next step is mediation with a neutral third party. If mediation is fruitless, the third step is binding arbitration with a written decision. The company pays the mediation and arbitration costs.[13]

The major advantage of ADR programs is that they can settle disputes more quickly than traditional methods. Accordingly, morale is boosted—even when decisions go against the employees. Quick closure keeps the employee from continued grumbling, which can lower morale and productivity for everyone.

UNION AND MANAGEMENT TACTICS

If the union and management are unable to settle their grievances, one or both may resort to tactics, legal or illegal, to force the other to come to a settlement. The following tactics are used when there appear to be no other alternatives.

ACTION PROJECT 15–2

A GRIEVANCE AT MERRILL ELECTRONICS (GROUP EXERCISE)

Consider a middle-sized electronics company of about 300 employees. About half the employees are members of a union, and most of the labor disputes have been solved by collective bargaining through this particular union.

John McIntyre works in a department that is completely dominated by the union. All 15 employees of this department are members of the union. Gene Rosefeld, sharp, intelligent, and union trained, is the shop steward. Peter Longnecker, a reasonable and dependable veteran with the company, is John's supervisor.

John is the most experienced technician in the department and is responsible for setting up all new assembly runs and doing all the necessary experimental tests. There have been too many experimental test runs lately, which is the point of the dispute. John feels that he is always asked to work overtime with no consideration for his personal life. Company business always comes first and he is tired of working 50 hours a week.

Peter, his supervisor, says that there is no one else who can do the experimental test runs and that by working on Saturday, John has fewer interruptions by fellow employees. John has talked the problem over with his supervisor, but he is still asked to work 8 to 10 hours on Saturday. As a tired, frustrated employee, John McIntyre goes to the shop steward.

PROCEDURE

Form groups of five persons. If possible, have one person who scored as a management person in the "union attitude" project, given earlier in this chapter, act as the supervisor, Longnecker. Have a person who scored as a union person act as the shop steward, Rosefeld. The part of the overworked employee, McIntyre, can be played by anyone. The other two persons will act as observers.

Role-play the parts, with McIntyre and Rosefeld coming to the supervisor to discuss the grievance. See if a solution can be reached within 10 minutes. If no solution can be reached, see if the situation might affect more than the one employee. Perhaps this may be a problem to take to a union representative or the department head. The two observers now become the union representative and the department head. The meeting may only be between the union representative and the department head; however, many times all five participants are involved in the discussion. Another 10 minutes are allowed to establish some solution to the problem.

RESULTS AND FOLLOW-UP DISCUSSION

1. What is the final solution? ____________________
2. Was it a compromise solution? ____________________
3. How would the observers rate the supervisor's attitude? (Circle one.)

   Exclusion   Containment   Acceptance

   Accommodating   Cooperative
4. How would the observers rate the shop steward's attitude? (Circle one.)

   Exclusion   Containment   Acceptance

   Accommodating   Cooperative
5. When the two new people entered the situation, did the tone of the discussion change? How? ____________________

(continued)

ACTION PROJECT 15–2

(CONTINUED)

6. Was the second group more agreeable to a solution? ____________
7. How would you rate the union representative? (Circle one.)
   Exclusion Containment Acceptance
   Accommodating Cooperative
8. How would you rate the department head? (Circle one.)
   Exclusion Containment Acceptance
   Accommodating Cooperative
9. Such meetings are often seen as a win-or-lose situation rather than the best solution to the problem. If asked, who would you say won? ____________
   Whose side were you on? ____________
   What was the group consensus? ____________
10. Most important, was it worth the employee's time and effort to go through this grievance procedure? Why? ____________

STRIKES

1. *Primary strike.* Workers fail to show up for work.
2. *Sympathy strike.* A strike called by one union for the benefit of another union.
3. *Sit-down strike.* Workers sit down on the job and fail to perform their duties.
4. *Slowdown strike.* Workers perform their tasks at a slower rate.
5. *Wildcat strike.* Some union members go on strike without the authorization or knowledge of the international union.
6. *Jurisdictional strike.* Forcing the company to recognize one union over another.

Sympathy, sitdown, wildcat, and jurisdictional strikes can be illegal.

PICKETS

1. *Primary picket.* Union members walk around the place of employment with placards to inform the public of unfair practices of the management.
2. *Mass picket.* So many union members are picketing around the company that it restricts entrance and exit of people on the company grounds. Such activity is illegal.

BOYCOTTS

A union tries to get the public to refuse to buy products or do business with the firm.

MANAGEMENT TACTICS

1. *Lockout.* Employees are not allowed to come into the plant until they accept the employer's terms.
2. *Layoff.* Employees are released from employment due to lack of work. Employees are allowed to collect unemployment, but would not be able to if they were fired.

3. *Injunction.* A court order requiring certain action. A mandatory injunction requires performance of a specific act, such as requiring workers to return to work. A prohibitory injunction orders the other party to refrain from certain acts, such as ordering the union to stop mass picketing.
4. *Yellow-dog contract.* As a condition of employment, a person agrees not to join a union. Outlawed by the Norris-LaGuardia Act, it is still practiced in some areas.
5. *Blacklisting.* A list of troublemakers is made available to other companies. Employment is not given to blacklisted union organizers. This activity is also illegal, but still used on occasion. Other management weapons include inventory buildup for use during a strike, doing work at other plant locations, and subcontracting.

These tactics have been employed by unions or management at some time in the history of the labor movement. Some are still being used and are respectable insofar as they are effective, if not always productive. The tactics used by unions today are generally aimed at production disruptions and, hence, the company's financial resources.

Management uses tactics aimed at the resources and solidarity of the union or the financial resources of the workers. With very few exceptions, labor disagreements today are relatively mild compared with the confrontations of 50 to 75 years ago. Nevertheless, these disagreements can have powerful economic repercussions if not dealt with promptly and effectively.

GUIDELINES FOR PRESERVING OR RESTORING A UNION-FREE WORKPLACE

Steps that may discourage union organizing include the following:

1. Manage fairly.
2. Hold frequent meetings with employees. Instead of telling or questioning employees, listen to them. Try to allay their hostility. You might just stand up and be honest by saying, "I blew it, help me." Ask what they think can be done to correct the problems.
3. Don't intimidate, interrogate, promise, or threaten. All these make the union seem like a good alternative.
4. Continue to inform employees with facts that favor your position. Gary Dessler offers several guidelines for employers wishing to stay union free:[14]

   - Practice preventive employee relations. Ensure fair discipline; open worker-management communications; offer fair salaries, wages, and benefits.
   - Recognize the importance of location. Unions have been weaker in the South and Southwest than in the North, Northeast, or far West.
   - Seek early detection. Detect union-organizing activity as early as possible; remember that your best source is probably your first-line supervisors.
   - Do not volunteer. Obviously, never voluntarily recognize a union without an election supervised by the NLRB.
   - Beware the authorization cards. When confronted by a union official submitting authorization cards, get another manager as a witness and do not touch (or, worse, count or examine in any way) the cards; call your lawyer (and get ready for the NLRB to supervise your election).
   - Consider your options. Consider the option of not staying union free; some employers do opt to let the union in.

"Union membership may make health benefits available at group rates that many employers could not afford, and industry- or association-wide wage agreements can remove the burden of having to negotiate salaries and raises with each of your employees. Some unions may be easier to get along with than others, if you have a choice. Therefore, consider your options."[15]

TODAY'S UNIONS

The worker of today is vastly different from the worker of even 10 or 15 years ago. American workers have opportunities for advancement and change that their parents couldn't have imagined. Today's workers are not particularly concerned with job permanence, are less inclined to conform to the decisions of higher authority, and are less likely to put up with uncomfortable working conditions. Workers' attitudes are in part responsible for current changes in unions, but there are other reasons.

WAGES AND BENEFITS

Union members are the offensive team.

The part of the collective bargaining agreement traditionally of most concern to employees is wages. With few exceptions, the direction of wages has been upward, and the burden of the argument for this change has been carried by the unions. Employers do not usually argue against wage increases, but against the amount of wage increase the union demands.

Leading unions set the trend for wages.

The general amount of wage increases for an industry is usually determined by settlements arrived at by the leading unions and large companies. Whatever settlement is made between the United Auto Workers and any one of the "Big Three" American automobile manufacturers negotiated with first becomes the pattern for the industry. Sometimes one firm in a locality is recognized as the pacesetter and other settlements follow it in much the same way.

Fringe benefits is a misnomer for the pension, hospitalization, supplementary unemployment, holidays, and vacation package, which now runs 20 to 33 percent of the per-employee wage cost paid by the employer. To make comparisons with what other employers and unions are doing, estimates of benefits are calculated as a per-hour expense, so that benefits have a dollar value.

MERGERS

Union power will continue to grow through consolidation into fewer and larger unions with more centralized control. The same difficulties that are involved in corporate mergers are evident in union mergers as well. Old rivalries and animosities often combine with ordinary merger problems to cause further delay. However, since the merger of the American Federation of Labor and the Congress of Industrial Organizations in 1955, the realization that union strength can be increased through a broad political base has impressed more and more union leaders.

SOCIAL AND TECHNOLOGICAL CHANGE

More minorities in unions.

There has been an increase in "urban unions" composed of teachers, hospital workers, police personnel, firefighters, and sanitation workers. Trade and white-collar unions are becoming increasingly comprised of ethnic minorities adding a different social base and political outlook, which is considerably different from the traditional union of 20 years ago.

Women are also finding recognition in unions. Females are wielding more clout in the labor movement these days, both at the local level and the national level, because union women are more numerous and active than ever before. Of every 10 union members, at least four are women, meaning there are almost six million women union members.

The issue of automation has been around for more than 30 years and, for the most part, unions have become begrudging converts to automation. Union members recognize that business must become more efficient to compete in today's market. Therefore, a company must automate or it will be out of business.

QUALITY OF WORK LIFE

Cooperative efforts between union and management have led to several new programs. Unions and management have come to realize that they must work together for the enterprise to succeed. Together, they have encouraged worker participation in business decisions and a greater emphasis on job security. The United Auto Workers, the Communications Workers of America, and many other unions, working with their counterparts in management, have reaffirmed their commitment to quality of work life (QWL). The Service Employees International Union (SEIU) wants a health care industry that is equitably funded, cost effective, and has a high degree of availability.[16]

The goal of QWL programs is to enhance work by making it more fulfilling and productive. These programs are implemented through semiautonomous work teams or management committees. The tasks of QWL are to

1. Improve quality control
2. Improve work schedules
3. Improve compensation systems
4. Improve self-fulfillment

The growth of "quality of work life" programs.

There seems to be an increased demand by workers for QWL programs. Companies such as GM, Procter & Gamble, Exxon, General Foods, TRW, Eastman Kodak, and Polaroid are all trying such programs. Another issue is whether QWL programs are unfair labor practices on the part of management under the NLRA, a topic discussed in the next section.

EMPLOYEE INVOLVEMENT PROGRAMS

Employee involvement teams (EIT) allow workers and management to jointly address issues that impact workers' well-being, but the NLRB sometimes considers such programs illegal. Congress periodically proposes legislation, such as Teamwork for Employees and Management (TEAM) Act, which would make these forms of involvement legal. With a Republican president in 2001, business groups will most probably seek to enact this type of law.[17]

Ninety-six percent of large employers have incorporated EIT to some extent, yet many companies were attacked by the NLRB for violation of Section 8(a)(2) of the NLRA. The statute makes it an unfair labor practice for an employer to "dominate or interfere with the formation or administration of any labor organization or contribute financial or other support to it." When broadly defined, even two employees could be considered an illegal, employer-dominated work group if they discuss workplace issues with management in an effort to resolve problems.

Laws like the TEAM Act would clean up the problem by removing restrictions on team-based employee involvement. The president of one labor policy organization asks: "Why shouldn't employees be allowed to work with management to improve the workplace?"[18]

SPIRIT OF COOPERATION

Although the element of conflict is ever present between union and management, perhaps an equally omnipresent spirit of cooperation can be developed. Sensitive observers increasingly call our attention to the fact that human beings are not machines and that they have feelings and emotions that must be respected to get the highest degree of cooperation in the workplace and in labor/management relations. The present emphasis on individual and group relationships is a recognition that, along with the solution of technical problems, there must be increasing concern for human elements in production.

THE GLOBAL ECONOMY AND UNIONS

Foreign unions are often more socialistic and lack strong central support.

Multinational business has involved American business managers with foreign labor unions, which cannot be dealt with in the same way as American unions. By and large, foreign unions are more steeped in tradition, are more socialistically oriented, and lack strong centralized power. Workers have not always agreed with their union leaders on whether to stress collective bargaining or political action, but generally American unions have opted for collective bargaining, whereas unions in many other countries have relied more on political action.

Strikes may be ineffective if local or global competition provides a market for labor resources. The United Auto Workers found that to be true in 1992 when it struck Caterpillar. The UAW was prepared to spend $800 million from its strike fund, but that did not work. Caterpillar told more than 12,000 employees with considerable seniority that they would be replaced—easy enough to do in a climate of global competition, high unemployment, and readily available replacement workers.

Union membership and density, as a percentage of population, is lower in the United States than in most other major economic countries except France, but unions play quite different roles in other countries. Many of the unions in these countries have strong political action agendas and, in some cases, strong government ties. Even in the United States there is sentiment that one of the major reasons for union decline is the passage of laws by governments, thus nullifying the need for unions.

The European and Asian (Japanese) models of labor-management cooperation have had a positive and profound effect on U.S. labor relations. New United Motor Manufacturing, Inc. (NUMMI), a joint venture of General Motors and Toyota, adopted Japanese practices emphasizing fewer job classifications, more teamwork and job rotation, and continuous improvement programs. These practices tend to replace direct supervision as the primary mechanism for obtaining high productivity and quality.

Labor relations have major effects on abilities to compete globally.

Even in our own hemisphere, labor relations have major effects on our abilities to compete globally. Canada and Mexico both have relatively strong and fairly stable unions. Canadian employers have "neither the will nor the opportunity to attack unions to the extent that they do in the United States."[19] In Mexico there is a close relationship between the government and the labor movement.

UNIONS, TECHNOLOGY, AND COLLECTIVE BARGAINING

According to many economists, including Federal Reserve Chairman Alan Greenspan, the use of new technologies has fundamentally changed our economic system. They argue that computers have increased labor output so much that historically low unemployment rates do not create inflationary pressures. Instead, productivity gains permit employers to maintain price levels and still improve employee compensation. As Greenspan explained, "The major contribution of advances in information technology and their incorporation into the capital stock has been to reduce the number of worker hours required to produce the nation's output, our proxy for productivity growth."[20]

Assume Greenspan and the "new economy" advocates are correct in their analysis. How should the productivity gains be distributed among workers, owners, and managers? The fact is that most wage earners over the past two decades have experienced stagnant or declining real wages, while executives, college graduates, and some white collar employees have increased their incomes. Particularly in high-level managerial jobs, income gains far exceed those in other sectors. Do you think those results are good or bad for society as a whole? Why do you think workers are falling behind? If unions help to ensure equitable distribution of wealth through collective bargaining, should we pass laws to make them stronger? What kinds of laws?

INTERNET ACTION PROJECT 15–3

Visit the Web sites for the AFL-CIO www.aflcio.org.home.htm and the Economic Policy Institute www.epinet.org/ for further information.

THE ETHICS OF LABOR LAW

By now you know that workers enjoy certain legal rights to join and form unions and engage in collective bargaining. Many legal scholars argue that the decline in union membership density can be attributed to employers' violations of workers' rights, such as intimidating, coercing, and discriminating against workers who try to form a union in the workplace. The evidence for this view is a substantial increase in meritorious unfair labor practice complaints during the 1980s and early 1990s. Union advocates further contend that the remedies for labor law violations are not strong enough to discourage employers from engaging in unlawful activities.

Assume that if a company becomes unionized, its labor costs will increase by about 15 percent; assume also that you as a manager could defeat a union drive by threatening and firing workers and taking a hard line against collective bargaining (that is, making clear to workers that under no circumstances would you enter into a labor agreement). Based on your cost-benefit analysis, you decide it is cheaper to violate the law than to obey it. Would you use illegal methods to defeat the union? What if you were convinced the price of the company's shares would fall if the union won the election? What if you believed that your own career with the company would suffer as a result of a union victory? As an ethical matter, do you sometimes disobey the law because you think either you won't be caught or the punishment is trivial? What about speed limits and traffic signals? Is there any difference between exceeding the speed limit on an interstate highway and firing a worker for trying to form a union? What is the difference?

SUMMARY

Most people think of unions in terms of the blue-collar movements because most union members are in such fields. Yet, although many union members belong to the blue-collar unions, the white-collar and public employees sector has the greatest potential for organized employee representation. Today less than 14 percent of the workforce are members of unions.

Management attitudes toward unions can range from total exclusion to cooperation. Many people feel that having a union on company grounds develops a dual or divided loyalty on the part of the employee. Sometimes those loyalties are in conflict. Poor morale and perceived low wages encourage employees to join unions. When a company becomes highly structured, it can be a breeding ground for unions.

The shop steward is sometimes a powerful adversary on the floor and can have a direct effect on the attitudes of the workers. The supervisor also affects the attitudes of the workers. If a supervisor misinterprets the relationship with either the shop steward or the workers, it can mean a breakdown in working relationships.

Good supervisors understand their relationship with workers as one in which they have the authority to ensure that the work that has to be done is done, but not the authority to decide arbitrarily that some of the workers are transferred to other areas or shifts. Nor do they have the power to discipline an employee without that disciplinary action being questioned by the shop steward.

Collective bargaining is probably the most complicated area of labor-management interaction. The tensions involved are frequently excessive on both sides of the table. Without a good understanding of the demands of the other, neither of the parties will be able to come to terms with the issues. Cooperation on both sides may curtail a number of the problems.

The tactics used by both unions and management to express their dissatisfaction can be seen in many ways. Unions use strikes, such as primary, sympathy, sitdown, slowdown, and wildcat strikes. They also use pickets and boycotts. Management methods include lockouts, layoffs, injunctions, yellow-dog contracts, and blacklisting. Many methods affecting both union and management are illegal, but that has not stopped their use.

International influences are being felt in bringing about more cooperative union-management relationships. Perhaps the element of conflict is always present between union and management, but a spirit of cooperation can be developed. Sensitive observers increasingly call attention to the fact that humans are not machines, that they have feelings and emotions that must be respected. Mutual respect must be brought about between union and management for higher production and mutual satisfaction.

CASE STUDY 15-1

FIREHOUSE UNION

Culver is a small, pleasant town with two modern and attractive fire stations. Most of the firefighters employed at these stations grew up together and now live within the city limits. They all get along well and frequently have family get-togethers. In spite of these conditions, the firefighters are far from happy.

For quite some time, the firefighters have been in conflict with the city's board of administration over obtaining a wage increase. The firefighters feel that their wages are too low and that the board is spending money unnecessarily. They feel that this money is being spent on fire equipment to impress the community instead of paying them a reasonable salary in line with the amount being paid in neighboring communities.

Previous attempts to obtain a significant wage increase from the board have been futile. The only occasion when the firefighters managed to obtain an increase over 6 percent was when they hired a lawyer for an evening during negotiations at a cost of $400 of their own money. Tomorrow the firefighters will go into negotiations with the board. There is talk within the ranks that if their request for a 9 percent wage increase is turned down, as it is expected to be, they will contact the local Teamsters Union and request an election for union representation.

Those who speak in favor of joining the union argue that the union would have more leverage in dealing with the board. If the board refuses to cooperate with the union, the firefighters could go on strike with the financial support of the union. In addition, the union could stop all trucking in the town to support a firefighters' strike if need be.

The firefighters against joining the union point out that the union requires what they consider high fees and that the firefighters might be called on to strike in support of other union members in the town. Additionally, a neighboring community fire station recently went on strike and, in that community, hostility was being expressed against the firefighters. If you were one of the firefighters, what would you do?

1. Recommend accepting the wage increase offered by the board?

2. Recommend hiring another lawyer?

3. Recommend joining the union?

4. Quit and find a better fire station in some other community?

DISCUSSION AND STUDY QUESTIONS—TO KEEP YOU THINKING

1. What were the original needs for unions? Have they all been met?

2. Where are unions going? What are their options?

3. Why is labor union membership declining? Are there employment sectors that are exceptions to the trend?

4. What are the social changes affecting unions today?

5. Are unions part of a productivity problem or are they part of a productivity solution?

6. What are guidelines for preserving or restoring a union-free workplace? Is a union-free workplace always desirable? What are the exceptions, if any?

NOTES

1. Albert Karr, "Labor Letter: Raising Union Dues," *The Wall Street Journal*, February 1, 1994, A1.
2. Raymond L. Hogler. *Labor and Employment Relations* (St. Paul, MN: West Publishing Co., 1995), 299, 306–308.
3. Edward Miller, "The Proposed New Role of the NLRB," *Journal of Labor Research* (winter 1996): 69–75.
4. Peter F. Drucker, "Reinventing Unions," *Across the Board* (September 1989): 12, 14.
5. Ibid., 14.
6. "Trends in U.S. Labor Movement," *The Futurist* (January–February 1996): 44.
7. Richard Freeman, "Is Declining Unionization of the U.S. Good, Bad, or Irrelevant?" in *Unions and*

Economic Competitiveness, ed. Lawrence Hishel and Paula B. Voos (Armonk, NY: M. E. Sharpe, 1992), 143–169.

8. Ibid., 167.
9. Yitchak Haberfield, "Why Do Workers Join Unions?" *Industrial & Labor Relations Review* (July 1995): 656–670.
10. Bill Vlasic, "Bracing for the Big One," *Business Week* (March 25, 1996): 34–35.
11. Brian Bremmels, "Shop Stewards' Satisfaction with Grievance Procedures," *Industrial Relations* (October 1995): 578–592.
12. Michael B. Shane, "The Difference Between Mediation and Conciliation," *Dispute Resolution Journal* (July–September 1995): 31–33.
13. Dominic Bencivenga, "Fair Play in the ADR Arena," *HR Magazine* (January 1996): 50–56.
14. Adapted from Gary Dessler. *Human Resource Management*, 6th ed. (Upper Saddle River, NJ: Prentice Hall, 1994), 558–559.
15. Ibid., 559.
16. Betty Bednarczyk, "The SEIS: A Partner for Change in U.S. Healthcare," *Modern Healthcare* (February 19, 1996): 25.
17. Steve Bartlett, "Teamwork: The Illegal Management Tool," *Management Review* (April 1996): 7; see also Dwane Baumgardner, "There Ought to Be a Law," *Industry Week* (April 1, 1996): 16.
18. Gillian Flynn, "TEAM Act: What It Is and What It Can Do for You," *Personnel Journal* (February 1996): 85, 87.
19. Hogler, *Labor and Employment Relations*, 1995, 34.
20. Quoted in John Cassidy, "The Productivity Mirage," *The New Yorker* (November 27, 2000): 110.

CHAPTER 16

Managing Change

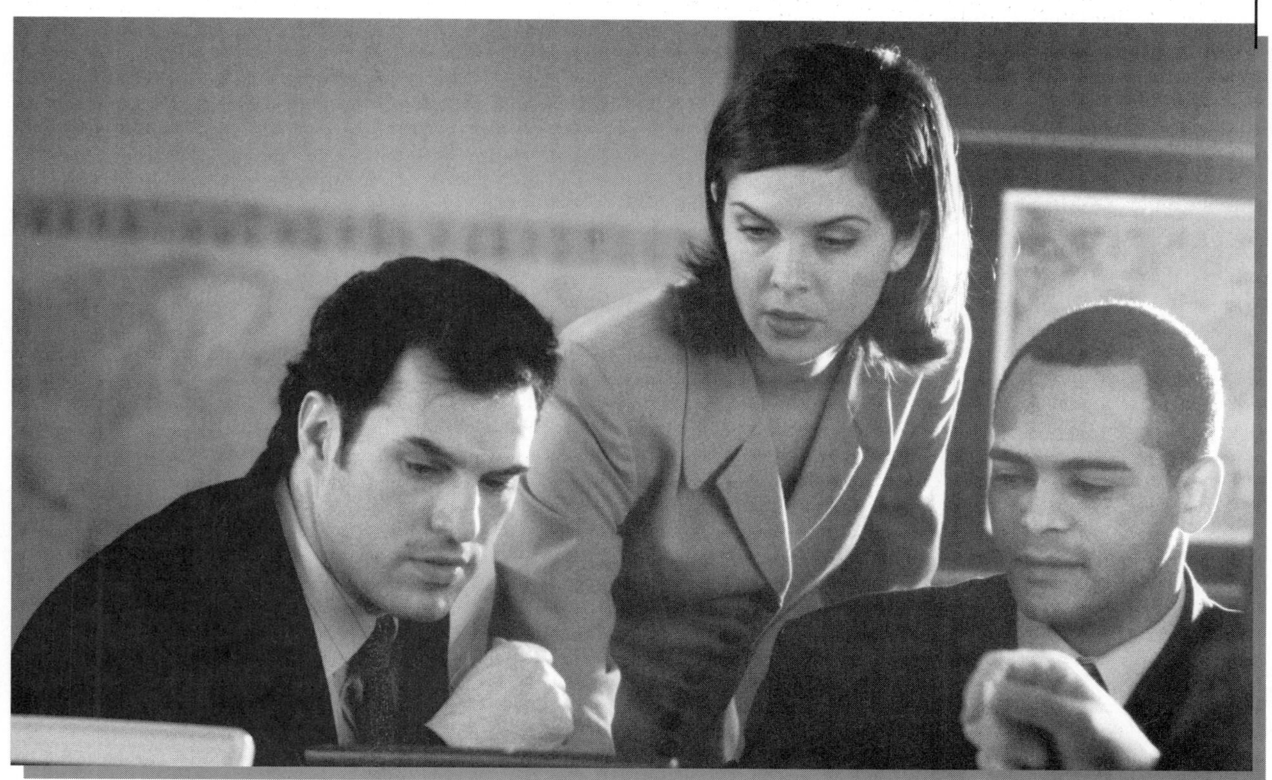

TO START YOU THINKING

Look at these questions before reading the chapter. Think about your answers as you read the chapter.

- Is your first reaction "It will never work" when you are asked to change the way you are doing something that you are used to doing a certain way?
- Do certain kinds of change upset or threaten you?
- When it is clear that change must take place, do you try to hinder or help it? Do you know how to implement change?
- Can change be mandated? Can it be managed?
- What makes change successful in some cases and unsuccessful in others?
- What are some of the changes facing us today?
- What are some diagnostic techniques for studying organizations?

LEARNING GOALS

After studying this chapter, you should be able to:

1. Discuss psychological resistance to change.
2. Explain, in your own words, how change takes place.
3. List economic reasons for avoiding change.
4. Discuss the advantages and disadvantages of change through mandate as opposed to change through participation.
5. Describe the keys to a successful change.
6. Explain the characteristics of organization development and how it relates to group dynamics.
7. Define and apply the following terms and concepts (in order of first occurrence):

KEYWORDS

- **change**
- **force-field analysis**
- **driving forces**
- **restraining forces**
- **high tech/high touch**
- **mandated change**
- **group dynamics of change**
- **organization development (OD)**
- **OD intervention**
- **Murphy's law**

INNOVATIVE DECISIONS REQUIRE CHANGE

Once a decision is made, it must be implemented. Implementation often requires changing individual attitudes and skills as well as organizational procedures and culture. This chapter focuses on changing individual behavior and that of organizations.

Things change. Economic systems, technology, and social systems all change. The rate of change in business is increasing, making change a permanent part of the business landscape.

Change may be defined as a function of effort over time to learn new methods. The Change equals Effort over Time (CET) model makes it easier to consider change in a useful way. The model separates change into four phases: (1) the *excitement* phase; looking forward to the positives that change will bring (2) the *hard work* phase where existing habits, patterns, and culture must be changed; (3) the *turning-point* phase where change becomes easier; and (4) *institutionalized* change where it takes no more effort to do things the new way than it did the old.[1]

Effort needed in phase 2 is usually underestimated.

It is important to note that phase 1 is usually overemphasized and that the effort in phase 2 is underestimated. To make the CET model work, realistic analyses and more effective communication of needed change are required. Too many attempts at change do not succeed because the process is not managed properly. Key risk factors include:

- Novelty of the product or service
- Novelty of the system technology
- Need for speed in development
- Gradual versus rapid phase-in
- Degree of user/system staff interface
- Commitment of the development team to the project[2]

These factors affect the likelihood of successful implementation of change.

RATES OF CHANGE

In the past, technological changes occurred over centuries. Today's technology has gone from changing within a decade to every 6 months. Mini-mill steel plants produce steel with the kind of minute precision and customization that only computers can achieve. Computers dispatch freight trains and control railcar inventories. Loan officers now conduct instant credit checks. We carry pocket-sized audio and video players as well as cellular telephones.

However, some new technologies do not always achieve their promise in the workplace. In the face of rapid change, many managers are preoccupied with the technical issues and neglect the equally important human issues. Managers undertaking change should keep in mind eight key points:

1. Technological change is inevitable.
2. Resistance to change is natural.
3. Change must make sense to most everyone involved.
4. Organizational settings vary.
5. Change takes time.
6. Change results in role overload.
7. Change requires ongoing technical support.
8. All change involves learning.[3]

Need for a commitment to ongoing change.

Managers must take into account the inevitability of change and recognize that a commitment to innovation and technology—things over which they have little control—is a commitment to ongoing change.

Technological change has always been equated with progress, and who is against progress? Yet when we examine the dynamics of change, we find that while many people favor progress, their actual behavior reveals contradictory and ambivalent feelings about the value of change. No matter how drastic our technological changes have been, are, or will be, social changes are even more dramatic. Peter Drucker notes that the social impacts of information may be greater than the technological impacts.[4]

Figure 16–1 describes a general model for change. The model begins with the perception that change is needed. The change process is not linear; rather, it is continuous and cyclical. Initiating changes in the work environment may cause resistance, which may be expressed openly or covertly, and directed against supervisors or work activities. The manner in which resistance is expressed depends on how much can be expressed safely without endangering job security. Resistance can take many forms including sloppy effort, slowdowns, lip service, or a combination of apathy and apple polishing, without actual change in behavior.

WHEN TO EXPECT AND PREPARE FOR RESISTANCE

Expect resistance to vague or unclear changes.

Usually, we fear the unknown. The outcomes of change are unknown; so, sometimes, we fear change. If the elements of a proposed change are not made clear to the people who are going to be affected by it, resistance can be expected. When changes are ambiguous or unclear, resistance is greater.

Often, the amount of resistance is related to the amount of participation that people have in the timing and direction of the change. Resistance will tend to be less when employees have the most to say and greater when they have the least to say.

FIGURE 16–1 *A General Model for Change*

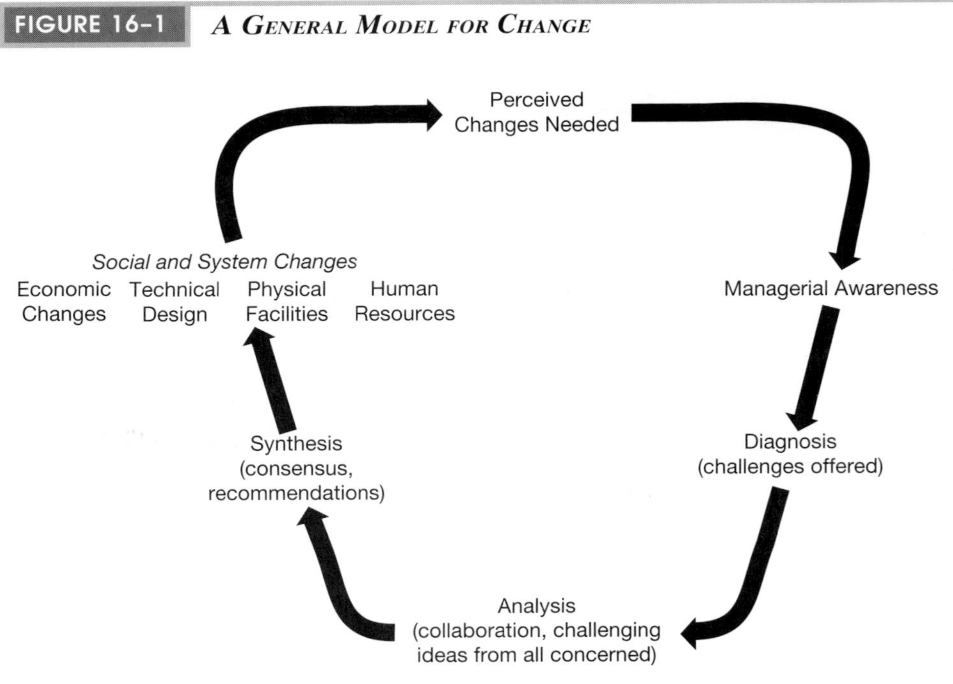

Preparing and involving employees in the change process are key to avoiding negative resistance.

INDIVIDUAL CHANGE

When we want an individual to do something different than before, we are seeking to modify one or more of the forces that make the individual behave as he or she does. Consider the model of an individual shown in Figure 16–2. To change an individual, we can alter one or more of the forces affecting his or her behavior; thereby, perhaps producing a change in the individual's behavior.

External and internal pressures can precipitate change.

Pressure often evokes change as indicated by the saying "necessity is the mother of invention." Any of the influences in Figure 16–2 can induce change in behavior, but the resulting change is not always easy or smooth, and the outcome of the various pressures can produce unexpected behaviors. For example, social adjustment to a new work environment can be difficult for someone who belongs to a tightly knit group. The process of breaking social ties with those at the old workstation and making new acquaintances can be threatening.

Conflict between individual beliefs and peer loyalties can produce unpredictable results.

Studies have shown that resistance to change often results from a conflict of individual and group loyalties (Figure 16–3). An individual may want to please the boss, yet be restrained by group pressure. In other words, peer pressure may induce a person to resist change even if he or she believes in it, because group acceptance is more important.

As illustrated in Figure 16–4, the force field analysis developed by Kurt Lewin, shows the pressure for and against change. For example, a new employee might produce more than the quota but is dissuaded from doing so by the other workers: "Hey, Charlie, we don't want a 'rate-buster' in our shop. Sure, we can all produce more parts than is required, but why? If we all did that, the guys in the head office would raise the standard and then where would we be? No bonuses and increased expectations.

FIGURE 16–2 *Various Influences on an Individual*

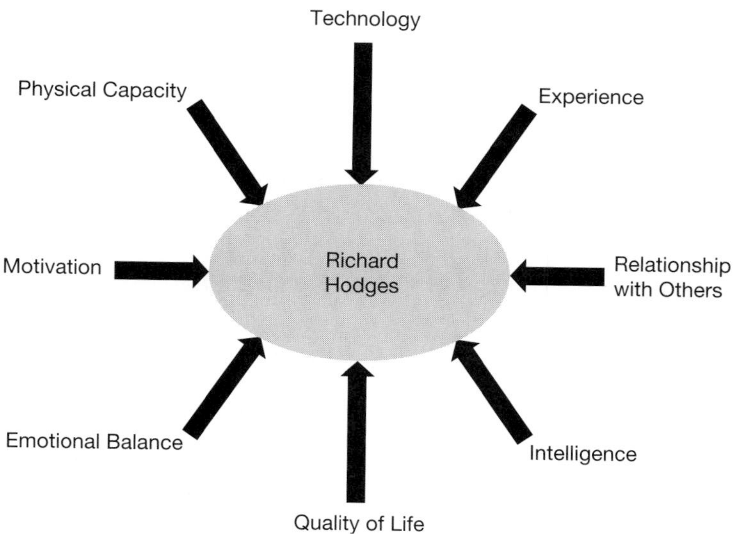

FIGURE 16-3 *Various Counterforces Can Produce an Unpredictable Change*

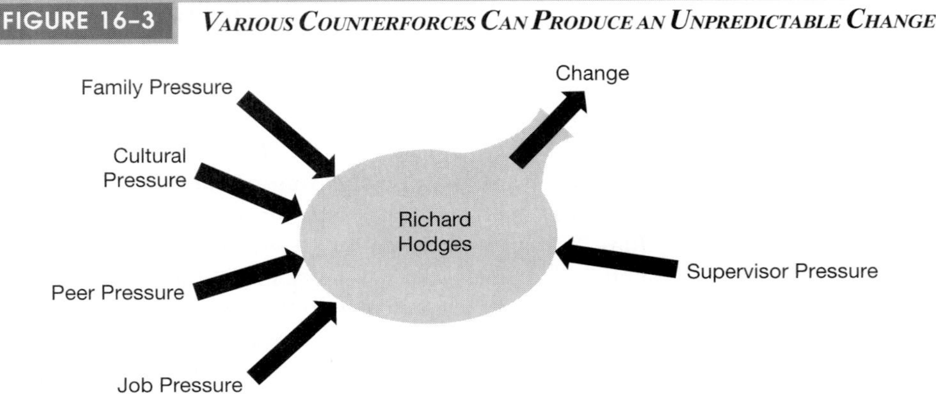

Be a nice guy, Charlie, and don't make waves. When you come in late, we will cover for you, so relax. Don't be an 'eager beaver.'"

Force-field analysis is a useful technique to assess the current state or equilibrium (the horizontal line), as well as the positive and negative forces working to change that equilibrium. The level of production can be raised by the forces below the line or reduced by the forces above the line. The greater the opportunity for a promotion for Charlie, the more likely he will become a "rate-buster." On the other hand, if the turnover is high within the department, it is less likely that group pressure will influence Charlie's production.

PSYCHOLOGICAL RESISTANCE

When stable patterns are disturbed, people may exhibit direct opposition or subtle resistance to the change. Psychologically, people may feel that the change threatens their status within the organization. Status involves comparison, and major organizational change usually brings in its wake the unintended side effect of lowering and raising the status of one or more individuals or work units. Naturally, the people who will be downgraded resist any such organizational change.

FIGURE 16-4 *Force-Field Analysis of Change*

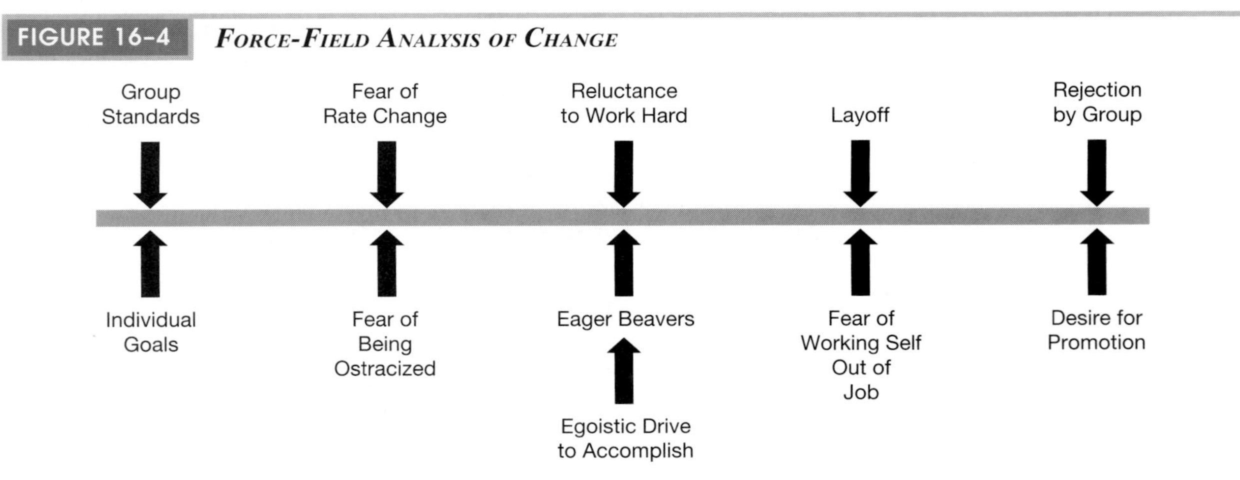

Psychological responses include "It will never work," or "I don't have time for this" or "We have always done it this way." Most telling is the response "No one asked me if this was a good idea."

As a result, managers and team leaders often expend a great deal of energy and determination just dealing with naysayers.

Yet change can be facilitated by recognizing and coping with these common barriers to change: (1) the surprise element, (2) fear of obsolescence, (3) inertia, (4) insecurity, and (5) personality conflicts. Knowing barriers exist and modifying their impact can lessen resistance and facilitate change.[5]

ECONOMIC RESISTANCE

Economic reasons for resisting change are much easier to isolate than psychological ones. Economic reasons usually include one or more of the following: (1) fear of technological unemployment; (2) fear of reduced work hours and, thus, less pay; (3) fear of demotion and, thus, reduced wages; and (4) fear of increased production expectations, thereby reducing real wages.

Managers must assess organizational readiness for change.

According to two change agents, as organizations continue to downsize, restructure, and make other transitions, managers must assess the organization's readiness for change. They advocate that managers use diagnostic instruments to get the "lay of the land." These diagnostics include questions about mission, vision, strategy, culture, and systems that facilitate people's work. They advocate determining "strategic intent," or the organization's ability to use its core competencies, such as intellectual assets, to position itself for new challenges. "Developing strategic intent is crucial, not just for profitability and productivity but also for long-term viability and vitality."[6]

DRIVING FORCES AND RESTRAINING CHANGE

Think back to the force-field analysis. Forces inducing change are called **driving forces**. Forces inhibiting change are called **restraining forces**. In Figure 16–5 the forces that increase production (new machinery and specific instructions and supervision in its use) are the driving forces; the forces keeping production down are the restraining forces. Additional driving forces might be the desire of some members to qualify for promotions or higher salaries. These forces would be balanced by the group's fear of layoffs; these restraining forces may manifest in the form of hostility or even ostracism of the offending group members.

Notice in Figure 16–5 that one category of forces acts against the other group of forces. Managers need to accept that give and take must occur between employees and the organization. Basically, change involves *unfreezing* (thawing current ways of doing things). Then change is implemented, followed by *refreezing* into new patterns of behavior. There must be some stability in the organization.

Change occurs when an imbalance develops between the restraining and driving forces. Such imbalance unfreezes the pattern and the group struggles to achieve a new balance of equilibrium.

Change agents work to unfreeze the existing pattern and develop a new pattern.

Once found, the new equilibrium will be made up of different components; that is, the group refreezes at a new and different equilibrium level. Studies show that when efforts are made to change a work group by increasing the driving forces, the most common response of the group is to increase restraining forces to maintain the same balance. By weakening the restraining force, the patterns are more easily unfrozen and the group experiences little difficulty moving on to new and different patterns of balance.

FIGURE 16-5 *The Change Process from Status Quo to New State(s) of Equilibrium via Driving and Restraining Forces*

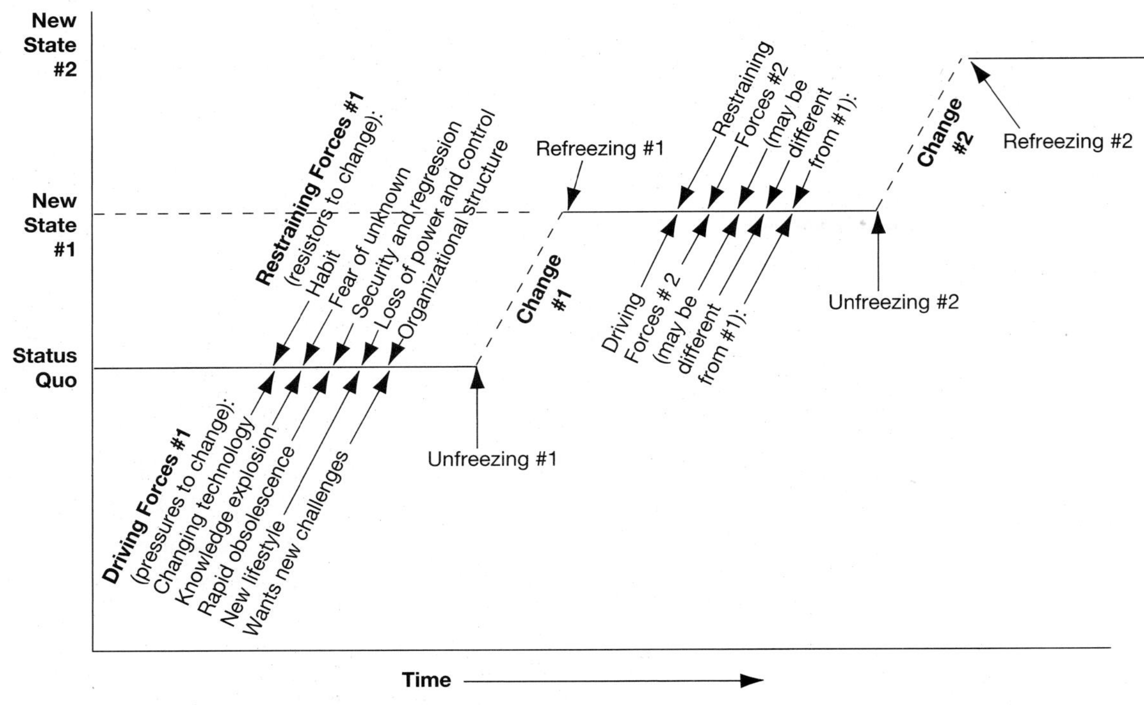

TECHNOLOGICAL RESISTANCE

Although it is true that technological innovation paved the way for the standard of living that we enjoy in the United States today, it is also true that the quality of our life has not always been enhanced by these changes. The environmental/ecological movements that have gained popularity in the past decades are one indication that growing numbers of people no longer believe that unchecked progress is the best course to follow.

Will the future be technology versus quality of life?

In the near future, we may see a balance between technological innovation and technological containment. It is increasingly the case that the major issue in the information revolution is not technology but people and quality of life. Progressive social change may come to mean greater emphasis on the quality of life for the total population and less emphasis on the kinds and quantities of the goods produced.

As the information age develops, we recognize that it brings a change in working conditions including working more at home than at the plant or in the office for some people. The shift from an industrial to an information society is centered on five points:

1. The information society is an economic reality, not an intellectual abstraction.
2. Innovations in communication and computer technology will accelerate the pace of change by collapsing information float (i.e., the amount of time information spends in the communication channel).

3. New information technologies will first be applied to old industrial tasks; then, gradually give birth to new activities, processes, and products.
4. In this literacy-intensive society, we need basic reading and writing skills more than ever before; our education system is in danger of turning out an increasingly inferior product.
5. The technological advances of the new information age are not guaranteed. They will succeed or fail according to the principle of high tech/high touch.[7]

There is a need to be together.

High tech/high touch means that in the age of technological information, where individuals work alone at home or telecommute, there must be corresponding human responses. There is, as John Naisbitt says, "a need to be together."[8] Technology enables employees to be more productive on their own, but their belonging needs remain strong.

EXPRESS YOUR OPINION

Suppose your company is moving 50 miles away. It is likely that you will keep your job, but you will need to be retrained. What will bother you the most? Will you attempt to change employers? Will you move or commute? Will you resist being retrained? Why?

ACTION PROJECT 16–1

THE OFFICE RELOCATION (INDIVIDUAL EXERCISE)

Because of budget cuts, it is necessary to close one of two offices. The employees from the closed office will be relocated to the remaining office. The question is, which office should be closed? The situation is this:

1. The offices are 70 miles apart.
2. Office A's characteristics are
   - Fifteen employees
   - Building is 10 years old
   - Located in a small town
   - High cost of living
3. Office B's characteristics are
   - Twenty employees
   - Building is 25 years old
   - Located in a large city

Go through the exercise twice: once as a member of office B, then as a member of office A.

(continued)

ACTION PROJECT 16–1

(CONTINUED)

WHICH SITUATION WOULD YOU RESIST THE LEAST?

1. The main office decides that the new location of the two offices should be office A. One reason was based on the age of the offices. Do you resist?
2. The main office asks for feedback from employees of both offices concerning which would be the best site. What would you suggest? Give pros and cons for your decision.
3. The main office sends you a copy of all the suggestions made by employees of both office sites. In looking over the material, you see that 17 people are in favor of office A and 17 are in favor of office B. You cast the deciding vote. Which would you choose? Why?

Would your answer be different (especially to situation 3) if you were a member from office A? You, your instructor, and other class members may want to discuss your reactions to the three situations.

OVERCOMING RESISTANCE

PARTICIPATION

There is a greater chance for success when all involved participate.

Management theorists, such as Kurt Lewin, Peter Drucker, and Leonard Sayles, have created an impressive body of evidence indicating that, when all the parties affected by change participate in planning the change, it is more likely to be successful. People tend to cooperate, rather than resist, when presented with the opportunity to evaluate a situation and participate in planning for change (see Figure 16–6). Social psy-

FIGURE 16–6 *GROUPS EVERYWHERE TEND TO COOPERATE RATHER THAN TO RESIST WHEN PRESENTED WITH THE OPPORTUNITY TO PARTICIPATE IN PLANNING FOR THE CHANGE*

chology theory has established that the least effective way to motivate people to change is through threat of punishment. In the past few decades, behavioral scientists have stressed the fact that force in human affairs, just as in physics, results in counterforce.

For the most part, employees want to participate in change. Participation in the process of change motivates the individual by (1) fulfilling the developmental needs of a healthy personality, (2) promoting security through knowledge of the environment and exercising control over it, and (3) reducing basic fears of the unknown that cause resistance to change. In fact, there is an inverse relationship between resistance to change and the degree of participation. As participation increases, resistance to change decreases.

Another good reason for encouraging employees to take part in planning for change is that they usually have useful information to contribute. Unfortunately, if they are not asked, they usually will not volunteer that information because they often believe that their input will not be wanted or accepted.

BEHAVIOR MODIFICATION

As technological sophistication increases in the workplace, employees may resist the technology. This provides a starting point for a reward system to encourage acceptance of the new technology. Remember from the chapter on motivation that behavior modification can change individual behavior. This implies that selected reinforcement through reward systems can encourage employees to adopt the new technology.[9]

Behavior modification can change attitudes, but it does require people to keep records. Keeping records helps to clarify the behavior involved. Supervisors who note on paper every time they criticize an employee or point to some mistake will see how much criticism they issue during the day. Supervisors who keep a record of every time they commend the employee will see the degree to which they praise others. If more commendations are issued, the supervisor will likely see improved employee performance (Figure 16–7).

FIGURE 16-7 *INITIATING CHANGE REQUIRES CERTAIN PERSONALITY TRAITS*

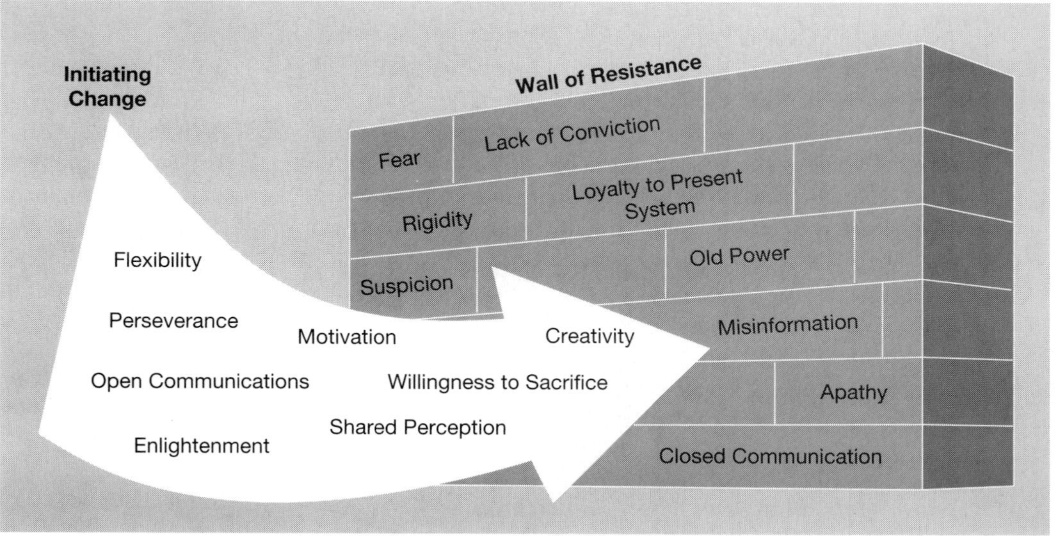

MANDATING CHANGE

Mandated change is fast but may be ineffective in the long term.

Mandated change is change demanded by someone in authority. Some changes are mandated by law, or for safety, health, and economic reasons. For example, company economics may mandate a factory closing. The main advantage of mandating change from above is that change can take place quickly and efficiently.

Mandating change is a top-down approach in which the leader is responsible for major decisions. Resistance can be handled by firing or transferring uncooperative employees or by ignoring employee concerns. Resistance can be minimized because the leader assumes the burden of risk. In fact, the leader will often go to great lengths to protect employees from doubts or worries, fearing the resulting confusion. Mandating change can be very effective in certain circumstances, like turnaround or bankruptcy, where decisions need to be made quickly. Nevertheless, resistance is to be expected when employees are pressured without a chance to contribute their own input.

EXPRESS YOUR OPINION

We have read about force-field analysis and how there are pressures to bring about change and pressures to resist change. Mandating appears to cause sudden change. By contrast, behavior modification encourages making changes slowly.

If situations change and a new direction is needed, which of these methods will encourage the fastest change? Will the pressures in both directions be greater under mandated change or behavioral modification? Once behavioral modification has changed people's actions, will it work as a stronger pressure to resist change in the opposite direction? Express your opinion with examples of changes that were mandated and changes that were effected by the behavioral modification method.

TIME ALLOWANCE

Even if there is no resistance to the change itself, it takes time to refreeze new patterns of behavior. If the supervisor loses patience with the amount of time that a subordinate needs to learn how to handle a procedural change, the subordinate will begin to feel pushed. That feeling of being pushed can breed resistance where there was none before.

Quantifying the need for change into timetables may help overcome resistance to change. Doing so may point out pitfalls and allow for modifications in the change process.

Managers and supervisors need to become much more aware of how human relationships affect the rate at which change can take place. Often, in the name of speed and efficiency, and without understanding the rhythms involved in creating the necessary atmosphere for change, management simply creates obstacles that later take much time and labor to overcome.

GROUP DYNAMICS OF CHANGE

Implementing change requires guidance.

The process of implementing change requires guidance. The influence of groups in bringing about change often yields amazing results. Recall that *group dynamics* refer to the effect that individuals collectively have on each other. The sense of belonging, prestige, and shared perceptions can dramatically affect an individual's behavior.

The term **group dynamics of change** refers to those forces of change operating in groups. Because change is an integral part of group life, it is desirable to study the group as a medium of change.

KEYS TO SUCCESSFUL CHANGE

There are several stages or key steps to follow to achieve change. As seen in Figure 16–8, the first step is to make clear the need for change, which involves communication and understanding. In addition to the steps in Figure 16–8, we can add education, training, goal setting, and outcomes assessment as keys to successful change.

To begin a program of planned change, Ralph Kilmann, author of *Managing Beyond the Quick Fix*, says:

> The first step in developing a completely integrated program for improving organizations entails identifying at least three sets of elements: (1) all the controllable variables—pinpointed via a systems' perspective—that determine organizational success, (2) all the multiple approaches—techniques, instruments, and procedures—that can alter these controllable variables, and (3) all the ongoing activities that drive organization-wide change.[10]

Techniques for achieving organization change include team building, modifying the organizational culture, and altering reward systems. Implementation of the program must be flexible and adapt to feedback from all stakeholders (employees, customers, and suppliers).

FIGURE 16–8 *KEYS TO A SUCCESSFUL CHANGE*

Need	1. Make clear the need for change.
Objectives	2. State the objectives clearly.
Participation	3. Encourage relevant group participation to clarify the needed changes.
Broad guidelines	4. Establish broad guidelines to achieve the objectives.
Details by group	5. Leave the details to the group that will be most affected by the change.
Benefits of change	6. State the benefits or rewards expected from the change.
Give rewards	7. Keep the promise of rewards to those who helped in the change.

Source: Goodwin Watson and Edward M. Glaser, "What We Have Learned About Planning for Change," *Management Review* (November 1965): 34–36.

ORGANIZATIONAL CHANGE

Organization development (OD) can be defined as a long-term, systematic, and organization-wide change effort designed to increase the total organization's effectiveness. OD advocates maintain that the organization must be dealt with as a whole. This includes all the personalities and issues that make the organization what it is.

The whole organization must change.

OD assumes that the entire organization, not just select individuals, must work for change. Organization development also recognizes the vulnerability of new employees who enter established work environments.

Develop skill sets.

Organization development has two major objectives: (1) to develop the skill sets that make it possible for employees to do their jobs well and (2) to develop employees' interpersonal skills, including giving and receiving assistance, listening and communicating, and dealing with people and organizational problems.

Organizational objectives may give way to individual goals.

OD is based on the belief that, as organizations grow in size, organizational objectives give way to individual goals. When this happens, the organization begins to decay. OD also recognizes that people have needs and desires that must be considered part of organizational objectives. If all members of the organization participate in forming group goals and, in the process, subscribe to them, then a great deal of energy is available for employees to move toward a common purpose.

CHARACTERISTICS OF ORGANIZATION DEVELOPMENT

Goal Setting: OD subscribes to goal setting. It recognizes some purpose or direction for both the company and the individual.

Time and Money: OD is a dynamic, ongoing process. It takes time to develop and requires a considerable investment of time and money. OD practitioners have a strong belief in training programs.

Psychology: OD relies on psychological ideas. If the company has a motivation problem, for example, management will investigate how other organizations have solved similar problems.

Mutual Trust: OD encourages the development of mutual trust between managers and employees.

Team Building: OD believes in team building and recognizes that one work group affects all others. One group cannot be changed without it impacting others. Thus, a development program must be a company-wide effort.

Experience Based: OD is experience based. If the goal is to improve intragroup communication, the group activity will provide opportunities for the members to gain insight into developing effective communication skills.

TYPES OF OD INTERVENTIONS

An **OD intervention** is a systematic attempt to correct an organizational deficiency. It may focus on individuals, groups or teams, a department, or the total organization. The overall objective is to positively impact the entire organization. Interventions may be carried out using one or a combination of several approaches:

Intervention	Description	Focus
Life/career planning	Self-analysis; planned development	Individual
Skill development	How to perform or improve performance on a job	Individual
Role analysis	Prescriptive—the jobs that people ought to be doing	Group
Team development	Building groups into effective teams	Group
Survey feedback	Using a questionnaire to gather data, analyzing those data, and feeding them back to employees so they can improve	Organization
Grid OD	A multiphased program that utilizes the managerial grid to change organizational leadership	Organization

MURPHY'S LAWS AND OTHER THINGS THAT CAN GO WRONG

In concluding this chapter, it is worthwhile to mention some of **Murphy's laws**:

1. If anything can go wrong, it will.
2. Everything takes longer than it should.
3. Nothing is as simple as it looks.

For example, take a plan by a local school board to change the date of monthly paychecks from the first of the month to the end of the month. Instead of receiving their paycheck on the first of the next month, employees would receive it at the end of the present month. Certainly everyone would like to be paid one day early. Surely there would be no resistance to such an administrative change, but the school board found out differently after informing the school employees of its plan.

Immediately, the county school office was informed of the income tax problem. Instead of receiving twelve paychecks the first year, each employee would receive thirteen, thereby having to pay income tax on a larger income. The solution: The teachers would be paid on the first day of January and the last day of February. Every month after that they would be paid on the last day of the month, except for December at which time they would be paid on January 1. Yes, everything takes longer than it should. This plan took 2.5 years to implement, and a few things did go wrong, but were ultimately fixed.

Involving employees in change allows the results to be more effective, but can take longer to implement. Specifically, managers should (1) look deeper and ask questions, (2) allocate time for confusion and resistance, and (3) be prepared with action and contingency plans.

Effectively planning for change and otherwise managing an organization requires leadership, but there is more to change than the process itself. We need balance

Balance the change process with end results.

between process and results—too much emphasis in either direction is not helpful. Some managers are too results oriented, while other managers are too process oriented. While humorous to some degree, managers will fail if they adopt the following attitude:

> You'll be needing a positive, can-do attitude (like mine), so I'll require you to participate in my favorite personal-growth experience, which happens to be a fire-walking seminar. Beckoning you onward from the far end of the glowing pit will be that big poster of . . . . me. . . .
>
> And so on. You may think you resent some of this, but I know better. You're just "experiencing some natural discomfort with the change process." Pretty soon you'll be transformed. Happier. More productive. Brimming with team spirit. Aligned. Just like me. Sure you will.[11]

SUMMARY

Once a decision is made, it must be implemented. The implementation process often requires changing people's attitudes. Managers can expect resistance to vague or unclear changes. Resistance will be less when employees have the most to say about procedural matters and greater when they have the least to say. By encouraging participation in change, managers can overcome resistance.

Studies show that restraining and driving forces impact change. First, existing patterns need to be unfrozen. Then a new pattern, made up of different components, is implemented. Finally, the group refreezes at a new equilibrium.

Change can also be encouraged by behavioral modification. Managers need to reward people for changing by commending them on how well they are doing in achieving the new goal.

Organization development is change throughout the entire organization. Concentrating on the whole organization allows many changes to occur at once rather than on a piecemeal basis. OD emphasizes education and training.

CASE STUDY 16-1

GROUP PRESSURE—"RATE BUSTING"

Engineer Frank Gonzales came to set up a new piece of equipment in the plant. According to Mr. Krieger, the plant manager, the new machine would improve the production rate of the assembly crew. Leon Robbins, the informal group leader, doesn't like the idea of the new machine. "What they're really after is a way to get more out of us without paying us any more than they have to. When they are done, you and I will be without a job. Just wait and see, one day this company won't need skilled people anymore; all they will need is a few button pushers."

When Frank completed the installation of the new machine, he asked for a volunteer to operate it. With the approval of the supervisor of the assembly department, John O'Neil began operating the machine under Frank's supervision. At the end of the day, the operator far exceeded Frank's anticipated increase in production.

"What effect will these new machines really have on our jobs?" asked one worker.

"According to the plant manager, if the system works out well, we'll all be either running the machines or we'll have some other related task," replied O'Neil.

"Well, we know we don't have to worry about losing our jobs, that's one of the first things we were told," said another worker.

"I've been around a long time, friend—you haven't. Let's wait and see what happens," retorted Leon Robbins in a disgusted way.

During the second day of testing, Frank chose another person to operate the new machine. After giving the operator instructions on how to run the machine, Frank began to supervise the employee's performance. Throughout the day Frank felt that the man was performing at less than an appropriate speed. In fact, Frank got the feeling that the man was stalling. At the end of the day, the operator's rate was only marginally higher than the average production rate using the old machine.

Playing the role of Frank, you are convinced that the machine is superior to those already in the plant. You also feel that some people do not want to learn the operation of a new machine and are quietly sabotaging any possibility of a really successful run on the machine. What would you do?

1. Go to the employee's supervisor?
2. Go to management and complain about your suspicions?
3. Spend more time with the employees through informal chats?
4. Call for a general meeting with the employees to explain the merits of the machine?
5. Keep trying in the same manner, but be sure that you are picking those employees to work on the machine who are willing to ignore the group pressure?

CASE STUDY 16-2

THE OVERQUALIFIED EMPLOYEE'S DILEMMA

Leslie Fisher has been employed as an administrative assistant in a large food service industry for almost 2 years. Recently, the chain suffered a serious financial crisis and the marketing division where she works experienced an 80 percent layoff. Leslie was not laid off but was transferred involuntarily to the corporate planning and development division.

The new position has less responsibility and status, but her pay was not reduced. She has become bored by the new job because the tasks involved offer less variety. She is also frustrated by the lack of opportunity for advancement within the division, and the company currently has a "no-growth" policy.

To advance and stay within the corporation, Leslie applied and was selected for a promotional transfer into the personnel department. However, her supervisor was not aware of her request. Mr. Sullivan, the vice president of corporate planning and development, refused to allow her to transfer to personnel. He claimed that he had a rush project in his department that Leslie was handling and would not be able to complete within the next few weeks.

This week Leslie had her annual review and had hoped for a merit increase. Her immediate supervisor told her that, although her job performance has been up to standard, because she is overqualified and overpaid for her job, she will not receive an increase in pay.

CASE QUESTIONS

1. What are Leslie's alternatives?
2. Should Leslie ask Mr. Sullivan why her transfer was denied?

3. How can a corporation best handle a situation of this type?
4. Do you feel that the corporation should have a policy regarding transfers? If so, how should it be worded?
5. What is the best solution for Leslie?

DISCUSSION AND STUDY QUESTIONS—TO KEEP YOU THINKING

1. Describe how participation can help overcome resistance to change.
2. Describe how behavior modification can help supervisors be more effective in implementing change.
3. Differentiate between driving and restraining forces in making changes.
4. What are the key characteristics of organization development?

NOTES

1. Clay Carr, "Following Through on Change," *Training* (January 1989): 39–44.
2. Joseph T. Gilbert, "Reducing the Risks from Innovation," *Journal of Systems Management* (January–February 1996): 12–15.
3. Lloyd P. Steier, "When Technology Meets People," *Training & Development Journal* (August 1989): 27–29.
4. Peter Drucker, "Information and the Future of the City," *The Wall Street Journal*, April 4, 1989, A10.
5. Bryan W. Armentrout, "Have Your Plans for Change Had a Change of Plan?" *HR Focus* (January 1996): 19.
6. Bill Trachant and W. Warner Burke, "Traveling Through Transitions," *Training & Development Journal* (February 1996): 41.
7. John Naisbitt. *Megatrends: Ten New Directions Transforming Our Lives* (New York: Warner Books, 1982), 19.
8. Ibid., 45.
9. Gerard George and Warren S. Stone, "Employee Technophobia: Understanding, Managing, and Rewarding Change," *Journal of Compensation & Benefits* (March–April 1996): 37–41.
10. Ralph H. Kilmann, "A Completely Integrated Program for Creating and Maintaining Organizational Success," *Organizational Dynamics* (summer 1989): 5–6.
11. Jack Gordon, "Employee Alignment? Maybe Just a Brake Job Would Do," *The Wall Street Journal*, February 13, 1989, A10.

INDEX